ETHICS IN PUBLIC POLICY AND MANAGEMENT

Ethics in Public Policy and Management: A global research companion showcases the latest research from established and newly emerging scholars in the fields of public management and ethics. This collection examines the profound changes of the last 25 years, including the rise of New Public Management, public governance and public value; how these have altered practitioners' delivery of public services; and how academics think about those services.

Drawing on research from a broad range of disciplines, *Ethics in Public Policy and Management* looks to reflect on this changing landscape. With contributions from Asia, Australasia, Europe and the USA, the collection is grouped into five main themes:

- theorising the practice of ethics;
- understanding and combating corruption;
- managing integrity;
- ethics across boundaries;
- expanding ethical policy domains.

This volume will prove thought-provoking for educators, administrators, policy makers and researchers across the fields of public management, public administration and ethics.

Alan Lawton is Professor of Management at Federation Business School, Federation University Australia.

Zeger van der Wal is Assistant Dean and Associate Professor at the Lee Kuan Yew School of Public Policy, National University of Singapore.

Leo Huberts is Professor of Public Administration at the Department of Political Science and Public Administration of VU University Amsterdam, the Netherlands.

Ethics in Public Policy and Management challenges traditional boundaries and provides the global perspective necessary for understanding the ethical issues confronting public managers in the 21st century. The multi-national scope of the chapters and diverse analytical frameworks place ethics at the forefront of good governance.

Danny L. Balfour, *Professor, Grand Valley State University, USA*

An excellent collection covering an eclectic range of issues from public service motivation to the ethics involved in space exploration. It poses a series of thoughtful questions for global ethics research.

Dr James Downe, *Reader, Public Policy & Management,*
Cardiff Business School, UK

ETHICS IN PUBLIC POLICY AND MANAGEMENT

A global research companion

Edited by
Alan Lawton, Zeger van der Wal
and Leo Huberts

Routledge
Taylor & Francis Group

LONDON AND NEW YORK

First published 2016
by Routledge
2 Park Square, Milton Park, Abingdon, Oxon OX14 4RN

and by Routledge
711 Third Avenue, New York, NY 10017

Routledge is an imprint of the Taylor & Francis Group, an informa business

British Library Cataloguing in Publication Data
A catalogue record for this book is available from the British Library

Library of Congress Cataloging in Publication Data
Ethics in public policy and management: a global research companion /
    edited by Alan Lawton, Zeger van der Wal and Leo Huberts.
    pages cm
    Includes bibliographical references and index.
    1. Political ethics. 2. Policy sciences. I. Lawton, Alan.
    JA79.E826 2016
    172 – dc23
    2015005693

ISBN: 978-0-415-72528-6 (hbk)
ISBN: 978-1-315-85686-5 (ebk)

Typeset in Bembo and Stone Sans
by Florence Production Ltd, Stoodleigh, Devon, UK

CONTENTS

FIGURES

TABLES

CONTRIBUTORS

Marcel Becker is Assistant Professor of Philosophical Ethics at the Radboud University, Nijmegen, the Netherlands. He teaches applied ethics to students of philosophy, business administration and law. In his research, he specializes in applied ethics, particularly ethics of public administration and ethics of the new media. Each of these fields he approaches from a virtue ethical background. He has made a DVD in which he elucidates the meaning of the cardinal virtues (temperance, courage, justice and prudence) for integrity debates in public administration.

Ken Coghill is an Associate Professor, Department of Management, and Co-Director of the Monash Parliamentary Studies Unit, Monash University, Australia. He was a Member of Parliament, Parliamentary Secretary of the Cabinet and Speaker (Victoria, Australia). His research and teaching interests include accountability, integrated governance, and professional development and codes of conduct for parliamentarians. He is the author of many submissions to parliamentary and government inquiries and a frequent commentator on parliamentary and governance matters. He is active in seeking policy reform to address climate change, including as a founding member of the climate action group Lighter Footprints.

Annelies De Schrijver holds a master's degree in Criminology (UGent, Belgium) and in Quantitative Analysis in Social Sciences (HUB, Belgium). In 2014, she obtained her PhD at the Leuven Institute of Criminology (University of Leuven, Belgium) on ethical competency of police recruits. This project was funded by the Research Foundation Flanders.

Ting Gong is Professor in the Department of Public Policy at City University of Hong Kong. She earned her MA and PhD from the Maxwell School of Citizenship and Public Affairs of Syracuse University, USA. She has done extensive research on corruption and anti-corruption enforcement, government integrity, and public governance. She is the author of the first English book-length study of China's corruption, and has also published widely in international and Chinese journals in the areas of political science and public administration.

Adam Graycar has recently (2015) taken up the post of Professor in the School of Social and Policy Studies at Flinders University, Adelaide, Australia. For five years before that, he was Professor of Public Policy at the Australian National University and also Director of the Transnational Research Institute on Corruption (TRIC) as well as Director of the Research School of Social Sciences. He acquired extensive policy experience over 22 years in the senior level posts he has held in Australian government, both federal and state. He has worked in many policy domains and has done extensive work on corruption prevention in Australia and internationally, and his latest book *Understanding and Preventing Corruption* (with Tim Prenzler) was published in the UK and US in 2013.

Leonie Heres is an Assistant Professor in Strategic Human Resource Management at the Institute of Management Research of the Radboud University in the Netherlands. Her primary research interests focus on leadership in the public and private sectors, organizational ethics and responsible organizational behaviour. She teaches courses in leadership and human resource management, organization sciences, and academic skills. Recent works have been published in *Public Management Review*, *International Journal of Leadership Studies* and *Journal of Change Management*. For more information about publications and recent activities, please visit www.leonieheres.com.

Paul M. Heywood is Sir Francis Hill Professor of European Politics in the School of Politics and International Relations, University of Nottingham. A Fellow of the Academy of Social Sciences and of the Royal Society of Arts, he has published extensively on issues relating to corruption and integrity. He is the author, co-author or editor of 15 books and more than 80 journal articles and book chapters. Among his most recent publications is the *Routledge Handbook of Political Corruption* (2015).

Alain Hoekstra studied Public Administration at Erasmus University, Rotterdam. He worked as a senior policy adviser at the Ministry of the Interior and Kingdom Relations, and is co-founder of the Dutch National Integrity Office. He participates in several international ethics networks and advises government organizations on the design and implementation of integrity management. He has published numerous articles and book chapters in this field, and is writing his PhD dissertation at the Rotterdam School of Management.

Leo Huberts is Full Professor of Public Administration at the Department of Political Science and Public Administration of VU University Amsterdam in the

Netherlands, with special responsibility for the VU research group on Integrity and Quality of Governance and the global IIAS Study Group on Quality of Governance. He is author or editor of 20 books on influence on governmental policy, on public corruption and fraud, on the integrity and ethics of governance, including *The Integrity of Governance: What It Is, What We Know, What Is Done, and Where to Go* (2014), published by Palgrave Macmillan.

Toon Kerkhoff is Assistant Professor at the Institute of Public Administration at Leiden University, the Netherlands. Following his master's degrees in History and Philosophy of Science (University of Amsterdam, the Netherlands), he obtained his PhD from Leiden University. His thesis concerned historical comparative research on ethics, public morality and corruption in Dutch public administration between 1750 and 1850, as part of a larger research project on the development of administrative values between 1650 and 1950. In his teaching and research, he focuses on corruption, integrity, public values, governmental reform and administrative history.

Alan Lawton is Professor of Management at Federation Business School, Federation University Australia. He has held a number of Professorial appointments in Australia, the Netherlands and the UK. He has advised governments in Europe and Africa on codes of conduct and ethics training, and has worked with a range of public bodies in the UK on developing ethical cultures. He has published extensively on public-sector management and public-sector ethics, and his current research interests include ethical leadership and ethical performance. His most recent book is *Ethics and Management in the Public Sector* (2013), with Julie Rayner and Karin Lasthuizen, published by Routledge.

Michael Macaulay is the Director of the Institute for Governance and Policy Studies at the VUW School of Government, Victoria University of Wellington, New Zealand, where he is also Associate Professor in Public Management. His research interests are in integrity, ethics and anti-corruption, and he has worked on international anti-corruption projects with numerous governmental agencies and NGOs such as the Council of Europe and Transparency International, and most recently for the United Nations Office on Drugs and Crime (UNODC). He is currently working on the Open Government Partnership for New Zealand. He is a Visiting Professor at the Universities of Johannesburg, Sunderland (UK) and York St John (UK), and he is the co-chair of the European Group of Public Administration (EGPA) permanent study group on ethics and integrity. He is the co-editor of the *International Journal of Public Administration* and sits on the editorial boards of several other journals, including *Public Management Review* and *Public Integrity*.

Jeroen Maesschalck studied Public Administration and Philosophy at the UGent (Belgium) and at the London School of Economics and Political Science (UK).

He holds a PhD in Social Sciences from the KU Leuven (Belgium). He is currently Professor at the Leuven Institute of Criminology of the KU Leuven, where he is Vice-Dean Research of the Faculty of Law. His research and teaching focus on public administration ethics and on management and policymaking in the criminal justice system. He has consulted on ethics management both within Belgium (local, regional and federal government) and internationally (e.g. OECD).

Heather Marquette is Reader in Development Politics, International Development Department, University of Birmingham (www.birmingham.ac.uk/idd) and is Director of the Developmental Leadership Program (www.dlprog.org) and the Governance and Social Development Resource Centre (www.gsdrc.org). She has extensive experience in research, policy advice, consultancy and training on the politics of development, governance, corruption, political analysis and aid policy. Her research includes work on Afghanistan, Ghana, India, Kenya and Nigeria, and has been published in *Third World Quarterly*, *Political Studies* and *Public Administration and Development*, among others, and she is the author of *Corruption, Politics and Development: The Role of the World Bank* (Palgrave Macmillan 2003).

Donald C. Menzel is President of Ethics Management International and Emeritus Professor of Public Administration, Northern Illinois University. He was the 2005–2006 President of the American Society for Public Administration. He holds a PhD from Pennsylvania State University, a master's degree from Miami University (Ohio) and a bachelor's degree in mathematics from Southern Illinois University. His most recent books are *Achieving Ethical Competence for Public Service Leadership* (co-editor with Terry L. Cooper – M.E. Sharpe 2013), *Ethics Management for Public Administrators: Building and Leading Organizations of Integrity*, 2nd edition (M.E. Sharpe 2012), *The State of Public Administration* (co-editor – M.E. Sharpe 2011) and *Ethics Moments in Government* (Taylor & Francis 2010). He resides in Tampa, Florida, USA.

Olivia Monaghan is a researcher at the Transnational Research Institute on Corruption. She has written a PhD on formulating anti-corruption policy for the police services, and is an independent consultant on organizational culture management and integrity building in both the public and private sectors. Past areas of research include transnational crime and human trafficking in Europe, and Italian organized crime syndicates.

Christopher J. Newman is a Reader in Public Law at the University of Sunderland and leads research within the Law Cluster. He has engaged in research examining corruption on a local and national level. In this field, he has provided a legal dimension to projects developed by academics from other specialisms. He has been active in the teaching and research of space law for a number of years and has worked with academics from other disciplines examining the legal, political and ethical aspects of space exploration. He has made numerous appearances on

British radio and television in relation to space law matters. He is a full member of the International Institute of Space Law and is also a member of the British Interplanetary Society.

Steven Parker has over 20 years of experience in local government as a social worker, policy and planning officer, and manager. He was awarded his doctorate in 2014 after studying at the School for Policy Studies at Bristol University. His research was on the relationship between the public service ethos and multi-agency collaboration. His research interests are the values of the public-sector professions and strategic partnership boards. He is a lecturer in the Faculty of Business and Law, De Montfort University, UK.

Caryn Peiffer is a Research Fellow at the Developmental Leadership Program in the International Development Department, University of Birmingham. She holds a PhD in Political Science from Claremont Graduate University. Her academic research has focused on the causes and consequences of corruption, developmental impact of state-business relations and democratic accountability. She has also carried out research for Transparency International, DFID, AFD and SIDA, and in India, Botswana and Zambia. With Professor Richard Rose, she is the co-author of *Paying Bribes for Public Services: A Global Guide to Grass-Roots Corruption* (Palgrave Macmillan 2015).

Julie Rayner is a Lecturer in Federation Business School, Federation University Australia. Prior to this, she worked at Monash University, Australia, and Durham University in the UK. She has published in the *Journal of Public Administration Research and Theory*, *Journal of Business Ethics* and *International Journal of Human Resource Management*. She is also co-author of *Ethics and Management in the Public Sector* (Routledge 2013), with Alan Lawton and Karin Lasthuizen. Her current research interests are in public service motivation and in sustainability and green human resource management.

Jonathan Rose is a postdoctoral fellow in the School of Politics and International Relations at the University of Nottingham. He completed his doctoral research, which was co-funded by the UK's Committee on Standards in Public Life and the Economic and Social Research Council (ESRC), on how citizens perceive the probity of their government. It was subsequently published as *The Public Understanding of Political Integrity* (Palgrave Macmillan 2014).

Ian Scott is Emeritus Professor and Fellow of the Asia Research Centre at Murdoch University and Visiting Professor in the Department of Public Policy at the City University of Hong Kong. He has written widely on politics and public administration in Hong Kong and Asia, most recently on corruption and administrative ethics. His latest books are *Gaming, Governance and Public Policy in Macao* (edited with Newman M.K. Lam) (2011) and *The Public Sector in Hong Kong* (2010), both published by Hong Kong University Press.

Helena Olofsdotter Stensöta is Associate Professor in Political Science at the University of Gothenburg. Her research centres on issues of gender, ethics, public policy and administration. She has theoretically elaborated on how ethics of care contributes to public administrating research (*Public Administration Review*, 2010), as well as how the perspective of public administration contribute to the ethics of care discussion (*Ethics and Social Welfare*, 2015). She is also interested in issues of front-line-level bureaucracy and attitudes (*J-Part*, 2012), as well as the institutional conditions that mediate relationships between gender and corruption (*Governance*, 2014).

Jitse Talsma is Project Researcher at the Radboud University in Nijmegen, the Netherlands, and advisor at the Dutch National Integrity Office (Bureau Integriteitsbevordering Openbare Sector) in The Hague, the Netherlands. In his research, he is interested in virtue ethics in public administration and organizational ethics. As an advisor at BIOS, he is concerned with strengthening the integrity, ethics and compliance policies of public organizations. Questions concerning the practical application of virtue ethics (with concepts such as eudaimonia, moral motivation, excellence, edification and practice) connect these two fields of interest with each other.

Zeger van der Wal is Assistant Dean (Research) and Associate Professor at the Lee Kuan Yew School of Public Policy, National University of Singapore. He teaches, studies and consults on organizational ethics and values, motivation and leadership, performance management, and strategic HR. He has (co)authored 70 publications, including books, journal articles and op-ed pieces in magazines and newspapers. Top-tier journals that have published his work include *Public Administration Review*, *Public Administration*, *Administration & Society*, *American Review of Public Administration*, *Public Management Review*, *International Public Management Journal* and *Journal of Business Ethics*. His main publications have been translated into Russian and Chinese. Currently, he is working on a textbook geared towards MPA, MBA and executive education classrooms, titled *The 21st Century Public Manager*.

Pieter Wagenaar is Assistant Professor at the Department of Political Science and Public Administration of the Faculty of Social Sciences, VU University Amsterdam. He holds a PhD from Leiden University, 1997, and in 1998 he became Assistant Professor at the Department of Public Administration at Leiden University, where he was part of Mark Rutgers' pioneer project *The Renaissance of Public Administration*. In 2001, he moved to the VU University Amsterdam. In 2006, he was co-applicant of a four-year research project on the development of administrative values over time. Since 1994, he has lectured in the departments of history and public adminis-tration for undergraduates, and graduates both Dutch and foreign. He has published on a range of topics concerning the informatization of public administration, and the history of public administration.

PREFACE

The front cover of the book shows a section from the frescoes *Allegory and Effect of Good and Bad Government*, created by Ambrogio Lorenzetti (1290–1348). The frescoes are in the Sala dei Nove, Palazzo Pubblico in Siena, Italy; they were commissioned by the council of nine ruling officials that governed Siena between 1287 and 1355. The section that we have chosen illustrates the rule of tyranny and the effects of bad government. The central horned figure represents tyranny, surrounded above by pride, avarice and vainglory, and below by cruelty, treason, force, fraud, war, fury and divisiveness. On an opposite fresco sits the figure of justice, and she is surrounded by peace, fortitude, prudence, concord, magnanimity, hope and temperance. The frescoes show the ruinous effects of bad government on the city and the countryside. Similarly, the effects on the city and countryside of good government are shown.

Clearly, a concern with good and bad government is nothing new, but to see them depicted in such a graphic way is rather startling, and reminds us of the impact of many of the issues that concern us today. In this book, our authors explore unethical behaviour, fraud and corruption, but also virtues, good behaviour and how organizations can promote good government. Lorenzetti reminds us of the appalling consequences that follow from bad government and the importance of justice to ensure good government. It is a lesson that is no less relevant today.

ACKNOWLEDGEMENTS

Zeger van der Wal would like to acknowledge the support of the National University of Singapore for providing him with an HSS Faculty Research Fellowship and the support of the Lee Kuan Yew School of Public Policy for providing him with a SRSS grant to work on the book. Leo Huberts acknowledges the continuing support of his colleagues in the VU research group on the Quality of Governance.

PART I

Introduction

1

THE SCOPE AND SCALE OF ETHICS IN PUBLIC POLICY AND MANAGEMENT

Alan Lawton, Zeger van der Wal and Leo Huberts

Introduction

The delivery, and deliverers, of public services have changed dramatically in the past 20 years, with the shift from government to governance, through a wide range of different types of organizations. Networked and collaborative forms of governance and direct provision of public services through private and voluntary organizations have changed the parameters of the public sector. This raises a number of issues, including the motivations of individual employees, the concept of acting in the public interest, and the wider issues of public-sector economy, efficiency and effectiveness in a time of austerity. It raises the question of whom or what constitutes the core public service. The casualization of the workforce in many areas of the public sector raises concerns over, for example, the quality of public services and the commitment of those who deliver them. At the same time, it raises ethical issues for the organization, the individual and the users of the services that they provide.

We might wonder at the extent to which there continues to exist a concept of public service as a vocation or whether, for both elected and appointed officials, public service has been replaced by the pursuit of private interests. Critics of postmodernism (e.g. Taylor 1991) describe the self-centred, self-improved and self-promoted individual as an example of the postmodern condition. One example of this might be, to paraphrase Von Clausewitz, 'Politics is the continuation of business by other means'. In Australia, billionaire businessman Clive Palmer, Federal Representative for Fairfax in Queensland, has been accused of using his political position in his dispute with Chinese company Citic Group Corporation in Beijing. It is alleged that Palmer siphoned off over $12 million of Chinese funds to bankroll his Palmer United Party's campaign for federal election in 2013. His commercial interests in China appear to have become entwined with his political ambitions. Palmer holds the balance of power in the senate.

Of course, we might consider the extent to which certain roles or professions in the public sector can make special claims to a certain understanding of ethical behaviour. A politician may argue that he or she is accountable to, and has responsibility for, those that elected him or her, or to the wider public rather than to individual constituents. Is it just a question of balancing out different priorities or do some commitments 'trump' others? A defence of arms sales to unsavoury dictators is that such sales are 'in the national interest'. A defence can be made of the 'dirty hands' of politicians. As philosopher and former leader of Canada's Liberal Party, Michael Ignatieff, puts it:

> I learned that you can't take refuge in moral purity if you want to achieve anything, but equally, if you sacrifice all principle, you lose the reason you went into politics in the first place. These are the essential dilemmas of political life, but they are what makes politics exciting.
>
> (2013, p. 150)

But what about civil servants who face different constituencies and accountability obligations, while at the same time having to loyally (but not necessarily obediently) serve their political masters (cf. van der Wal 2011)? They have always been operating in a minefield of competing values and loyalties (De Graaf and van der Wal 2010; van der Wal *et al.* 2011), and developing political astuteness and administrative virtues was key to their survival. However, we might wonder if the virtues of our public officials have been compromised in recent decades by the target-setting, performance-driven culture that is such a feature of the public services nowadays, from health care to university education.

The organizational dimension will provide a context for the ethical behaviour of public officials and will include those regulatory agencies that are used to police, educate and/or adjudicate ethical conduct on the part of public officials. These organizations increasingly take on different forms, have different resources and have different functions. The extent to which they form part of an integrity system, coherent and with clear jurisdictions, is a moot point.

However, different regulatory 'styles' will reflect social norms and values; a legalistic regulatory style may incline a country's institutions to formalized codes of conduct and approach ethics through compliance mechanisms.

Aims of this chapter

This first chapter serves several functions. First, it provides an overview of some of the key issues in public service ethics, integrity and governance. It is not the intention to provide a state-of-the-art summary of developments and research in the field over the past 20–30 years. Rather, it asks us to pause and reflect upon some of the key questions that researchers have been asking and considers whether we could have problematized our interests in different ways. Second, in so doing, we consider how different disciplines might offer different perspectives on the same problems. Indeed, the individual authors in the book are drawn from different disciplines, including philosophy, public administration, history, political science, economics, management and so on. Third, the Introduction indicates the different themes that emerge and link the individual chapters. Our approach has not been to impose a pre-conceived set of themes for individual authors to follow. Rather, we recognize that researchers follow their own instincts and pursue their own curiosities, and this is what gives the subject richness and vibrancy. Nonetheless, five common themes have emerged, inductively as it were: theorizing the practice(s) of ethics; understanding and combating corruption; managing integrity; ethics across boundaries; and expanding ethical policy domains. We introduce each of the chapters in turn and add our own commentary. We leave consideration of future research themes and directions, and the extent to which they are international or even global, to the concluding chapter of this volume.

Problematizing ethics in public policy and management

Many of the issues that concern us are problematized as either/or and offer a black-and-white picture of the issues that may not be useful. We are asked to choose between the public and private delivery of public services; between a compliance or an integrity approach regulating ethics; between public policy for the lifetime of the government or for future generations; between individual interests or common interests. Even the simple choice between consequentialist ethics, the ethics of ends, and deontological ethics, the ethics of means, is not helpful. Life is much more complex.

Thus, it is extremely difficult to put a boundary around the private lives of, in particular, elected politicians, and any attempt can be challenged. In the UK, for example, former Mayor of London, Ken Livingstone, was found guilty by the regulatory body, the Standards Board for England, of bringing his office into disrepute. On leaving a civic function, he was approached by a newspaper reporter, there was an exchange of words and Mr Livingstone accused the reporter of being like a Nazi war criminal. The reporter is Jewish. A complaint was made to the Standards Board by the Board of Deputies of British Jews on the grounds that Mr Livingstone had brought his office into disrepute. The Standards Board found that Mr Livingstone was still acting in an official capacity and had breached the code of conduct, and was suspended by the Standards Board for four weeks. Mr Livingstone appealed to the High Court of Justice, and Mr Justice Collins found in favour of Mr Livingstone and ruled that the Standards Board decision be quashed.

In terms of organizational status, it is the case that public services are delivered by a range of different types of organizations, both private and voluntary, sometimes acting alone and sometimes in collaboration. It is too simplistic to suggest that individuals working in different organizational types will have different motivations and this could impact, adversely, the quality of public services.

We have already hinted that the boundaries of ethics are contestable, and while we do distinguish between ethical and unethical behaviour, we constantly come up against the thorny problem of cultural relativism. At the same time, cross–cultural and global research does indicate that certain 'virtues' such as integrity seem to be regarded highly in just about all of the countries researched. Also, our understanding of ethical and unethical behaviour changes over time, and what might be acceptable in one period is deemed unacceptable in the next period. We explore this in more detail in the concluding chapter.

The study of corruption sees corruption as either an individual action problem or a systemic problem of the 'commons'. Both approaches reflect the economists' concern with rational action. Can the problem of corruption be seen in a different way? We might distinguish between the ideal and the needs of ordinary life, between our goals and our moral capabilities. That is, perhaps by focusing upon what is required to survive within a particular set of norms, customs and values, rather than upon some abstract ideal state of affairs, we might not be so disappointed with the lack of progress in curbing corruption.

Finally, we turn to that old chestnut of rules versus values, and the recognition, increasingly, that most integrity regimes will include a combination of both. What we do not know is which configuration and combination of the different tools, institutions and processes works best in any given situation. Is it ethical leadership that makes the difference? Is it the code of conduct that is the most effective trick in our repertoire?

Themes to the book

We grouped and categorized the contributions to this edited volume under five broad themes: (1) theorizing the practice(s) of ethics; (2) understanding and combating corruption; (3) managing integrity; (4) ethics across boundaries; and (5) expanding ethical policy domains. Here, we describe each theme and highlight the key contributions and contents of each chapter.

1. Theorizing the practice(s) of ethics

It is always tempting to 'cut to the chase' and commence with the realities of corruption, ethical and unethical behaviour, (un)ethical leadership, codes of conduct, ethics training and so on. However, the more fundamental discussions concerning the nature of ethics itself still engage our attentions and are a precursor to understanding the issues as ethics gets played out in the practice of policymaking and management. We include three chapters under this theme, which challenge the reader to reflect upon their own understandings and assumptions of ethics.

Helen Stensöta introduces the public ethics of care as a general public ethic and builds on the idea of human interdependency. In this way, she is able to move beyond a simple distinction between universal and particularistic ethics. Following on from Carol Gilligan's groundbreaking work, Stensöta builds upon her own previous research and outlines a public ethics of care that has four central notions: interdependence, the significance of relations, responsibility and context sensitivity.

In line with several of our other contributors, she argues that rule following provided insufficient guidance and finds that under New Public Management, care has been commodified. Stensöta argues that a public ethics of care can inform a diverse range of policy areas, including housing and city planning such that policy goals can sustain relations with the environment and accommodate future generations. It can underpin political responsibility and accountability; indeed, it is a matter of common interest that it does so.

Our second contribution under this theme is from Marcel Becker and Jitse Talsma, who take a virtues approach to understanding the practice of ethics, and identify its usefulness in ethics training and education for public officials. In their view, virtue ethics bears twenty-first-century relevance as it is instrumental in contemporary integrity vocabulary, which has highly dualistic tendencies. In their view, on the one hand, popular integrity concepts often revolve around, and reinforce, the dichotomy between right and wrong. On the other hand, a stream of literature has emerged that intends to describe integrity in a more gradual and positive way. Their chapter discusses the merit of virtue ethics as one of these positive approaches. After arguing how the concepts of integrity, the grey area and the dilemma can lead to overly negative and oversimplified, black-and-white distinctions, they discuss in-depth three concepts from virtue ethics (the excellent mean, the development of virtues and shared practices), which enable graduality and a positive approach to ethics and integrity. The authors provide practical suggestions for how these three concepts may serve as valuable and practical enrichments to current integrity discourse, and dilemma workshops and ethics training programs.

Our final chapter in this section is from Michael Macaulay, who applies a critical philosophical perspective to the way in which the field of public administration has developed in recent decades. In particular, he argues that there has been an absence of a coherent philosophical underpinning as such. Macaulay commences his discussion by looking at the power of myth and offers an example of how myth underpins key policy areas such as the myth of the deserving and undeserving poor. Such myths are often used to propagate dichotomies, black or white views of the world, and he argues that we should be seeking to broaden our views and not necessarily seek to reconcile opposing views. Drawing upon the work of the German idealists, and Hegel in particular, he calls for an intersubjective philosophy of public administration that can maintain the link between politics and administration.

2. Understanding and combating corruption

Given all the anti-corruption measures that have been put in place around the world and given the continued growth of corrupt activities, is it time to re-conceptualize corruption? The contributors under this theme take different approaches and offer fresh contributions to our understanding of corruption.

Toon Kerkhoff and Pieter Wagenaar argue for an often missing historical approach to administrative ethics, taking into account time and context. Contingency and contextuality of social phenomena, including corruption, seem to be underestimated in our research and theories. The authors argue that the dominant present approach seems currently to be the near exclusive domain of organization science, (new) public management or policy studies. The historical study of cases of corruption provides an opportunity to investigate discussion, disagreement and public value-conflict that make up public ethics at different times and places. In addition, they argue in this chapter that a historical approach also offers insight into important practical and normative questions in today's policy and research concerning good governance, corruption and public integrity. Kerkhoff and Wagenaar are critical of a research community that seems to be dominated by 'universalism', with an abundance of (quantitative) research based on corruption indexes, etc., resulting in an 'anti-corruption industry' that has pushed 'particularistic' research (by anthropologists and historians) to the fringe of corruption studies. As a consequence, we seem to be left with serious problems. The authors argue that ignoring the significance of context and time will have important normative consequences for today's research and policy on 'good governance', corruption and public integrity, in line with Samuel Huntington's statement: 'what is universalism to the west is imperialism to the rest' (1997, p. 184).

In the second contribution in this section, Olivia Monaghan and Adam Graycar provide a new typology for understanding integrity violations and expanding current definitions of corruption, which they illustrate with four vignettes from different governance settings. They conclude their chapter with an overview of specific policy instruments and their supposed effectiveness for the three main types of integrity violations they distinguish: corruption, misconduct and maladministration. First, the authors focus on this differentiation between the three phenomena as a means through which more targeted integrity processes and preventive strategies can be built. Second, they identify some challenges to organizational integrity. By considering the factors (both internal and external) that affect an organization's integrity, an organizational culture can be more effectively safeguarded. Third, they relate these challenges to a number of integrity-building processes and preventive strategies that can be easily adopted into an organization's operational system. An applicable, practical method of building integrity in the public sector reduces the risk of a band-aid approach. Such an approach assumes that corruption, misconduct and maladministration take the same form in every organization and that they can be targeted through a similar approach. The analysis of the three phenomena highlights some of the problems with this assumption.

Caryn Peiffer and Heather Marquette, in their contribution, suggest that part of the explanation for the continuing failure of programmes to curb corruption lies in the inappropriate theoretical foundations that underscore their design. Such programmes are overwhelmingly influenced by principal-agent theory, which assumes that there are 'principled principals', and which relies on a theory of rational individual action. In contrast, Peiffer and Marquette examine corruption through the lens of collective action theory, which relies on intra-group trust and engagement with the wider society. However, the authors argue that the two approaches are not substitutes for each other, but should complement each other.

At the same time, Peiffer and Marquette recognize the complexity of the anti-corruption debate and provide a number of examples to illustrate the circumstances when corruption may serve certain functions that are deemed defensible by those involved.

Our final chapter in this section is from Paul Heywood and Jonathan Rose. They, too, make the point that reducing the level of corruption appears to have met with only modest success, and anti-corruption programmes do not appear to be working. They ask us to consider the difference between an anti-corruption strategy and a pro-integrity strategy, arguing that too often the response to corruption has been a rules-based compliance approach. Such an approach may help to minimize corruption and to provide public visibility for the fight against corruption. However, it does not promote high integrity, which they see as a reflexive, self-conscious 'thick' morality. The authors also present data from a small-scale study of the senior civil service in the UK, which shows a greater desire for a values-based approach to promoting integrity.

3. Managing integrity

Part III of this book turns to the issue of managing integrity: what do more than two decades of evidence tell us about what works and what hurts in various organizational and institutional contexts? What are key recent developments in developing new instruments and approaches to integrity management, ethical leadership, and our insights in the effectiveness of integrity management?

The first chapter in this part from Alain Hoekstra presents a thorough and useful overview of perspectives and best practices of institutionalizing integrity management in public-sector organizations in developed countries. He frames his discussion in the context of the various financial crises of the past seven years and the austerity measures governments around the world have implemented since. Severe cutbacks can hamper attention (and resources devoted) to integrity management while at the same time exacerbating the chances of unethical conduct by public employees in terms of motive and opportunity. Risk assessment and management will become an important tool in future efforts of governments to manage integrity while cutting costs at the same time. One innovative contribution of the chapter is an analysis of network strategies employed by public- and private-sector actors as they collaborate in the area of integrity management, a relatively new phenomenon fuelled by decreasing resources.

Another area that certainly needs more research, according to Hoekstra, concerns the impact of austerity measures on ethical behaviour, and on integrity management in the public sector. The existing circumstantial evidence should be classified as alarming, but has to be examined in much greater detail. Recent developments, signalling that the financial crisis might be on its return in some countries, provide all the more reason not to wait with this kind of research since a relapse may be possible. More generally, we should improve resilience for future economic crises.

In the next chapter, Leonie Heres presents new data on a relatively understudied area in ethical leadership: the expectations and perceptions of various followers and stakeholders. Heres posits that extant, abundant research into ethical leadership does have an important caveat: it is predominantly leader-centred. Unlike studies on, for instance, servant or responsible leadership, those studying ethical leadership typically focus on a leader's characteristics and behaviour, and pay little attention to the role of stakeholders in the constitution and development of ethical leadership. The apparent lack of attention to stakeholders is surprising when we consider that ethical leadership is by definition an ascribed and subjective phenomenon that exists only by virtue of the buy-in of such stakeholders. Heres presents the results of a multi-method study into follower expectations of ethical leadership in settings with different task complexities, resulting in five types of ethical leadership: the safe haven creator, the practicing preacher, the moral motivator, the social builder and the boundaries setter. Heres then proceeds with presenting her FEEL model, which suggests a baseline of minimum ethical leadership requirements that leaders should meet, regardless of their followers' personal characteristics or the structural characteristics of their work: when these baseline requirements are not met, the model suggests, leaders are less likely to build a strong reputation for ethical leadership. The FEEL model points out that followers first and foremost use aspects related to safety, approachability, learning from mistakes, and personal accountability to distinguish ethical leaders from ethically neutral leaders. Furthermore, it implies that explicit and proactive discussions about ethics, values and moral principles may be less relevant when followers' moral task complexity is low and their work is more straightforward.

In describing her future research agenda, Heres indicates that we need to look beyond ethical leaders themselves and explore the nature of the relationships between the leaders and their many stakeholders.

Don Menzel makes our third contribution under this theme. He first provides a context to the unethical conduct in the US and provides data on the size and scale of the problem. He distinguishes between strong ethics, bent ethics and broken ethics, and argues that we also need to know what motivates people to do good, as well as understanding why they might stumble from the path of ethical behaviour. Menzel uses six vignettes to illustrate how and in what circumstances public officials in the US have demonstrated strong, bent or broken ethics. While there are ethically minded officials who act out their values, Menzel also reminds us of the institutionalization of unethical behaviour, where the problem is not the 'bad apple', but the 'bad barrel'.

In the final chapter in this section, Jeroen Maesschalck and Annelies De Schrijver reflect on ethics training as a popular instrument of integrity management in organizations, and point to the scarce research that has been done on what works. The studies that do exist generate conflicting findings, which also has to do with significant conceptual confusion. Moreover, the outputs and the outcomes that are measured differ substantially, and as a result hypotheses about the impact of training on those outputs and outcomes are often difficult to falsify or corroborate.

The chapter reviews the empirical literature on the effectiveness of ethics training and then proposes a theory about types of ethics training and their expected outcomes. Basically, the authors propose to be more specific about both the independent and the dependent variables in ethics training research, offering a conceptual framework that can be used for the evaluation of very different ethics training programmes with various training objectives. A training that emphasizes rules might in fact undermine another ethical sub-competence, 'moral sensitivity'. Such a systematic investigation not only of the intended effects but also of the un-intended and often undesirable side effects might offer an important and evidence-based complement to the unconditional enthusiasm about ethics training that is not uncommon among actors in what has been labelled the 'ethics industry'.

4. Ethics across boundaries

As we have indicated above, the focus for public service ethics and policy is on shifting sands as public services are delivered by a whole host of different organizations interacting with each other in different ways. What does this mean for the commitment to some kind of a public service ethos that is said to charac-terize traditional public officials?

The first chapter in this section is from Alan Lawton and Julie Rayner, who explore the implications of networked organizations for public service motivation or PSM. In drawing together the literatures on public service motivation and networks and partnerships, the authors offer five propositions for future research.

Lawton and Rayner show how the original work on public service motivation has grown and expanded, and indeed has almost created an industry in its own right. The authors pose the question: is public service motivation the same for all those delivering public services, irrespective of their institutional or industry context? At the same time, with the increase in the number of partnerships and networks, do network characteristics influence the motivation of those who are delivering public services through them? Lawton and Rayner present propositions that need to be sharpened through research in case studies before developing an instrument that measures public service motivation under network circumstances.

The second chapter in this section is from Steven Parker, who explores the extent to which the concept of the public service ethos is contested between individuals with different professional backgrounds. His case study is a multi-agency strategic partnership board in the UK where different agencies work together in providing services for disabled children. Parker draws upon interviews from officials 'on the ground' as it were to explore the meaning of the public service ethos in practice. He is interested in the extent to which there is a common view of a public service ethos, and public service accountability, among a diverse range of public service professionals. Parker offers us a framework of analysis that operates at the micro, macro and applied levels, and suggests a future research agenda that utilizes such a framework.

In a contribution from Asia, Ting Gong and Ian Scott examine a timely and intriguing topic: the differences in problems associated with identifying and classifying conflicts of interest and unethical behaviour in the public sector and between mainland China and Hong Kong. After outlining what the authors consider key issues in such a task, they discuss measures that the respective governments have taken to try to address various conflict of interest issues. Gong and Scott argue that the pervasiveness, uncertainty, diversity and increasing frequency of conflicts of interest mean that rule-based approaches to prevention are unlikely by themselves to succeed. Supplemental value-based approaches offer greater prospects of reducing serious conflicts of interest but much depends on the extent that, and the ways in which, governments support such approaches. The authors' assessment of value-based integrity management initiatives in mainland China and Hong Kong is based on interviews with officials with specific responsibilities for integrity and on an administrative ethics survey focusing on the values of senior public servants, which was conducted in both places. One innovative contribution to existing classifications is the notion of 'ultra-organizational' relationships (next to societal, inter-organizational and intra-organizational relationships), which concern conflicts of interest that may arise due to post-public-sector employment of officials, often in the private sector.

Gong and Scott argue that approaches to controlling conflicts of interest in both countries have focused on rule compliance. In some cases, intruding new rules where necessary may be a desirable first set (e.g. the rules governing the ethical standards of Hong Kong Legislative Councillors). And yet, a values approach is also required; in post-public employment, for example, in both mainland China and Hong Kong, the rules were observed but perceived unethical behaviour still occurred.

5. Expanding ethical policy domains

There are new challenges for public officials and new policy domains that open up. Often, we are slow to recognize the ethical implications of policy areas involving new technologies. As John Gray has put it, 'Science and technology are cumulative, whereas ethics and politics deal with recurring dilemmas' (2014, p. 75).

We are also sometimes slow to recognize the responsibilities that we have to future generations and to recognize that these responsibilities are collective in nature.

The first chapter in this section is by Ken Coghill, who addresses the 'Great moral challenge of our time' in his exploration of the ethics involved in climate change. He provides a background to climate change deliberations and policy in recent years, and argues for integrated governance to address the issue. Coghill points to the interlocking nature of the state, the market and civil society, and asks us to consider the role of deliberative democracy in ensuring that communities participate in the fundamental decisions that affect their lives both now and in the future. Coghill points to the importance of learning from ancient traditions and responsibilities, and also identifies the ancient principles of fiduciary duties and trusteeship to guide us. Coghill argues that we should learn, and take inspiration, from those cultures in which it is unethical to damage their environment.

Our second contribution under this theme is from Christopher Newman, who argues for the importance of establishing an ethical standpoint for space exploration. Like Coghill, he argues for the shared heritage of humankind and proposes that there has to be a shift from state actors to a multi-sectored space sector. Hitherto, space exploration has reflected national and regional priorities rather than global ones, and it is crucial to reconcile competing state, and growing commercial, activities. The environment of space is fragile and is under threat increasingly from, for example, the detritus of space activity.

Much of the activity in space has been regulated by 'soft' law in the form of guidelines, and Newman argues for a code of conduct to underpin ethical discussions, which is binding upon all of the national space agencies and their governments.

Conclusion

This book aims to present current thinking by prominent scholars into ethics and integrity issues in public policy and public management, with a global focus. Contributions from Asia, Australasia, Europe and the US show a rich variety of approaches in the field of administrative ethics and integrity management, and presents new frameworks for evaluating ethical policies. Our authors represent both the worlds of academia and political and administrative practice, and the book combines empirical data from public, non-profit and private-sector organizations and managers, and innovative approaches to the field.

References

De Graaf, G. and van der Wal, Z. (2010) 'Managing conflicting public values: Governing with integrity and effectiveness', *The American Review of Public Administration*, 40(6): 623–30.

Gray, J. (2014) *The Silence of Animals: On Progress and Other Modern Myths*, London: Penguin.

Huntington, S.P. (1997) *The Clash of Civilizations and the Remaking of World Order*, New York: Simon & Schuster.

Ignatieff, M. (2013) *Fire and Ashes: Success and Failure in Politics*, Cambridge, MA: Harvard University Press.

Taylor, C. (1991) *The Ethics of Authenticity*, Cambridge, MA: Harvard University Press.

van der Wal, Z. (2011) 'The content and context of organizational ethics', *Public Administration*, 89(2): 644–60.

van der Wal, Z., De Graaf, G. and Lawton, A. (2011) 'Competing values in public management: Introduction to the symposium issue', *Public Management Review*, 13(3): 331–41.

PART II

Theorizing the practice(s) of ethics

2

A *PUBLIC* ETHICS OF CARE

Bringing ethics of care into public ethics research

Helena Olofsdotter Stensöta

Introduction

The rise of scholarly discussion of public ethics is often described as a reaction to the first phase of New Public Management (NPM) reforms (Osborne and Gaebler 1992), which arguably led to a bias favouring efficiency and a consequent neglect of values and ideals (Cooper 2004; Frederickson and Hart 1985). Notably, many of these observed shortcomings have been found in care-oriented policy areas. Reports have illustrated how the marketization of care services has created inhuman conditions for both clients and customers (Grimshaw *et al.* 2002; Ranson and Stewart 1994). Drawing on such empirical patterns, scholars have argued that ethical risk-taking increases with public-sector entrepreneurialism (Eimicke *et al.* 2000; Hebson *et al.* 2003) and that public ethics can serve as a vehicle for improving government and governance.

Given the care-oriented context of these critiques, it is odd that the ethics of care has not been considered a useful concept in the emergent field of public ethics. The ethics of care was originally presented by Carol Gilligan (1982) as complementing the ethics of justice and was thereafter developed into a broader field emphasizing care as a *political* issue (Hankivsky 2014; Tronto 1995). Contemporary ethics of care theory highlights care ethics as important in its own right and comprehensively explores the processes of giving and receiving care, in both private and public institutions, as well as how the care perspective can serve as a critical lens through which to view contemporary politics and policy.

In this chapter, I introduce the ethics of care to the research area of public ethics. I accordingly introduce the concept of a *public ethics of care* (PEC) understood as a *general, public* ethics intended to facilitate policy formation and implementation (Stensöta 2010). By *public*, I mean that the PEC concept transforms activities based on political decisions, regardless of whether they take place in public administrative bodies or in contracted-out settings. By *general*, I mean that the concept is valid in many policy areas and is not limited to what we normally consider 'care' in the everyday understanding of the term, but also relates to policies that affect our abilities to build, nurture, sustain and protect relationships in a broad sense. This includes housing, infrastructure and environmental policies, as well as law enforcement and prison management. Care ethical considerations may inform both individual public employees making decisions based on judgements as well as policymakers organizing the context of relationships.

PEC builds on the central idea in current ethics of care theory, i.e. that humans are *interdependent*, which leads to an understanding of *relationships* as crucial for human well-being. However, I expand on the concept of relationships by not only considering relationships between humans, but also acknowledging that we as humans are embedded within a wider set of relationships with nature and, through our children, with the future. Highlighting the importance of relationships in a well-functioning society, PEC emphasizes something overlooked by other theories informing public ethics approaches. The PEC perspective provides a theoretical apparatus addressing relationships in a thick way, including a view of why relationships are crucial to human well-being and survival, as well as detailed ideas about how necessary processes for *building, nurturing, sustaining and protecting relationships of different kinds* are characterized.

The chapter starts by defining PEC, noting four interesting and central notions, namely interdependence, significance of relationships, responsibility and context sensitivity. I then outline what PEC means for public tasks and the policy process, as well as how it contributes to the public ethics discussion. I examine in greater depth what is 'public' about PEC, as well as how PEC allows for more general interests to be addressed. I finally illustrate PEC by citing three main types of interactions addressed through policy and to which PEC is relevant.

Defining a public ethics of care: PEC

Initial ideas on care ethics

The initial understanding of care ethics formulated by Carol Gilligan (1982) argued that ethics of care differed from ethics of justice in three important ways: (1) it saw moral development as a question of responsibility and relationships rather than of principles and rights; (2) it located moral problems in conflicting responsibilities rather than in conflicting rights; and (3) it argued that situated (i.e. context-sensitive) rather than principled reasoning was required in order to solve these problems. Gilligan described the mature human as practising both an ethics of care and an ethics of justice, but claimed that girls, through their shared gender with the primary caregiver (usually the mother), started by developing an ethics of care, whereas boys did not.

These ideas were refined by the second generation of care ethics scholars, starting with Joan Tronto (1995), who presented the ethics of care as a normative perspective in its own right and argued that it was relevant to *humans*, broadening the earlier association with women. She also argued that the division of care responsibilities reflected power imbalances in society along sex, class and racial lines, and that ethics of care was therefore a *political* concept. Later, care ethics scholars also stressed the political responsibility to satisfy care needs, using the perspective as a critical lens through which to evaluate welfare state policies (Sevenhuijsen 1998; Williams 2001).[1]

Grounding the content of PEC

In defining PEC, I start with Tronto's (1995) general definition, which states that care is 'everything we do to maintain and reproduce ourselves and "the world" so that we can live in it as well as possible' (p. 103). Care is understood as a process consisting of several ethical elements: attentiveness to relevant problems, responsibility to address them, competence to perform the task of caring and responsiveness to ensure that care needs have been met satisfactorily (Tronto 1995). In my understanding, these elements may apply to individuals caring for each other and to the policy process of providing care to citizens.

In addition to this basic understanding, I bring in Selma Sevenhuijsen's (1998) idea of how we can 'judge with care'. Sevenhuijsen understands care as informing action, which means that it plays an important role in making judgements, having a place among the common ways of making judgements in the public sector (e.g. through applying distance and impartiality). I use these ideas when I argue that care is relevant to judgements made by policymakers and public employees. According to Sevenhuijsen (1998), the problem of judging with care that transcends the particular can be addressed through deliberative arrangements allowing for communication. Julie White (2000) further develops these ideas by providing a framework for institutionalizing a democratic politics of care. White discusses this from the perspective of paternalism, arguing that many definitions of paternalism make it impossible to provide any care at all; however, if we define paternalism as 'the process of speaking for others in the course of defining needs' (White 2000, p. 15), then deliberative structures allowing for needs to be defined in dialogue between professionals and the person in need can serve as a way to democratize care. This approach can therefore serve as a way to ensure that care does not address individual demands only, but is incorporated into catering to more general interests.

On these grounds, PEC can be understood as a public ethics through four core notions: (1) the ontological view of human *interdependence*, according to which it is (2) important to establish, nurture, sustain and protect *relationships* of various kinds. PEC further (3) stresses *responsibility* in a broader sense and (4) sees *context sensitivity* as fundamental. These four core notions are elaborated on below.

Interdependence: The ethics of care is a normative perspective that starts from the ontological notion of humans as interdependent, that is, mutually dependent. The PEC perspective endorses the view that full autonomy or independence is a chimera. Dependency can be illustrated across the human life span, as we are more dependent as children and during old age, but are dependent at specific points in life when we are sick or otherwise unable to provide for ourselves. Extending the perspective, humans can be understood as interdependent at all points in time, as we are connected through relationships with other people and with our surroundings, and without these relationships we would definitely die.

Significance of relationships: The concept of interdependence leads to the view that relationships, in their own right, are fundamental to human existence. Thus, PEC endorses the goals of establishing, nurturing, sustaining and protecting relationships that are important for human survival. PEC therefore brings these goals into policy and policy implementation. The notion of protection can be attached to the goal of 'not-hurting', which has been presented as the other side of care (Pettersen 2008). Daniel Engster (2009, p. 54) has argued that preventing harm is integral to the ethics of care because one aim of caring is to help individuals avoid or to relieve suffering and pain. Relationships have been emphasized in care ethics theory from the beginning, but previous theory has not expanded on relationships beyond those between humans.

Formal administrative models, such as those concerning bureaucratic and management organizations, provide thin concepts of relationships. From a bureaucratic perspective, the quality of relationships can be seen as defined by the exercise of impartiality, which means that public employees should treat all citizens in the same situation in an equal manner, thereby disregarding the individual properties of citizens that are not specifically mentioned in applicable law. From the NPM perspective, relationships are essentially seen as agreements between sellers and buyers. In NPM, care is further commodified, for example, in the form of 'care packages' that individuals in need are given; this concept allows individuals in need to shop around and purchase care from a range of providers. In care ethics theory, managerial accounts have been criticized for assuming that people dependent on care can always make rational decisions about their care (Barnes 2012; Tronto 2010).

Many policy tasks, however, rely on thicker concepts of relationships. In discretionary policy such as law enforcement, teaching and social work, rule following provides insufficient guidance for the judgements and actions that employees fulfilling public duties actually perform in their everyday work. Formal models therefore need to be reinforced by other guiding frameworks, which is where public ethics in general comes in. The specific contribution of PEC is that it is particularly directed towards establishing, nurturing, sustaining and protecting *relationships* that arise through or are affected by public policy.

Responsibility: Assuming responsibility for common problems may be what politics is ultimately about. Public ethics in general can be understood as promoting a wider scope of responsibility than is the case when the more limited principles of rule following or management efficiency are the guides. Several understandings of public ethics take general rules, such as the UN's Universal Declaration of Human Rights, as a point of departure, claiming that public employees may act responsibly in relation to such broader rules even when laws at lower levels do not allow for this (Lundquist 1997).

Gilligan (1982) argues that responsibility is central to care ethics, just as rules are central to justice ethics. This means that care ethics proposes a deeper understanding of responsibility as attached to addressing contextualized problems. Tronto (2013) recently made responsibility central to her discussion of how to improve democracy, arguing that assigning care responsibilities should be at the heart of democracy.

In the PEC framework, it is essential to assume responsibility for establishing, nurturing, sustaining and protecting contextualized relationships. This may direct attention to 'new' and broader types of political problems, such as environmental problems that concern our relationships with the environment and with the future. The notion of responsibility also addresses public employee judgement in the act of implementation.

Adopting a broad notion of responsibility raises the problems of limits and restrictions. Indeed, Held (2010) has argued that an ethics of care builds on the principle of unconditionality. This may seem to entail serious problems in applying an ethics of care perspective to public administration, as it appears to circumvent any notion of accountability. However, both internal and external mechanisms of accountability can be attached to PEC.

One solution to this problem can be found in the notion of interdependence. Because one central human need is to belong, to be included in a web of relationships, actions that might endanger this inclusion are typically avoided. The basic PEC accountability mechanism starts from the conviction that people need to feel incorporated into a community with other people and that this is our basic individual motivation for honesty – an accountability mechanism partly situated within the client him or herself.

Second, an external (i.e. institutional) accountability solution promoted by a number of care ethics scholars is that of deliberative arrangements, as discussed above (Sevenhuijsen 1998; White 2000). Needs could be assessed in deliberative discussion between claimants or persons/entities in need and other involved people, such as professionals, experts, politicians and ordinary people. This suggestion has certain similarities with more participatory ideas of implementation, though with some crucial differences. Participatory democracy assigns no particular value a prominent role, but is instead an argument about form. Deliberation could proceed without having any concern for interdependence or relationships. In contrast, the ethics of care framework focuses on the deliberative discussion of these concerns. The deliberative structures used in defining needs can therefore be seen as central to accountability, as understood from the citizen's perspective.

Context sensitivity: In Gilligan's original ethics of care concept, moral problems were considered within their specific contexts. Since then, the ethics of care has provided a theoretical framework for addressing moral and political problems in a situated way, considering the particular circumstances of a given situation. Context sensitivity is fundamental to the way problems are comprehended from a PEC perspective.

Context sensitivity is important to the implementation of policies in several ways. It can inform situations in which employees fulfilling public duties enjoy discretion that allows them to influence how rules are implemented, for example, in human processing areas whose goal is often to transform clients' behaviour and encourage them to return to work after unemployment or sick leave. As discussed above, these matters do not necessarily concern care, but are relevant more generally when relationships are affected or created by policies. Furthermore, context sensitivity is not relevant only at the individual level. Political issues such as environmental problems and global warming require that situational circumstances be taken into account if they are to be addressed efficiently. Context sensitivity is an important part both of reformulating problems in the language of PEC and of assuming responsibility for political problems in a wider sense; it also helps employees fulfilling public duties to make discretionary decisions in a context-sensitive manner.

Bringing PEC into public ethics discourse

How can PEC be positioned within a general discussion of public ethics? In the discourse of public ethics in general, the concept of 'public' is central, and several definitions of it have been proposed. Barry Bozeman (1987, p. 8) defined 'public' as the degree of public authority of an institution, anchoring the concept in specific institutions. An alternative proposition, found in the governance literature, instead defines 'public' as grounded in the authority of the *duties* that agencies or institutions fulfil (Pierre 2011). According to the latter proposition, all agencies and institutions performing governmental, that is, publicly agreed-on, tasks could be included in the definition of 'public', regardless of whether the task is performed by a public organization or contracted out to market agents. This understanding fits approaches that treat contemporary public ethics as mixing former private and public values (Grimshaw *et al.* 2002; Lawton 2005).

In defining 'public' in PEC, I use Pierre's (2011) definition grounded in the *authority of the duties* that agencies or institutions fulfil. Admittedly, there may be differences in how well the transformative power of a PEC can take hold in a public versus a private organization, but no theoretical limitations are established beforehand based on how the organization positions itself relative to the public–private divide.

Regarding the distinction between ethics and values, Bozeman (1987, 2007) argues that public values are not drawn from a specific branch of ethics (e.g. consequential, deontological, utilitarianism or virtue ethics), but usually combine various ideas in a pragmatic way. Following Bozeman, we regard values as easier to apply in everyday public administrative contexts. *Care* ethics, however, is still more pragmatic (Tronto 1995), as it uses contextual sensitivity instead of principled reasoning. This is also reflected by the fact that care is usually understood as a process, that is, an activity, rather than a principled standpoint.

PEC is *political* as it is a matter of common interest, which is why politics and public administration should deal with it, and because it is intertwined with power relationships. PEC is *general* as it informs not only what we normally consider 'care' areas, but also policy areas that generally involve judgements and organize/affect relationships between people.

What does PEC mean for public tasks and the policy process? In contemporary public ethics discourse, there are several views of how public ethics should be applied in practice: as ethical decision-making by individual public employees, as the ethical content of laws, as organizational performance ethics and as the ethical environment of public administration (for an overview, see Menzel 2005, p. 16). PEC can be thought of as a source of norms that: (1) encourage policymakers to design policies and institutions in line with PEC goals; and (2) encourage public employees to make judgements in line with PEC goals. The general character of PEC distinguishes it from professional or policy-limited ethics.

Care in previous public ethics discourse and why it is insufficient

The rich range of contemporary public ethics research offers some concepts that touch on the concerns of an ethics of care. In one of the first articles to treat public ethics in relation to public servants, Frederickson and Hart (1985) suggested that the central motive of civil servants should be the 'patriotism of benevolence'. This was understood as comprising 'regime values' and regarded as more general than policy ethics. Patriotism was defined as the love of one's country, associated with democratic values represented by benevolence and understood as 'the extensive and non-instrumental love of others' (Frederickson and Hart 1985, p. 547). This concept identifies a value, but does not delve theoretically or empirically deeper into what 'love of others' may actually entail or what operations are necessary in order to practise it. It is also difficult to think of how a public employee might 'love' others professionally.

Bozeman's (1987, 2007) scholarship provides a rich account of the importance of public values in public administration. Fundamentally, he draws on ideas of the common good as advocated by Aristotle and argues, both theoretically and empirically, that public values differ from private values and that the former are vital. Of Bozeman's values, it is the value of altruism that especially relates to care. Altruism, however, is also a concept that has not been problematized in any deep way concerning what it may mean in theory and practice when it concerns professionals.

There are also more empirically oriented ideas that relate to care ethics, for example, in the approach to public service motivation of Perry and Hondeghem (2009), whose aim is to map out and measure public employee motivation. Perry (1996; Perry and Wise 1990) applies a tripartite division of motivations as rational, normative and affective. The affective component is associated with the compassionate public employee labelled the 'Samaritan' (Perry 1996), who is described as being 'strongly motivated to help other people' (Perry 1996, p. 10). The operationalization of Samaritan motivation includes affective motives (e.g. feelings and being moved), belief in the centrality of social programmes, altruistic tendencies, thinking of people as dependent and not connecting care with conditions. As Waerness (1987) has pointed out, grounding care ethics in the motivations of 'feelings' and being emotionally 'moved' and distinguishing it from rational calculations implies that care cannot be rational, hence that it is irrational. Discussing homeworkers, Waerness has shown how their work is truly rational, however, attaining to other goals than economic efficiency.

In an updated version of Samaritans, Brewer *et al.* (2000, p. 258f) acknowledge that all three motives are present in all types of motivations: Samaritans, communitarians, patriots and humanitarians. Samaritans see themselves as 'guardians of the underprivileged and are moved emotionally when they observe people in distress'. The characteristics of the Samaritan are close to what the PEC concept brings to public ethics and administration.

Several questions that these scholars do not problematize are discussed in contemporary care ethics theory. First, care ethics views care as a process and a relationship, permitting deeper analysis of both the person in need and the person providing care, which is necessary if the values discussed here are to be useful in practice. Second, it is difficult to believe that care as a professional task should be as associated with feelings and being moved, as Perry suggests. In care ethics theory, care is conceptualized as an important goal that may benefit from various motives and motivations, and that is clearly rational in that people striving for it choose the best possible opportunity to practise it. Third, feminist ethics of care research argues against the idea that care flows 'naturally' from the disposition of particular groups of people (e.g. women), instead conceptualizing it as a competence that is learned in a process including experiences, rational operations and emotions.

A typology of relationships affected by policies

Expanding the relevance of PEC from care policies only to encompass a broader range of policies proceeds through elaborating on the types of relationships that are important to humankind. I propose that policies can affect these relationships in three major ways:

1 policies may *directly* affect citizens' relationships;
2 policies may *indirectly* affect citizens' relationships by organizing the (a) contemporary context of interactions and (b) the future as context; and
3 policies may create a *relationship between an employee performing public tasks and a citizen*, where the citizen can be in the relationship (a) voluntary or (b) as a result of coercion (i.e. in policy areas such as law enforcement and prison management or compulsory care for drug addiction or psychiatric problems, where the patient may be subject to care he or she does not desire).

The 3(b) category forms a separate subcategory, as persons coerced into them may need to be protected from themselves and to be restrained in some way to protect those around them. Furthermore, we can imagine that people in general do not want those who have committed crimes and are incarcerated to receive unlimited care, as this would counter the idea of punishment.

The four core notions, discussed above, are associated with the policy formulation and implementation processes in the following ways: the notion of *interdependence* informs the formulation of policy problems in the language of care; *responsibility* addresses the scope of policy, as well as ways to demand accountability; and *context sensitivity* addresses how context is related to within policy, in both problem formulation and everyday discretionary tasks. Finally, the importance of establishing, nurturing, sustaining and protecting *relationships* guides activities in all these respects, both directly and indirectly.

Directly regulating relationships between citizens

Sevenhuijsen (1998) provides an example of how to judge, from a care perspective, relationships between citizens and a third party (i.e. children). She argues that a rights perspective starts from the right to have a child and does not concern itself with whether or not functioning relationships are present between the child and the person responsible for him or her. The care perspective starts the other way around, encouraging parents to develop good relations with the child and claiming that, once such relations are established, 'rights' can be exercised (Sevenhuijsen 1998, p. 111). These considerations can be broadened in at least two ways. First, we may broaden relationships so as to consider not only fulfilled care duties, but also *non-fulfilled* ones. For example, if one partner fails to provide economic support for his or her child, in the Swedish context, the state gives the other partner compensation. In this case, it is not only the partner who receives the money who is dependent on the state; in addition, the partner who does not provide economic support depends on the state to do the work he or she otherwise would have been obliged to perform. Second, this logic may be extended to other areas as well. For example, a firm's inability or unwillingness to care for the environment can be interpreted using the same model, as the firm makes itself dependent on another party to complete a task made necessary by the firm's inaction.

These directly regulated relationships are mainly of interest to policymakers. They illustrate how PEC *reformulates goals*, which also has implications for the deeper scope of *responsibility*.

Indirectly affecting relationships through local context

1. The contemporary context

Policies that organize our physical space – for example, housing, city planning, infrastructure and local business policies – affect how we interact with each other on a daily basis. From a PEC perspective, these policies should therefore be thought of as taking responsibility for establishing, nurturing, sustaining and protecting these relationships.

PEC may be able to *reformulate goals* within these policy areas. If a PEC perspective were integrated into housing policies, opportunities to care for ourselves and close relatives and friends would be considered when planning new housing areas. We would therefore consider how far people needed to travel each day, especially when taking care of their children and other relatives. PEC would accordingly favour shorter distances and more locally organized community building. These concerns would also become a matter of city planning and infrastructure policies, as the establishment of zones where people walk or cycle would facilitate interaction between them. City planning that takes account of opportunities for people to interact directly in their local environment – such as local centres accessible on foot – would be preferable, as such centres improve people's opportunities to interact face-to-face.

These local concerns would also extend into policies regulating business arrangements. Accordingly, PEC would give preference to policies that encourage local merchants to favour local farmers or local production. This could mean more local food products in stores and enhance local production networks, for example, carpentry or other services. Many of these reformulated policy goals also apply to relationships with the environment and with the future. Ecological policies often favour local production, as this results in a reduction in transportation of goods over great distances. Moreover, places where people tend to walk or cycle are usually child-friendly and sustainable from the perspective of the future.

Another context that involves responsibility for the environment and for the future is that of waste disposal. PEC may be used to inform discussions of this in order to bolster the view that what is locally produced should also be disposed of locally. This would mean that no locally created waste problems would be transported to other geographical areas. Reorganizing policies concerning local space could reformulate our understandings of the boundaries of political *responsibility*.

The notion of increased responsibility also addresses matters of *accountability*. In the above cases, stakeholders representing local merchants, the environment and the future could be invited to take part in policy formulation processes. However, as these processes are guided by PEC concerns, the actors would be encouraged to consider specific PEC values in their deliberations.

Several policies affecting how our relationships are fostered through the organization of context are implemented using considerable discretion. PEC can help local public employees establish procedures for local businesses and their waste disposal in a manner that takes PEC concerns seriously. However, PEC is also intended to have a more general influence on public employees in their everyday work. For example, applying a PEC perspective as a bus driver would entail prioritizing responsible and safe driving over following the timetable.

A number of conflicts are highlighted by these examples. PEC favours the local over large-scale alternatives. According to PEC, we should refrain from organizing higher-level contexts in ways that harm local contexts. Prioritizing the local also collides with efficiency requirements, as 'large-scale solutions' are often said to be more efficient. The idea of favouring local producers goes against the idea of free movement of goods.

2. Affecting human relationships with the future

The central notion of contextual sensitivity points to the future as a relevant context. Although the PEC perspective does a great deal to promote concern for human-kind, it is becoming increasingly clear how important it is to include subjects other than humans when discussing what relationships are important for human well-being and survival. Concern for the environment might be included in additional policy areas through the application of PEC, owing to its broad notion of respons-ibility. As the consequences of policy decisions affecting the environment might not be evident today, but only in the future, the application of PEC would be appropriate as it reinforces a long-term outlook. In this context as well, delibera-tion would offer a way to negotiate claims, provided the stakeholders included representatives of the environment and the future (Kronsell and Stensöta, in press).

With regard to the future, which can be thought of as requiring the prolongation of environmental care, Elena Pulcini (2009) has argued that the care perspective provides the only basis for solidarity with future generations, as it is superior to a rights perspective. Her account specifically criticizes what she calls the unlimited individualism of today's world, and she claims that, through care, we can transform 'fear' and 'anxiety' – the dominant emotions in the world today – into care (Pulcini 2009).

There is a conflict between short-term and long-term considerations. Possible negative consequences of policy decisions concerning the environment might not be evident today, but only in the future. PEC promotes anticipating such consequences, taking a long-term view. How long this time frame should extend into the future depends on the policy in question. For example, a discussion of nuclear waste would not be set in the same time frame as would a discussion of household waste. Determining what time frame is suitable for various decisions must be a matter of judgement in each case. For example, with regard to local planning, it is recommended that global warming issues be included in the process of planning new housing areas or infrastructure investments.

Relationship between citizens and employees fulfilling public tasks

Relationships also arise between citizens and employees fulfilling public duties. These relationships do not only concern 'care' as we understand it in an everyday sense; rather, the important thing is that a relationship is established and the public employee has some discretion in shaping it. Here, applying PEC would serve to reinforce the ethical elements of care in everyday decision-making. As several of the problems in this category are found in the subcategory of relationships established under coercion, I discuss these matters further in the next section.

Relationship between citizens and employees fulfilling public tasks under coercion

This subcategory concerns relationships between citizens and public employees mandated to use coercion. This involves both particular public employees, such as law enforcement officers, who create relationships with citizens in which they may use force, and treatment under coercion, such as imprisonment and compulsory psychiatric care.

Stensöta (2004) traced ideas about care in current law enforcement policy, arguing that several ideas connected to 'community policing' can be thought of as care-oriented. She provides a local-level account of what context sensitivity, seen from a care perspective, may entail if it is applied to law enforcement and community policing. For example, trying to prevent crime rather than prosecuting after a crime has been committed may be considered a way of preventing harm. Furthermore, establishing and nurturing relationships may be viewed as an important tool in crime prevention. Using such approaches, crime is prevented when law enforcement nurtures relationships within the local environment. From a PEC perspective, community policing may be seen as a reformulation of what law enforcement should aim for and do.

Coverdale (2014) has argued that caring should be part of punishment based both on principled argument and on more political and pragmatic arguments. Penal practice causes indirect harm by, for example, reducing inmates' chances of having a home or a job to return to after punishment. She further argues that these ideas are already being put into practice in bottom-up alternative criminal justice (in the UK) and in restorative justice. Coverdale argues that many of the operations that are necessary to keep order in a prison can be thought of as care practices, if Tronto's care ethical elements (i.e. awareness, responsibility, competence and responsiveness) are applied, as they include maintaining relationships and being sensitive to context. Furthermore, prison management works well when good relationships prevail between staff and inmates.

Prison management can be considered an example of a context where the problem of striking a balance between deliberation to define needs and professional judgement regarding these needs is crucial. Deliberation represents a way to protect against the paternalism that professionals may exercise. However, there is also that danger that professionalism cannot be exercised at all. Initiatives such as deliberative democracy in schools that give pupils and parents more of a say, as well as managerial demands regarding contracted-out services that shift the accountability structure to citizens 'voting with their feet', arguably diminish the influence of professional judgement. In some sense, NPM alternatives respond to some of the criticism of the bureaucratic treatment of clients as too rigid. However, managerialist models of accountability relying on client choice have several disadvantages. First, they are not suited to administering treatments that clients might not choose for themselves, such as drug addiction rehabilitation or compulsory psychiatric care. Second, the accountability mechanism gives all the power of accountability to the clients, which seriously limits the opportunities to create and sustain a public spirit or public ethics. In sum, what seems to be demanded is an accountability mechanism that is flexible in accommodating citizens' varying needs yet does not relinquish all power to the clients.

Public ethics in general can serve to make rules less rigid and managerial accounts more value-laden. It can serve as an accountability structure that is flexible within limits but that does not relinquish all the power of the actual professional engaged in the activity.

Although I argue that we should view prison management and incarceration as incorporating relationships that need to be cared for, there are probably limitations to how much care could be given without eroding the role of prisons to punish earlier wrongdoings. Needs assessment must be of a special kind, which restricts deliberation. In these situations, deliberation should be framed by professional judgement, meaning that responsiveness should also be restricted by professional judgement.

Conclusion

The main contribution of this chapter has been to advocate a public ethics of care (PEC) as a *general* public ethics that is useful for improving government and governance in policy areas that extend much further than what we normally consider 'care'-oriented.

A crucial question has been how an ethics of care, as a particularistic ethics at the individual level, can incorporate more general interests. In answering this question, I have drawn on later decades of care ethics research that views care ethics as a political issue involving power and that locates the responsibility for satisfying care needs at the centre of democracy. My contribution has been to put relationships in the centre of care ethics and to systematize the types of relationships created or affected by policy, arguing that these are all relevant to care considerations. In doing this, I have also drawn on the notions of how care ethics inform judgements.

Note

1   There is also a third generation of care ethics scholars who extend care ethics beyond the nation state (Robinson 2006). In this context, care structures and patterns are seen as mirroring power differences in an intersectional sense, arguing that our position in the intersection of socio-economic conditions, gender and race affects how we relate to care (Hankivsky 2014).

References

Barnes, M. (2012) *Care in Everyday Life: An Ethic of Care in Practice*, Bristol: Policy Press.

Bozeman, B. (1987) *All Organizations Are Public: Bridging Public and Private Organizational Theories*, San Francisco, CA: Jossey-Bass.

Bozeman, B. (2007) *Public Value and Public Interest*, Washington, DC: Georgetown University Press.

Brewer, G.A., Coleman Selden, S. and Facer II, R.L. (2000) 'Individual conceptions of public service motivation', *Public Administration Review*, 60(3): 254–64.

Cooper, T.L. (2004) 'Big questions in administrative ethics: A need for focused, collaborative effort', *Public Administration Review*, 64(4): 395–407.

Coverdale, H.B. (2014) *Punishing with Care: Treating Offenders as Equal Persons in Criminal Punishment*, London: Department of Law, London School of Economics & Political Science.

Eimicke, W.B., Cohen, S. and Perez Salazar, M. (2000) 'Ethical public entrepreneurship', *Public Integrity*, 2(3): 229–45.

Engster, D. (2009) 'Rethinking care theory: The practice of caring and the obligation to care', *Hypatia*, 20(3): 50–74.

Frederickson, H.G. and Hart, D.K. (1985) 'The public service and the patriotism of benevolence', *Public Administration Review*, 45(5): 547–53.

Gilligan, C. (1982) *In a Different Voice: Women's Conceptions of the Self and of Morality*, Cambridge, MA: Harvard University Press.

Grimshaw, D., Vincent, S. and Willmott, H. (2002) 'Going privately: Partnership and outsourcing in U.K. public services', *Public Administration*, 80(3): 475–502.

Hankivsky, O. (2014) 'Rethinking care ethics: On the promise and potential of an intersectional analysis', *American Political Science Review*, 108(2): 252–64.

Hebson, G., Grimshaw, D. and Marchington, M. (2003) 'PPPs and the changing public sector ethos: Case-study evidence from the health and local authority', *Work, Employment and Society*, 17(3): 481–501.

Held, V. (2010) 'Can the ethics of care handle violence?', *Ethics and Social Welfare*, 4(2): 115–29.

Kronsell, A. and Stensöta, H.O. (in press) 'The green state and empathic rationality', in A. Kronsell and K. Bäckstrand (eds), *The Green State Revisited*, London: Palgrave.

Lawton, A. (2005) 'Public service ethics in a changing world', *Futures*, 37(2–3): 231–43.

Lundquist, L. (1997) *I demokratins tjänst: Statstjänstemannens roll och vårt offentliga Etos* [*In Service of Democracy: Civil Servants and Our Public Ethos*], SOU [Swedish Public Investigations] 28, Fritzes.

Menzel, D.C. (2005) 'State of the art of empirical research on ethics and integrity in governance', in H.G. Frederickson and R. Ghere (eds), *Ethics in Public Management* (pp. 16–46), New York: M.E. Sharpe.

Osborne, D. and Gaebler, T. (1992) *Reinventing Government: How Entrepreneurial Spirit Is Transforming Government*, New York: Plume.

Perry, J.L. (1996) 'Measuring public service motivation: An assessment of construct reliability and validity', *Journal of Public Administration Research and Theory*, 6(1): 5–22.

Perry, J.L. and Hondeghem, A. (eds) (2009) *Motivation in Public Management: The Call of Public Service*, Oxford: Oxford University Press.

Perry, J.L. and Wise, L.R. (1990) 'The motivational bases of public service', *Public Administration Review*, 50(3): 367–73.

Pettersen, T. (2008) *Comprehending Care: Problems and Possibilities in the Ethics of Care*, Plymouth: Rowman & Littlefield.

Pierre, J. (2011) 'Stealth economy? Economic theory and the politics of administrative reform', *Administration & Society*, 43(6): 672–92.

Pulcini, E. (2009) *Care of the World: Fear, Responsibility and Justice in the Global Age*, Bologna: Springer.

Ranson, S. and Stewart, J.D. (1994) *Management for the Public Domain: Enabling the Learning Society*, Basingstoke: Macmillan.

Robinson, F. (2006) 'Care, gender and global social justice: Rethinking ethical globalization', *Global Ethics*, 2(1): 5–25.

Sevenhuijsen, S. (1998) *Citizenship and the Ethics of Care: Feminist Considerations on Justice, Morality and Care*, London: Routledge.

Stensöta, H.O. (2004) *Den empatiska staten: Jämställdhetens inverkan på daghem och Polis 1950–2000* [*The Empathetic State: The Impact of Equality on Child Care and Law Enforcement, 1950–2000*], University of Gothenburg no 85, Gothenburg, Sweden.

Stensöta, H.O. (2010) 'The conditions of care: Reframing the debate about public sector ethics', *Public Administration Review*, 70(2): 295–303.

Tronto, J.C. (1995) *Moral Boundaries: A Political Argument for an Ethic of Care*, New York: Routledge.

Tronto, J.C. (2010) 'Creating caring institutions: Politics, plurality and purpose', *Ethics and Social Welfare*, 4(2): 158–71.

Tronto, J.C. (2013) *Caring Democracy: Markets, Equality, and Justice*, New York: New York University Press.

Waerness, K. (1987) 'On the rationality of caring', in A.S. Sassoon (ed.), *Women and the State: The Shifting Boundaries of Public and Private* (pp. 207–34), London: Unwin Hyman.

White, J.A. (2000) *Democracy, Justice, and the Welfare State: Reconstructing Public Care*, University Park, PA: Pennsylvania State University Press.

Williams, F. (2001) 'In and beyond New Labour: Towards a new political ethics of care', *Critical Social Policy*, 21(4): 467–93.

3

ADDING COLOURS TO THE SHADES OF GREY

Enriching the integrity discourse with virtue ethics concepts

Marcel Becker and Jitse Talsma

Introduction

Today's integrity vocabulary has highly dualistic tendencies. On the one hand, popular integrity concepts often revolve around, and reinforce, the dichotomy between right and wrong. On the other hand, a stream of literature has emerged that intends to describe integrity in a more gradual and positive way. This chapter discusses the merit of virtue ethics as one of these positive approaches. We first show how the concepts of integrity, the grey area and the dilemma can lead to overly negative and oversimplified, black-and-white distinctions. We subsequently present three concepts from virtue ethics (the excellent mean, the development of virtues and shared practices), which are capable of expressing graduality and lead to a positive approach. These are suggested as valuable and practical enrichments to the current integrity discourse.

A dualistic concept of integrity

Today, 'integrity' has come to be used in a very broad field, stretching from anti-corruption efforts to professional and personal ethics (Huberts 2014). The word derives from the Latin *integritas*, meaning both purity and wholeness. This original meaning of integrity is highly dualistic. Purity is lost by the slightest contamination; wholeness is lost by the slightest damage. In an ethical context, it implies an absolute division between right and wrong. With such 'dualistic moral reasoning', the real moral issue obviously disappears out of sight. 'It is important to realize that the consideration is rarely about black or white, that in the practice of governance and business it is more often about *graduality*: more or less integrity . . .' (Huberts 2012, p. 36) (emphasis in original). Moreover, a dualistic concept leads to the conclusion that if something is not absolutely right, it must be wrong. Yet, even in everyday situations, it is humanly impossible to be completely right, pure and whole. As a consequence, a dualistic concept of integrity easily leads to a negative approach.

The original meaning of 'integrity' is clearly present in public opinion. A public figure whose integrity is questioned will have a hard task to rehabilitate him or herself: once contaminated, forever contaminated. This is visible in the way integrity scandals are handled: 'There is a search for a final and ultimate judgment: is someone good or bad, is he or is he not a person of integrity' (Huberts 2012, p. 35, our trans.). Even worse, the dualistic interpretation tends to seep through to the workplace. Policymakers are mostly concerned with the negative side of integrity, penalizing unethical behaviour but rarely rewarding ethical behaviour, and causing employees to be preoccupied with trying to avoid doing anything wrong (Karssing 2006). Very real phenomena disappear out of sight: 'Positive examples from daily practice are hardly ever recognized. Yet they do exist' (Van Tankeren 2012, p. 403, our trans.). Such gaps in integrity policies obviously do not enhance their legitimacy, which is regrettable, since most integrity officers are in want of more legitimacy (Treviño *et al.* 2014).

An important contribution to counter this dualistic interpretation of the concept integrity was made by Paine (1994). She developed the distinction between 'compliance-based' and 'integrity-based' approaches to ethics management. Under the flag of the latter, scholars and practitioners have endeavoured to develop an approach that is both motivational to good conduct and able to recognize the graduality in professional ethical life (for instance, Karssing and Spoor 2009; Vandekerckhove 2014). From a broader view, several research fields have focused their attention on related subjects, such as good work (Gardner and Mucinskas 2013), public service ethos and motivation (Rayner *et al.* 2011) and public values (Bozeman 2007; van der Wal 2009). And much to our interest, in organizational and business ethics, several authors have turned towards virtue ethics (Hoekstra 2006; Moore and Beadle 2006; Oakley and Cocking 2001; Overeem 2014; Solomon 1993; Tholen 2011). We will make a similar move, in arguing for the practical use of several concepts found in virtue ethics.

But first, we must acknowledge that dualistic moral reasoning is persistent in discussions about integrity issues. In our view, this is not only caused by the dualistic roots of the word 'integrity'. Two other popular integrity concepts, the 'dilemma' and the 'grey area', lead us in dualistic patterns as well. Although seemingly nuanced, they will prove to be essentially dualistic, oversimplifying and inherently steering towards a negative approach.

The grey area

In professional ethics, a much-used concept is the 'grey area'. As it is said to be a gradual intermediate between right and wrong, escaping both extremes, the concept seems to be promising at first glance. However, on a closer look, the concept of the grey area brings about three problems.

First of all, the use of the grey area turns out to confirm the absolute distinction between black and white. The grey area depicts a foggy terrain. Within this area, it is hard to determine where one passes from acting with little integrity into acting with too little integrity. Though the boundary is not very visible, it is still there. The metaphor expresses the idea that the distinction between right and wrong is difficult to locate. The grey area turns out not to be a nuance, but a refinement (and in that sense a confirmation) of thinking in black and white.

The second problem is that the grey area immediately brings about a negative connotation. It is generally considered to be a sign of integrity when someone makes a decision in a difficult situation. Such a decision is above all praiseworthy. The metaphor of the grey area does no justice to this. It primarily brings about the question why the grey area actually arose, and why one did not stay away from it. After all, a foggy terrain is something to be evaded.

The third problem of the grey area is that in the current use, it only allows for thinking about integrity in terms of 'more or less'. Whether one is brave, vain, honest or wilful, the grey area calls for an undifferentiated reduction of all such qualifications into the same category, namely more or less integrity. This is one-dimensional, implying that there are only different shades of grey, and leaving out the possibility that there are different colours altogether within one situation. Yet, in integrity issues, there is a need for such different colours, since moral judgements are a composition of qualifications of different kinds. Let us explain this idea with an example.

An administrator of a public housing corporation chose a Maserati as his company car. When asked about this choice, he stated that it was allowed by the existing rules (this car was in the same price range as the large German cars that some of his peers drove) and therefore permitted. He simply enjoyed driving such a car, even though it was not very practical.

The choice of the administrator is reason for generally shared indignation. In the Netherlands, a housing corporation is a semi-public organization that provides housing for people with a low income. The public deems it wrong that money is spent on an expensive sports vehicle, instead of on houses for vulnerable people. As the other administrators allowed themselves expensive cars as well, all administrators were doing something wrong. But the Maserati-administrator was subject to significantly more criticism than his 'colleagues'.

This criticism lays bare different dimensions in integrity issues. The administrator is deemed not only to have acted excessively, but also selfishly, because he used the means of the housing corporation solely for his own pleasure. Furthermore, even if the Maserati would have been cheaper and very practical, such a sports car radiates a luxury that does not suit the social role of a housing corporation. The administrator should have realized this, which makes his choice, besides excessive and selfish, inappropriate as well.

Integrity issues have a multidimensionality that is not done justice when expressed in a dualism of doing (more or less) right or wrong. Excessiveness, selfishness and inappropriateness are moral wrongs of different kinds. In the grey area, one is tempted to add them up into one category, and talk solely in terms of more or less, without acknowledging that, in reality, these aspects are incommensurable.

Dilemmas

Another popular concept in thinking about integrity is the 'dilemma'. A lot of integrity training programmes and popular discussions about integrity issues revolve around this concept. It serves as a tool to explicate and solve integrity issues. A dilemma frames such issues as choices between two options, both morally valuable but mutually exclusive. These options can be either equally right or equally wrong. The latter is sometimes called a 'tragic dilemma'. Within the framework of the dilemma, acting with integrity means correctly weighing these options against each other, and carrying out the chosen option.

This framing is problematic in several ways. To start with, it suggests that there is always a moral price to be paid, and so a negative vocabulary lurks just around the corner. If moral damage is inevitable, then how can one resolve a dilemma? Moreover, the framing narrows the process of moral reasoning. The bifurcation offers only two possible solutions. As a consequence, the dilemma hinders creative thought about morally complex matters. Of course, it is possible that deliberation about a dilemma leads to a third solution, but the dilemma structure itself does not evoke this option. And the dilemma is narrow in another sense: it is oriented at actions. But actions are the outcomes of a process in which perception, attitude and influence of the environment are also involved. The dilemma framework easily ignores these aspects, even though they are generally considered to be highly relevant for integrity issues. The following case illustrates this.

The City Council is developing plans for a new shopping mall. Peter, one of the councillors, owns a business, and is considering opening a new shop there. Because of this, he experiences his situation as a dilemma: should he have a say in the council meetings about this topic, or should he step back? After some consideration, he decides to withdraw from the meetings, starting from the first moment the plans are discussed.

In situations such as these, councillors are divided about this choice. On one hand, some of them think Peter is doing the right thing. The municipal government and its officials should pursue the public interest, and in the course of this decision-making process Peter might develop a personal interest. On the other hand, there are councillors who think Peter is doing the wrong thing. Of all the councillors, precisely he has the most expertise on this subject. With Peter's knowledge and help, the City Council could come to a better plan.

By introducing his issue in terms of a dilemma, Peter only allows for two possible options. Whichever option he chooses, the result will be moral damage. Peter will harm the public interest, either by lowering the quality of the decision-making process, or by risking a conflict of interests. Nevertheless, the dilemma demands that one of the options is decided to be the right thing to do. By inference, the lesser option can only be wrong, and one cannot act with integrity by doing the wrong thing. Paradoxically, where we started with two equally valuable options, the decision model turns one of these options into its negative.

Now, we do not want to deny the existence of dilemmas. Situations where only two options are possible do exist, and recognizing them is an important moral ability. But we think it is problematic to reduce every moral issue to a dilemma, as is often done in everyday vocabulary and in many training sessions. Luckily, Van Es (2011) provides a useful distinction between three kinds of moral issues: moral questions (concerning gaps in relevant moral knowledge, such as the details on a whistle-blowing procedure), moral problems (concerning moral challenges that have to be dealt with, with the help of knowledge, skills and prudence) and moral dilemmas or moral aporias (concerning inevitable moral conflict and damage). So, not every moral issue is a dilemma. What appears to be a dilemma could very well be a moral problem or even just a moral question. In line with this, Badaracco (1998) describes dilemmas as 'defining moments', acknowledging their heavy weight. We agree that the concept of 'dilemma' should only be used in the gravest of choices. It takes a thorough scrutiny to discern what kind of moral issue one faces. Unfortunately, this is not necessarily always done well, especially if the dilemma is actively and solely put to the fore as a framework for moral issues.

The distinction made by Van Es could be a helpful guide for Peter. He might first frame his issue as a moral question: are there relevant regulations? Though some City Councils have formulated guidelines on conflicts of interest, this would probably not be very helpful to Peter. He has not yet developed a personal interest (though it could arise in the near future). Moreover, the limitations of rules in such complex situations have been broadly recognized (Hoekstra 2006; Vandekerckhove 2014). They call for interpretation, prudent application and are most of the times not yet adapted to new situations. Peter therefore probably faces a moral problem, which requires him to broadly reflect on his situation. In the next paragraphs, we will provide Peter the means for such reflection.

Virtue ethics concepts

The concepts of integrity, the grey area and the dilemma harbour a dualistic framing within them, tempting people to oversimplify moral issues. This dualistic framing is mostly demotivating, focusing on the negatives. Meanwhile, the overall goal of professional integrity and ethics is worthwhile: to stimulate good conduct and to prevent bad behaviour in organizations. Therefore, alternative concepts are required, which should be able to deal with the positive aspects of integrity, and express the graduality and complexity of moral reasoning. To this end, we introduce three concepts based on virtue ethics and compare these with other developments in the field.

Though the claim *that* virtue ethics could be fruitful for professional ethics is not new, there is still much to be done to put this into practice (Tholen 2011, p. 38). In the next three sections, we focus on *how* a virtue ethics approach can be put to use in integrity issues. Three virtue ethical concepts will be highlighted: 'the excellent mean', 'the development of virtues' and 'shared practices'. From a virtue ethical perspective, it is a bit artificial to isolate three concepts, since they are connected to each other in the virtue ethics framework. Yet, the reason we do so anyway is because of their practical worth: each of these has its own merit.

Excellent mean

The most urgent moral issues usually revolve around the question: what should I do? The classic virtue ethical answer to that question is given by the progenitor of virtue ethics, Aristotle: the right thing to do is to achieve 'the excellent mean' (Aristotle 2002, NE 1107a1-5). As every situation is different, one cannot overly rely on standardized rules and procedures. Instead, one must find the excellent mean. Where this excellent mean lies depends on the situation: 'what is virtuous in a specific setting cannot be determined in advance, using some rule or algorithm. The specific context and setting have to be taken into consideration' (Tholen 2011, p. 39).

Aristotle's use of the term 'mean' has tempted many people to associate virtue with 'average' or 'moderate' actions. Yet, the goal is to find the *excellent* mean. Such associations are therefore not justified. The mean should not be confused with becoming dull or average. Instead, Aristotle says that achieving the excellent mean is 'a rare thing, a proper object of praise, and something fine' (Aristotle 2002, NE 1109a31). Virtuous actions represent the ideals of a good life by high standards. They are excellent actions, and signs of an excellent character.

The fact that a virtue ethics approach aims for the excellent mean does not imply that any other action than the perfect one is morally unacceptable. On the contrary, it implies that there is room for lesser options. Aristotle uses the image of an archer, trying to hit a target in the bullseye (Aristotle 2002, NE 1094a23-24). As the archer receives points for hitting the target, the reward increases the closer he or she gets to the centre, with the bullseye as the highest score. In virtue ethical terms, to judge an action is to measure it in relation to the excellent mean at which it should be aimed. The closer the better, but there is a wider margin in which the action is acceptable.

The ability of the excellent mean to take into account moral graduality can be demonstrated in the case of Peter and the shopping mall. We saw that a description of his situation as a dilemma forces him to condemn either withdrawing or participating. But Peter could also ask: what is the excellent mean in this situation? Thus framed, it becomes a moral problem instead of a moral dilemma (Van Es 2011). This immediately opens a moral space from 'acceptable' to 'excellent', giving Peter room for different actions. Virtue ethics challenges him to take the best possible decision, while acknowledging that a near-perfect act is good and praiseworthy as well. For instance, there could be a certain period of time in which it would be better, but not necessary, for Peter to withdraw from the decision-making process. During this time, both withdrawing and not withdrawing would be morally acceptable. The excellent mean makes it possible to ask what the best moment to withdraw would be, within the period of time in which this would be acceptable.

This gradual way of reasoning seems to be possible in the grey area as well. Yet, there are two important differences. First of all, the concept of the grey area focuses at the black in the transition zone between black and white. Contrastingly, the excellent mean is oriented at the white area. It is a positive, motivating approach, staying away from the bad by focusing on the good. Second, and more importantly, compared to the grey area, the excellent mean brings the complexity of acting with integrity much more to the fore. As Aristotle phrases it, the person of virtue acts 'to the extent one should, when one should, for the reason one should, and in the manner one should' (Aristotle 2002, NE 1109a26-28). It is self-evident that to hit the excellent mean, one must take into account many different aspects of the situation: one can miss the target in many ways. Recall Aristotle's comparison of the virtuous person with an archer. He or she must take into account all aspects of the situation to hit the bullseye. These aspects can differ from shot to shot. First, there is wind, then there is rain, and then there is maybe some fog (the archer probably lives in England). So to hit the mean three times in a row, the archer has to take into account all the relevant, different aspects of each new situation.

In the example of Peter, the concept of the excellent mean clarifies that his moral issue is not only about finding the best moment to withdraw. It is also about doing so with the right collegial manners, the right amount of (media) attention, the right tone of voice and using the right (formal and informal) procedures. Moreover, perhaps Peter can withdraw partly, for example only from the voting, or only from the debates. These aspects of the situation are all of a different kind. They cannot all be compared on one scale, nor can they be reduced to each other. Approaching an issue in terms of a grey area tends to reduce all moral aspects into one category. Contrastingly, the excellent mean encourages one to take all these different aspects into consideration, creating room for a broad moral investigation.

The development of virtues

The question of how one can hit the excellent mean seems to be a question about an action. But since the excellent mean is different in every situation, we must focus our attention on the person who has to have the *ability* to act well in all those situations (Upton 2014, p. 166). In Aristotle's example, the archer must take into account many aspects of the situation, differing from shot to shot. What is necessary all the time is that he or she is an excellent archer. This is the main argument of virtue ethics: that we must focus 'upon what sort of person one is rather than upon what sorts of actions one performs' (Van Hooft 2014, p. 3).

A virtue is, according to Aristotle's classical definition, 'a disposition issuing in decisions, depending on intermediacy of the kind relative to us, this being determined by rational prescription and in the way which the wise person would determine it' (Aristotle 2002, NE 1107a1-5). The most important feature of a virtue is that it is a character trait, encompassing all aspects of behaviour and attitude: 'beliefs, desires, emotions, patterns of reasoning, strength of will, and so on' (Upton 2014, p. 166). In other words, character traits are both 'deep' and 'broad' (Russell 2013, p. 17). The first means that character traits are steady and reliable. A person can be characterized by his or her character traits, because they are present over a longer period of time. 'Broad' implies that character traits show themselves not only in action, but in one's entire attitude, values and emotions.

Virtues are a specific kind of character trait: they are morally praiseworthy, since they are those the 'wise person' would have. They are 'excellences of character that consist in both caring about the right sorts of things and having the wisdom and practical skills to judge and act successfully with respect to those things' (Russell 2013, p. 7). For example, honesty is considered to be a virtue. It means that one cares about telling the truth, but also has the practical skills to assess when, where and how one can tell the truth. In addition, it also means that one has an emotional appreciation of truth and of other truth-telling people.

This raises the question of which virtues are key to the professional life. Van Tongeren (2012) and Overeem (2014) focus on the classic (cardinal) virtues of courage, justice, temperance and prudence. MacIntyre recognizes a different set of virtues as the core professional virtues: justice, courage and truthfulness (2014, p. 226). Solomon gives yet another analysis of the 'supervirtue' of integrity (1993, p. 174), stressing openness, cooperation, loyalty and autonomy. A final fruitful suggestion is offered by Swanton's notion of 'dialogical virtues'. As she points out, ethics is not a matter of individual judgement, for virtuous judgement is informed by wisdom, and part of wisdom is the awareness that each of us only possess a limited perspective. So, ethical decision-making is and ought to be collective. To be able to do so, several 'dialogical virtues' are necessary (Swanton 2003). The most important of these is of course *phronésis*, the moral wisdom that Aristotle treats in book VI of his *Nicomachean Ethics*. For now, we will conclude that a focus on actions is one-sided. The richness of the concept of integrity can only be captured by understanding what it means to be a person of integrity. That is, by understanding which virtues are relevant to his or her profession, and in which way these virtues express themselves. This seems to be a fruitful approach, although further investigation is necessary to see whether this approach can be maintained.

Character traits exist in different degrees. For instance, someone can be outstandingly courageous, or courageous to a certain degree, or downright cowardly. A core idea of virtue ethics is that character traits can grow and can be developed. This process of character building requires exercise and training, of a specific kind:

> the way we learn things we should do, knowing how to do them, is by doing them. For example people become builders by building, and cithara-players by playing the cithara; so too, then, we become just by doing just things, moderate by doing moderate things, and courageous by doing courageous things.
>
> (Aristotle 2002, NE 1103a33–b1)

Paradoxically, virtues are developed by repeatedly acting with virtue. This moral development can be difficult at the start, but 'over time we develop an understanding of what a particular virtue demands and some level of comfort and satisfaction in acting virtuously' (Hartman 2013, p. 249). Aristotle compares virtue to bodily fitness, which also requires continuous exercise (for instance, Aristotle

2002, NE 1099a3-4, 1104a15, 1106b3). Virtue requires constant exercise and has to go on all the time. It is a process that takes effort, time and is never over. Moral development is never completed. A virtue ethics approach is therefore critical of training forms that are one-time events. 'Moral education must be of continuous concern, of internalization, and moulding character' (Tholen 2011, p. 41). All in all, virtue ethics argues that organizations should provide a learning environment 'hospitable to virtue' (Hartman 2013, p. 254).

A growing number of authors confirm the idea that the development of moral character plays a positive role in strengthening integrity, for instance with the help of a concept such as competence. Macaulay and Lawton consider virtue and competence as 'equally valid routes to the successful implementation of a new ethical culture within local government' (2006, p. 709). Whitton (2009) discusses competence in a way that resembles virtue ethics as well. He defines ethical competence as a set of knowledge, skills, values and attitudes, and describes six different stages, starting with problem identification skills (ethical sensitivity) and ending with 'attitude and commitment' (wanting to act right). This last element especially could be understood (better) in a virtue ethics approach.

There is a body of knowledge on the effectiveness of integrity training forms. Often, trainings have a limited character, giving priority to 'cognitive programmes in ethical decision-making' (Lawton et al. 2013, p. 130). They offer transference of knowledge on relevant laws and regulations, transference of the values of an organization, and development of the skill to analyse and weigh dilemmas (Maesschalck 2012). Such training methods primarily affect the intellectual dimension, instead of all the different emotional and motivational aspects of a character. Whitton identifies this as a serious gap in the current practices in professional moral development: 'perhaps the most problematic area of developmental intervention in ethics is achieving commitment to the application of standards. Notoriously, knowledge of norms does not itself guarantee conforming conduct' (2009, p. 242). So there is a growing recognition of the importance of a right attitude. This recognition is also visible in Huberts' distinction of the different goals that moral trainings should pursue: moral awareness, moral judgement, moral motivation and ethical behaviour (Huberts 2014, p. 170). In a virtue ethics approach, daily practice would be the centrepiece of moral education, taking place in response to the requirements of highly concrete, practical situations (Sherman 1999, p. 257). Still, training forms encompassing all four of Huberts' goals would certainly be helpful to the moulding of a good character.

Another interesting parallel development can be found in the distinction between intrinsic and extrinsic motivation. That is, in doing something either because 'it is inherently interesting or enjoyable' or because 'it leads to a separable outcome' (Ryan and Deci 2000, p. 55). A virtue ethics approach argues that a person of integrity is intrinsically motivated to act with integrity. This correlates with empirical evidence, indicating that if there is a distinct motivation to work in public service, this positively relates to 'a range of desirable organizational attitudes and behaviours' (Lawton et al. 2013, p. 58; cf. Bozeman 2007, p. 181).

Shared practices

Moral development has a strong social dimension. This idea is supported by a third virtue ethics concept: 'shared practices'. Aristotle's famous statement that 'man is a social animal' (Aristotle 1990, Politics 1253a4) means that the development of virtue only succeeds when it is facilitated and stimulated by a social environment, in a community where people share basic norms and values (MacIntyre 2014, p. 217). A virtue ethics approach to integrity and ethics management takes it as a starting point that organizations are 'first of all communities, social groups with shared purposes' (Solomon 1993, p. 131). Professional integrity has to be understood from within these communities of professionals. Cox *et al.* bring precisely this idea to the fore: 'Professional integrity is not a matter of remaining true to oneself; it is, very roughly, a matter of remaining true to the fundamental role and character of one's profession – to its principles, values, ideas, goals and standards' (2003, p. 104).

Moral education is therefore a moral upbringing to the standards of the profession. But what are these standards of a profession? Where can one find them?

This question can be answered excellently with MacIntyre's concept of a practice. In his view, a practice is 'a coherent and complex form of socially established cooperative human activity through which goods internal to that form of activity are realized' (2014, p. 218). Examples of practices are making music, providing health care or playing football. What separates a practice from other forms of human activity is that the practice contains goods that are 'internal to that form of activity'. Think, for instance, of musicians, playing together for the pleasure of playing together. The internal good of making music characterizes what making music is all about. Likewise, professional practices can be characterized by their internal good. Health care is about caring for people's health; law is about ensuring lawfulness; science is about gaining knowledge. To be clear, practices are no moral islands, separated from society. Every practice is embedded within society. This gives a normative orientation. Practices are supposed to play a worthwhile role in society – providing music, health, legality, knowledge, so that society as a whole can flourish. This distinguishes the 'practice' of criminality from the practice of policing. Internal goods 'make for an achievement for the whole community' (Tholen 2011, p. 39).

Practices involve 'standards of excellence and obedience to rules as well as the achievement of goods' (MacIntyre 2014, p. 221). This means that in a virtue ethics approach, rules have a natural place. For instance, musicians obey certain explicit rules (i.e. the instructions of the conductor) and follow implicit norms (i.e. to listen attentively to each other's music), to achieve the internal good of playing music together. In much the same way, physicians ideally follow the rules and standards of their practice to achieve good health care. If professional integrity consists of remaining true to the role of one's profession, professionals must be focused on the rules that follow from the internal good: 'to play the game is to accept . . . the rules that define them' (Solomon 1993, p. 120). Values find their place in a practice as well. They should stem from the internal goods of the profession. In law, given the internal good of 'justice', highly valued values should be accuracy and impartiality, since these are the values that contribute to the good of the profession. Lastly, practices involve virtues as well as standards of excellence. 'The virtues enable the individual to achieve the goods internal to practices' (Moore and Beadle 2006, p. 372). Becoming virtuous means becoming able to engage in a practice, acting according to its standards and realizing its internal goods.

A practice is also characterized by 'external goods': material means, power and prestige. 'External goods can be the individual's property and possession. They are typically the object of competition and zero sum game' (Tholen 2011, p. 39). Organizations and institutions are focused on external goods, since money, influence and power are necessary for any organization to exist. But a professional should primarily be working towards the internal goods. This creates an inevitable tension in professional life: 'the essential association and tension between practices and institutions, and internal and external goods, gives the texture of organizational life a central dilemma' (Moore and Beadle 2006, p. 371). A focus on power, personal prestige and money will have a corrupting influence on behaviour. But, in a morally healthy organization, the external goods are subordinated to the internal goods of its practice (MacIntyre 2014, p. 226).

The distinction between external and internal goods provides us with a vocabulary to discuss organizational goals. Knowledge of the internal goods within a practice can provide more clarity to which goals, values, standards and rules are worth pursuing. For instance, it provides a moral foundation for criticizing the attitude of the 'Maserati-administrator'. He lost track of the purpose of his organization (providing housing for vulnerable people), and his desire for money and prestige prevailed over his responsibility for the internal goods of the organization.

Practices do not only provide direction for moral criticism. They are also open for discussion themselves. 'Practices are not fixed and unchanging sets of activities; they have a history and evolve' (Tholen 2011, p. 39). Over time, professions change, and so do their standards (Cox et al. 2003, p. 104). This is a gradual, social process, informed both by the professionals from within, and the societal demands from outside the profession. Aristotle explains this process by pointing out that man is a political animal in a community characterized by *logos* (rationality). In other words, people live in a community where there is an ongoing discussion and debate about its moral standards. This is (maybe even more so) true for present-day societies.

For integrity policies, it is important to remain aware of this aspect of practices. If practices are explicated, it could be tempting to fixate them in some sort of code. But practices must stay connected to societal changes and allow themselves to change: 'Professions must remain open to broader social influences, to remind each profession of its constitutive ideals that it has been entrusted to serve' (Oakley and Cocking 2001, p. 90). If a practice becomes overly fixated in processes, codes, rules, regulations and moral codes, it would turn out to be counterproductive.

Another aspect of practices is equally instructive for integrity policies. As internal goods differ, the face of integrity is different between different professions.

This is particularly important when we talk about the civil service, an umbrella concept for a wide range of different professions: from police officers to health policy advisors, from community councillors to controllers in finance departments. Integrity is not exactly the same for all of them. Nevertheless, there is a tendency to standardize integrity policy models in civil services. 'The ethical significance of the distinctive goals of different professions is often ignored by contemporary approaches to professional ethics' (Oakley and Cocking 2001, p. 84). A virtue ethics approach warns for the development of such an overly uniform approach. There should always be enough room for the inevitable differences between professions. Without this, integrity policies could be harmful, instead of advancing the moral quality of civil services.

The concept of practice has serious consequences for the widely recognized importance of ethical leadership as well. There is a growing literature on the impact of leadership on organization ethics and ethics management leadership, with consensus on the important role of the leader (Bird and Waters 1989; Huberts 2014; Lasthuizen 2008; Treviño et al. 2000). A virtue ethics approach stresses that the leader has to 'protect the practice'. It is up to the leader and senior management to let the external goods be put to use for the internal goods. This means both resisting the temptations of the external goods (fraud, corruption, self-enrichment or unnecessary enrichment of the organization) and defending the practice from overly financial, political and efficiency-driven goals.

It also implies attention for inexperienced employees. They should 'be able to learn from those more experienced. Role models must be identified. That might be leaders or superiors, but also others' (Tholen 2011, p. 42). Mentoring new or junior colleagues by senior employees could also be an effective instrument (Goosen and Van Vuuren 2005, p. 69). It should be emphasized that teaching newcomers in their profession is not a non-committal happening, but entails very real requirements to those newcomers:

> In the initial stages of their professional lives novices experience many externally imposed obligations. As time goes by virtuous habits are developed, which is to say that the underlying values and principles that define good practice within a given professional sphere have been internalized.
>
> (Becker 2004, p. 57)

All in all, a profession must be able to provide a moral upbringing to its members.

The concept of shared practices can be seen as complementary to current developments that refer to morally motivated behaviour. The constructs of public service motivation (PSM) and public service ethos (PSE) bear remarkable likenesses to the concept of practice. They combine individual motivation, organizational rules and processes, and the organizational goals, indicating 'a belief system that may explain "why" individuals are motivated by it, "how" they deliver public services in accordance with its values, and "what ends" they perceive it to endorse' (Rayner et al. 2011, pp. 29–30). Though PSM and PSE lack the normative and critical aspect of 'practice', their empirical descriptions could possibly strengthen our understanding of particular practices. This calls for further research.

Karssing and Spoor (2009) describe integrity as professional responsibility. They consider a 'third-generation conception' of integrity, consisting of acting according to the standards of the profession, and connected to motivation, learning and autonomy. Yet, the notion 'professional responsibility' lacks an underlying conceptual framework. Virtue ethics could provide this, by showing how the moral orientation of professional behaviour is connected to both human motivation and the normative orientation of societies.

In a similar way, virtue ethics is complementary to the public values approach. Starting with Moore's *Creating Public Value* (1995), this approach turned out to be a welcome counterbalance to the dominance of public management approaches rooted in assumptions of economic individualism. The public values approach argues that management is not a technical affair. Instead, it should be oriented towards the public values that are generally shared in society. There are many similarities between virtue ethics and a public values approach, but they should not be identified with each other. The starting point of the latter are the values that are generally shared in society and public interest. Importantly, it stresses the consensus about these values. For instance, Bozeman refers to the values that are 'endorsed by the social collective' (2007, p. 15). As pointed out before, virtue ethics empha- sizes that society is characterized by ongoing discussions about its values, virtues, goods and standards, and that practices are constantly evolving. Furthermore, a virtue ethics approach has a different starting point. The focus is not on policy problems (as is the case in Bozeman 2007), but on the professional within his or her professional practice.

Another complementary line of research is focusing on 'organizational values' (van der Wal 2009, 2012). Values are the denominators of what is important to an organization. This is not far removed from the described orientation on internal goods. In fact, the establishment of internal goods is often served by expression of core values. But values remain rather abstract ideas, which gain their precise meaning only when they are understood and 'practised' in a practice. Virtue ethics offers the tools to discover these precise moral meanings in real organizational life. It explains how values are realized in one's character (i.e. as virtues) and one's actions (i.e. in virtuous actions).

Furthermore, virtue ethics provides a normative viewpoint, which can be both contrasted and supplemented by descriptive value research (such as Rayner *et al.* 2011; Vandenabeele *et al.* 2006; van der Wal 2009). For instance, the fact that empirical research shows a 'value solidity' (van der Wal 2009, p. 231) provides support for the idea that practices exist with a certain moral stability. And it is highly valuable to know which values are present in a profession or organization. Still, such insights do not provide an adequate moral ground for judging which values should be present and how they should be ranked. The concept of practice, guided by an internal good, does provide for such moral reasoning. For instance, a pressing question is which values are instrumental, and which values are intrinsic to a practice (Bozeman 2007, pp. 119–20). A virtue ethics approach enables one to make this distinction. Moreover, it enables one to criticize or approve existing value sets in organizations.

A last line of discussion that is related to virtue ethics concerns the distinction between intrinsic and extrinsic motivation. However, two different types of extrinsic motivation are discerned. People 'can perform extrinsically motivated actions with resentment, resistance, and disinterest or, alternatively, with an attitude of willingness that reflects an inner acceptance of the value or utility of a task' (Ryan and Deci 2000, p. 55). This means that knowing that a task contributes to the internal good could provide sufficient external motivation to 'will' the task, even when the task itself is not 'inherently interesting or motivating'. In such cases, dedication to the internal goods is characterized by extrinsic motivation. Therefore, MacIntyre's distinction between internal and external goods cannot be understood as synonymous with the distinction between intrinsic and extrinsic motivation. Still, there is an interesting interplay between both distinctions. In our view, this calls for further research, since it could provide a connection between descriptive psychological insights and the normative moral theory of virtue ethics.

Conclusion

In this chapter, we have analysed three popular integrity concepts: integrity, the dilemma and the grey area. We came to the conclusion that these concepts bring about a strong tendency towards dualistic moral reasoning. Though we do not deny that in many cases a clear judgement about right and wrong is appropriate, at least part of our moral vocabulary should be able to recognize more colours than black, grey and white. Too often, the current concepts lead us, even if we are unaware of this, to dualistic patterns. We run the risk of losing sight of the very real graduality and complexity of integrity issues. Even worse, it overly emphasizes the negative side of these issues, causing demotivation and fear. This does not enhance the credibility of integrity discussions, nor the legitimacy of integrity policies.

A virtue ethics approach enables people to express and to deal with moral graduality and complexity in the workplace. It proves to be of practical value to the field of integrity, avoiding the inherent negativity that dualistic concepts entail. We showed this with the help of three concepts from a virtue ethics approach: the excellent mean, the development of virtues and shared practices.

First, the idea of the excellent mean provides professionals with a concept to investigate a situation as a moral problem, instead of a moral dilemma. Looking for the excellent mean is positive and motivating, since it is oriented at the perfect action. This creates space for professionals to find different ways and different gradations of acting with integrity.

Second, the concept of developing virtues provides the possibility to discuss *to what extent* someone is a person of integrity. It makes way for a gradual character approach to integrity. Instead of the two options one has within the dualistic approach (to be or not to be), one can ask which virtues one has, to what extent and how they can be developed further. It brings about a vocabulary that is intrinsically aimed at improvement, while acknowledging what such training requires. Clearly, this is a positive approach to integrity.

And third, the notion of shared practices reminds us that professional integrity is closely related to the role and purpose of an organization. It leads to a better understanding of the moral role of the manager: to serve and protect the practices in his or her organization. Moreover, the idea of shared practices makes us realize that integrity has as many faces as there are professions. Internal goods could provide the much-sought-for moral compasses in current practices and organizations. Integrity policies should tap into this source of moral motivation.

We showed that a virtue ethics approach has connections to several other developments in the field of integrity. This interplay is, should and will be subjected to critical discussion. In this, virtue ethics provides a unique and normative perspective. Therefore, we think virtue ethics offers a promising way of thinking about the advancement of integrity, and we have glimpsed such an approach. But at the very least, with the help of the three concepts we presented, a virtue ethics approach can bring some colour into our black and white thinking.

References

Aristotle (1990) *Politics*, trans. H. Rackham, Cambridge, MA: Harvard University Press.

Aristotle (2002) *Nicomachean Ethics*, trans. S. Broadie and C. Rowe, Oxford: Oxford University Press.

Badaracco, J.L., Jr. (1998) 'The discipline of building character', *Harvard Business Review*, 76(2): 114–25.

Becker, M. (2004) 'Virtue ethics, applied ethics and rationality twenty-three years after *After Virtue*', *South African Journal of Philosophy*, 23(1): 48–62.

Bird, F.B. and Waters, J.A. (1989) 'The moral muteness of managers', *California Management Review*, 32(1): 73–88.

Bozeman, B. (2007) *Public Values and Public Interest: Counterbalancing Economic Individualism*, Washington, DC: Georgetown University Press.

Cox, D., La Caze, M. and Levine, P. (2003) *Integrity and the Fragile Self*, Aldershot: Ashgate.

Gardner, H. and Mucinskas, D. (2013) 'Educating for good work: From research to practice', *British Journal of Educational Studies*, 61(4): 1–18.

Goosen, X. and Van Vuuren, L.J. (2005) 'Institutionalising ethics in organisations: The role of mentoring', *Journal of Human Resource Management*, 3(3): 61–71.

Hartman, E. (2013) 'The virtue approach to business ethics', in D.C. Russell (ed.), *The Cambridge Companion to Virtue Ethics* (pp. 240–64), Cambridge: Cambridge University Press.

Hoekstra, A. (2006) 'Integriteit vanuit deugdenethisch perspectief', *Filosofie in bedrijf*, 2 (June): xx.

Huberts, L.W.J.C. (2012) 'Visies op integriteit', in J.H.J. Van Den Heuvel, L.W.J.C. Huberts and E.R. Muller (eds), *Integriteit: Integriteit en integriteitsbeleid in Nederland* (pp. 21–37), Deventer: Kluwer.

Huberts, L.W.J.C. (2014) *The Integrity of Governance*, Basingstoke: Palgrave Macmillan.

Karssing, E.D. (2006) *Integriteit in de beroepspraktijk*, Assen: Van Gorcum.

Karssing, E.D. and Spoor, S. (2009) 'Integriteit 3.0, Naar een derde generatie integriteitsbeleid', *Jaarboek Integriteit 2010*, The Hague: CAOP.

Lasthuizen, K. (2008) *Leading to Integrity: Empirical Research into the Effects of Leadership on Ethics and Integrity*, Enschede: Printspartners Ipskamp.

Lawton, A., Rayner, J. and Lasthuizen, K. (2013) *Ethics and Management in the Public Sector*, London: Routledge.

Macaulay, M. and Lawton, A. (2006) 'From virtue to competence: Changing the principles of public service', *Public Administration Review*, 66(5): 702–10.

MacIntyre, A. (2014) *After Virtue: A Study in Moral Theory*, 3rd edn, London: Bloomsbury.

Maesschalck, J. (2012) 'Integriteitstrainingen', in J.H.J. Van Den Heuvel, L.W.J.C. Huberts and E.R. Muller (eds), *Integriteit: Integriteit en integriteitsbeleid in Nederland* (pp. 325–46), Deventer: Kluwer.

Moore, G. and Beadle, R. (2006) 'In search of organizational virtue in business: Agents, goods, practices, institutions and environments', *Organization Studies*, 27(3): 369–89.

Moore, M.H. (1995) *Creating Public Value: Strategic Management in Government*, Cambridge, MA: Harvard University Press.

Oakley, J. and Cocking, D. (2001) *Virtue Ethics and Professional Roles*, Cambridge: Cambridge University Press.

Overeem, P. (2014) 'Naar een beter integriteitsbegrip: Van deontologie naar deugdethiek', *Liberaal Reveil*, 3: 124–8.

Paine, L.S. (1994) 'Managing for organizational integrity', *Harvard Business Review*, 72(2): 106–17.

Rayner, J., Williams, H.M., Lawton, A. and Allinson, C.W. (2011) 'Public service ethos: Developing a generic measure', *Journal of Public Administration Research and Theory*, 21(1): 27–51.

Russell, D.C. (ed.) (2013) *The Cambridge Companion to Virtue Ethics*, Cambridge: Cambridge University Press.

Ryan, R.M. and Deci, E.L. (2000) 'Intrinsic and extrinsic motivations: Classic definitions and new directions', *Contemporary Educational Psychology*, 25(1): 54–67.

Sherman, N. (1999) 'The habituation of character', in N. Sherman (ed.), *Aristotle's Ethics: Critical Essays*, Lanham, MD: Rowman & Littlefield.

Solomon, R.C. (1993) *Ethics and Excellence: Cooperation and Integrity in Business*, Oxford: Oxford University Press.

Swanton, C. (2003) *Virtue Ethics: A Pluralistic View*, Oxford: Oxford University Press.

Tholen, B. (2011) 'Public virtue approaches', in M.S.S. De Vries and P.S. Kim (eds), *Value and Virtue in Public Administration* (pp. 33–46), Basingstoke: Palgrave Macmillan.

Treviño, L.K., Hartman, L.P. and Brown, M. (2000) 'Moral person and moral manager: How executives develop a reputation for ethical leadership', *California Management Review*, 42(4): 128–42.

Treviño, L.K., Den Nieuwenboer, N.A., Kreiner, G.E. and Bishop, D.G. (2014) 'Legitimating the legitimate: A grounded theory study of legitimacy work among ethics and compliance officers', *Organizational Behavior and Human Decision Processes*, 123(2): 186–205.

Upton, C. (2014) 'What virtues are there?', in S. Van Hooft (ed.), *The Handbook of Virtue Ethics* (pp. 165–76), Durham: Acumen.

Vandekerckhove, W. (2014) 'Virtue ethics and management', in S. Van Hooft (ed.), *The Handbook of Virtue Ethics* (pp. 341–51), Durham: Acumen.

Vandenabeele, W., Scheepers, S. and Hondeghem, A. (2006) 'Public service motivation in an international comparative perspective: The UK and Germany', *Public Policy and Administration*, 21(1): 13–31.

van der Wal, Z. (2009) 'A two-pronged methodological approach for measuring public and private sector organizational core values: The importance of content and context', in R.W. Cox (ed.), *Ethics and Integrity in Public Administration: Concepts and Cases* (pp. 212–35), Armonk, NY: M.E. Sharpe.

van der Wal, Z. (2012) 'Waarden en integriteit', in J.H.J. Van Den Heuvel, L.W.J.C. Huberts and E.R. Muller (eds), *Integriteit: Integriteit en integriteitsbeleid in Nederland* (pp. 87–102), Deventer: Kluwer.

Van Es, R. (2011) *Professionele Ethiek: Morele besluitvorming in organisaties en professies*, Deventer: Kluwer.

Van Hooft, S. (ed.) (2014) *The Handbook of Virtue Ethics*, Durham: Acumen.

Van Tankeren, M.H.M. (2012) 'Integriteit in de politieorganisatie', in J.H.J. Van Den Heuvel, L.W.J.C. Huberts and E.R. Muller (eds), *Integriteit: Integriteit en integriteitsbeleid in Nederland* (pp. 391–416), Deventer: Kluwer.

Van Tongeren, P. (2012) 'Integriteit als deugd', in J.H.J. Van Den Heuvel, L.W.J.C. Huberts and E.R. Muller (eds), *Integriteit: Integriteit en integriteitsbeleid in Nederland* (pp. 55–67), Deventer: Kluwer.

Whitton, H. (2009) 'Developing the "ethical competence" of public officials: A capacity-building approach', in R.W. Cox (ed.), *Ethics and Integrity in Public Administration: Concepts and Cases* (pp. 236–56), Armonk, NY: M.E. Sharpe.

4

DISCOURSES OF DECEIT

Political myth and ideological capital in public administration[1]

Michael Macaulay

Introduction

It is many decades since public administration was denounced for arriving at 'shallow and spurious answers' (Waldo 1948, p. 102), and arguably it has suffered from that same canard ever since. More recently, it has been claimed that public administration is a Sisyphean task, in which academics and practitioners are doomed to have the same conversations for eternity (Stivers 2008b). More recently still, Pollitt argued that public administration has comparatively little coherence as an academic discipline; indeed, he refers to public administration as 'a community of interest' that is brought together by 'its subject—the state, the public sector, and the public realm—not its aims, theories, or methods' (Pollitt 2010, p. 292). That public administration, and administrative ethics more specifically, are multidisciplinary fields cannot seriously be questioned. Yet, that same multidisciplinary perspective can be a positive force, enabling a multiplicity of perspectives to be looked at simultaneously; not through a grand unifying theory, but through the recognition of difference. The aim of this chapter is to explore this concept through a discussion on political myth and the notion of ideological capital.

Both of these concepts spring from ideas on narrative and storytelling in public administration, and while political myths are not new, they are increasingly prevalent as one of several 'discourses of deceit'. I will show that political myths display five interlocking components (see Table 4.1), which work together to ideological positions. I will then suggest that the notion of competing myths is unhelpful to understanding ethical, political and administrative debates as they seek to overcome complexity with reductionism. Instead, an intersubjective approach will be put forward to recognize and acknowledge myriad perspectives. In so doing, this chapter does not seek to denigrate the notion of political myth, but to critically assess its application. Finally, it will reinterpret an old myth to suggest a potential path for the development of an intersubjective philosophy of public administration. That is equally valid for administrative ethics (see also Macaulay 2009).

Political myth and discourses of deceit

As Farazmand (2012) has argued, public administration is facing unprecedented challenges both practical (financial crises, global security, climate change) and theoretical (the balance between openness and security). Indeed, it has been argued that we are living in 'dark times' (Stivers 2008a). Both the breadth and depth of these challenges are indeed enormous, although it is difficult to state for certain how comparable they are to the global challenges brought into being by the nineteenth and twentieth centuries, and therefore we face a further challenge today of looking towards a new philosophy of public administration in order to begin to conceptualize a response to the problems currently facing us. One of the responses is the development of political myths.

At its essence, a myth of any kind is a form of story, a narrative, and of course political discourse (and by extension discourse regarding public administration) has always been driven by storytelling: political parties create narratives around individual politicians, events and policies that are either accepted and repeated, or else investigated and (occasionally) exposed by the media. In the still vastly unregulated world of social and digital media, such stories can rise and/or fall exponentially more quickly.

There is little intrinsically wrong with such an approach, and the use of narrative has become evermore popular within the field of public administration itself. Bevir (2011) has recently produced a spirited defence of public administration as storytelling: that too often, studies were founded on a modern empiricist paradigm that is far more accessible through interpretive analysis of the construction of meaning. Such an argument builds on a substantial body of work, including Bevir et al. (2003), Pollitt (2013), Rhodes and Brown (2005) and many others. Creating and interpreting stories in the public realm, therefore, is nothing new.

Yet, the dominance of narrative approaches raises a number of troubling questions. First, who creates the narrative? Pollitt (2010) suggests that another issue for the field of public administration is that there are competing voices not only from within academia, but from without, particularly business schools and the world of consultancy, all of whom seek to create their own narratives. Second, what is the basis for accepting a particular narrative? As Weston (2007) demonstrates in his study of the psychology of electoral campaigns, messages that are simple and have greater emotional resonance are far more likely to be embraced. Tellingly, this works equally for positive and negative emotions, for aspiration as well as fear. More importantly, these points lead to a third consideration: to what extent are such stories true, and does this even matter? Herein lies the discourse of deceit: a narrative that may either be partially true or completely false, which nevertheless garners broad acceptance. It should be noted that these discourses also have a long-established heritage: one of the earliest examples in Western political philosophy,

Plato's *Republic*, argued for the development of the 'noble lie' – a fiction that would quell too much questioning or dissatisfaction from the populace. In a more modern setting, Arendt pioneered the discussion on the use of falsehoods as propagandistic drivers to great effect. Perelman and Obrechts-Tyteca (1969) outlined the 'new rhetoric' that sought to persuade an audience towards an 'adherence' to future action. Parker (1972) discussed exploitative rhetoric and the ability for narrative to be used for manipulation. More recently still, Oborne (2005) suggested that, in the UK at least, there had been an increase in both the quantity and quality of political lies, while Poole (2006) has examined the way in which language continues to be manipulated by the political class. How, then, do myths fit within these discourses?

Myths are seemingly everywhere in public administration. They can be found underpinning the public sector reforms of innumerable nations as diverse as New Zealand (Lodge and Gill 2011), the Republic of Ireland (Wallis and McLoughlin 2010), the US (Stillman 1990), and in parts of Africa (Smoke 2003). There are myths about individual fields within public administration: the myth of account-ability (Downey 1986; Lam 2009), the myth of performance management (Modell 2004), myths about e-government (Bekkers and Homburg 2007; McCue and Roman 2012), myths of convergence (Goldfinch and Wallis 2010; Pollitt 2001), and even public policy (Christensen and Lægreid 2003; Ukeles 1997) or NPM itself (Lane 2006). It may be noted that these myths are often found to be reconsidered and repeated from time to time.

It may seem counter-intuitive to suggest that myth presents absolutes when it is an interpretive medium. Frequently, a myth is portrayed simply as a story, largely or entirely fictional, that can be exposed and falsified. This is certainly the approach behind opponents of the 'myths' of foreign policy and entry into the wars of the last decade. Moreover, some recent books have looked at specific political leaders and have sought to deconstruct the mythology that has evolved (or has been deliberately constructed) around their particular life stories – perhaps the most pertinent example of this has been the biography of Reagan, whose very title exhorts the reader to *Tear Down This Myth* (Bunch 2009; there is clearly a long tradition of such works; see, for example, Dunn 2011 for a similar exposé of Sarah Palin). This approach is also the fallback position for many of the academic papers cited above: their subjects of interest are mythical in the sense that they are untrue. But this is hardly the point. Of course, myths are stories, and frequently do rest on falsehoods, but this is by no means their only defining characteristics. Myth may be fictional, but fiction is not, necessarily, myth. Telling stories is one thing; constructing myths is quite another.

Related to this is the way in which myth can be created and sustained. Of course, to philosophers of history such as Skinner (1969), mythology can be the parvenu for those who neglect proper historical method, to the extent that commentators on the history of ideas frequently fall prey to mythologizing their subjects. This occurs through the development of the myth of *doctrines* (which attributes doctrinal expectations from the historians' own perspective on to a given theorist); the myth of *coherence* (which attributes coherence to a set of unconnected ideas, often by intricate analysis of hidden meanings by which to create the coherence); or the myth of prolepsis (which retroactively attributes teleological meaning to a particular theory or doctrine). Thus, for example, Rousseau's proclamation for the 'tyranny of the majority' becomes falsely attributed as the progenitor of twentieth-century totalitarianism.

What is crucial – particularly to the discourse of deceit – is that even though they do not necessarily report facts, myths of all types become reified so as to be seen as expressing essential truths. Whether or not they are true is beside the point; as Sorel (1960) suggests, the importance of myths (specifically political myths) is that they become so entrenched in the world view of a particular group that the myth 'cannot be refuted'.

Deconstructing political myths

At this stage, it may be useful to clarify our terminology. I do not wish to expand the chapter into an overview of mythology itself, but specifically *political* myths in public administration. Sorel's argument, therefore, serves to provide a further crucial distinction for my argument. Political myths are not to be belittled in any way, nor do I seek to argue *against* the use (or misuse) of political myth simply on the basis that such accounts are not truthful. As previously suggested, such argumentation is self-defeating as the power of a myth is not, ultimately, its evidential basis. Besides which, myths play a vital and positive role throughout the tradition of Western political philosophy from Plato onwards: the myth of the cave (although this is perhaps better understood as a parable) still provokes discussion today about the nature of reality, of knowledge, and of what it may mean to have enlightened government. While there is no need, of course, to revisit all of the instances where such myths have been used, it may be worth noting that so many of the concepts still held dear in liberal democracies – rights, justice, property, liberty, etc. – are themselves still frequently debated through the prism of myth: most notably, the myth of the social contract, whether this is through the English tradition of Hobbes and Locke or the continental European tradition of Pufendorf, Rousseau and others. Again, it may be worth noting that it is unimportant that such social contracts are fictitious; what these accounts have provided are an invaluable store of debate and dialogue that have proven to be continually beneficial for the advancement of political thought. To 'tear down' this particular myth would be counterproductive to the point of absurdity. And yet the appeal of these myths prevails even now.

Thus, what I am arguing here is, first, that there are other levels to understanding political myths; and, second, the way in which myth solidifies and underpins key assumptions in UK public policy and administration. As previously stated, the reality of a myth is beside the point: the interpretation and promulgation of the myth is all-important. In addition to the questions asked previously, therefore, the success of a political myth may perhaps be summed up in a relatively simple question: who is the *interpreter* of the myth?

TABLE 4.1 The components of political myths

Five components of political myths
1. Presented as narratives or stories
2. Largely, often entirely, untrue accounts
3. Designed to address practical issues
4. Most successful when used as interlocking narratives with other myths
5. Connect ideology and narrative

The first two elements of the political myth are already before us: they are largely (often entirely) untrue accounts that are presented as narrative. A third key element emerges from Tudor's (1972) seminal exposition, that political myth is entwined with practical thinking and real-life problem-solving:

> The understanding it provides is a practical understanding; that is to say, an understanding in which men consider the world that confronts them, not as the object of disinterested curiosity but as the material for their activity . . . No doubt some distortion of fact does occur. But, when practical considerations are foremost, men tend to believe what, at that moment, they find it convenient or necessary to believe.
>
> (Tudor 1972, p. 123)

Again, therefore, truth, if not wholly irrelevant, is only of secondary importance to the utility of myth. Gill (1980, cited in Flood 2002) further suggests that political myths rarely succeed in isolation and become bound up in an interlocking series of mythological discourse, each strand acting as reinforcement of the central theme. Christensen and Lægreid (2007, p. 1062) suggest that a mythical interpretation of public management 'sees reforms and their main concepts mainly in terms of myths, symbols, and fashions'. This explanation may be somewhat tautological but it hints at the interlocking nature of the appeal of myth.

Finally, and crucially, Flood argues that a political myth is the connection between ideology and narrative, and it 'is an ideologically marked account of past, present or predicted political events and which is affected as valid in its essentials by a social group' (2002, p. 42).

Political myths are manifestations of ideological positions, and therein lay their power. As we have suggested, the importance of myth lies in its interpretation; a political myth, therefore, is presented with the interpretation already embodied in the narrative. We know who controls the myth.

In such a way, I suggest that the fundamental power of political myth is that it helps create and sustain *ideological capital*. Like other forms, most notably Bordieu's economic, cultural and social capital, ideological capital is a resource that can be used to persuade people to accept and follow political leadership. Similar concepts have been discussed previously. Aldrich (2012) discussed the idea of social capital serving three purposes: bonding, bridging and linking, the latter of which relates explicitly to connecting people to political officials and leaders. Ideological capital achieves a similar link, through the delivery of a specific narrative in order to foster commitment to political decisions. This form is ideological in two of its best-recognized forms: both in terms of promoting a world view but also in the critical sense of normalizing elite perspectives (Lukes 2005). The more widely a myth is regarded as an uncontested truth, the more powerful its ideological capital.

Building ideological capital in the UK

Perhaps the most likely policy arena in which we may expect to find political myths is in foreign policy. To be fair, there is no shortage of discussion about the myths surrounding the Iraq and Afghanistan wars, which usually congregate around the fictional role of Saddam Hussein, or the creation of the misleading (if not downright fraudulent) UK dossier on the weapons capability of Iraq. These are all fascinating, if well worn, debates, although they are often framed in the sense of a simple untruth rather than the more nuanced, fivefold definition that I have outlined above. However, to reiterate, it is my contention that, in the UK at least, political myths significantly underpin ideas that drive both public policy and also attitudes towards public administration.

One of the more infamous recent examples has been used as a justification for welfare reform, which is currently being restructured and cut to an unprecedented degree. In 2009, before he was Secretary of State for the Department of Work and Pensions (DWP), Ian Duncan Smith made a speech that addressed the supposed fact that there are many families in the UK of whom three generations had never worked and had lived solely off state benefits: 'Life expectancy on some estates, where often three generations of the same family have never worked, is lower than the Gaza Strip. It suggests that unemployment can be explained by "cultures of worklessness" and "welfare dependency"'.

This image became deeply lodged in debates around welfare and remains so today. It is, I suggest, a political myth in every sense of the term. First, the statement is, at best, a gross and unsubstantiated generalization; at worst, it is entirely fictional. Recent longitudinal research has clearly demonstrated that even in the most deprived post-industrial areas of the UK, there is no evidence to support the notion of three generations of workless families (Shildrick *et al.* 2012). It is crucial, however, to not simply attack the claim here as false; as we have suggested, the truthfulness of a myth is secondary (at best) to its efficacy and resilience. What is more interesting is to see how far it corresponds to the other aspects of political myth, which elevates it from simple untruth to mythical status. The second critical area of success of the myth is that it is presented as an image: Duncan Smith offered no data to support his claim; rather, he relied on the narrative force of the image: grandparents, parents and children all living a life off the state and taxpayers' money.

Third, this narrative provides a very practical understanding of the supposed issues of welfare dependency. Nuance is not needed: generations are affected; welfare must be stopped. Fourth, the myth appears to be deeply ideological, and is better understood as part of an interlocking series of myths. It could be argued that this myth is an extension of old arguments of deserving versus undeserving poor (De Swaan 1988), which was restated in the 1980s by both US and UK governments, although its origins are much older (Beito 1993). In the UK, the debate is also bound up alongside accounts of benefit cultures and misleading (if not entirely mythical) accounts from senior politicians such as the then Prime Minister David Cameron's claim that 5 billion GBP is lost each year due to fraud and error. In actual fact, 80 per cent of that total was due to error alone, although, again, the veracity of a particular idea does not necessarily mean that it cannot be widely embraced. Even common language in the UK reflects the depth to which these myths have taken hold: from the use of the word 'chav' to denote somebody who is from what we may call (reluctantly) the underclass, to the universal acceptance of 'benefit scrounger' for people who claim welfare payments. Currently, welfare reform is deliberately positioned as 'strivers' versus 'shirkers'. The myth has certainly taken hold in the UK. A 2012 national survey found that the public thought that 41 per cent of welfare spending was on the unemployed and that 27 per cent of the entire welfare budget subjected to fraudulent claims. The actual figures are 3 per cent and 0.7 per cent, respectively.[2]

Of far greater significance, however, is that the myths underpinning these aspects of public policy are also interconnected with another myth, the myth of public administration in the UK. This myth could not be simpler, which is perhaps why it has persisted like a champion for so long. This is simply the myth of public administration as bureaucratic monolith. In the UK at least, the myth persists, and not as a relic of bygone debates, but as a living justification for continued change in public services. Why? Precisely because it *is* a myth, and therefore the lack of foundational truth or evidential basis truth is irrelevant.

Its most recent incarnation can be found in the *Open Public Services* White Paper that seeks to restructure (and radically cut) public services in health, education and welfare. This is premised in a jaundiced view of public administrators:

> Too many of our public services are still run according to the maxim 'the man in Whitehall really does know best'. Decades of top-down prescription and centralisation have put bureaucratic imperatives above the needs of service users, while damaging the public service ethos by continually second-guessing highly trained professionals. The idea behind this view of the world – that a small group of Whitehall ministers and officials have a monopoly on wisdom – has propagated a lowest common denominator approach to public services that implicitly favours the wealthy by allowing them to move to find pockets of excellence or to opt out altogether. Our vision of open public services turns this presumption on its head and places power in the hands of people and staff.
>
> (*Open Public Services* White Paper 2011, para. 1.9)

A more recent iteration emphasizes this view again:

> This means replacing top-down monopolies with open networks in which diverse and innovative providers compete to provide the best and most efficient services for the public. It means re-thinking the role of government – so that governments at all levels become increasingly funders, regulators and commissioners, whose task it is to secure quality and guarantee fair access for all, instead of attempting to run the public services from a desk in Whitehall, city hall or county hall.
>
> (*Open Public Services* 2012, p. 3)

I suggest that this is the embodiment of another political myth, in all five essential ways. First, the claims about top-down monopolies and the 'man in Whitehall' are not made with reference to evidence: indeed, they fly in the face of the overwhelming evidence about, for one example, networks in the public sector. If the government's claims are accurate, then there at least needs to be an admission that many decades of reform have been utterly without merit. Second, it presents a gripping narrative, albeit one that has clinically been dissected (see, for example, Lynn 2001). Third, as we have seen, the myth is entwined with other narratives of public service reform, which, taken collectively, give a clear demarcation of heroes and villains, with the bureaucrat and the welfare scrounger firmly in the latter camp. Fourth, the myth is painted in practical colours. Reform will be for more 'efficient services' and simply to 'secure quality'.

Finally, in Flood's terms, the myth is startlingly ideological. It is not only ideological in the Marxist sense, although it is most avowedly that too, but in the more commonly understood sense that it reflects a specific political perspective: in this case, the continuation of a New Right position that has its roots in the 1970s and 1980s. As Aucoin (2013) has shown, this view rests on key aims: to strengthen central government; to increase the power over staffing in the public services; to increase central control by continuing to dichotomize administration (or management) and policy. Two examples may suffice to illustrate this. The 1988 Educational Reform Act officially introduced the concept of parental choice in the UK state school sector; it also granted the Education Secretary 488 new powers to directly intervene in state schools. In 2013, state schools are being offered a choice to turn into privately run 'academy schools', except that that choice can be (and is being) forced on to some schools directly by the Education Secretary.

My point here is not to attack government policies; far from it, the entrenched nature of these political myths can be seen as a major success. What is crucial here is that there is only black and white, a public policy approach that is both created and reified by myth, and one which inherently succeeds on its own terms by trying to cast public administration in a particular (in this case, wholly negative) light. The stakes in grounding a philosophy of public administration have therefore risen. Our intersubjective lens must be shifted to allow us to gaze at political myth. But simply *refuting* such myths will not suffice: they stand or fall without recourse to facts or evidence. Instead, as philosophers of public administration, we must embrace a different philosophical perspective: one that is simultaneously both critical and constructive. We also need to understand that an intersubjective approach requires us to reinterpret and create myths ourselves.

Intersubjectivity: an alternative approach to myth making?

Nabatchi (2010) has suggested that public administration needs to recapture the *political* aspects of public administration; that instead of being concerned with structures and processes, we look back towards relationships between citizen and state: what is actually meant by the *public*? What forms of participation will emerge to bolster our teetering representative democracies? Honig (2009) also highlights the political dimensions of public administration and ties these to the dynamism of the political realm. The development of public administration is equally dynamic: the shift from different forms of governance is equally the evolution of the role and understanding of the citizen: as sovereign, subject, service user, consumers, customer, and, most recently, co-creators of public services. Public administration is a fluid entity, and we should recognize that we are all surely Heracliteans now? What philosophy best reflects such flux and change? One that, I would suggest, acknowledges different realities simultaneously; one that walks the line between our dual notions of institutionalism and contextualism. In other words, to approach public administration through the lens of intersubjectivity (Macaulay 2009), which Stivers (2008b, p. 1010) usefully defines as:

> The reality that emerges from the interactions among people in a shared space. It spans several levels of consciousness, including explicit, tacit, and unconscious. It is talk and action, whether collaborative or competitive. It produces, sustains, and transforms shared (or disputed) meaning, norms and understandings about what is going on, carried primarily but not exclusively in language.

Stivers (2008b, p. 1011) mentions many theorists who have investigated the nature of social reality either from a philosophical or empirical intersubjective basis, including Husserl, Merleau-Ponty, Goffman and Weick. Picking any of these theorists as a starting point may seem slightly arbitrary but, nonetheless, I will aim to anchor this discussion with a specific thinker: Hegel.

This may seem an unusual choice to some. After all, Hegel is most frequently viewed as a Christian philosopher and German idealist, particularly in the Anglo-American tradition, not helped by his later seemingly conservative views regarding the end of history and the (as he perceived it) success of the Prussian state. This is by no means the only interpretation of Hegel, however, and it is one that disregards much of the critical force – and overt critique of Christianity as the unhappy consciousness – of the Jena *Phenomenology*. Hegel's work need not be read as the development of abstract rationality towards the ideal. To do so would be to overlook the interplay between subject and object, and ignore the complex reality of intersubjectivity; such a reading fails to recognize our full (universal and particular) human selves. Hegel's philosophy seeks to expand on the development of knowledge, from sense perception to self-consciousness, through a series of intersubjective steps between object and subject. It drives the movement of *geist* through the process of unfolding recognition (Macaulay 2009).

Recognition, in the Hegelian sense, may be viewed as a normative concept in itself: the necessity of constitutive mutual recognition is a key element of moral judgement and ethical life; and its counterpart, misrecognition, is potentially the cause of much unethical behaviour. Second, recognition serves as a dialectical trigger to move between competing perspectives: rational and non-rational; deontology and consequentialism; compliance and integrity. This is the real meaning of *geist* for Hegel: not God's revelation, but human intersubjectivity: 'the unity of the different independent self-consciousnesses which, in their opposition, enjoy perfect freedom and independence: "I" that is "We" and "We" that is "I"' (Hegel 1992 *Ph Sp* §177).

Hegel's dialectic will no doubt be familiar to many as the triad of *thesis–hypothesis–synthesis*, a formulation that is usually presented as an attempt to provide unity through opposition (Kainz 1998). Hegel, in fact, did not use this formulation (Inwood 1992, p. 81), but it remains a popular interpretation. Yet, Hegel's dialectic constitutes a more subtle and fluid way of thinking. It can be applied both internally and externally. Internally, it charts the progress of consciousness from its earliest stages of understanding through to its final stages of knowledge and self-consciousness. Externally, as will be seen, the dialectic refers to the movement of *geist* throughout history. In both instances, recognition acts as a trigger to move from opposing (but not necessarily opposite) moral viewpoints, allowing for new perspectives on familiar situations. The triadic formula implies that a synthesis is a simple resolution between two extreme positions, which suggests that any compromise or agreement could be the result of a dialectical interaction. What the dialectic really addresses is parallax rather than paradox (Žižek 2006).

Parallax is not to be confused with paradox, which 'in the primary and most important meaning, is an *apparent* contradiction; to repeat, the contradiction is only apparent, and indeed it expresses a profound truth' (Kainz 1998, p. 12) (emphasis in original). A parallax, on the other hand, occurs when there are opposite, but not necessarily opposing, points of view:

> the apparent displacement of an object (the shift of its position against a background), caused by a change in observational position that provides a new line of sight. The philosophical twist to be added, of course, is that the observed difference is not simply 'subjective', due to the fact that the same object which exists 'out there' is seen from two different stances, or points of view.
>
> (Žižek 2006, p. 17)

The parallactic shift is not one that allows us to resolve contradictions or point out the unity of seemingly dichotomous positions, but rather one that broadens our view, allowing us to encompass a number of disparate perspectives all at once. The parallactic shift, then, does not turn the two sides of a coin inward to face each other; it rotates the coin so that we can see both sides at once, and thus grasp the wider reality, in much the same way as Hegelian recognition acts as a dialectical mechanism that allows us to move between parallaxes. The dialectical process allows us to see the intersubjectivity of different realities during the state of flux – again, it is the spinning of the coin. It does not seek to attain a paradoxical resolution as a traditional linear end point, but to provide a deeper understanding by revealing different positions as they unfold along a broader whole. It is this dynamic rather than any conclusion that is the key. Ultimately, then, utilizing intersubjectivity allows for parallactic shifts of perspectives of the type that run through the foundations of public administration: the public good, the public interest, the nature of the demos. There is no thesis or antithesis, nor are there any forced and false syntheses in these debates.

Reinterpreting myths[3]

There is, of course, a well-known myth that recounts the intersubjective nature of social reality in some detail: Hegel's master–slave dialectic (Hegel 1992 *Ph Sp* §178–198; and which finds re-expression in *Enc* §413–439).[4]

The master–slave dialectic famously describes the first meeting of two primeval human beings. Both have a sense that they are unique, conscious, individual beings while simultaneously being vaguely aware that they each belong to a universal species. Crucially, they only suspect that their particular and universal natures are true but they do not know for certain; they cannot be sure until they gain recognition of another human consciousness. Unfortunately, when they meet they do not know how to engage in such a reciprocal act as recognition, and thus they attempt to overcome each other physically through a fight to the death in which each seeks to subsume the other's human identity. As the fight progresses and one overwhelms the other, the loser has a moment of sudden self-realization: that death would categorically negate his all-too-precious human life, and therefore submits. As a result, a relationship is forged in which the victor is the master over the loser, who thus becomes a slave.

Yet, the fight for recognition continues as both human consciousnesses still require recognition in order to make sense of their identity and status. Yet, their relationship is extremely one-sided: the master cannot acknowledge the humanity of the slave, seeing instead the mere extension of his or her self; the slave simply enacts the orders of the master, and thus does not act as a self-determining individual human being – 'what the slave does is really the action of the master' (Hegel 1992 *Ph Sp* §191). Conversely, the slave undergoes a process of self-realization. The slave is a creative being, even if his creations are, initially, for the benefit of somebody else (i.e. the master). Through his work, he objectifies his own essential nature. The production of objects and the creative labour involved allows the slave to recognize his own true self: his existence for himself and also for another. For Hegel, misrecognition is the driving force of history: the fate of Anitgone (Hegel 1992 *Ph Sp* §470) was sealed by adherence to the universal (divine law) at the expense of the particular; the Romans sought to create a society that did not adequately address the universal. The unhappy consciousness of Christianity projects its own human essence as an external God to worship (Hegel 1992 *Ph Sp* §207–213), and onwards until the attainment of absolute being, howsoever this may be interpreted.

Eschatological schemata aside, what the master–slave myth reveals is the intersubjective relationship of power and fulfilment: not simply that self-consciousness is only attained through struggle (Sartre famously suggesting that the master–slave serves as the template for all human relationships), but that multiple perspectives develop from the difficulties in coming to terms with intransigence. The unwavering belief of the master is precisely what fuels the servant's journey of enlightenment – he understands not only himself, but the nature of his master and the relationship that governs them both. He achieves the parallax perspective. Hegel himself seemed to recognize the implications of this for public servants, who 'necessarily have a deeper and more comprehensive insight into the nature of the State's institutions and requirements and, moreover, a greater skill in the habituation of government, so that they can achieve what is best (Hegel 1960 *Phil Right* §309).

It is precisely those engaged in public administration that have the knowledge and expertise to distinguish between competing individual and social claims, and the protection of rights arguably allowed the universal aspects of our common humanity to coexist with our particularized existence as individuals. Fundamentally, a philosophy of public administration cannot simply be the provenance of academics; it must come from those engaged in practice, the very people who are already on the journey of knowledge.

Conclusion

How, then, does this myth relate to political myth and discourses of deceit? It suggests that regarding politics and public administration as a series of competing narratives is, at best, an intellectual cul-de-sac. Complexity is not best understood through reductionism, which promotes partial recognition. We can see the interplay of contrary perspectives in the very foundations of public administration itself, with Wilson's (1887) notion of administration being separate to politics, essentially distinguishing between *public* (i.e. political) and *administration* (technical, non-political). It could be argued that the developments from NPM and beyond have emphasized the technical, apolitical aspects of public administration: managerial efficiency has trumped political expediency. Yet, equally the development of these models could be seen as ideologically driven; the expansion of a market-driven world view. In the UK at least, while academics may attempt to disclose and enunciate multiple realities in public administration, public discussion (without which the philosopher's task is surely meaningless) is intellectually restricted. Far from recognizing multiple realities, public policy is dominated by narratives that propose absolute realities. The fact that these propositions are demonstrably false does not stop them from being the drivers of public policy. Public administration has little room for philosophy at the minute as it is dominated by political myth.

Public administration, public management, public governance, all exist in a world of flux, complexity and an increasing blurring of boundaries. As Gregory (2013) suggests, we require simultaneous types of analyses, both empirical and normative, in order to craft our understanding. It is little wonder, then, that political myths continue to hold such privileged positions in public policy in the media and in popular debate. They are more than mere stories. Myths provide a more tangible narrative anchor upon which to base decisions and form opinions. Their power lies in their capacity to be internalized as an authentic vision of reality (Bennett 1980; see also Girling 1993). When this authenticity is bound up in other myths, and reflects an ideological position (explicitly or implicitly), then the victory of the *political* myth is complete. A political philosophy of public administration needs to be fluid, to be able to both acknowledge the power of political myth while creating alternatives to it. It is not enough to tear down a myth; any philosophy must be equally constructive and critical. An intersubjective approach allows for such dynamism to be properly understood by reflecting on the relationships between perceptions, as well as perception itself. Of course, there are numerous methodological questions still to debate (see Brincat 2011 for a recent formulation of these issues), but until we acknowledge that public administration is not a series of either/or choices, the distinctions between politician and public official, between citizen and state, between private and professional identities, are false dichotomies. Unless the complexity and intersubjectivity of experiences are addressed, public administration will be doomed to be at the mercy of myth rather than philosophy.

Notes

1 This chapter is based on a conference paper delivered to the American Society for Public Administration, in New Orleans, March 2013.
2 See www.guardian.co.uk/politics/2013/jan/09/skivers-v-strivers-argument-pollutes.
3 This section is adapted from a previous discussion (Macaulay 2009).
4 Recent translations have classified this as Lordship and Bondage, but I am sticking to the better-known terminology simply because it *is* better known. Two further points. First, some commentators, not least of whom is the indomitable Hegel scholar Kojeve, who may argue that far from being a mythic account, Hegel actually meant this story to be taken as real. To which it may be replied social contract theorists may, in quitter moments, have thought that their accounts were true as well, but this does not make them so, nor does it account for their longevity and lasting power. Second, it could be argued that this account is not, according to our previous definition, a *political* myth. Such a comment would be accurate, but this does not mean it may be useful for interpretation.

References

Aldrich, D.P. (2012) *Building Resilience: Social Capital in Post-Disaster Recovery*, Chicago, IL: University of Chicago Press.

Aucoin, P. (2013) 'The political administrative design of NPM', in T. Christensen and P. Lægreid (eds), *The Ashgate Research Companion to New Public Management*, Farnham: Ashgate.

Beito, D.T. (1993) 'Mutual aid, state welfare and organized charity: Fraternal societies and the "deserving" and "undeserving" poor 1900–1930', *Journal of Policy History*, 5(4): 419–34.

Bekkers, V. and Homburg, V. (2007) 'The myths of e-government: Looking beyond the assumptions of a new and better government', *Information Society*, 23(5): 373–82.

Bennett, W.L. (1980) 'Myth, ritual and political control', *Journal of Communication*, 30(4): 166–79.

Bevir, M. (2011) 'Public administration as storytelling', *Pubic Administration*, 89(1): 183–95.

Bevir, M., Rhodes, R.A.W. and Weller, P. (2003) 'Traditions of governance: Interpreting the changing role of the public sector', *Public Administration*, 81(1): 1–17.

Brincat, S. (2011) 'Towards a social-relational dialectic for world politics', *European Journal of International Relations*, 17(4): 679–703.

Bunch, W. (2009) *Tear Down This Myth: How the Reagan Legacy Has Distorted Our Politics and Haunts Our Future*, New York: Free Press.

Christensen, T. and Lægreid, P. (2003) 'Policy: The challenge of turning symbols into practice', *Public Organization Review*, 3(1): 3–27.

Christensen, T. and Lægreid, P. (2007) 'The whole-of-government approach to public sector reform', *Public Administration Review*, November/December: 1059–66.

De Swaan, A. (1988) *In Care of the State: Healthcare, Education and Welfare in Europe and the USA in the Modern Era*, Cambridge: Polity Press.

Downey, G. (1986) 'Public accountability: Fact or myth?', *Public Money and Management*, 6(1): 35–9.

Dunn, G. (2011) *The Lies of Sarah Palin: The Untold Story Behind Her Relentless Quest for Power*, New York: St Martins Press.

Farazmand, A. (2012) 'The future of public administration: Challenges and opportunities – a critical perspective', *Administration & Society*, 44(4): 487–517.

Flood, C.G. (2002) *Political Myth*, London: Routledge.

Girling, J. (1993) *Myths and Politics in Western Societies: Evaluating the Crisis of Modernity in the United States, Germany and Great Britain*, New Brunswick, NJ: Transaction.

Goldfinch, S. and Wallis, J. (2010) 'Two myths of convergence', *Public Administration*, 88(4): 1099–115.

Gregory, R. (2013) 'Normativity and NPM: A need for some theoretical coherence', in T. Christensen and P. Lægreid (eds), *The Ashgate Research Companion to New Public Management* (pp. 375–90), Farnham: Ashgate.

Hegel, G.W.F. (1960) *Philosophy of Right*, trans. T.M. Knox, Oxford: Oxford University Press.

Hegel, G.W.F. (1992) *Phenomenology of Spirit*, trans. A.V. Miller, Oxford: Oxford University Press.

HM Government (2011) *Open Public Services White Paper*, cm 8145, July, London: The Stationery Office.

HM Government (2012) *Open Public Services 2012*, London: Cabinet Office.

Honig, B. (2009) *Emergency Politics: Paradox, Law, Democracy*, Princeton, NJ: Princeton University Press.

Inwood, M. (1992) *A Hegel Dictionary*, Cambridge: Cambridge University Press.

Kainz, H.P. (1998) *G.W.F. Hegel: Philosophical System*, Athens, OH: Ohio University Press.

Lam, J.T.M. (2009) 'Political accountability in Hong Kong: Myth or reality?', *Australian Journal of Public Administration*, 68: S73–S83.

Lane, J.E. (2006) 'Osborne's trilogy: A critique of the management philosophy of David Osborne', *Halduskultur*, 7: 6–14.

Lodge, M. and Gill, D. (2011) 'Toward a new era of administrative reform? The myth of post-NPM in New Zealand', *Governance*, 24(1): 141–66.

Lukes, S. (2005) *Power: A Radical View* (2nd edn), Basingstoke: Palgrave Macmillan.

Lynn, L.E., Jr (2001) 'The myth of the bureaucratic paradigm: What traditional public administration really stood for', *Public Administration Review*, 61(2): 144–60.

Macaulay, M. (2009) 'The I that is we: Recognition and administrative ethics', in R. Cox III (ed.), *Ethics and Integrity in Public Administration: Cases and Concepts* (pp. 26–40), New York: M.E. Sharpe.

McCue, C. and Roman, A.V. (2012) 'E-procurement myth or reality?', *Journal of Public Procurement*, 12(2): 221–48.

Modell, S. (2004) 'Performance measurement myths in the public sector: A research note', *Financial Accountability & Management*, 20(1): 39–55.

Nabatchi, T. (2010) 'The (re)discovery of the public in public administration', *Public Administration Review*, 70: 309–11.

Oborne, P. (2005) *The Rise of Political Lying*, London: Free Press.

Parker, D.H. (1972) 'Rhetoric, ethics and manipulation', *Philosophy & Rhetoric*, 5(2): 69–87.

Perelman, C. and Obrechts-Tyteca, L. (1969) *The New Rhetoric*, Notre Dame, IN: University of Notre Dame Press.

Pollitt, C. (2001) 'Convergence: The useful myth?', *Public Administration*, 79(4): 933–47.

Pollitt, C. (2010) 'Envisioning public administration as a scholarly field, 2020', *Public Administration Review*, 70(December): 292–4.

Pollitt, C. (2013) 'The evolving narratives of public management reform', *Public Management Review*, 15(6): 899–922.

Poole, S. (2006) *Unspeak*, London: Little Brown.

Rhodes, C. and Brown, A.D. (2005) 'Narrative, organizations and research', *International Journal of Management Reviews*, 7(3): 167–88.

Shildrick, T., MacDonald, R., Furlong, A., Roden, J. and Crow, R. (2012) *Are 'Cultures of Worklessness' Passed Down the Generations?* York: Joseph Rowntree Foundation.

Skinner, Q. (1969) 'Meaning and understanding in the history of ideas', *History and Theory*, 8(1): 3–53.

Smoke, P. (2003) 'Decentralisation in Africa: Goals, dimensions, myths and challenges', *Public Administration and Development*, 23(1): 7–16.

Sorel, G. (1960) *Reflections on Violence*, New York: Collier.

Stillman II, R.J. (1990) 'The peculiar "stateless" origins of American public administration and the consequences for government today', *Public Administration Review*, 50(2): 156–67.

Stivers, C. (2008a) *Governance in Dark Times*, Washington, DC: Georgetown University Press.

Stivers, C. (2008b) 'Public administration's myth of Sisyphus', *Administration & Society*, 39(8): 1008–12.

Tudor, H. (1972) *Political Myth*, London: Pall Mall.

Ukeles, J.B. (1977) 'Policy analysis myth or reality?', *Public Administration Review*, 37(3): 223–8.

Waldo, D. (1948) *The Administrative State*, New York: Ronald Press.

Wallis, J. and McLoughlin, L. (2010) 'A modernization myth: Public management reform and leadership behavior in the Irish public service', *International Journal of Public Administration*, 33(8/9): 441–50.

Weston, D. (2007) *The Political Brain: The Role of Emotion in Deciding the Fate of the Nation* (6th edn), New York: Public Affairs.

Wilson, W. (1887) 'The study of administration', *Political Science Quarterly*, 2(2): 197–222.

Žižek, S. (2006) *The Parallax View*, Cambridge, MA: MIT Press.

PART III

Understanding and combating corruption

5

HISTORY, PUBLIC ETHICS AND THE ANTI-CORRUPTION INDUSTRY

Toon Kerkhoff and Pieter Wagenaar

Introduction

Among the difficulties of studying developments in public ethics in the day-to-day practice of public administration, three seem particularly striking. First, to assess developments, one needs to look into the past and consider a much longer time frame than is usually done. Second, when doing so, one needs to find appropriate material. After all, it is only since the late 1990s that we have been able to use more readily available and relatively explicit sources such as public value statements and codes of conduct and good governance from which to deduce thinking on public ethics. Third, one somehow needs to get past the window dressing of such formal statements. Often, what organizations and individuals profess in public (or in interviews and surveys for that matter) differs from what they do in the day-to-day running of public administration. Obviously, people are not always willing or able to be open about the choices they themselves and others make, especially when it concerns matters of integrity or a lack thereof. Therefore, what is actually considered acceptable or unacceptable behaviour in 'the trenches' of public administration is usually not explicitly spelled out and remains unseen.

In this chapter, we aim to show how a historical approach to public ethics offers solutions to both aforementioned sets of problems and how it allows for new and valuable perspectives on public-sector ethics. Such an approach, in short, especially takes into account time and context. It uses primary source material to provide an in-depth analysis – usually qualitative and interpretive – that allows for contingency and contexuality of social phenomena. Such an approach is all the more useful for the study of public-sector ethics as the latter seems currently to be the near exclusive domain of organization science, (new) public management or policy studies, as well as – of course – philosophical reflection (cf. Beck Jørgensen 2009; Correlje and Groenewegen 2009; De Vries and Kim 2011; Lynn 2006; Moore 1995; van der Wal 2008; van der Wal and Van Hout 2009; Veeneman *et al.* 2009).

We argue that a historical approach offers appropriate but often-ignored tools to map and understand developments in public ethics. More specifically, we aim to show how historical research into corruption of the past provides promising avenues for research and analysis. Especially as public ethics – prior to the late 1990s – is usually not very explicit, research of when things go wrong brings implicit assumptions, values and ideas to the fore. Alasdair Roberts wrote how public ethics can be regarded as 'the product of social struggles and popular arguments about proper conduct' (1994, p. 412). Historical analysis of such 'struggles', inevitably surrounding cases of corruption, therefore seems fitting. The historical study of cases of corruption provides an opportunity to investigate discussion, disagreement and public value conflict that make up public ethics at different times and places. Consequently, this enables us to start answering theoretical and empirical questions as to when, why and how developments in public ethics actually occur (cf. Beck Jørgensen and Bozeman 2007, pp. 355, 357–8; Beck Jørgensen and Vrangbæk 2011, p. 486; Beck Jørgensen *et al.* 2009, pp. 452–5; Moynihan 2009, p. 820).

In addition to the aforementioned methodological, empirical and theoretical advantages, we argue in this chapter that a historical approach to public ethics also offers insight into important practical and normative questions in today's policy and research concerning good governance, corruption and public integrity. There are those, of course, who would agree with the idea that public ethics is inherently contextual and contingent, and thereby particularistic. Still, there seem to be at least as many who adhere to the opposite position of universalism. We argue that a historical approach to public ethics ends any lingering confusion and leads us to discard the latter and embrace the former. Furthermore, we aim to show some potential negative ramifications in policy and research that are attached to a *non*-historical and universalist attitude to public ethics.

In the remainder of this chapter, we will proceed as follows. We first provide a brief overview of universalist and particularistic approaches to the study of public ethics and corruption. We then focus on the use of historical approaches to public ethics and corruption, and elaborate on results from recent research. In the next section, we try to find an answer to the question why – despite the obvious usefulness of particularistic approaches – it is universalist approaches to corruption that are so dominant.

Universalism and particularism: two main approaches to public ethics and corruption

Studies on public ethics and corruption are sometimes divided into two categories (cf. Wagenaar 2011b). One is 'universalist' research, which holds that there are universally held norms on public ethics. This implies that there is also a universal understanding about what corruption is. The other is 'particularistic' work in which authors, on the contrary, think that views on public ethics, and what constitutes corruption, vary widely between cultures and over time. In the following, we will briefly discuss each category in turn, before we take a closer look at historical studies.

Universalist approaches to public ethics and corruption

Until the 1990s, scholarly attention on corruption was quite scarce (Hough 2013, p. 14), as data were lacking and defining corruption posed a huge problem. The surge in publications after that period usually took an economic perspective (Krastev 2003, pp. 117–22), and thus departed from an economic definition of corruption: 'the abuse of public power for private benefit' (Tanzi 1998, p. 564). Corruption was regarded as economically rational behaviour that occurred under the influence of certain incentives (Krastev 2003, pp. 117–22). Pushing back government's influence on the economy, consequently, was a way to deny politicians and bureaucrats the means to follow these incentives (Hough 2013, pp. 22–5). Naturally, it was the economic effect of corruption that was the most important object of study to scholars adhering to this perspective (Rose-Ackerman 2007).

After a while, though, the adherents to an economic perspective on corruption shifted their focus to the incentive structure itself. If corrupt behaviour was incentive-driven, then fighting corruption was a matter of changing the incentives. Since this shift in attention coincided with the coming into being of corruption perception indices, such scholars now had the data on which they could found their research (Krastev 2003, pp. 117–22). Thus, quantitative cross-country studies emerged, in which – through regression analysis – an answer was sought to the question of which institutional structures further corruption. Were presidential systems more prone to corruption than parliamentary ones? What were the effects of first-past-the-post systems as compared to proportional representation? Was decentralizing a good idea if one wanted to roll back corruption (Andersson and Heywood 2009, p. 755; Rose-Ackerman 2007, pp. xxi–xxv)? Fighting corruption now became a matter of the right institutional design (Hough 2013, pp. 31–5).

Naturally, the works of scholars adhering to an economic perspective on corruption was usually universalistic to the extreme, but it was not the only place in the field of corruption studies where absolutism was to be found. The few scholars in the discipline of organization studies dealing with corruption – some of the articles in Ashforth, Gioia, Robinson and Treviño's special issue of the *Academy of Management Review* (Ashforth *et al.* 2008) are a good example – took a similar stance. As they usually dealt with contemporary corruption in but one culture, and as they were often looking for universals, departing from a given set of norms was the obvious thing to do.

Particularistic approaches to public ethics and corruption

Since the rapid increase in scholarly attention in the 1990s, most corruption studies are universalistic in nature. Yet, there also is a small body of particularistic studies, in which cultural and temporal variance in public ethics is emphasized. Some of these have a distinctly Weberian outlook. The work of Weber has been of crucial relevance to the study of public ethics and corruption even though the latter seems not to have been an explicit topic for Weber himself. In *The Protestant Ethic and the*

Spirit of Capitalism, Weber, for instance, wondered how banking and other moneymaking pursuits became honourable at some point in the modern age 'after having stood condemned or despised as greed, love of lucre, and avarice for centuries past?' (cf. Hirschman 1977, pp. 9, 130–1; Weber 1958, p. 74). Weber already noticed that acts are judged differently throughout time and depending on context. In the scale of medieval values, frugality and thrift were, for instance, ranked lower than honour and courage. Other questions of Weber's (compare also the work of Norbert Elias) essentially concerned diversity, change and continuity of public ethics. From a Weberian perspective, developments in public ethics and corruption can be studied as a phase on the route from patrimonial to rational legal authority (Hoetjes 1977, pp. 53–5; cf. Rubinstein 1983, p. 493). In short – theoretically speaking – when a society becomes more bureaucratic, old, patrimonial practices come to be defined as corruption because of the growing amount of and adherence to bureaucratic rules and regulations and (possibly) because of coinciding evolving ideas on, for instance, neutrality, common good and public versus private interest. This is why for Weber – as Rubinstein and Von Maravić write – 'corruption was the hallmark of an earlier, more "primitive" stage of society, and would eventually vanish with the triumph of a professionalized bureaucracy' (2010, p. 21). Weber has often mistakenly been regarded as a universalist. In reality, the use of his ideal type of bureaucracy does not prevent – and actually stimulates – a particularistic approach. With it, we can describe and explain how certain practices slowly came to be perceived as corrupt in different times and places (cf. Kerkhoff 2011; Schattenberg 2009). Because bureaucracy and bureaucratization are still contingent, use of Weber's model does not imply a universalist approach to either public ethics or corruption.

A second example of particularistic approaches can be found in structural-functionalism, which holds that society is a collection of more or less coherent systems in which all societal phenomena have a function. Scholars adhering to this approach ask which function corruption fulfils in a specific society (De Zwart 2010; Hoetjes 1977, pp. 55–7, 1982, pp. 67–9). Corruption can, for instance, provide protection and influence for groups in society that possess material wealth but lack political influence (Waquet and McCall 1991, p. 62). Similarly, brokerage – to some a form of corruption – can serve to facilitate action between central and local levels (Blockmans 1985; Huiskamp 1995; Welskopp 2010, p. 222). A closer look at the actual function of corruption can provide some distance between 'real political scenarios' (i.e. how things actually work in everyday practice) and 'moral-philosophical fiction' (i.e. how things are believed or supposed to be working) (Welskopp 2010, p. 221). Taking such an approach is particularistic since it means that what is considered corruption at any point in time has not always necessarily been perceived as such in earlier times. Likewise, it can explain differences of opinion on public ethics between various groups and actors in society.

With structural-functionalism, we have arrived at yet another important example of a particularistic approach: the work of Fred Riggs. He has emphasized how behaviour is judged in the context of the normative order of any given society in which different value systems can coexist. As soon as 'new' or 'external' values and ideas are imported or exist alongside an 'old' and existing 'internal' social and normative order, two conflicting value systems can have validity at the same time (cf. De Zwart 2010; Riggs 1964, p. 12). This leads to what Riggs calls 'poly-normativism'. While new values and ideas on proper behaviour are internalized by some, others strictly adhere to existing standards. Then, there are those who mix things up as they see fit and depending on the situation. This is why Riggs' actors often support merit-based appointments while at the same time practising and stimulating nepotism or cronyism (Riggs 1964, p. 230).

Other examples of particularistic approaches to public ethics and corruption can be found in anthropological work. In this discipline, public ethics and corruption are not seen as phenomena that carry universally valid meanings or definitions. Instead, they are regarded as social constructs that vary geographically, culturally and over time. Various examples of anthropological approaches can be found in a volume by Haller and Shore (2005), which presents studies of the meaning and representation of 'corruption' (and therefore public ethics) in various environments. These anthropological studies see corruption as a highly normative social construct. Therefore, they focus on language as well as on social context, and emphasize particularism rather than universalism. Likewise, Tänzler (2007a, 2007b) advocates a cultural (anthropological) approach as he investigates the social realities of how corruption is perceived. Sissener (2001) also advocates an anthropological perspective as he discusses how cultural differences (between 'Western' and 'non-Western' societies, for instance) influence opinions on what is corrupt.

Political scientists adhering to constructivist approaches emphasize how the meaning of public ethics and corruption is constructed through power struggle, conflict and societal 'disagreement' and discussion. The core of these approaches is a focus on the contextual and contingent nature of corruption and its various definitions (De Graaf et al. 2010, p. 99). Among its proponents, we find, for example, Johnston (1996, 2005). Johnston has written how:

> as the scope of politics broadened, our conception of corruption has . . . narrowed. Societies have become secularized and fragmented; many are seen more as arenas for contention among groups and interests than as embodying any coherent system of values; and ethical issues in politics now seems to revolve more around maintaining the fairness of this competition than around the pursuit of fundamental moral goals.
>
> (Johnston 1996, p. 322; see also Johnston 2005, pp. 62–3)

Johnston views corruption and improper public official conduct as a political and moral issue, and not solely as individual acts of public officials. He has a view that is broad enough to encompass wrongful individual behaviour, as well as the political and social processes that define it as such. Any definition or idea of political corruption at any point in time should, according to Johnston, not just look at specific individual actions, but also at the broader contextual processes of consent, influence and authority (Johnston 1996, pp. 329–31).

Johnston's constructivist, historical and contextual approach stresses the important notion that corruption is defined through the contestation of concepts in specific times and places. The use of this is that corruption or public values acquire their 'true' meaning in clashes between different views held by various groups and individuals on what is right or wrong. Such a contextual and historical understanding of corruption rules out any universal understanding or specific definition. Only value judgements that change in time, place and setting determine what constitutes public ethics and corruption in any practical sense. Thus, the meaning of corruption must be understood in relation to its social setting, or its 'syndrome of corruption' (Johnston 2005). This means that its content differs between societies and groups, and between individuals within societies and over time.

Examples of this are abundant. Gift giving or spending private money on one's public electoral campaign (Johnston 2005, p. 69) can, for instance, be construed as wrong and corrupt in one context, but legitimate and appropriate in another, depending on time and who one asks. In some contexts, as Scott already acknowledged, the 'parochial corruption' in which 'ties of kinship, affection, caste, and so forth determine access to favors of power holders' (1972, p. 88) can quite easily lead to different interpretations of what is deemed acceptable or appropriate. As De Zwart, in his study on transfer of Indian civil servants, noted:

> No one who has a friend, or a friend of a friend, working at the railway station buys tickets at the booking-office, even if it would be quicker and easier than to suffer the obligatory rituals (drinking tea) and indebtedness that the help of a friend inevitably entails. It would be improper to pass him by; he would feel offended if he came across his friend at the booking-office. And for the friend (or friend of a friend) it would be improper not to help with a ticket, even if it cost him time and led to complaints from his boss. Often both parties feel uncomfortable, but the situation is somehow unescapable.
>
> (1994, pp. 111–12)

This is reminiscent of Clifford Geertz, who wrote how 'placing morality beyond culture is no longer possible' (2000, pp. 45–6).

The use(s) of history to assess public ethics and corruption

In the previous section, we outlined the main particularistic approaches to the study of public ethics and corruption. In this section, we focus on a final subset: historical studies. The use of history for the study of public administration has been widely discussed in recent decades (see, among many others, Caldwell 1955; Raadschelders 1994, 2010; Raadschelders *et al.* 2000; Tilly 2008; Vaughn 1985). As Raadschelders and others have pointed out, the study of public administration benefits from historical research because the latter has 'at its core the insight that a phenomenon can only be studied holistically, precisely because of its contingent qualities in time and space' (2000, p. 782). Similarly, a historical approach is thought to be useful because it helps to show limits and possibilities of generalization in understanding and explaining long-term social processes (cf. Caldwell 1955, p. 454; Raadschelders *et al.* 2000, p. 781).

Argumentation of this kind becomes apparent in the work of various scholars such as Luton (1999, p. 206), Mahoney and Rüschemeyer (2003b), Pierson (2003, 2004), Pierson and Skocpol (2002), Raadschelders (1994), Skocpol (2003), Skocpol and Somers (1980), Thelen (1999, 2002, 2003), or Tilly (2008). The latter, for instance, argued 'that explanatory political science can hardly get anywhere without relying on careful historical analysis' (2008, p. 418), as it is taking a historical approach that provides knowledge of the context of human action, conduct and experience. This 'enhances insight in the meaning of human behaviour in relation to the contextuality of human action to circumstances of space and time' (Raadschelders 2000, p. 9), and means that:

> for a proper understanding of contemporary structures and relations in public administration a geographical and historical setting is of great importance . . . Without knowledge of the geographical and historical context, we are not able to assess the uniqueness or the comparability of societal phenomena.
> (Raadschelders 2000, p. 9)

Similarly, it has been argued that it is through comparative historical analysis that we are able 'to derive lessons from past experiences that speak to the concern of the present (Mahoney and Rüschemeyer 2003a, p. 9). It provides a long-term perspective, which is essential to 'see through political and administrative fads and fashions of the day and enables us to get a perspective on more fundamental differences and similarities between present and obsolete structures, operations and policies' (Raadschelders 2000, p. 13). Lynn uses administrative history in precisely this way when he argues that 'history can reveal the fundamental dynamics of state building' (2006, p. 22).

We argue that the aforementioned general advantages of historical research for the study of public administration also apply to the specific research areas of public ethics and corruption. A long-term historical perspective enables us to see the more fundamental how's and why's, and offers possibilities to assess motives, intentions and context of public ethics at certain moments in time (cf. Moodie 1989, pp. 875–6). This has been acknowledged by others as well – compare Johnston's historical-constructivist approach discussed earlier – but in a limited way. In a rare case of attention for the use of historical research into public ethics within the discipline of public administration, Beck Jørgensen (2009, pp. 452–5) has stressed how adherents to various theoretical approaches to public values often fail to study them in their relevant political-ideological, philosophical (and thus historical) context. Similar calls have been heard earlier and elsewhere, for instance in Beck Jørgensen and Bozeman's 'public values research agenda', where investigating the origins of public values was first on their to-do list (2007, p. 355). The disadvantage of quoting values out of historical context has, according to them, led to the removal of values 'from the message or argument of which they form a part, thus robbing them of specific meaning' (Beck Jørgensen and Bozeman 2007, pp. 357–8). Likewise, Moynihan (2009, p. 820) noted how 'we need better historical accounts of the debate over administrative values, capable of linking these debates to the broader environment'.

Historians on public ethics and corruption

While it is important that the aforementioned is said within public administration in general and the growing academic 'industry' on ethics, integrity and corruption in particular, to most historians such arguments are hardly new or surprising. As a result, from the 1990s onwards and in line with the surge of academic interest in corruption, integrity and public values, historians have used their discipline to approach these specific topics. Their work, we argue, provides an especially welcome opportunity to investigate and support a constructivist and particularistic notion that discussion, disagreement and public value conflict make up public ethics differently at different times and places.

From important edited volumes by Engels (2009) or Grüne and Slanička (2010), the usefulness of historical research on public ethics and corruption quickly becomes apparent. These volumes show different kinds of historical work on public ethics and corruption. One kind focuses on specific national contexts over relatively long periods of time (such as, but not limited to, Bajohr 2009; Bernsee 2013; Bösch 2009; Engels 2006, 2008, 2009; Harling 2003; Kerkhoff 2014; Kerkhoff et al. 2010; Lerner 2011; Nützenadel 2009; Rivers 1991; Rubinstein 1983; Schattenberg 2009; Wagner 2005; Wilson 2007). A second kind focuses on specific case studies on (scandals surrounding) corruption from which to deduce developments in public ethics (such as, but not limited to, Ebhardt 2013; Hoenderboom 2013; Hoenderboom and Kerkhoff 2008; Kerkhoff 2013a; Kerkhoff et al. 2013; Krischer 2011; Kroeze 2008; Kroeze and Klein 2013; Von Thiessen 2009, 2010; Wagenaar 2011a).

These contributions have much to offer. In the landmark volume of Engels (2009), corruption is, for example, seen as a highly normative concept, that thus has to be researched within the semantics and the value system(s) of its time. Plumpe, in his contribution on theory and models in that volume, for instance, argues how norms shift over time, and argues this is why universal definitions of corruption are useless to historians (Plumpe 2009). An example of the practical use of such insights for the present is provided by historians such as Von Thiessen or Nützenadel, who use historical research to explain the impact of existing parallel norms – informal face-to-face, on the one hand, and formal legal, on the other – on problems of finding a proper balance between them (Nützenadel 2009, pp. 121–42; Von Thiessen 2009, pp. 94–8, 2010, pp. 205–20; see also Wagenaar 2011a, pp. 1–2).

The use of a historical approach in current debates becomes apparent from other examples of comparative historical research of scandals of corruption as well. In a recent special issue of the *Journal of Modern European History* (cf. Kerkhoff *et al.* 2013), it is, for instance, argued how processes of modernization in the long nineteenth century in various Western European states (the Netherlands, England, France and Germany) have led to a slow but steady replacement of early modern value parallelism and pluralism in favour of dominant and more coherent value systems in 'modernity'. These, however, became contested as well, when emerging political ideologies started to clash. Yet, and this is key also in contemporary debates, this was not a straightforward or inevitable process, and could even be reversed in many cases. Most notably, public opinion, politicization and proto-democratic sentiments, rather than legal regulation or a monopoly on state violence, seems to have been the primary catalysts for moral reform (cf. Bayly 2004, pp. 245–84; Kerkhoff 2013b, p. 178, 2014). Likewise, historical studies show the impact of discussions on a diminishing public–private divide (Ebhardt 2013) or the influence of trade and industry on perceptions of corruption (Ebhardt 2013; Kroeze and Klein 2013), discussions that still frequently occur today.

Another, and final, example of practical insight for the present, derived from historical approaches to public ethics and corruption, is offered in a recent book by Engels (2014). He shows us how historical corruption research adds nuance, context and thus perspective to our current perceptions of corruption. Engels explains how our present-day corruption discourse is derived from European debates in the *Sattelzeit* of the late eighteenth and early nineteenth centuries. Critique of corruption was then used by reformers to define 'modernity' by juxtaposing it with 'premodern' ideas that needed to be overcome. The 'new world' had to be bureaucratic, in a Weberian sense. This discourse still deeply influences current discussions concerning so-called 'non-Western' or 'developing' countries. The 'othering' of these countries by means of criticizing their supposed corruption already started in the mid nineteenth century. Engels describes how this critique of corruption is still very much alive, while 'modernity' itself has long since lost most of its appeal and credibility. As a result, 'Western' ideals are still regarded as the general norm in many debates on corruption despite their outdatedness (2014, pp. 15, 58, 177, 211–14, 250–1, 357–8, 370, 372).

From studies such as the aforementioned, the use of historical approaches should become clear. After all, they provide information to assess mostly hidden, incremental and unpredictable developments in public ethics, especially when it concerns combinations of in-depth historical cases of corruption and explicit theoretical, thematic and/or methodological frameworks and thus alleviate limitations in temporal and geographic scope (cf. Raadschelders 2000, p. 49; Skocpol and Somers 1980, pp. 174–97). They also acknowledge and study the possible existence of grand processes and mechanisms in public ethics' developments, and at the same time leave room for contingency and detail. Historical work on public ethics is thus especially well suited to show that values, expectations, norms and rules are contextually and temporally determined. This enables us to begin to see how and why public ethics develops, and in what way – if any – the past constrains or enables present-day thinking on public ethics. It thereby contributes to a deeper and, we argue, more realistic understanding of the incremental, unpredictable and long-term nature of such developments. In addition, a historical perspective on public morality that underscores context could (or should) also lead to an important realization of ethical relativism: current times are not necessarily more or less corrupt than past times and different public moralities acquire meaning in their own contextual frames of reference. One might do well to take such a historical vantage point and realize their own context-bound morality before entering into discussions over someone else's values. This, we will also discuss in the following section.

History, good governance and the 'anti-corruption industry'

If particularistic, and especially historical, approaches to public ethics come with such advantages, why is it that universalistic approaches to corruption have so much appeal? The answer is to be found in a short history of the 'good governance movement', and the accompanying 'anti-corruption industry'.

The term 'good governance' was first used in 1989–1990, not in academia, but by international development assistance organizations, the World Bank especially. And the end of the Cold War was an important part of the cause. Formerly, policy had been to keep clear away from the domestic affairs of non-Western allies against communism, but after the fall of the Berlin Wall, this was not necessary anymore (De Sousa *et al.* 2012, p. 1; Doornbos 2001, pp. 93, 96–9). It had now become possible to criticize the governments of developing countries for the way they squandered development funds. At first, the admission that ineffective governance was an important barrier to successful development assistance led to a desire to diminish the role of the state in so-called 'Third World countries' in favour of the market. Yet, during the 1990s, the state was 'brought back in'. The idea emerged that effective markets could not exist without strong government institutions (Beekers and Van Gool 2012, p. 2). 'Good governance' was thus of the essence.

What 'good governance' actually meant remained unclear. Yet, its opposite was more easily defined. The term 'corruption' looked less elusive, and this paved the way for anti-corruption policies to further good governance (Beekers and Van Gool 2012, p. 3; Santiso 2001, pp. 3–4, 5, 10). The real take-off for the anti-corruption movement came in 1993, when former World Bank employees founded Transparency International, and in 1996, when World Bank president James Wolfensohn delivered an anti-corruption speech (Brown and Cloke 2004, pp. 278–9; Hough 2013, p. 15; Krastev 2003, pp. 110–16; Michael and Bowser 2009; Polzer 2001; Sampson 2010, pp. 273–6, 2012, p. 175). Now, in several phases, a veritable 'anti-corruption industry' came into being (Michael 2004; Michael and Bowser 2009; Sampson 2010, pp. 262, 271), consisting of many and diverse actors, the most important being the UN, Transparency International, the World Bank, the OECD, the EU, USAID and the IMF (Brown and Cloke 2004, pp. 275–6;

Bukovansky 2006, pp. 86–194; De Sousa *et al.* 2012, p. 2; Sampson 2010, pp. 268–9, 2012, pp. 174–5). These organized conventions, drew up founding documents, signed treaties and installed monitoring mechanisms (Sampson 2010, pp. 268–9). Soon, the industry started growing spectacularly. Michael and Bowser (2009) estimate that between 2003 and 2009, anti-corruption programmes in the former Warsaw Pact countries grew from 100 million to 5 billion dollars, to give but an illustration of the pace of growth. The consequences for developing countries were huge, as they were confronted with 'aid conditionality' and 'selectivity' (Santiso 2001). They either had to meet a whole range of conditions before receiving aid, or they were only eligible for it if they already did (Doornbos 2001, pp. 100–3; Sampson 2010, p. 265). Every development assistance agreement now came to contain a section on fighting corruption (Sampson 2005, pp. 110–12).

Before the 1990s, scientific attention for corruption had been meagre, but when the anti-corruption industry got into gear academe woke up (Harrison 2006, p. 15; Hough 2013, p. 14). Scientific input was required for the drawing up of indicators for corruption, and for the cross-country comparisons these enabled. Naturally, this put a bonus on taking quantitative approaches to corruption, and on departing from a given corruption definition, instead of trying to find out what 'corruption' means in a particular context, in a particular period, at a particular place (Harrison 2006, p. 16; Sampson 2010, pp. 268–71). Transparency International, and especially its Corruption Perceptions Index, which was quantitative and comparative by definition, even reinforced this development (Andersson and Heywood 2009, pp. 755–6; Hough 2013, p. 17). Corruption research – a quickly expanding field – became the domain of scholars adhering to a public choice or an institutional design approach. Their quantitative, universalist and economic views on the problem of corruption and its solutions came to be the standard, completely replacing the particularistic views of the past (Hough 2013, pp. 22–5, 31–5; Krastev 2003, pp. 106, 117–22).

Naturally, there still are scholars who hold the view that corruption is indefinable, as it is a fluid, context-dependent, local practice, surrounded by local discourse from which it derives its meaning (Brown and Cloke 2004, pp. 284–5; Sampson 2005, p. 106). Various scholars point to the fact that practices defined as corruption by scholars taking a universalist approach – forms of patronage, for instance, or 'solidarity networks' – can be considered to be legitimate by the people actually living with them (Beekers and Van Gool 2012, pp. 4, 7, 11, 25; Harrison 2006, pp. 21–2; Ruud 2000; Sissener 2001). Naturally, also, we do not mean to imply there is no reflection on context by the 'industry' at all. Yet, for the reasons mentioned above, adherents to universalist approaches at current dominate both science and policy. Many use but one definition of corruption, cross-culturally, and have standard antidotes against it. 'Good governance' and anti-corruption therefore often boil down to imposing Western values on non-Western countries (Brown and Cloke 2004, p. 289; Bukovansky 2006, p. 198; Doornbos 2001, pp. 99–100; Harrison 2006, p. 19). Unsurprisingly, there is no indication that this approach has actually reduced corruption (Bracking 2007; Doig and Marquette 2005, p. 201;

Hough 2013, pp. 22, 29–31; Michael and Bowser 2009). It is true that scholars using particularistic approaches to corruption have very little to offer in the way of solutions either, but at least they have not wasted enormous amounts of tax money legitimizing something that simply does not work.

Conclusion

When we try to study the development of public ethics in practice, we are confronted with a lack of reliable material, and with 'window dressing'. A way out of the deadlock is looking at corruption scandals. During those, after all, it is often explicitly spelled out what the standards are or should be, and also how these are being violated in practice. Naturally, approaching public ethics in this manner means we can neither depart from a priori notions of public ethics, nor from a given definition of corruption. Quite on the contrary: what we are looking for is how those were defined in the past, how they developed over the course of time and how they differed between actors. This approach, sometimes called 'particularism' by corruption researchers, is mainly followed by anthropologists and historians. It has led to interesting analyses of the evolution of public ethics in the course of time, but it remains a very small field.

The 'universalistic' approach to corruption, on the other hand, which departs from a given corruption definition, has led to an abundance of research since the 1990s. This has largely been caused by the coming into being of corruption perception indices, which made the kind of quantitative data available that is required if one wants to do regression analyses. Having lists and clear rankings is, furthermore, often considered more helpful than more nuanced but 'difficult' observations usually attached to particularism. The funding that can be obtained for such research since the World Bank put corruption on the agenda is another cause: a veritable 'anti-corruption industry' has come into being, in which many academics – especially economists and public choice political scientists – participate.

The enormous quantity of output of such universalistic approaches has pushed particularistic research to the fringe of corruption studies. As a consequence, we seem to be left with serious problems. First, attention for continuity, change and diversity in public ethics has relatively diminished. This is a pity since, as we have argued in this chapter, a long-term perspective (while not losing sight of the 'nitty-gritty' nature of corruption) and a historical understanding of the contingent and contextual nature of public ethics and corruption offer much better tools for mapping, understanding and explaining both. Second, a denial of the particularistic nature of corruption and public ethics and the embrace of universalism has offered very little in practical terms. Simply put: a lot of very expensive policies have been implemented in the non-West and the not-so-very-West that have not been adjusted to local notions of public ethics. That these policies, exactly because of their universalistic pretences, meet with so very little success can hardly come as a surprise. Finally, historical research on public ethics has – in addition to methodological, empirical, theoretical and practical advantages – important normative consequences for today's research and policy on 'good governance', corruption and public integrity. Samuel Huntington once wrote that 'what is universalism to the west is imperialism to the rest' (1997, p. 184). This is something the 'anti-corruption industry' should take to heart.

References

Andersson, S. and Heywood, P.M. (2009) 'The politics of perception: Use and abuse of Transparency International's approach to measuring corruption', *Political Studies*, 57(4): 746–67.

Ashforth, B.E., Gioia, D.A., Robinson, S.L. and Treviño, L.K. (2008) 'Re-viewing organizational corruption', *Academy of Management Review*, 33(3): 670–84.

Bajohr, F. (2009) 'K'orruption in der NS-Zeit als Spiegel des nationalsozialistischen Herrschaftssystems', in J.I. Engels, A. Fahrmeir and A. Nützenadel (eds), *Geld, Geschenke, Politik: Korruption im neuzeitlichen Europa* (pp. 231–48), Munich: Oldenbourg.

Bayly, C.A. (2004) *The Birth of the Modern World, 1780–1914: Global Connections and Comparisons*, Malden, MA: Blackwell.

Beck Jørgensen, T. (2009) 'Value dynamics and infrastructure reform', *International Journal of Public Policy*, 4(5): 449–57.

Beck Jørgensen, T. and Bozeman, B. (2007) 'Public values: An inventory', *Administration & Society*, 39(3): 354–81.

Beck Jørgensen, T. and Vrangbæk, K. (2011) 'Value dynamics: Towards a framework for analyzing public value changes', *International Journal of Public Administration*, 34: 486–96.

Beck Jørgensen, T., Vrangbæk, K. and Sørensen, D-L. (2009) *The Historical Development of Values in Danish Administrative Reform*, paper presented at the EGPA conference 'The public service: Service delivery in the information age'.

Beekers, D. and Van Gool, B. (2012) 'From patronage to neopatrimonialism: Postcolonial governance in Sub-Sahara Africa and beyond', African Studies Centre Working Paper 101/2012, Leiden, the Netherlands.

Bernsee, R. (2013) 'Corruption in German political discourse between 1780 and 1820: A categorisation', *Journal of Modern European History*, 11(1): 52–71.

Blockmans, W.P. (1985) 'Corruptie, patronage, makelaardij en venaliteit als symptomen van een ontluikende staatsvorming in de Bourgondisch-Habsburgse Nederlanden', *Tijdschrift voor sociale geschiedenis*, 11: 231–47.

Bösch, F. (2009) 'In defence of the taxpayers: Korruptionspraktiken und -wahrnehmungen im Edwardischen Grossbritannien', in J.I. Engels, A. Fahrmeir and A. Nützenadel (eds), *Geld, Geschenke, Politik: Korruption im neuzeitlichen Europa* (pp. 175–202), Munich: Oldenbourg.

Bracking, S. (ed.) (2007) *Corruption and Development: The Anti-Corruption Campaigns*, Basingstoke: Palgrave Macmillan.

Brown, E. and Cloke, J. (2004) 'Neoliberal reform, governance and corruption in the South: Assessing the international anti-corruption crusade', *Antipode*, 36(2): 272–94.

Bukovansky, M. (2006) 'The hollowness of anti-corruption discourse', *Review of International Political Economy*, 13(2): 181–209.

Caldwell, L.K. (1955) 'The relevance of administrative history', *International Review of Administrative Sciences*, 21: 453–66.

Correlje, A.F. and Groenewegen, J.P.M. (2009) 'Public values in the energy sector: economic perspectives', *International Journal of Public Policy*, 4(5): 395–413.

De Graaf, G., Von Maravić, P. and Wagenaar, F.P. (eds) (2010) *The Good Cause: Theoretical Perspectives on Corruption*, Opladen & Farmington Hills, MI: Barbara Budrich.

De Sousa, L., Larmour, P. and Hindess, B. (2012) 'Introduction', in L. De Sousa, B. Hindess and P. Larmour (eds), *Governments, NGOs and Anti-Corruption: The New Integrity Warriors* (pp. 1–15), London: Routledge.

De Vries, M. and Kim, P.S. (2011) *Value and Virtue in Public Administration*, Basingstoke: Palgrave Macmillan.

De Zwart, F. (1994) *The Bureaucratic Merry-Go-Round: Manipulating the Transfer of Indian Civil Servants*, trans. G. Benton, Amsterdam: Amsterdam University Press.

De Zwart, F. (2010) 'Corruption and anti-corruption in prismatic societies', in G. De Graaf, P. Von Maravić and F.P. Wagenaar (eds.), *The Good Cause* (pp. 36–46), Opladen & Farmington Hills, MI: Barbara Budrich.

Doig, A. and Marquette, H. (2005) 'Corruption and democratisation: The litmus test of international donor agency intentions?', *Futures*, 37(1–2): 199–213.

Doornbos, M. (2001) '"Good governance": The rise and decline of a policy metaphor?', *Journal of Development Studies*, 37(6): 93–108.

Ebhardt, C. (2013) 'In search of a political office: Railway directors and electoral corruption in Britain and France, 1820–1870', *Journal of Modern European History*, 11(1): 72–87.

Engels, J.I. (2006) 'Politische Korruption in der Moderne, Debatten und Praktiken in Grossbritannien und Deutschland im 19. Jahrhundert', *Historische Zeitschrift*, 282(2): 313–50.

Engels, J.I. (2008) 'Corruption as a political issue in modern societies: France, Great Britain and the United States in the long 19th century', *Public Voices*, 10(2): 68–86.

Engels, J.I. (2009) 'Revolution and Panama: Korruptionsdebatten als Systemkritik in Frankreich vom 18. Jahrhundert bis zur Dritten Republik', in J.I. Engels, A. Fahrmeir and A. Nützenadel (eds), *Geld, Geschenke, Politik: Korruption im neuzeitlichen Europa* (pp. 143–74), Munich: Oldenbourg.

Engels, J.I. (2014) *Die Geschichte der Korruption: Von der Frühen Neuzeit bis ins 20. Jahrhundert*, Frankfurt am Main: S. Fischer Geschichte.

Geertz, C. (2000) *Available Light: Anthropological Reflections on Philosophical Topics*, Princeton, NJ: Princeton University Press.

Grüne, N. and Slanička, S. (eds) (2010) Korruption: Historische Annäherungen an eine Grundfigur politischer Kommunikation, Göttingen: Vandenhoeck & Ruprecht.

Haller, D. and Shore, C. (2005) *Corruption: Anthropological Perspectives*, London: Pluto Press.

Harling, P. (2003) 'Parliament, the state, and "old corruption": Conceptualizing reform, c. 1790–1832', in A. Burns and J. Innes (eds), *Rethinking the Age of Reform: Britain 1780–1850* (pp. 98–113), Cambridge: Cambridge University Press.

Harrison, E. (2006) 'Unpacking the anti-corruption agenda: Dilemmas for anthropologists', *Oxford Development Studies*, 34(1): 15–30.

Hirschman, A.O. (1977) *The Passions and the Interests: Political Arguments for Capitalism before Its Triumph*, Princeton, NJ: Princeton University Press.

Hoenderboom, M.P. (2013) *Scandal, Politics and Patronage: Corruption and Public Values in the Netherlands (1650–1747)*, Amsterdam: Vrije Universiteit, Amsterdam.

Hoenderboom, M.P. and Kerkhoff, A.D.N. (2008) 'Corruption and capability in the Dutch republic: The case of Lodewijk Huygens (1676)', *Public Voices*, 10(2): 7–24.

Hoetjes, B.J.S. (1977) *Corruptie in het openbare leven van ontwikkelingslanden: een verkenning van theorie en onderzoek, in het bijzonder gericht op India sinds 1947*, Leiden: Leiden University.

Hoetjes, B.J.S. (1982) *Corruptie bij de overheid: een bestuurlijk en politiek probleem, sociaal-wetenschappelijk beschouwd*, Vuga: s-Gravenhage.

Hough, D. (2013) *Corruption, Anti-Corruption and Governance*, Basingstoke: Palgrave Macmillan.

Huiskamp, R. (1995) 'Tussen centrum en periferie: Giften en corruptie in de vroegmoderne politiek', *Volkskundig bulletin*, 21(1): 27–58.

Huntington, S.P. (1997) *The Clash of Civilizations and the Remaking of World Order*, New York: Simon & Schuster.

Johnston, M. (1996) 'The search for definitions: The vitality of politics and the issue of corruption', *International Social Science Journal*, 149(3): 321–36.

Johnston, M. (2005) *Syndromes of Corruption: Wealth, Power and Democracy*, Cambridge: Cambridge University Press.

Kerkhoff, A.D.N. (2011) 'Organizational reform and changing ethics in public administration: A case study on 18th century Dutch tax collecting', *Journal of Public Administration Research and Theory*, 21(1): 117–35.

Kerkhoff, A.D.N. (2013a) 'Changing perceptions of corruption in the Netherlands: From early modern pluralism to modern coherence', *Journal of Modern European History*, 11(1): 88–108.

Kerkhoff, A.D.N. (2013b) *Hidden Morals, Explicit Scandals: Public Values and Political Corruption in the Netherlands (1748–1813)*, Leiden: Leiden University.

Kerkhoff, A.D.N. (2014) 'Early modern developments in Dutch public administration: Patriot and Batavian authors on public morality (1770s–1813)', *Administrative Theory & Praxis*, 36(1): 73–94.

Kerkhoff, A.D.N., Kroeze, D.B.R. and Wagenaar, F.P. (2013) 'Corruption and the rise of modern politics in Europe in the eighteenth and nineteenth centuries: A comparison between France, the Netherlands, Germany and England – Introduction', *Journal of Modern European History*, 11(1): 19–30.

Kerkhoff, A.D.N., Hoenderboom, M.P., Kroeze, D.B.R. and Wagenaar, F.P. (2010) 'Dutch political corruption in historical perspective: From 18th century value pluralism to a 19th century dominant liberal value system and beyond', in N. Grüne and S. Slanička (eds), *Korruption: Historische Annäherungen an eine Grundfigur politischer Kommunikation* (pp. 443–68), Göttingen: Vandenhoeck & Ruprecht.

Krastev, I. (2003) 'When "should" does not imply "can": Making of the Washington Consensus on Corruption', in W. Lepenies (ed.), *Entangled Histories and Negotiated Universals: Centers and Peripheries in a Changing World* (pp. 105–26), Frankfurt: Camous.

Krischer, A. (2011) 'Korruption vor gericht: Die Fälle Francis Bacon (1621), Warren Hastings (1788–1795) unde der Strukturwandel bei der Bewertung politischer Delinquenz in England', in N. Grüne and S. Slanička (eds), *Korruption: Historische Annäherungen an eine Grundfigur politischer Kommunikation* (pp. 307–26), Göttingen: Vandenhoeck & Ruprecht.

Kroeze, D.B.R. (2008) 'Political corruption scandals in the Netherlands in the nineteenth century: The letters affair of 1865', *Public Voices*, 10(2): 25–43.

Kroeze, D.B.R. and Klein, A. (2013) 'Governing the First World War in Germany and the Netherlands: Bureaucratism, parliamentarism and corruption scandals', *Journal of Modern European History*, 11(1): 109–29.

Lerner, M. (2011) 'The search for the origins of modern democratic republican political thought in early modern Switzerland', *Modern Intellectual History*, 8(3): 647–58.

Luton, L.S. (1999) 'History and American public administration', *Administration & Society*, CCCB, 2: 205–21.

Lynn, L.E., Jr. (2006) *Public Management: Old and New*, New York: Routledge.

Mahoney, J. and Rüschemeyer, D. (2003a) 'Comparative historical analysis: Achievements and agendas', in J. Mahoney and D. Rüschemeyer (eds), *Comparative Historical Analysis in the Social Sciences* (pp. 3–38), Cambridge: Cambridge University Press.

Mahoney, J. and Rüschemeyer, D. (eds) (2003b) *Comparative Historical Analysis in the Social Sciences*, Cambridge: Cambridge University Press.

Michael, B. (2004) 'Explaining organizational change in international development: The role of complexity in anti-corruption work', *Journal of International development*, 16(8): 1067–88.

Michael, B. and Bowser, D. (2009) *The Evolution of the Anti-Corruption Industry in the Third Wave of Anti-Corruption Work*, paper presented at the Proceedings from the Konstanz Anti-Corruption Conference, Constanz.

Moodie, G.C. (1989) 'On political scandals and corruption', in A.J. Heidenheimer, M. Johnston and V.T. LeVine (eds), *Political Corruption: A Handbook* (pp. 873–86), New Brunswick, NJ, & Oxford: Transaction.

Moore, M. (1995) *Creating Public Value: Strategic Management in Government*, Cambridge, MA: Harvard University Press.

Moynihan, D.P. (2009) '"Our usable past": A historical contextual approach to administrative values', *Public Administration Review*, 69(5): 813–22.

Nützenadel, A. (2009) '"Serenissima corrupta": Geld, Politik und Klientelismus in der späten venetianischen Adelsrepublik', in J.I. Engels, A. Fahrmeir and A. Nützenadel (eds), *Geld-Geschenke-Politik: Korruption im neuzeitlichen Europa* (pp. 121–42), Munich: Oldenbourg.

Pierson, P. (2003) 'Big, slow-moving, and . . . invisible: Macrosocial processes in the study of comparative politics', in J. Mahoney and D. Reuschemeyer (eds), *Comparative Historical Analysis in the Social Sciences* (pp. 177–207), Cambridge: Cambridge Univeristy Press.

Pierson, P. (2004) *Politics in Time: History, Institutions, and Social Analysis*, Princeton, NJ: Princeton University Press.

Pierson, P. and Skocpol, T. (2002) 'Historical institutionalism in contemporary political science', in I. Katznelson and H.V. Milner (eds), *Political Science: The State of the Discipline* (pp. 693–721), New York & London: W.W. Norton & Company.

Plumpe, W. (2009) 'Korruption: Annäherungen an ein historisches und gesellschaftliches Phänomen', in J.I. Engels, A. Fahrmeir and A. Nützenadel (eds), *Geld, Geschenke, Politik: Korruption im neuzeitlichen Europa* (pp. 19–47), Munich: Oldenbourg.

Polzer, T. (2001) 'Corruption: Deconstructing the World Bank Discourse', *Development Studies Institute (DESTIN) Working Paper Series 01-08*, London School of Economics.

Raadschelders, J.C.N. (1994) 'Administrative history: Contents, meaning and usefulness', *International Review of Administrative Sciences*, 60(1): 117–29.

Raadschelders, J.C.N. (2000) *Handbook of Administrative History*, New Brunswick, NJ: Transaction.

Raadschelders, J.C.N. (2010) 'Is American public administration detached from historical context? On the nature of time and the need to understand it in government and its study', *American Review of Public Administration*, 40(3): 235–60.

Raadschelders, J.C.N., Wagenaar, F.P., Rutgers, M.R. and Overeem, P. (2000) 'Against a study of the history of public administration: A manifesto', *Administrative Theory and Practice*, 22(4): 772–91.

Riggs, F.W. (1964) *Administration in Developing Countries: The Theory of Prismatic Society*, Boston, MA: Houghton Mifflin Company.

Rivers, I. (1991) *Reason, Grace, and Sentiment: A Study of the Language of Religion and Ethics in England, 1660–1780*, Cambridge: Cambridge University Press.

Roberts, A.S. (1994) 'Systems of Survival: A Dialogue on the Moral Foundations of Commerce and Politics, Jane Jacobs (book review)', *Journal of Policy Analysis and Management*, 13: 410–14.

Rose-Ackerman, S. (2007) 'Introduction and overview', in S. Rose-Ackerman (ed.), *International Handbook on the Economics of Corruption* (pp. xiv–xxxviii), Cheltenham: Edward Elgar.

Rubinstein, W.D. (1983) 'The end of "old corruption" in Britain 1780–1860', *Past and Present: A Journal of Historical Studies*, 101: 55–86.

Rubinstein, W.D. and Von Maravić, P. (2010) 'Max Weber, bureaucracy, and corruption', in G. De Graaf, P. Von Maravić and F.P. Wagenaar (eds), *The Good Cause: Theoretical Perspectives on Corruption* (pp. 21–35), Opladen & Farmington Hills, MI: Barbara Budrich.

Ruud, A.E. (2000) 'Corruption as everyday practice: The public–private divide in local Indian society', *Forum for Development Studies*, 2(2): 271–94.

Sampson, S. (2005) 'Integrity warriors: Global morality and the anti-corruption movement in the Balkans', in D. Haller and C. Shore (eds), *Corruption: Anthropological Perspectives* (pp. 103–30).

Sampson, S. (2010) 'The anti-corruption industry: From movement to institution', *Global Crime*, 11(2): 261–78.

Sampson, S. (2012) 'Corruption and anti-corruption in Southeast Europe: Landscapes and sites', in L. De Sousa, B. Hindess and P. Larmour (eds), *Governments, NGOs and Anti-Corruption: The New Integrity Warriors* (pp. 168–85), London: Routledge.

Santiso, C. (2001) 'World Bank and good governance: Good governance and aid effectiveness – the World Bank and conditionality', *Geo. Public Pol'y Rev/Georgetown Public Policy Review*, 7(1): 1–137.

Schattenberg, S. (2009) 'Die Ehre der Beambten oder: Warum die Staatsdiener nicht korrupt waren: Patronage in der russischen Provinzverwalting im 19. Jahrhundert', in J.I. Engels, A. Fahrmeir and A. Nützenadel (eds), *Geld, Geschenke, Politik: Korruption im neuzeitlichen Europa* (pp. 203–30), Munich: Oldenbourg.

Scott, J.C. (1972) *Comparative Political Corruption*, Englewood Cliffs, NJ: Prentice Hall.

Sissener, T.K. (2001) *Anthropological Perspectives on Corruption*, Bergen: Chr. Michelsen institute (CMI).

Skocpol, T. (2003) 'Doubly engaged social science: The promise of comparative historical analysis', in J. Mahoney and D. Reuschemeyer (eds), *Comparative Historical Analysis in the Social Sciences* (pp. 407–28), Cambridge: Cambridge University Press.

Skocpol, T. and Somers, M. (1980) 'The uses of comparative history in macrosocial inquiry', *Comparative Studies in Society and History: An International Quarterly*, 22(2): 174–97.

Tanzi, V. (1998) 'Corruption around the world: Causes, consequences, scope, and cures', *International Monetary Fund Staff Papers*, 45(4): 559–94.

Tänzler, D. (2007a) *Cultures of Corruption: An Empirical Approach to the Understanding of Crime*, Konstanz: University of Konstanz.

Tänzler, D. (2007b) *Korruption als Metapher*, Konstanz: University of Konstanz.

Thelen, K. (1999) 'Historical institutionalism in comparative politics', *Annual Review of Political Science* 2(1): 369–404.

Thelen, K. (2002) 'The explanatory power of historical institutionalism', in R. Mayntz (ed.), *Akteure, Mechanismen, Modelle* (pp. 91–107), Frankfurt: Campus Verlag.

Thelen, K. (2003) 'How institutions evolve: Insights from comparative historical analysis', in J. Mahoney and D. Reuschemeyer (eds), *Comparative Historical Analysis in the Social Sciences* (pp. 208–40), Cambridge: Cambridge University Press.

Tilly, C. (2008) 'Why and how history matters', in R.E. Goodin and C. Tilly (eds), *The Oxford Handbook of Contextual Political Analysis* (pp. 417–37), Oxford: Oxford University Press.

van der Wal, Z. (2008) *Value Solidity: Differences, Similarities and Conflicts between the Organizational Values of Government and Business*, Amsterdam: VU Amsterdam.

van der Wal, Z. and Van Hout, E.T.J. (2009) 'Is public value pluralism paramount? The intrinsic multiplicity and hybridity of public values', *International Journal of Public Administration*, 32(3): 220–31.

Vaughn, S. (ed.) (1985) *The Vital Past: Writings on the Uses of History*, Athens, GA: University of Georgia Press.

Veeneman, W., Dicke, W. and Bruijne, D. (2009) 'From clouds to hailstorms: A policy and administrative science perspective on safeguarding public values in networked infrastructures', *International Journal of Public Policy*, 4(5): 414–34.

Von Thiessen, H. (2009) 'Korruption und Normenkonkurrenz: Zur Funktion und Wirkung von Korruptionsvorwürfen gegen die Günstling Minister Lerma und Buckingham in Spanien und England im frühen 17. Jahrhundert', in J.I. Engels, A. Fahrmeir and A. Nützenadel (eds), *Geld-Geschenke-Politik: Korruption im neuzeitlichen Europa* (pp. 91–120), Munich: Oldenbourg.

Von Thiessen, H. (2010) 'Korrupte Gesandte? Konkurrierende Normen in der Diplomatie der Frühen Neuzeit', in N. Grüne and S. Slanička (eds), *Korruption: Historische Annäherungen an eine Grundfigur politischer Kommunikation* (pp. 205–20), Göttingen: Vandenhoeck & Ruprecht.

Wagenaar, F.P. (2011a) 'Extortion and abuse of power in the Dutch republic: The case of bailiff Lodewijk van Alteren', *International Journal of Public Administration*, 34(11): 731–40.

Wagenaar, F.P. (2011b) 'Aktuelle Korruptionsforschung: ein Ueberblick' [Recent corruption studies: A review], *Neue Politische Literatur*, 56(1): 61–9.

Wagner, P. (2005) *Bauern, Junker und Beamtelokale Herrschaft und Partizipation im Ostelbien des 19. Jahrhunderts*, Göttingen: Wallstein.

Waquet, J.C. and McCall, L. (1991) *Corruption, Ethics and Power in Florence, 1600–1770*, Cambridge: Polity Press.

Weber, M. (1958) *The Protestant Ethic and the Spirit of Capitalism*, trans. T. Parsons, New York: Scribner.

Welskopp, T. (2010) 'Ehrbare Bestechung' [Honest graft], in N. Grüne and S. Slanička (eds), *Korruption: Historische Annäherungen an eine Grundfigur politischer Kommunikation* (pp. 221–45), Göttingen: Vandenhoeck & Ruprecht.

Wilson, B. (2007) *The Making of Victorian Values: Decency and Dissent in Britain, 1789–1837*, New York: Penguin Press.

6

BUILDING INTEGRITY IN PUBLIC-SECTOR OPERATIONS

Olivia Monaghan and Adam Graycar

Introduction

Corruption has been the focus of much academic scrutiny. Increasingly, these literatures are focusing on the role of corruption in effective governance and public administration (Anechiarico and Jacobs 1996; Brown and Head 2005; De Lancer Julnes and Villoria 2014; Della Porta 2004; Kim and Lee 2012; Larmour and Barcham 2006; Menzel 2005; Mills 2012; Mulcahy 2012; Smith 2005; Warburton and Baker 2005). The three integrity violations of corruption, misconduct and maladministration are, in many ways, three sides of the same coin. All involve a misuse of office, all entail some deviation of public duty, and all contribute to political pressures and, in some cases, uncertainties. Their differences, however, should not be overlooked. In understanding these differences, and the various ways in which corruption, misconduct and maladministration manifest in public administration, more effective integrity-building processes can be incorporated into public-sector operations.

This chapter focuses on this differentiation between the three phenomena – corruption, misconduct and maladministration – as a means through which more targeted integrity processes and preventive strategies can be built. It does this across three sections. First, it dissects the three phenomena so as to allow them to be better understood. Second, it identifies some challenges to organizational integrity. By considering the factors (both internal and external) that affect an organization's integrity, an organizational culture can be more effectively safeguarded. Third, this chapter identifies a number of integrity-building processes and preventive strategies that can be easily adopted into an organization's operational system. An applicable, practical method of building integrity in the public sector reduces the risk of a band-aid approach. Such an approach assumes that corruption, misconduct and maladministration take the same form in every organization and that they can be targeted through a similar approach. Our analysis of the three phenomena at the start of this chapter highlights some of the problems with this assumption.

Corruption, misconduct and maladministration are different types of integrity violations. When creating integrity-building processes and preventive strategies for the public sector, these differences need to be understood and considered. The literature contains many definitions of corruption, with writers either seeking a comprehensive term or a focus on a particular topic. Morgan (1998, pp. 11–12) notes the tendency towards a minimalist definition is because it is both concise and broad enough to be applied to most instances of corruption. The definition provided by the World Bank and Transparency International is an example of this, with corruption being defined as 'the abuse of public office for private gain' (Larmour and Wolanin 2001; Transparency International 2013; Transparency International UK 2014; World Bank 1997). Where corruption, misconduct and maladministration differ, however, is in the notion of personal gain. In the examples of misconduct and maladministration discussed in this chapter, it is shown that intent is not necessary, and personal gain was not a desired outcome. These nuances make it problematic to apply traditional anti-corruption strategies to public services affected by misconduct or maladministration and expect positive reform.

This section will first expand upon the definitional aspects of the three phenomena, using definitions adopted in Australian legislation. Following this, it will highlight these definitional differences through the use of four real examples – 'driving licences', 'welfare checks', 'soliciting architecture' and 'Board of Elections'. These vignettes are drawn from examples reported by anti-corruption agencies in Australia and the US.

These four vignettes highlight the different forms that integrity violations can take. A large number of cases of corruption, misconduct and maladministration exist, and they exist in all countries, jurisdictions and cultures. With this in mind, the four chosen cases represent both the different types of integrity violations and span different countries and regions, and adequately show different strategies are needed for different types of unethical behaviours. 'Driving licences' is from a case heard by the Independent Commission Against Corruption (ICAC) in New South Wales, Australia, involving a clear case of corruption. Two examples of misconduct are provided to illustrate the issue of intent in integrity breaches. 'Welfare checks' involves the misuse of police power in Victoria, Australia, as reported by the Victorian Independent Broad-Based Anti-Corruption Commission (IBAC), and 'soliciting architecture' involves a Construction Project Manager for the New York City Department of Housing Preservation and Development. The complexities of integrity-building techniques and preventive strategies are also highlighted in the 'Board of Elections' example involving the New York City elections in 2011.

This chapter first identifies the definitional differences between corruption, misconduct and maladministration in both literature and policy. It then applies these definitions to the above vignettes. Organizational factors that precipitate integrity breaches are then discussed, and used to shape the integrity-building processes and preventive strategies proposed in this chapter. To demonstrate how these processes and strategies can be used in practice, they are then applied to the vignettes.

Defining corruption, misconduct and maladministration

Perhaps the most commonly cited definition of corruption is the 'abuse of public office for private gain' definition provided by the World Bank (1997) and Transparency International (2013). This is a clear concept – a public official who uses his or her office to receive a personal advantage. There remains, however, significant definitional debate surrounding the notion of corruption. The literature contains a number of views on what acts constitute corruption (Graycar and Prenzler 2013; Roebuck and Barker 1974; Transparency International UK 2014; Wood 1997), the causes of corruption (De Lancer Julnes and Villoria 2014; Mills 2012; Morgan 1998; Rose-Ackerman 1999; Treisman 2000), and how corruption in public administration can be best understood and approached (De Lancer Jules and Villoria 2014; Ede *et al.* 2002; Findlay and Stewart 1992; Gorta 2000, 2006; Hooker 2009; Hossain *et al.* 2010; Mills and Cooper 2007; Mulcahy 2012; Redlawsk and McCann 2005). Further adding to the definitional discomfort is the fact that the major global convention on corruption, the United Nations Convention against Corruption (UNCAC), chooses not to define the phenomenon (UNODC 2003). This chapter will not detail definitional debates, other than to acknowledge the usefulness of allowing understandings of corruption to evolve so as to remain relevant to an ever-changing phenomenon.

Max Weber argued that analyses should not begin with a definition, but should derive the definition by looking at specific examples, allowing a definition to be tailored to the purposes at hand (Klitgaard 1988; Weber 1958). It is this that this chapter seeks to do – provide case studies of corruption, misconduct and maladministration that demonstrate the nuances of the phenomena. Through demonstrating how these three phenomena manifest and the differences in their manifestations, we can create a sound basis from which preventive strategies can be drawn.

With this in mind, however, a provisional understanding of some of the legal definitions of corruption, misconduct and maladministration is important in creating an awareness of the architecture in which anti-corruption efforts operate. Through understanding the existing framework, reforms can be tailored to produce a best 'fit' for the purpose required.

There are a number of existing anti-corruption agencies in Australia, both independent and state-run, most of which operate under different protocols and legislations. This makes providing any cohesive definitions for corruption, misconduct and maladministration difficult. Nonetheless, these definitions provide clear understandings of the general approach to corruption, misconduct and maladministration of public administration systems in Australia.

Corruption

The New South Wales ICAC is Australia's oldest independent anti-corruption organization. According to Sections 7, 8 and 9 of their Act, corrupt conduct occurs when:

- A public official improperly uses, or tries to improperly use, the knowledge, power or resources of their position for personal gain or the advantage of others
- A public official acts dishonestly or unfairly, or breaches public trust
- A member of the public influences, or tries to influence, a public official to use his or her position in a way that is dishonest, biased, or breaches public trust

(NSW 1988)

This definition shows that corruption can involve more than a misuse of office for personal gain. By also encompassing 'the advantage of others', it demonstrates that personal gain does not necessitate lining your own pockets. Further, by including the notion of breaching public trust, this definition shows that corruption in public administration ultimately relates to a deviation from proper and official conduct.

Misconduct

This notion of deviating from official conduct is central to the legal definitions of misconduct in Australia. The definition of serious misconduct as adopted by Regulation 1.07 of the Fair Work Regulations (2009) is conduct that includes:

- Wilful or deliberate behaviour from an employee that is inconsistent with the contract of their employment;
- Conduct that causes serious or imminent risk to the health or safety of a person or the reputation, viability or profitability of the employer's business;
- The employee, in the course of the employee's engagement, engaging in theft, or fraud, or assault;
- The employee being intoxicated at work;
- The employee refusing to carry out a lawful and reasonable instruction that is consistent with the terms of the employee's contract of employment.

(Government of Australia 2009)

This can be reduced to conduct that causes serious and imminent risk to the health, safety, reputation, viability or profitability of the employer's business. The key difference between misconduct and corruption is that explicit personal gain does not need to be involved.

Maladministration

The South Australian Independent Commissioner Against Corruption Act (2012) is one of the few pieces of anti-corruption legislation in Australia that outlines the offence of maladministration. According to Section 5 of the Act, maladministration is:

- Conduct of a public officer or practice, policy or procedure of a public authority that results in irregular and unauthorised use of public money, or

- Conduct of a public officer involving substantial mismanagement in or in relation to the performance of official functions.

(Government of South Australia 2012)

This definition shows that, despite involving a deviation of official duties, there is scope for the act of maladministration to be unintentional – finances can be mismanaged as a result of incompetence, not intent. This differs to corruption, where intent is key. Further to this, there is no specification of personal gain in the above definition of maladministration.

Applying definitions to cases

As the following three examples demonstrate, corruption involves clear intent to deviate from one's duties for a personal gain.

Four examples are included below – one each for corruption and maladministration, and two for misconduct. Two examples are provided for misconduct ('welfare checks' and 'soliciting architecture') to demonstrate the nuances of the phenomenon. Notably, the two examples are chosen to illustrate the role of intent in integrity breaches; whereas in some cases of corruption, misconduct and maladministration, such as bribery of an official, intent plays a clear and active role, in others the public official may be of the opinion that he or she is acting with integrity when he or she is in fact acting outside the rules of an organization or the laws of a state.

Corruption (driving licences)

In 2007, a manager of the Roads and Transport Authority (RTA) – the agency responsible for driving licences – in New South Wales, Australia, was found by the New South Wales ICAC (ICAC 2007) to have corruptly issued driving licences to individuals who failed to meet RTA standards. The manager, Paul MacPherson, failed to sight adequate identification, issued licences to those who had failed their practical tests, and gave test answers to individuals in exchange for payments in either cash or marijuana.

Mr MacPherson was also found to have approached a driving instructor, Komate Jaturawong, and established a system of collusion. Between December 2002 and August 2006, the Commission found that Mr McPherson colluded with Mr Jaturawong to improperly provide the correct answers to licence applicants undertaking the driver knowledge test and unfairly advantage applicants undergoing a practical driving test (ICAC 2007). The Commission also found that Mr Jaturawong sought and received cash payments from licence applicants as a reward or inducement for arranging the provision of unlawful assistance to them by Mr McPherson during the driver knowledge test and practical driving test (ICAC 2007). As a result of the ICAC's investigation, Mr MacPherson was jailed for three years for corruption, and Mr Jaturawong received 20 months for aiding and abetting.

Considering the above definition of corruption as when a 'public official improperly uses, or tries to improperly use, the knowledge, power or resources of their position for personal gain or the advantage of others' (NSW 1988), this is a clear case of corruption. Both Mr MacPherson and Mr Jaturawong have abused their positions for personal gain. They acted with intent in deviating from their duties, breached public trust, and engaged in an unauthorized trading of their entrusted authority.

Misconduct (welfare checks)

In 2007, a Victorian police patrol attended a residence to conduct a routine welfare check on a woman who had recently attempted suicide. At the end of his shift, one of the officers, Officer Quach, returned to the residence in plain clothes and with some groceries. The woman (unnamed in the verdict) was aware that Quach was a police officer. Intimate activity occurred, involving the officer ultimately abusing his position and her vulnerability.

What makes this a clear example of misconduct is the fact that the officer would not have known of the woman and would not have been able to abuse his power had it not been for his job as a public official. Although he was off duty, and despite the offer of goodwill in bringing the groceries, Quach used the power awarded him by his job to take advantage of the woman's vulnerability. Further, as Justice Redlich stated in his verdict, the

> use of knowledge or information acquired by the office holder in the course of his or her duties for a private or other impermissible purpose may be inconsistent with the responsibilities of the office and calculated to injure the public interest.
>
> (Supreme Court of Victoria – Court of Appeal 2010)

This is consistent with the above definition of misconduct, whereby the wilful behaviour is inconsistent with the terms of employment and negatively impacts the reputation of the organization.

Misconduct (soliciting architecture)

In 2013, a Construction Project Manager for the New York City Department of Housing Preservation and Development (HPD), Patrick Enright, solicited an architect and a construction labourer over whose work he had authority to perform architectural and carpentry services at his daughter's home and at his summer home. In each case, the work was performed and paid for (DOI 2013). The manager in question was found to have violated a section (2604 (b)(3)) of the City's conflict of interest law (New York City 1986), stating:

> No public servant shall use or attempt to use his or her position as a public servant to obtain any financial gain, contract, license, privilege or other private or personal advantage, direct or indirect, for the public servant or any person or firm associate with the public servant.

In this case, despite an absence of any evidence that Enright received any special treatment from the person or firm whose work was solicited, he was found to have misused his connections to obtain a personal benefit. The above section of the conflict of interest law safeguards against the possibility that a public servant's judgement with respect to the public matter over which he or she has authority will be compromised because of the business relationship that he or she has established with the private party involved in the matter. This prohibition means that Enright had the entire pool of architects and carpenters in the metropolitan area available to him, except those with whom he dealt in his City work.

This case is different to the two presented above insomuch as there was no evidence to suggest that Enright intentionally misused his position – he paid for the architectural work, received no special treatment and did not take advantage of anyone as a result of his position. Where this case is similar to that of 'welfare checks' is in the misuse of knowledge gained in the course of one's official duty. As Enright used the connections obtained during the course of his official work for an advantage, he placed himself in a position whereby he had a private business relationship with one of the contractors whose work he was duty-bound to oversee, risking the reputation and viability of the employer's business.

Given that Enright paid for the services of the architect and carpenter and that the harms were minimal – it was an act committed out of convenience rather than a desire for personal advancement – this activity might not be regarded as inappropriate or be seen as misconduct in many jurisdictions, whereas not reporting conflicts of interest, or creating the perception of conflicts of interest, may constitute misconduct in others. The arrangement between Enright and those whose work he solicited created the perception of possible favourable treatment in assessing their future work, thus risking the reputation and viability of his employer.

Maladministration (Board of Elections, New York City)

In April 2013, the New York City Board of Elections (BOE) was found by the Department of Investigations (DOI) to have wasted at least $2.4 million of NYC funds by failing to consolidate election districts and to reduce staffing numbers during the 2011 off-year elections (DOI and Hearn 2013). In advance of the election, the BOE was warned of low turnout at public hearings and in the media and was urged to consolidate districts, which it is legally permitted to do when anticipated voter turnout is low, and which had been done in the past (DOI and Hearn 2013).

The BOE ignored the risks, and fully staffed its polling sites with 28,279 workers assigned to 6,102 election districts. Approximately 90 per cent of the 1,357 polling sites in the five boroughs had 10 or fewer voters for every poll worker assigned. There was an average turnout of six voters for every poll worker, and at least 12 sites had more poll workers than voters.

In this case, the BOE ignored the identified risks and acted poorly in the administration of its duties, resulting in a significant financial loss to the City (DOI and Hearn 2013).

The financial mismanagement in this case, resulting from BOE ignoring the risks, makes this a clear case of maladministration. While the use of public money by the BOE was authorized, the loss of $2.4 million is in accordance with the above definition of maladministration, 'conduct of a public officer involving *substantial mismanagement* in or in relation to the performance of official functions' (Government of South Australia 2012) (emphasis added).

It is this – the substantial mismanagement in or in relation to the performance of official functions – that highlights the key difference between misconduct and maladministration. Whereas misconduct involves an act by a public official that contradicts his or her terms of employment or risks the reputation and viability of his or her employer, maladministration involves individual mismanagement. The public official may be acting in accordance with the terms of his or her employment, and he or she may not be seeking or receiving advantage, yet his or her actions can still result in mismanagement.

Precipitating factors in the literature

The above vignettes demonstrate how integrity violations are defined, and how they manifest. Some, such as Caiden et al. (2001) and Mills and Cooper (2007), identify organizational factors that precipitate integrity breaches. Understanding these factors helps to build preventive strategies that can be applied to a variety of organizations.

Mills and Cooper (2007) classify corruption risk factors as being individual, institutional or environmental. These factors (individual, institutional and environmental) are not mutually exclusive in contributing to corrupt conduct. They are often found to coexist and/or interact with each other. Mills and Cooper's (2007) analysis of corruption risk factors are drawn from an analysis of cases investigated by the New South Wales ICAC.

This section will focus on Mills and Cooper's (2007) three corruption risk factors – individual, institutional and environmental. Following this, these precipitating factors will be applied to the case studies to demonstrate how precipitating factors can be targeted when drafting integrity building strategies and preventive measures.

Individual factors

In their analysis of cases investigated by the New South Wales ICAC, Mills and Cooper (2007) found that the most common activities where public officials acted alone in corruption were contracting, engaging in secondary employment, and regulating (licensing and certification). However, they also found that corrupt public officials are more likely to be managers or elected officials than staff without supervisory or management functions. Out of the 63 investigations considered between 1988 and 2006, 30 involved findings of corrupt conduct against public-sector managers or supervisors, and 10 were against elected officials (Mills and Cooper 2007).

In regard to corrupt behaviours with individual perpetrators, Mills and Cooper (2007) determined that the most common behaviours were acceptance of bribes, gifts and secret commissions, and collusion. These mostly relate to relationships between public officials and those outside the public sector.

Individual relationships were found to be important, leading to the conclusion that relationships facilitate corruption by providing the opportunity for exchange of power between individuals who are looking for ways to get something they want (Mills and Cooper 2007). The corruption risk is enhanced when the public official in question has regulatory or decision-making authority, and if he or she had a pre-existing relationship with his or her non-public-sector accomplice. Another common scenario involved public-sector perpetrators who had developed inappropriate relationships with clients whom they had met through their work (Mills and Cooper 2007). As discussed above, this behaviour qualifies as both corruption and misconduct.

Also, people who are more dependent on their employing organization, in the sense that they have few options for alternative employment, are more likely to engage in unethical behaviours that they see as vital to protecting or enhancing their career. Further, individuals with a dependence on alcohol or gambling are also at risk of corrupt practices. The same is said for those who feel dissatisfied or perceive unfairness in their workplace (Mills and Cooper 2007).

So, from this analysis we can determine that a number of factors create corruption risks for individual perpetrators; namely, the amount of discretion and autonomy their position holds, the level of power afforded them by their position, pre-existing relationships, job insecurity or dissatisfaction, and individual dependency issues (such as with drugs, alcohol, gambling, etc.).

In a study of corruption in New York City, Graycar and Villa (2011) found that, of the 100 cases examined, three-quarters were of people acting alone. This is not to say that organized corruption did not exist or was not found, but rather highlights the strength of individual factors in encouraging acts of corruption, misconduct and maladministration.

Institutional factors

Mills and Cooper (2007) found that organizations are more susceptible to unethical conduct when the individual role of the employee is uncertain or the organization is destabilized in some way. For example, organizations were found to be at risk if they are large, intensely competitive (both internally and externally), prioritize the bottom line, operate in industries or sectors with a culture of misconduct, and are experiencing a state of dynamic change such as corporate restructuring or diversification, or in the case of government, budget cutbacks and mission drift. Financial problems faced by the organization may also be related to, and encourage, unethical conduct (Mills and Cooper 2007).

There are two types of internal factors that might influence employee conduct: system failures (i.e. poor supervision, oversight or procedural rules) and socialization factors (i.e. conduct of peers and management within an organization). System failures involve cases where the agencies had no policies or procedures that addressed the conduct, or where perpetrators failed to follow adequate procedures, but the failure was not identified because monitoring was inadequate. In some cases, agencies had adopted policies and procedures, but they were so complex or outdated that they made it easier for employees to engage in corruption and harder for managers to supervise or monitor their activities because it was not clear how things should be done (Bozeman 2000; Mills and Cooper 2007, p. 19).

Socialization factors mostly relate to poor supervision and management. Two forms were identified. One, organizational incompetence, involve cases where there is a failure to monitor performance, implementation and supervision. The second relates to how management responds to ethics issues. This includes behaviour on the part of managers that tolerate or reward unethical behaviour, not acting on corruption and behaving inconsistently, and emphasizing the bottom line of the organization over other values (Mills and Cooper 2007; Treviño *et al.* 2000).

When a number of staff are found to have acted inappropriately within the one organization, it was mostly in an environment where they were not effectively supervised and were allowed a high degree of autonomy. They were also frequently highly trusted and respected for their knowledge, and were thus allowed to assume high levels of personal discretion as a result of seniority, long service, trust and popularity (Mills and Cooper 2007).

From this analysis, we can determine that there are particular elements of an organizational culture that contribute to institutional corruption. These are identified as being: the size of the organization, the degree to which competition is valued and expected, the importance of the bottom line as a key performance indicator, an uncertain future for the organization, poor supervision and management, the way management demonstrates its stance against corrupt behaviours, impracticability of existing codes of conduct or integrity measures, and stagnation in leadership.

Environmental factors

According to Mills and Cooper (2007), environmental factors are those that originate in the environment in which the organization operates and have a demonstrable impact on it while being outside the control of the agency. Some of these factors are: the potential for significant personal gain (financial or otherwise), a highly competitive working environment, the nature of the agency's work, significant change imposed on the organization (i.e. organizational restructure, allocation of new funds by the government, the need to operate on a commercial basis), inadequate legislative provisions, and poor understanding of proper agency functioning by some sectors of the community.

Operating in a competitive environment – such as regulation of property development, liquor licensing or universities competing to attract students – can result in an environment that has a tendency to see increased profits as a goal orientation, without consideration of organizational values (Mills and Cooper 2007).

Preventive measures targeting environmental factors should thus consider the ethical standards of those engaged in third-party contracting by an organization, as well as the external pressures placed on employees.

Building integrity processes and preventive strategies

Daniel Kaufmann, former Director of the World Bank Institute, recently stated, 'we can no longer fight corruption by simply fighting corruption alone' (Kaufmann 2012). It is with this in mind that these integrity-building processes and preventive strategies are designed. The processes and strategies are created to allow for an easier tailoring of integrity reform within an organization. In this sense, the processes and strategies 'fit' with the categories of 'individual', 'institutional' and 'environmental' factors as outlined by Mills and Cooper (2007). The integrity-building processes focus on the restructuring of the values and goals of an organization, and how these can be best communicated to employees and relating publics. Preventive strategies, however, focus on methods an organization can adopt to minimize the risk of corruption.

These processes and strategies are designed to assist a situational approach to reducing levels of corrupt behaviours in an organization. Not every process and strategy will apply to each case of corruption. For example, if misconduct is the main unethical activity occurring in a workplace, it would be pointless to adopt strategies targeting bribery.

This section outlines some integrity-building processes (Table 6.1) and preventive strategies (Table 6.2) that can be adopted to target levels of corruption, misconduct and maladministration in public administration. These processes and strategies have been adapted from a number of different sources, both public (Crime and Corruption Commission 2008; Crime and Misconduct Commission 2013; ICAC 2001, 2002, 2014; NSW Auditor-General 2015; OPI 2009; Queensland Police Service 2013; Robinson and Queensland Transport 2007) and private sectors (Goodson *et al.* 2012; McCusker 2006; University of Western Sydney 2010). They are here provided as a guide to tailoring a 'best-fit' approach to integrity reform.

This section will first outline the identified integrity-building strategies and preventive measures before demonstrating how they support Mills (2012) and Mills and Cooper's (2007) precipitating factors. The four case studies of driving licences, welfare checks, soliciting architecture and Board of Elections will be used to demonstrate how Mills and Cooper's (2007) factors, in addition to the integrity-building strategies and preventive measures, can create a multi-angulated approach to reducing levels of corruption in public administration systems.

Integrity-building processes

The following processes have been adapted from a number of reports written by Australian independent and state-run anti-corruption organizations, in addition to

TABLE 6.1 Integrity-building processes

Individual factors

- Include integrity issues in induction, education and awareness programmes
- Include integrity issues in organizational discussions
- Establish leadership mentoring programmes that focus on integrity issues
- Clearly communicate the people management resources available to leadership and ensure that they are used appropriately
- Ensure leadership takes responsibility for their team
- Ensure leadership effectively manages work performance issues as they arise, and that outcomes are communicated to all parties involved

Institutional factors

- Evaluate current organizational culture through ongoing review
- Use structured anonymous surveys to evaluate organizational culture
- Use survey results to identify implementation issues or possible areas for improvement
- Establish clear and reasonable behavioural expectations through codes of conduct, performances and building processes
- Involve all employees in the development of organizational values to ensure they are practical and consistent
- Establish a system of confidential reporting of issues
- Adopt an internal communication plan that reinforces behavioural standards and outlines how they are enforced
- Employ values and public interest principles in recruitment, selection and performance review criteria
- Establish a system for screening potential employees, suppliers and/or customers
- Consider public interest when reviewing internal policies and procedures
- Utilize systems of mentoring and review to ensure public resources are used appropriately and effectively

Environmental factors

- Ensure decision-making processes are transparent to the public and open to review
- Make copies of organizational values, codes of conduct, complaints and disciplinary policies publically available
- Communicate the importance of organizational values to key stakeholders

Source: Adopted from Crime and Corruption Commission (2008), Crime and Misconduct Commission (2013), ICAC (2001) and OPI (2009).

research conducted into integrity processes in an Australian state government (Crime and Corruption Commission 2008; Crime and Misconduct Commission 2013; ICAC 2001; OPI 2009). Not all are appropriate in every circumstance, and these can be used to form a technique bank from which one can draw a diagnosis of a problem.

TABLE 6.2 Preventive measures

Individual factors

- Support those who identify corruption or unethical behaviour
- Provide specialist support services to all staff members (e.g. alcohol, drug and gambling support, senior human support officers, pastors)
- Recognize good work, encourage and reward good work practices
- Provide customized training to staff involved in cash handling

---

Institutional factors

- Utilize risk management and regularly review operational risks
- Consider the risks faced and identified by similar organizations
- Implement staff rotation in high-risk functional areas
- Address the corruption prevention outcomes your organization wants to achieve, identify what your organization is already doing to achieve these outcomes, and target the gap between where you are and where you want to be
- Engage all staff in the creation of integrity policies, procedures and systems to ensure they are practical
- Maintain a database of corrupt or unethical incidents and regularly review to identify emerging patterns or trends
- Strengthen an ethical culture through training, education and public accountability
- Relevant staff receive regular training in the agency's procurement processes
- Establish effective and appropriate complaint management
- Encourage staff to report misconduct, corruption or maladministration
- Embed ethical standards into the recruitment strategies of human resources
- Establish systems of promotion that consider demonstrated ethical conduct
- Minimize internal competition
- Undertake regular research into corruption prevention strategies

---

Environmental factors

- Demonstrate public accountability by providing appropriate, accurate and timely information to the government and public
- Engage in procurement planning to manage purchasing patterns
- Incorporate monitoring and evaluation of performance of contractors and products into each tender or purchasing decision
- Communicate proper organizational functioning to both staff and public
- Allow for scrutiny and review of systems and practices
- Focus on public accountability and duty rather than bottom line

---

Source: Adapted from ICAC (2002, 2014), McCusker (2006), NSW Auditor-General (2015), Robinson and Queensland Transport (2007), Queensland Police Service (2013), and University of Western Sydney (2010).

Preventive measures

These preventive measures have also been adapted from a number of Australian independent and state-based anti-corruption institutions (ICAC 2002, 2014; McCusker 2006; NSW Auditor-General 2015; Robinson and Queensland Transport 2007; Queensland Police Service 2013; University of Western Sydney 2010), and have been explored in Graycar and Sidebottom (2012).

The preventive measures target the roots of corruption, misconduct and maladministration in a given organization. By categorizing them into individual, institutional and environmental factors, it becomes easy to see how these factors encourage or facilitate corruption and the different ways in which these factors can be addressed.

Applying processes and strategies to vignettes

If we consider the opening examples of corruption, misconduct and maladministration, we can see how these processes and strategies are applied.

Corruption (driving licences)

For example, in the case of the RTA manager accepting cash and drugs to pass people who would otherwise have failed their licence or who failed to provide insufficient identification, individual factors were at play. The manager was not prompted into corrupt behaviour from a rotten culture – he saw a scheme and he went with it. The bribes were being paid to circumvent the policies and systems of the organization, but because applicants did not meet the standards, not because the policies and systems were overly arduous or complex.

The following preventative strategies can be applied to this case: provide specialist support services to all staff members; recognize good work; encourage and reward good work practices.

Integrity-building processes relevant to this case are those focusing on human resources management (HRM) and incentivizing proper conduct. Processes that emphasize public interest are not entirely relevant to this case because the activities of the individual in question benefited a particular public (those attempting to sit their driving test). As such, the relevant processes are:

1   *Include integrity issues in induction, education and awareness programmes.* If standards of promotion involve demonstrated proper behaviour, this will help negate the risk of individuals seeking bribes. Further, by demonstrating that the organization is serious about integrity, employees may be deterred from engaging in corruption in the future.

2   *Establish a system for screening potential employees, suppliers and customers.* This point is really limited to 'screening potential employees' in this case. This individual was employed to score driving tests; as such, the organization has little control

over who the customer is, they could be anyone sitting a test. However, incorporating integrity standards into recruitment through interview questions would flag potential rotten apples.

3 *Clearly communicate the people management resources available to leadership, and ensure they are used correctly.* In this case, the individual involved was a manager. However, by communicating to his superiors the people management resources available, suspect or problematic behaviour may have been addressed sooner.

Misconduct (welfare checks)

Individual factors are clearly present in this example of misconduct. The police officer in question acted alone in misusing information obtained through his position (the existence, location and vulnerability of the woman) to then return to the property after work and out of uniform. While in the past the institutional trappings of being a police officer may have given licence for all sorts of inappropriate behaviour, that is not the case now, and it is unlikely that institutional factors would have played a role here (unless there were deep-seated, localized cultures of corruption). Institutionally, it could be that the officer was not given enough training on ethical conduct and was therefore not aware of proper conduct, but this is more likely an individual case of misconduct. Given the existence and promotion of codes of conduct in the Victorian police force and that the officer has targeted a vulnerable individual, it is reasonable to assume that further promoting the behavioural guidelines of the police force would have done little to prevent this act from occurring.

As such, the following preventive strategies can be applied to this case: provide specialist support to all officers; utilize risk management and regularly review operational risks.

Integrity-building processes focus on human resources management (HRM), staff management and incentivizing good conduct:

1 *Include integrity issues in recruitment, education and awareness programmes.* Not only does this demonstrate that the organization is committed to best practice, but it allows staff members to raise any questions they may have about proper conduct.

2 *Establish clear and reasonable behavioural expectations through codes of conduct, performance measures and business processes.* Although in this case the organization has a well-established and well-promoted set of behavioural guidelines, ensuring that they are both reasonable and understood among all employees, and ensuring that promotion considers good practice, incentivizes good behaviour.

3 *Employ values and public interest principles in recruitment, selection and performance review criteria.* This allows human resources to risk assess any future and current employee of the organization through asking targeted, integrity-focused questions.

Misconduct (soliciting architecture)

As the architect and carpenter agreed to engage in the work, and as Enright acted alone but not from a desire to seek special treatment, the factors involved in this case are a mixture of individual, institutional and environmental.

Applicable preventive strategies are: provide customized training to staff involved in cash handling; utilize risk management and regularly review operational risks; engage all staff in the creation of integrity policies, procedures and systems to ensure they are practical; strengthen an ethical culture through training, education and public accountability; incorporate monitoring and evaluation of performance of contractors and products into each tender or purchasing decision; communicate proper organizational functioning to both staff and the public.

As Enright was not found to have achieved any special treatment from the architect and carpenter, and that the only advantage he received from his public office was knowledge of the work of these individuals, it suggests that integrity-building strategies should focus on education and awareness. Further, as no public resources were diverted or mismanaged in this case, integrity-building strategies focusing on public accountability and resource management are not applicable. Applicable strategies are:

1   *Involve all employees in the development of organizational values to ensure that they are practical and consistent.* This ensures that staff members are aware of behavioural standards while providing an opportunity for leadership to become aware of any risks caused by impractical policies.
2   *Adopt an internal communication plan that reinforces behavioural standards and outlines how they are enforced.* This can be in the form of advertising (i.e. on noticeboards, via email) or through less formal forms of communication such as conversations with immediate supervisors.
3   *Include integrity issues in induction, education and awareness programmes.* Providing employees with situational cases to 'solve' or respond to can create awareness of the more complex elements of existing laws and regulations.
4   *Establish leadership mentoring programmes that focus on integrity issues.* This allows employees to raise questions they may have about proper conduct with superiors confidentially and without fear of reprimand.
5   *Communicate the importance of organizational values to key stakeholders.* This can be achieved either through ensuring that clients and stakeholders meet ethics/integrity standards (i.e. have their own code of ethics) or can involve the incorporation of behavioural expectations into contracts/agreements and communications.

See also DOI (2013).

Maladministration (Board of Elections, New York City)

The fact that this case involved financial mismanagement and the organizational disregard to identified risks points to institutional factors.

As such, the applicable preventative strategies are: utilize risk management and regularly review operational risks; strengthen an ethical culture through training, education and public accountability.

Only two preventive strategies are applicable here for a number of reasons. First, it was poor decision-making by leadership, not widespread malpractice, that caused the case of maladministration. Second, the nature of the BOE is such that it does not rely on practices of tendering or procurement and the 'key stakeholders' are the public who use its services. Third, the BOE did demonstrate public accountability and did allow for scrutiny and review by holding public hearings; it just chose to ignore all suggestions. This places the onus on BOE leadership. In this case, utilizing and properly responding to risk management and strengthening the ethical culture at the top are the only applicable preventive strategies.

In order to ensure that the BOE continues to effectively and efficiently use public resources in the future, the following integrity-building processes can be adopted:

1   *Evaluate current organizational culture through ongoing review.* This can be achieved through the use of anonymous surveys. By establishing systems of anonymous, ongoing review, you create a leadership that responds to the concerns of its employees and the leadership team is able to identify implementation issues or other possible areas of improvement. This ensures that the leadership culture is one that regularly considers best practice.
2   *Consider public interest when reviewing internal policies and procedures.* 'Public interest' can here refer to both the issues that arise in public forums and the taxpayer dollar. Considering both will reinforce the notion of public duty.
3   *Establish a system of confidential professional reporting of issues.* This allows staff members to flag efficiency or practical concerns of which leadership may otherwise be unaware.
4   *Ensure decision-making processes are transparent to the public and open to review.* This further ensures that an organization is committed to risk management and being responsible to the public.
5   *Utilize systems of monitoring and review to ensure public resources are used appropriately and effectively.* Same as point 4.
6   *Ensure leadership actively manages work performance issues as they arise and that outcomes are communicated to all parties involved.* If parties are private individuals, communication can occur in private. If, in this case, the parties involved are the public, the DOI, the City and the media, communicating review outcomes via a public forum (such as the media or the BOE website) shows that the organization is committed to reform and that investigations have been conducted. This is an important step in restoring public trust.

Conclusion

All cases of corruption, misconduct and maladministration are not the same. It is impossible to write a law or policy for every possible scenario in which corruption, misconduct and maladministration might occur. With this impossibility in mind, it becomes important to build integrity so people have a sense of what is acceptable and what is not. Building preventive strategies that are general and can be applied in specific cases allows for an easily adopted model of corruption, misconduct and maladministration prevention. This chapter has illustrated, with some real-life examples, how this can be done, and the complexity in so doing.

Returning to Weber's (1958) assertion, that analyses should not begin with a definition, but should derive the definition by looking at specific examples, this chapter has shown that definitions can be built from practice just as applying case study research to empirical work can build theory. No organization is impenetrable to integrity breaches, but integrity can be managed.

References

Anechiarico, F. and Jacobs, J.B. (1996) *The Pursuit of Absolute Integrity: How Corruption Makes Government Ineffective*, Chicago, IL: University of Chicago Press.

Bozeman, B. (2000) 'Technology transfer and public policy: A review of research and theory', *Research Policy*, 29(4): 627–55.

Brown, A.J. and Head, B. (2005) 'Institutional capacity and choice in Australia's integrity systems', *Australian Journal of Public Administration*, 64(2): 84–95.

Caiden, G.E., Dwivedi, O.P. and Jabbra, J.G. (2001) *Where Corruption Lives*, West Hartford, CT: Kumarian Press.

Crime and Corruption Commission (2008) *Misconduct Resistance: An Integrated Governance Approach to Protecting Agency Integrity*, Perth: Crime and Corruption Commission, available at: www.ccc.wa.gov.au/SiteCollectionDocuments/CCC-MR-complete.pdf (accessed 15 May 2014).

Crime and Misconduct Commission (2013) *Building Integrity*, Brisbane: Crime and Misconduct Commission, available at: www.cmc.qld.gov.au/topics/misconduct/misconduct-prevention/building-integrity-program (accessed 15 May 2014).

De Lancer Julnes, P. and Villoria, M. (2014) 'Understanding and addressings citizens' perceptions of corruption: The case of Spain', *International Review of Public Administration*, 19(1): 22–43.

Della Porta, D. (2004) 'Political parties and corruption: Ten hypotheses on five vicious circles', *Crime, Law and Social Change*, 42(1): 35–60.

DOI (2013) 'In the Matter of Patrick Enright, COIB Case No. 2012-469, Oath Index No. 1293/13', 7 August 2011, New York: The City of New York Department of Investigations, available at: www.nyc.gov/html/doi/downloads/pdf/q7-cityemp-enright.pdf (accessed 20 May 2014).

DOI and Hearn, R.G. (2013) 'Report on the Board of Elections' Staffing Levels and Costs for the November 8, 2011 "Off-Year" General Election', 1 April 2013, New York: The City of New York Department of Investigations, available at: www.nyc.gov/html/doi/downloads/pdf/2013/apr13/pr12boerpt_40113.pdf (accessed 20 May 2014).

Ede, A., Homel, R. and Penzler, T. (2002) 'Situational corruption prevention: A police study', in T. Prenzler and J. Ransley (eds), *Police Reform: Building Integrity* (pp. 210–16), Sydney: Federation Press.

Findlay, M. and Stewart, A. (1992) 'Implementing corruption prevention strategies through codes of conduct', *Corruption and Reform*, 7(1): 67–85.

Goodson, S.G., Mory, K.J. and Lapointe, J.R. (2012) 'Supplemental guidance: The role of auditing in public sector governance', The Institute of Internal Auditors (Global), January

2012, available at: https://na.theiia.org/standards-guidance/Public%20Documents/Public_Sector_Governance1_1_.pdf (accessed 10 June 2014).

Gorta, A. (2000) 'Research: A tool for building corruption resistance', in P. Larmour and N. Wolanin (eds), *Corruption and Anti-Corruption* (pp. 11–29), Canberra: Asia Pacific Press.

Gorta, A. (2006) 'Corruption risk areas and corruption resistance', in C. Sampford, A. Shacklock, C. Connors and F. Galtung (eds), *Measuring Corruption* (pp. 203–19), Burlington, VT: Ashgate.

Government of Australia (2009) *Fair Work Regulations (Fair Work Act) 2009*, Canberra: Commonwealth of Australia.

Government of South Australia (2012) *Independent Commissioner Against Corruption Act 2012*, Adelaide: Government of South Australia.

Graycar, A. and Prenzler, T. (2013) *Understanding and Preventing Corruption*, Basingstoke: Palgrave Macmillan.

Graycar, A. and Sidebottom, A. (2012) 'Corruption and control: A corruption reduction approach', *Journal of Financial Crime*, 19(4): 384–99.

Graycar, A. and Villa, D. (2011) 'The loss of governance capacity through corruption', *Governance: An International Journal of Policy, Administration, and Institutions*, 23(3): 419–38.

Hooker, J. (2009) 'Corruption from a cross-cultural perspective', *Cross Cultural Management: An International Journal*, 16(3): 251–67.

Hossain, N., Musembi, C.N. and Hughes, J. (2010) *Corruption Accountability and Gender: Understanding the Connections*, United Nations Development Fund for Women, New York, available at: www.undp.org/content/dam/aplaws/publication/en/publications/womens-empowerment/corruption-accountability-and-gender-understanding-the-connection/Corruption-accountability-and-gender.pdf.

ICAC (2001) *The First Four Steps: Building Organisational Integrity*, Sydney: Independent Commission Against Corruption, available at: www.icac.nsw.gov.au/documents/doc_download/1332-the-first-four-steps (accessed 15 May 2014).

ICAC (2002) *The Do-It-Yourself Corruption Resistance Guide*, Sydney: Independent Commission Against Corruption, available at: www.icac.nsw.gov.au/documents/doc_download/1314-do-it-yourself-corruption-resistance-guide (accessed 15 May 2014).

ICAC (2007) 'Report on an investigation into corrupt issuing of drivers licenses (Operation Sirona)', 20 September 2007, Sydney: Independent Commission Against Corruption.

ICAC (2014) *Corruption Prevention Plan*, Sydney: Independent Commission Against Corruption, available at: www.icac.nsw.gov.au/preventing-corruption/corruption-prevention-strategy/cp-plan/4871 (accessed 15 May 2014).

Kaufmann, D. (2012) 'Rethinking the fight against corruption', *The Huffington Post*, 28 November 2012, available at: www.huffingtonpost.com/danielkaufmann/rethinking-the-fight-corruption_b_2204591.html (accessed 20 May 2014).

Kim, S. and Lee, J. (2012) 'E-participation, transparency, and trust in local government', *Public Administration Review*, 72(6): 819–28.

Klitgaard, R.E. (1988) *Controlling Corruption*, Oakland, CA: University of California Press.

Larmour, P. and Barcham, M. (2006) 'National Integrity Systems in small Pacific island states', *Public Administration and Development*, 26(2): 173–84.

Larmour, P. and Wolanin, N. (eds) (2001) *Corruption and Anti-Corruption*, Canberra: ANU E Press.

McCusker, R. (2006) 'Review of anti-corruption strategies', *Technical and Background Paper*, Canberra: Australian Institute of Criminology, available at: www.aic.gov.au/documents/8/F/1/%7B8F179E8B-B998-4761-84B3-AD311D7D3EA8%7Dtbp023.pdf.

Menzel, D.C. (2005) 'Empirical research on ethics and integrity', in H.G. Frederickson and R.K. Ghere (eds), *Ethics in Public Management* (pp. 16–48), Armonk, NY: M.E. Sharpe.

Mills, A. (2012) *Causes of Corruption in Public Sector Institutions and its Impact on Development: Turning What We Know in to What We Do*, paper presented at the Expert Group Meeting on Corruption in Public Administration, May 2012, United Nations Public Administration Network, available at: http://unpan1.un.org/intradoc/groups/public/documents/un-dpadm/unpan049589.pdf.

Mills, A. and Cooper, D. (2007) 'Learning from experience: A project to maintain knowledge-based prevention policy', *CIES Working Paper*, Lisbon, Portugal: Centre for Research and Studies in Sociology (Portugal), available at: www.cies.iscte.pt/destaques/documents/CIES-WP29_MillsCooper__000.pdf (accessed 15 May 2014.).

Morgan, A. (1998) *Corruption: Causes, Consequences, and Policy Implications*, San Francsico, CA: The Asia Foundation.

Mulcahy, S. (2012) *Money, Politics, Power: Corruption Risks in Europe*, Berlin: Transparency International.

New York City (1986) 'The Administrative Code and Charter of the City of New York', Albany, NY: The City of New York, available at: http://72.45.128.254/nycnew/?Aspx AutoDetectCookieSupport=1 (accessed 22 June 2014).

NSW (1988) *Independent Commission Against Corruption Act 1988*, Sydney: NSW Government.

NSW Auditor-General (2015) *Better Practice Guide: Fraud Control Improvement Kit – Meeting Your Fraud Control Obligations*, July 2006, Sydney: New South Wales Auditor-General, available at: www.audit.nsw.gov.au/ArticleDocuments/197/Fraud_Control_Improvement_Kit_February_2015_2.pdf.aspx?Embed=Y.

OPI (2009) *A Guide to Building Workplace Integrity: Indicators and Practice*, Melbourne: Office of Police Integrity, available at: www.ibac.vic.gov.au/docs/default-source/opi-prevention-and-education/a-guide-to-building-workplace-integrity—-dec-09.pdf?sfvrsn= 2 (accessed 15 May 2014).

Queensland Police Service (2013) 'The QPS corruption prevention framework: A strategic approach', *Corruption Prevention Plan 2009–2013: "Integrity is Everyone's Business"*, Brisbane: Queensland Police Service, available at: www.police.qld.gov.au/Resources/Internet/services/reportsPublications/corrupt/document/CPP_page6to10.pdf (accessed 15 May 2014).

Redlawsk, D. and McCann, J. (2005) 'Popular interpretations of "corruption" and their partisan consequences', *Political Behavior*, 27(3): 261–83.

Robinson, R. and Queensland Transport (2007) 'Implementing a corruption prevention strategy in Queensland Transport: Freeways, speed-bumps and potholes', *Australian Public Sector Anti-Corruption Conference 2007*, Sydney: Queensland Transport, Queensland Government.

Roebuck, J.B. and Barker, T. (1974) 'Typology of police corruption', *Social Problems* 21(3): 423–37.

Rose-Ackerman, S. (1999) *Corruption and Government: Causes, Consequences and Reform*, Cambridge: Cambridge University Press.

Smith, R. (2005) 'Mapping the New South Wales public integrity system', *Australian Journal of Public Administration*, 64(2): 54–61.

Supreme Court of Victoria – Court of Appeal (2010) 'The Queen v Huy Vinh Quach (findings) [R v Huy Vinh Quach [2010] VSCA 106 (07 May 2010) (ASHLEY and REDLICH JJA and HANSEN AJA)]', 7 May 2010, Melbourne: Supreme Court of Victoria – Court of Appeal, available at: https://jade.barnet.com.au/Jade.html#!article= 147354 (accessed 20 June 2014).

Transparency International (2013) *Global Corruption Barometer 2013*, available at: www.transparency.org/gcb2013 (accessed 15 March 2014).

Transparency International UK (2014) *Corruption Typologies*, available at: www.ti-defence.org/corruption/typologies.html#tabs0291 (accessed 7 May 2014).

Treisman, D. (2000) 'The causes of corruption: A cross-national study', *Journal of Public Economics*, 76(3): 399–457.

Treviño, L.K., Hartman, L.P. and Brown, M. (2000) 'Moral person and moral manager: How executives develop a reputation for ethical leadership', *California Management Review*, 42(4): 128–42.

University of Western Sydney (2010) *UWS Corruption and Fraud Prevention Strategy*, Sydney: University of Western Sydney, available at: http://policies.uws.edu.au/download.php?id=541 (accessed 15 May 2014).

UNODC (2003) *United Nations Convention against Corruption*, Vienna: United Nations Office of Drugs and Crime.

Warburton, J. and Baker, G. (2005) 'Integrity systems and local government', *Australian Journal of Public Administration*, 64(2): 62–8.

Weber, M. (1958) *The Protestant Ethic and the Spirit of Capitalism [1904–5]*, New York: Charles Scribner's Sons.

Wood, J.J. (1997) *Royal Commission into the New South Wales Police Service: Final Report*, May 1997, Sydney, available at: www.pic.nsw.gov.au/files/reports/RCPS%20Report%20Volume%201.pdf.

World Bank (1997) 'Helping countries combat corruption: The role of the World Bank', *Poverty Reduction and Economic Management*, Washington, DC: World Bank, available at: www1.worldbank.org/publicsector/anticorrupt/corruptn/corrptn.pdf.

7

THEORETICAL (MIS)UNDERSTANDING?

Applying principal-agent and collective action theories to the problem of corruption in systemically corrupt countries

Caryn Peiffer and Heather Marquette

Introduction

In the past decade and a half, the effort to control corruption in the developing world has grown seemingly exponentially; it has attracted support from all major aid agencies and has inspired hundreds of reform projects, action plans, anti-corruption agencies and a growing class of in-demand experts. Depending on the source consulted, it has drawn anywhere from hundreds of millions to billions of dollars in investment (Michael 2004; Michael and Bowser 2009; Mungiu-Pippidi, 2006; Sampson 2010), leading to what has been called the birth of an 'anti-corruption industry' (Michael 2004; Mungiu-Pippidi 2006; Sampson 2010). Despite this investment, there seem to be few successful cases where countries have significantly reduced corruption (Johnsøn *et al.* 2012, p. 42). In short, most systemically corrupt countries are considered to be just as corrupt now as they were before anti-corruption interventions were rolled out (Hough 2013; Mungiu-Pippidi 2006; Persson *et al.* 2013).

For a growing number of authors, the wide-scale failure of anti-corruption programming lies in the inappropriate theoretical foundations that underscore its design. Anti-corruption programming is overwhelmingly influenced by principal-agent theory, which depicts corruption as occurring when public officials who have discretion over the provision of public services lack accountability. This emphasizes the rational choices that take place in individual incidents of corruption, assuming that corruption is 'solvable' with policies that can alter these individual calculations. Critics have recently argued that this assumption is flawed, especially in systemically corrupt contexts, where corruption is best understood to be a collective action problem instead (Bauhr and Nasiritousi 2011; Mungiu-Pippidi 2011; Persson *et al.* 2013; Rothstein 2011). From this perspective, the application of principal-agent theory mistakenly assumes that there will be 'principled principals' in civil society and in positions of power to actively oppose corruption and enforce the anti-corruption reforms. Instead, for these authors, systemic corruption persists because corruption is widely perceived to be the norm in such contexts, and individuals gain little from abstaining from or resisting corruption if they cannot trust that others will do the same. The roots of this insight are attributed to collective action theory.

In this chapter, we unpack this critique further. In doing so, we first aim to set out how principal-agent and collective action theories have been applied so far in the literature on corruption and anti-corruption, and describe in more detail the critique made that the application of principal-agent theory 'mischaracterizes' the nature of corruption in systematically corrupt contexts, and the ways in which a collective action theory lens is said to better capture the dynamics of corruption in that context. We argue, however, that this application of collective action theory to the issue of corruption has thus far been both incomplete and narrow. In addition to the insight that trust and perceptions of how others act influence decisions regarding whether to engage in or to resist corruption, the rich collective action theory literature also highlights the potential importance of a host of other factors, such as the salience of the good for the group and the feasibility through which members can monitor each other in contributing towards the collective good. Once the scope of potential contributions from collective action theory is widened, we argue that instead of the two theories being diametrically opposed, as they have been portrayed, they prove to be in fact complementary, and even overlap in some meaningful ways. This is particularly important, given the growing development policy interest in translating this research into practical policy recommendations.[1] Finally, we conclude with thoughts on how future research can better explore how each theory could be used to better inform anti-corruption interventions.

A principal-agent approach to corruption

The predominance of principal-agent theory in corruption research has been clearly demonstrated by a meta-analysis of 115 studies looking at corruption's impact on economic growth by Ugur and Dasgupta (2011, p. 43). They found that all studies considered 'adhered to an explicitly-stated principal-agent approach to corruption, or their account was closely related to that approach'. This illustrates that the principal-agent theory lens shapes our very understanding of how corruption impacts development. It is no wonder, then, that, as Persson *et al.* (2013) argue, the designs of most anti-corruption programmes reflect a principal-agent understanding of corruption, rather than any other alternative view.

The principal-agent approach finds its origins in theories of the firm, where the classic principal was the investor who had little confidence in the stockbroker.

A principal-agent problem stems from two assumptions: that the principal and agent have diverging interests and that the agent has more information than the principal (information asymmetry). Due to asymmetric information, the principal is unable to perfectly monitor the actions of the agent, and so the agent has some discretion to pursue their own interests. Moral hazard occurs when the interests of the principal and the agent are not aligned, and the agent pursues his or her own interests at the expense of the interests of the principal, hence the 'problem' (Harris and Raviv 1979; Ross 1973).

Corruption is often described as existing in society as a *double* principal-agent problem. In the first instance, a political leader is cast as the 'principal'; he or she is tasked with monitoring the actions of bureaucrats (agents) in order to keep them accountable. Without the ability to perfectly monitor their actions, however, rationally minded bureaucrats use their discretion over resources to extract rents when the opportunity arises. The second principal-agent problem occurs when public officials (bureaucrats or politicians) are conceptualized to be the 'agents' and the public, more generally, as the 'principal'. As the agent, the public official is able to abuse his or her office and discretion over public services to secure private rents from members of the public, and the public is unable to perfectly monitor or hold public officials accountable (Bardhan 1997; Klitgaard 1988; Rose-Ackerman 1978; Ugur and Dasgupta 2011). While one would expect that the latter principal-agent problem is more prevalent in countries where there are immense information asymmetries between the ruler and the ruled, even in those countries where there are well-developed democratic and legally enforced accountability mechanisms and a high degree of government transparency, the public is still unable to perfectly monitor officials' actions and hold them universally accountable.

In either case, viewing corruption through a principal-agent lens emphasizes the rational choices of individuals that take place in discrete incidences of corruption. This focus implies that corruption is 'solvable' with policies that alter the level of discretion given to agents and their individual incentive calculations. Consequently, anti-corruption interventions, guided by principal-agent models, have focused on reducing the discretion of civil servants, increasing monitoring mechanisms, promoting transparency in government, supporting anti-corruption civil society groups to serve as watchdogs, and strengthening sanctions on those who engage in corruption, so as to better align the incentives of potential 'agents' with those of their respective 'principals'.

However, a recent U4/DFID paper on mapping evidence gaps in anti-corruption programmes supported by donor agencies provides some pretty stark reading. The review found that '[o]nly in the case of [public financial management (PFM)] does the evidence clearly suggest that such measures reduce corruption' (Johnsøn et al. 2012, p. 42). In terms of public-sector reforms (other than PFM), oversight institutions, civil society, budget support, donors' own systems and multilateral agreements, all interventions in keeping with the principal-agent model, the evidence of their efficacy is weak or fair at best. After over a decade and a half, and significant investment in both time and resources, this is fairly shocking, though how much of this is down to failed interventions and how much is down to gaps or weaknesses in the evidence base itself (e.g. an overall lack of empirical research on anti-corruption work in fragile states) is unknown (Johnsøn *et al.* 2012, pp. 42–4). One answer given to the question of why the record of anti-corruption interventions has been so poor is that anti-corruption interventions are based on a theoretical misunderstanding of the nature of corruption; in other words, principal-agent theory has fallen short in providing viable solutions to the problem.

If principal-agent approaches depict the success of an anti-corruption intervention as a function of the abilities of principals to monitor and hold accountable agents for their actions, a lack of 'political will' of leaders to fully implement anti-corruption reforms is typically flagged as an explanation for the failure of anti-corruption efforts. The application of principal-agent theory to the issue of corruption has taken for granted that principals have the 'will' to serve the functions of monitoring and keeping agents to account. It is no wonder, then, that anti-corruption programming does not effectively grapple with the variable 'willingness' principals may have in holding agents accountable.

It's a collective action problem, *instead*?

Several authors (e.g. Bauhr and Nasiritousi 2011; Mungiu-Pippidi 2011; Persson *et al.* 2013; Rothstein 2011) have recently criticized the principal-agent view within anti-corruption policy on these grounds, as well as governance more generally (Booth and Cammack 2013). They have argued that, in certain contexts, corruption should instead be viewed as a problem of collective action, and that especially in a context of systemic corruption, viewing corruption as a principal-agent problem 'mischaracterizes' the issue of corruption completely (see Persson *et al.* 2013 for this particular turn of phrase). A classic collective action problem, according to Mancur Olson (1965), occurs when, even if it is in the best interest of all individuals in a group (or across groups) to act collectively towards a common goal, group members do not do so; instead, group members find it in their individual interest to not contribute at all or to limit their contributions, ensuring that the collective benefit is not realized to its fullest potential.

What impacts people's perceived interests and calculations to contribute towards the common good has been the subject of hundreds of studies. One potentially important factor that has been highlighted is the influential role that perceptions of how other group members act or, in other terms, trust within the group (see Elster 1985; Ostrom 1990; Seabright 1993 for examples). It is from this insight that the authors cited above root their application of collective action theory to the conceptualization of corruption. The following, from Persson *et al.* (2013, pp. 456–7), typifies the argument made:

> In particular, the rewards of corruption—and hence the strategy any rational actor is most likely to opt for—should according to this set of theories be

expected to depend critically on how many other individuals in the same society that are expected to be corrupt. Insofar as corrupt behavior is the expected behavior, everyone should be expected to act corruptly, including both the group of actors to whom the principal-agent framework refers to as 'agents' and the group of actors referred to as 'principals'.

Viewing corruption in this way highlights the collective, rather than individual, nature of corruption and the very difficult challenge that anti-corruption efforts face in changing levels of distrust in society and norms that reinforce persistent patterns of systemic corruption. There is much intuitive logic to this analysis, but collective action theory has potentially much more to contribute to our under-standing of corruption and the efficacy of anti-corruption interventions than on just the important role that a lack of intra-group trust plays in sustaining systemic corruption. Collective action theorists have highlighted the potentially important role of several other variables in influencing whether a group acts collectively.

So how does collective action theory apply to the study of corruption? While the study of collective action predates, and has developed significantly since Mancur Olson's (1965) book *The Logic of Collective Action*, its influence on framing the issue is still very prominent. Writing at a time when many scholars took for granted the idea that people will cooperate within groups and act collectively to achieve common goals, Olson's work was a strong counterpoint, as it suggested that collectives would sometimes not realise their full potential, becoming caught up in a collective action problem.

In his book, Olson specifically referred to the ability of collectives to work towards the production of public goods. These are goods that are impossible to exclude people from using (*non-excludable*) and where one person's use of the good does not reduce the availability of the good for others to enjoy (*non-rivalrous*). Street lighting and national defence are often referred to as examples of public goods. Olson's analysis has since been applied to other types of goods, such as common pool resources, which share in common with public goods their non-excludability, but not their non-rivalry (Ostrom *et al.* 1992). Unregulated or 'open-access' natural sites, such as certain fishing grounds, pastures and forests, are commonly cited examples of common pool resources; a person's access to an unregulated fishing ground is by definition not restricted ('non-excludable') but his or her fishing activity can reduce the stock available for other users to catch ('rivalrous').

Because both types of these goods are non-excludable, people who do not contribute towards their production can still benefit from them; beneficiaries of this sort are called 'free riders'. The potential for free riding is at the heart of an Olsonian collective action problem. Viewing individuals as maximizing rational agents, Olson argued that whenever a user cannot be excluded from enjoying the benefits of collective action, the individual incentive to contribute towards the production of that collective benefit is reduced. Put differently, people opt to free ride when they know their level of contribution towards the collective good does not impact their beneficiary status. Moreover, individuals feel less inclined to contribute towards the collective benefit when they know or anticipate that others will free ride on their efforts.

The resultant free riding is the collective action problem. When some free ride, and others do not, the collective benefit is not provided to its fullest potential; of course, if everyone decides to not contribute at all, then the collective benefit never materializes. In the case of common pool resources, where the consumption of the good by one reduces what is available for others, copious free riding can lead to the depletion of the resource, which harms all users in the long run. This phenomenon is commonly referred to as the 'tragedy of the commons' (Hardin 1968).

Ostensibly, in using collective action theory when thinking of corruption, corruption is the manifestation of free riding itself, as the motivation for engaging in corrupt behaviour is usually depicted as coming from putting personal interest ahead of the larger group's collective interest.[2] The group's collective benefit, in this case, can be conceptualized as being either abstract or quite concrete. In the case of the former, the choice to engage in corruption robs the group from having a 'corruption-free environment' or a good quality of government. According to Rothstein (2011), a good quality of government is one where all citizens are treated impartially, according to the established rule of law. A good quality of government is positively associated with a number of tangible health, economic and other social outcomes; however, it also represents something more abstract, which is a governance environment that citizens and foreign investors trust to be fair and reliable, and is associated with greater life satisfaction. Through this prism, the absence of corruption and the presence of an impartial government is a public good in and of itself (Rothstein 2011).[3]

In a more concrete sense, corruption is charged with causing the depletion of tangible resources, which is typical of a common pool resource. Corruption can lead to the bankrupting of the state or at least reduce its ability to provide public services effectively and efficiently. One might conceptualize the collective benefit here to be the percentage of the public purse allocated to the provision of services, and free riding – engaging in corrupt behaviour – as reducing or depleting the capacity of the state to take care of all citizens to its actual financial potential.

As noted earlier, trust/perceptions of free riding are only a couple of potentially important variables of the many explored in collective action literature. Agrawal (2002) listed more than 30 that scholars have identified as likely to affect whether a group will be able to overcome a potential collective action problem. While it is outside of the scope of this chapter to review all of those, we present a smaller list of 11 in Table 7.1; it draws from Ostrom's (2010) list of variables most frequently cited in the collective action theory literature (see also Ostrom 1998, 2007). Ostensibly, each of these variables can be important to the issue of corruption, though some seem more readily applicable than others.

The potential importance of any one of the variables listed in Table 7.1 is acknowledged to be completely contextual in the broader collective action theory literature (see Ostrom 2010, p. 164, for example). Moreover, it is also clear that

TABLE 7.1 How variables may affect collective action

Variable	Why?
Group size	In large groups, free riding is not easily noticed and group members may feel like their potential contribution will not make much of a difference to producing the collective benefit (Olson 1965). With more people, it may be more difficult to come to an internal agreement about how to coordinate activity to arrive at a collective benefit (Olson 1965). In the case of a common pool resource, more group members increases the chance of a resource becoming depleted (Ostrom *et al.* 1992).
	Groups of a very small size may not be able to mobilize the resources needed to engage effectively in collective action (Agrawal 2000); larger groups have more resources to draw upon to aid the collective effort (Marwell and Oliver 1993).
Group heterogeneity	When some members have a much stronger interest in seeing that the collective good be produced, they may be more willing to bear the burden of others free riding to make sure that the good will be produced (Olson 1965).
	Heterogeneity increases the difficulty and the likelihood of conflict occurring over coordinating and negotiating the distribution of the costs and benefits of collective action (Banerjee *et al.* 2005; Bardhan 1993; Hardin 1982; Isaac and Walker 1988; Kanbur 1992).
Face-to-face communication	Face-to-face communication gives group members a more intimate interaction, which can be used to persuade others to cooperate or discuss grievances of past interactions. Promises made to cooperate face-to-face are more easily trusted than those made by other means (Adolphs *et al.* 1996; Kerr and Kaufman-Gilliland 1994; Ostrom *et al.* 1994).
Repeated interaction	Repeated interaction between group members facilitates learning. Group members have the ability to figure out what strategies were successful or unsuccessful in garnering collective action. Moreover, reputations for whether group members would be willing to work collectively can be established through repetitive interactions (Miller 1992; Ostrom 2000; Schlager 1995).
Trust/good reputations	Group members who feel that they can trust other group members to act collectively, based on a good reputation of past collective action or on something else, will be more willing to contribute towards the common good (Elster 1985; Ostrom 1990; Seabright 1993).
Group interdependence	Direct and dependent linkages between individuals will likely increase the chances of collective action. When a person knows that his or her access to resources is dependent on others' contributions and/or that his or her contribution is being depended on by others, he or she will be more inclined to contribute (Cook and Hardin 2001; Yamagishi and Cook 1993).

continued . . .

TABLE 7.1 Continued

Variable	Why?
Voluntary group membership	If group membership is optional, then people will be more inclined to join groups that they already trust will work together towards the common good. Voluntary membership is therefore associated with groupings that have pre-existing higher levels of trust (Hauk and Nagel 2001; Orbell and Dawes 1991).
Heuristics/norms	Through personal experiences and from other people, individuals learn heuristic strategies for how to get certain outcomes and norms, which attach a certain value on any given strategy or outcome. Depending on the heuristics and norms learned, they can either work to enhance a person's willingness to forgo immediate individual goals in the interest of pursuing the collective good or not (Crawford and Ostrom 2005; Simon 1955, 1957, 1999; see Ostrom 2010 for a discussion on norms).
Monitoring/ transparency (contributions and collective good)	If contributions towards the collective good can be easily monitored, individuals will be less likely to free ride, out of a fear that their free riding will be detected (Ostrom 1990).

Monitoring could reveal that free riding is the norm and that the collective good is far from being achieved; if that is the case, then group members will be less likely to contribute towards the collective good. |
| Long time horizons | Contributing towards the collective benefit usually means that individuals forgo their immediate individual interests for the long-term interests of the group. Thus, individuals who do not discount the future, or have long time horizons, are more likely willing to contribute towards the collective good (Bendor and Mookherjee 1987; Ostrom 1990). |
| Salience of collective good | If the collective good is vital to group members' livelihood or survival, then group members have a greater incentive to act collectively (Agrawal 2002). |

any one of the potential influences on collective action is most certainly impacted by the influence of others. This not only means that the variables' interactive effects likely matter, but that their own causal relationships to each other matter as well. For instance, trust or distrust that people will abstain from corruption is influenced by the heuristics people have formed about how others will behave in society, which are in turn largely shaped by one's repeated interactions with others. Also, leaders with longer-time horizons have long been assumed to be more 'developmental' (see Clague *et al.* 1996; Olson 1993, pp. 567–77). For example, the Kagame regime in Rwanda is said to have spearheaded the taming of corruption because it not only has a perceived long time horizon of holding office, but also because corruption is understood by the regime to be a highly salient obstacle to the country's broader developmental goals, and fighting corruption is key for avoiding a return to genocide (Chene 2011; Kelsall 2011).

Transparency International's Integrity Pacts are arguably the archetypal example of a collective action anti-corruption approach. They involve written agreements between government and private bidders to refrain from bribery and collusion during the process of procurement bidding and a monitoring system that provides for independent oversight from civil society over the public contracting process (Transparency International 2009). In bringing all actors together to make a formal agreement, such exercises acknowledge that the most precarious risks for corruption often lie in collective dynamics. Consistent with the expectations set out by the literature on corruption and collective action, successful Integrity Pacts are built on trust within the group of actors involved (Transparency International 2009). However, as the wider collective action theory literature suggests (see Table 7.1), the success of an Integrity Pact is often challenged when other factors are also not in place, such as: transparency of information and the ability of actors to monitor each other throughout the process of procurement bidding; continuity of actors with time horizons long enough to last the process of procurement (i.e. low public service turnover); and the political will of the government to be involved at all (Transparency International 2009).

The current treatment of collective action theory by corruption/governance circles may leave readers with the sense that collective action tends to equal inclusive community engagement, awareness-raising campaigns, working with civil society to build trust in society, and so on. A collective action approach to anti-corruption programming may involve these things, but Table 7.1 illustrates that successful collective action also may be exclusive, exclusionary and hierarchical. After all, as noted in Table 7.1, having a small group size is often seen as beneficial to finding a resolution to a collective action problem, and collective action problems are thought to arise when there is no clear and legitimate leadership that can regulate public or common goods. Moreover, collective action may also be influenced by particularized trust dynamics – trust extended selectively to those in close social proximity – rather than or in addition to generalized trust – trust in people generally (Freitag and Traunmuller 2009, p. 783).[4] So it may be the case that the collective goals pursued are those that benefit a subgroup, such as an ethnic group or clan, which could come at the cost of other members of a superordinate group, as in other citizens of the wider national group.

Throwing the theoretical baby out with the bathwater?

Those that criticize the principal-agent approach to corruption and think that collective action theory brings a fresh insight often emphasize how these two approaches differ.[5] For instance, Persson *et al.* (2013, p. 450) tell us: 'as a collective action problem, systemic corruption reveals radically different characteristics than predicted by principal-agent theory. As such, they argue that it also demands radically different solutions'. On two issues are these theories thought to differ. First, principal-agent theory, from this critical perspective, mistakenly assumes that there will always be 'principled principals' who are willing to hold officials accountable for engaging in corruption; as discussed earlier, this is rightly not assumed in viewing corruption as a collective action problem. Second, unlike principal-agent theory, the application of collective action theory is able to make sense of the fact that in an environment where everyone is believed to be engaging in corruption, there are few incentives for individuals to abstain.

There are some fundamental flaws with this analysis, however, which have implications for the development of these 'radically different solutions'. First, this is actually a misunderstanding of the principal-agent model, rife within the policy-oriented academic literature on corruption, in which principals are motivated not by principles, but by interests. There is no such thing, in theory, as a 'principled principal'. The problem in applying the principal-agent model to government is that (in principle) officials do not own public assets or have a material stake in them. This is why the response to the principal-agent problem is to find ways of creating (a sense of) ownership and property rights in public management, and aligning the interests of agents with those of principals.[6] Principal-agent 'theory' does not assume that: (1) either the principal or the agent is principled (but does assume they have interests); or (2) the principal is willing to hold the agent accountable for not acting in his or her own interests. Where principals do not have a stake in the intended outcome, they will not be willing to play this role.

Second, a collective action approach is not necessarily wholly incompatible with a principal-agent interpretation of corruption. Both perspectives, for example, tend to approach systemic corruption solely as a problem, which fails to recognize that for some in certain contexts, corruption and patron-client networks function to provide solutions to problems they face, be it security (e.g. Gauri *et al.* 2011), access to resources in the face of a weak state (e.g. Walton 2013), a sense of social cohesion (e.g. Olivier De Sardan 1999) and/or political stability (Khan 2004, 2006). For example, Gauri *et al.* (2011, p. 27) observe that in Honduras, a history of violent conflict has shaped the way in which patron–client relations are viewed; rather than simply understood as a way in which to (corruptly) access public funds, they are understood to provide security and safety in a highly violent and unstable environment. Walton (2013) finds that in Papua New Guinea, many citizens excluded from state benefits believe that engaging in certain corrupt acts is the only way in which they can secure often-scarce social services. This means that it is important to recognize a lack of political will or the will of citizens to resist or refuse to be involved in bureaucratic corruption as not just a matter of no one wanting to make the first step towards reducing corruption, but rather that the present state of affairs may serve functions that seem defensible to those involved.[7]

Additionally, both theoretical lenses describe the same individual calculations made when deciding whether or not to engage in corruption. Both theories assume individual rationality, whether that be bounded or not, and understand that people engage in corrupt acts only when it is in their individual self-interest. Moreover, both theories recognize that the decision to engage in corruption is shaped by the perceived likelihood that one will not be held accountable for doing so. In collective action theory, with corruption as free riding, the decision to engage in corruption is motivated by the free rider's self-interest and knowledge that he or she will not lose his or her beneficiary status to a good (i.e. be held accountable) because he or she chose to engage in corruption. Similarly, in principal-agent terms, the logic behind an agent being corrupt is understood to be a function of the agent following his or her self-interests and the perceived unlikely chance that the principal can hold him or her to account for doing so.

A logical conclusion from both theories is actually that more effective monitoring and sanctioning can increase accountability and reduce corruption. Those that criticize the principal-agent approach to corruption downplay this. Persson *et al.* (2013), for example, argue that the principal-agent framework has led anti-corruption strategies down the wrong path by implying that anti-corruption reforms should focus on reducing the discretion of civil servants, increasing monitoring mechanisms and strengthening sanctions on those that engage in corruption. These remedies are indeed tightly linked to the principal-agent vision of corruption; the inability of the principal to perfectly monitor and punish (or hold accountable) the agent's engagement in corruption is at the heart of a corrupt principal-agent problem.[8] It follows from the application of principal-agent theory that when the principal is better able to monitor or sanction the agent, the incentive to engage in corruption will be reduced.

Arguably, however, similar conclusions could be drawn from some examples in the collective action literature. As Table 7.1 alludes, several examples within the collective action literature illustrate that when group members' actions are more easily and readily monitored, the incentive to engage in free ridership becomes reduced (Agrawal and Goyal 2001; Ostrom 1990). Institutional arrangements that increase the ability of the group to monitor and sanction individuals for free riding, while recognizably difficult to organize, are hypothesized to aid in the solution of the collective action problem (Ostrom 1990).[9]

In highlighting the ways in which the two theories overlap in their conceptualization of corruption, we do not mean to downplay the contributions of either theory. Rather, we suggest that, in different ways, each theory adds to the understanding of why corruption is sometimes so difficult to control. It strikes us as much more useful to think about how each theoretical lens can complement the other's contribution. For example, when taking into account different institutional and societal structures within society, it may be useful to make room for an interlinked theoretical understanding of corruption. One way forward may be to focus on what types of specific collective action problems influential principals face in deciding which anti-corruption reforms to pursue and whether they do so, as well as the challenges those principals face in implementation via their organizational agents in implementing those reforms.

For example, in politicized bureaucracies, recruitment patterns are usually rooted in clientelistic networking rather than meritocracy. There are a host of reasons, from a collective action theory perspective, why principals overseeing recruitment in a bureaucracy may not want to try to discipline reforms. They may believe that other people in similar positions are allowing un-meritocratic hiring, and therefore find some encouragement to do the same because 'everyone else is doing it'. Also, achieving a meritocratic bureaucracy may not be a particularly salient goal for them; as their own position is perceived to be subject to the political winds changing, they may not have a particularly long time horizon in their office. This will limit willingness to risk losing personal benefits from the status quo and/or exert energy to change things. Finally, the wider politicized organizational and even societal heuristics and norms may encourage them to allow this pattern of recruitment to continue. These issues address why political will might be absent, but it is important to note that these principals may also face classic principal-agent problems enforcing meritocratic recruitment patterns, such as not being able to monitor closely enough the specific recruitment procedures their agents are following. Those having the 'political will' to reform would still find this limitation in their capacity to manage their agents a significant challenge to overcome before achieving a meritocratic bureaucracy. Therefore, depending on the situation, both principal-agent and collective action lenses highlight different challenges present to anti-corruption.

As Persson *et al.* (2013) already argue, it is perhaps best to evaluate the utility of each theory's interpretation of corruption dynamics as being context-dependent. We would add that even in systemically corrupt contexts, certain institutions may be relatively safeguarded from the types and extents of corruption that exist in wider society, and thus may benefit from a principal-agent theory-inspired anti-corruption approach that emphasizes greater monitoring, oversight and higher sanctions. Thus, for us, it is important not to discard the usefulness of principal-agent theory's understanding of corruption carte blanche even in the context of systemic corruption.

Conclusion

In this chapter, we have shown how principal-agent and collective action explanations for the persistence of corruption are not necessarily competing, but are usefully complementary. Principal-agent theory's take on corruption highlights the rational calculations made by individuals at discrete points in time in a specific type of hierarchical structure. While collective action theory points to the role intra-group trust can play in influencing individual decisions, for example, it has more to contribute than just this insight. A collective action theory lens applied to corruption emphasizes the fact that the same individual decisions on whether or not to engage in corruption occur within a wider society, rather than in isolation of the behaviour of others. Thus, monitoring, transparency and sanctioning – all variables that impact upon individual calculations of whether or not to engage in corruption – are also weighed against the potential influence of group dynamics that may impact on the likelihood of free riding. Collectively, the two theoretical approaches to corruption teach us that corruption persists in highly corrupt countries because it is not only difficult to monitor and therefore difficult to prosecute, but also because, when it is systemically pervasive, people lack the incentives to initiate either countermeasure.

Together, these lenses highlight the multifaceted challenges that anti-corruption reformers in systemically corrupt countries face. This implies that effective anti-corruption efforts need to be tailored to context. This is hardly an original suggestion, but it cannot be over-emphasized. The context should drive efforts to tackle corruption, *not* the theory or model, regardless of whether these are inspired by principal-agent or collective action theories. For example, monitoring, transparency and sanctioning measures may have a big impact in contexts where incidences of corruption are relatively isolated; however, as Persson *et al.* (2013) note, transparency efforts in an environment of systemic corruption could expose the fact that corruption is wildly pervasive, and this may compel people to engage more in corruption, rather than fight against it.[10] Put differently, collective action theory-inspired anti-corruption approaches, such as values-based training or public awareness raising, should not be viewed as universally appropriate solutions to apply in all contexts. The lesson here is that we should learn from the history of (mis)applying principal-agent theory-inspired models of anti-corruption to inappropriate contexts, where political will was missing to implement the fixes prescribed.[11]

Moving forward, research should take up the task of unpacking these different depictions further. Instead of building arguments for how one theoretical lens explains the incidence of corruption over another, research should aim to further the understanding of the different contexts and circumstances under which each lens is most appropriate to apply. Research along these paths will not only further the theoretical debate on the social and political underpinnings of corruption, but will be vital for informing the development of more contextualized, and potentially more effective, anti-corruption programming in systemically corrupt countries.

Notes

1 See, for example, studies commissioned by the UK Department for International Development (Rao 2013; Rocha Menocal *et al.* 2015), the Norwegian Agency for Development Cooperation (Mungui-Pippidi 2011), and several papers by the World Bank (e.g., Gauri *et al.* 2011; Keefer 2012; World Bank Institute 2008).

2 We emphasize 'personal interest' here instead of the more commonly used 'personal gain' because the term 'gain' suggests that opportunities to engage in corruption are pursued in an opportunistic manner in order solely to benefit participants (e.g. monetary gain, career progression, etc.). 'Interest', to us, suggests something different. A customs officer who lets in cargo knowing there are illegal narcotics hidden inside may be incentivized by his or her personal gain, but he or she (and his or her family) may also be under threat by powerful drugs lords. It is in his or her interest to turn a blind eye, regardless of whether or not he or she personally gains.

3 Hughes and Hutchinson (2012), however, challenge the notion that developmental outcomes should be thought of as a public good – beneficial to everyone. They argue that even the most encouraging developmental trends – such as the achievement of 'good government' – should be understood to be the likely consequence of conflictual political

struggles between groups, where net 'positive' results often come at the cost of certain parties suffering, having to compromise their position and/or lose access to certain resources.

4 The wider it goes beyond a small group, presumably the more it will depend on generalized trust.

5 Booth and Cammack (2013: 15) arguably emphasize their differences but do acknowledge that they are somewhat complementary: 'principal-agent analysis still has some relevance to meeting development challenges, but it must be nested within an understanding of collective action challenges, not the other way around'.

6 Paradoxically, perhaps principal-agent approaches could be most relevant to patrimonial systems. We are grateful to Richard Batley for this insight, among others.

7 Though there is not space here to discuss in more detail, this may also explain why 'integrity management' approaches – such as values-based training, improving codes of conduct and so on, often devised in less corrupt contexts and then applied in systemically corrupt environments – tend also to disappoint. Current research by the authors, along with Paul Heywood and Nieves Zúñiga (University of Nottingham) looks at integrity management systems in different contexts, with case studies planned in Bolivia and Rwanda, and another in Papua New Guinea under discussion. This research is co-funded by ANTICORRP (an EU FP7 programme) and the Developmental Leadership Program (see www.anticorrp.eu and www.dlprog.org for more details).

8 There are other reasons, of course, for why principals will not act, other than ability, such as ownership, alignment of incentives, organizational capacity, capacity of agents to exercise influence, and so on (see, for example, Batley and Larbi 2004: 62–5).

9 To be fair, this is acknowledged by Persson et al. (2013, p. 456): 'collective action theories do not necessarily question the potential relevance of effective monitoring and punishment regimes as means to curb corruption'.

10 Ostrom (2010) puts forth a general framework linking several variables, which puts more structural variables such as the size and heterogeneity of a group as impacting upon a core set of variables, such as reputations and trust, which all have feedback loops and effects on each other and on collective action. 'It is the combination of these variables that evokes norms, helps or hinders building reputations and trust, and enables effective or destructive interactions and learning to occur' (Ostrom 2010, p. 164). Moreover, it should be noted here that collective action literature has been methodologically limited in testing many hypotheses when it comes to large groups. The study of collective action has been dominated by in-depth case study or lab experimental research, yielding fewer studies that are broadly comparative in nature or that have examined CA with respect to a large N scenario (i.e. the study of large groupings) (Poteete et al. 2010). Moreover, studies with larger Ns tend to be limited in geographical scope, which can limit the generalizations one can make with respect to lessons learned (Poteete et al. 2010).

11 Another valid critique of the development policy-oriented literature is its lack of engagement with the wider organizational culture literature, particularly with regard to public-sector and business ethics. Future research could usefully bring these literatures together. However, even if this were to be corrected, the lessons on the importance of context remain valid. As Rosen (2010, p. 81) points out: '[f]or Afghans to understand corruption as Americans do more or less entails their having to experience the whole web of religious, social and economic concepts that Americans have experienced. That really is asking too much'.

References

Adolphs, R., Damasio, H., Tranel, D. and Damasio, A. (1996) 'Cortical systems for the recognition of emotion in facial expressions', *Journal of Neuroscience*, 16(23): 7678–87.

Agrawal, A. (2000) 'Small is beautiful, but is larger better? Forest management in the Kumaon Himalaya, India', in C. Gibson, M. McKean and E. Ostrom (eds), *People and Forests: Communities, Institutions, and Governance* (pp. 57–86), Cambridge, MA: MIT Press.

Agrawal, A. (2002) 'Common resources and institutional sustainability', in E. Ostrom, T. Dietz, N. Dolsak, P. Stern, S. Stonich and E. Weber (eds), *The Drama of the Commons, National Research Council, Committee on the Human Dimensions of Global Change* (pp. 41–85), Washington, DC: National Academies Press.

Agrawal, A. and Goyal, S. (2001) 'Group size and collective action: Third-party monitoring in common pool resources', *Comparative Political Studies*, 34: 63–93.

Banerjee, A., Iyer, L. and Somanathan, R. (2005) 'History, social divisions, and public goods in rural India', *Journal of the European Economic Association*, 3(2–3): 639–47.

Bardhan, P. (1993) 'Analytics of the institutions of informal cooperation in rural development', *World Development*, 21(4): 633–9.

Bardhan, P. (1997) 'Corruption and development: A review of issues', *Journal of Economic Literature*, 35(3): 1320–46.

Batley, R. and Larbi, G. (2004) *The Changing Role of Government: The Reform of Public Services in Developing Countries*, Basingstoke: Palgrave.

Bauhr, M. and Nasiritousi, N. (2011) *Why Pay Bribes? Collective Action and Anti-Corruption Efforts*, QOG Institute, Working Paper 18, University of Gothenburg, Sweden.

Bendor, J. and Mookherjee, D. (1987) 'Institutional structure and the logic of ongoing collective action', *The American Political Science Review*, 81(1): 129–54.

Booth, D. and Cammack, D. (2013) *Governance for Development in Africa: Solving Collective Action Problems*, New York: Zed Books.

Chene, M. (2011) 'Anti-corruption progress in Georgia, Liberia, Rwanda', *U4 Expert Answer*, number 288.

Clague, C., Keefer, P., Knack, S. and Olson, M. (1996) 'Property and contract rights in autocracies and democracies', *Journal of Economic Growth*, 1(2): 243–76.

Cook, K. and Hardin, R. (2001) 'Norms of cooperativeness and networks of trust', in M. Hechter and K. Opp (eds), *Social Norms* (pp. 327–57), New York: Russell Sage Foundation.

Crawford, S. and Ostrom, E. (2005) 'A grammar of institutions', in E. Ostrom (ed.), *Understanding Institutional Diversity* (pp. 137–74), Princeton, NJ: Princeton University Press.

Elster, J. (1985) 'Rationality, morality and collective action', *Ethics*, 96: 136–55.

Freitag, M. and Traunmuller, R. (2009) 'Spheres of trust: An empirical analysis of the foundations of particularized and generalized trust', *European Journal of Political Research*, 48(6): 782–803.

Gauri, V., Woolcock, M. and Desai, D. (2011) 'Intersubjective meaning and collective action in "fragile" societies: Theory, evidence and policy implications', *World Bank Policy Research Working Paper 5707*, June, World Bank.

Hardin, G. (1968) 'The tragedy of the commons', *Science*, 162: 1243–8.

Hardin, R. (1982) *Collective Action*, Baltimore, MD: Johns Hopkins University Press.

Harris, M. and Raviv, A. (1979) 'Optimal incentive contracts with imperfect information', *Journal of Economic Theory*, 20: 231–59.

Hauk, E. and Nagel, R. (2001) 'Choice of partners in multiple two-person prisoner's dilemma games: An experimental study', *Journal of Conflict Resolution*, 45: 770–93.

Hough, D. (2013) *Corruption, Anti-Corruption and Governance*, New York: Palgrave Macmillan.

Hughes, C. and Hutchinson, J. (2012) 'Development effectiveness and the politics of commitment', *Third World Quarterly*, 33(1): 17–36.

Isaac, R. and Walker, J. (1988) 'Communication and free-riding behavior: The voluntary contribution mechanism', *Economic Inquiry*, 26(4): 585–608.

Johnsøn, J., Taxell, N. and Zaum, D. (2012) 'Mapping evidence gaps in anti-corruption: Assessing the state of operationally relevant evidence in donors' actions and approaches to reducing corruption', U4 Issues Paper No. 2012:7.

Kanbur, R. (1992) *Heterogeneity, Distribution and Cooperation in Common Property Resource Management*, background paper for the World Development Report.

Keefer, P. (2012) 'Why follow the leader? Collective action, credible commitment and conflict', *World Bank Policy Research Working Paper 6179*, August.

Kelsall, T. (2011) 'Rethinking the relationship between neo-patrimonialism and economic development in Africa', *IDS Bulletin*, 42(2): 76–87.

Kerr, N. and Kaufman-Gilliland, C. (1994) 'Communication, commitment and cooperation in social dilemmas', *J. Pers. Soc. Psychol.*, 66: 513–29.

Khan, M. (2004) 'State failure in developing countries and institutional reform strategies', in B. Tungodden, N. Stern and I. Kolstad (eds), *Toward Pro-Poor Policies: Aid Institutions and Globalization* (pp. 165–98), Oxford: Oxford University Press & World Bank.

Khan, M. (2006) 'Determinants of corruption in developing countries: The limits of conventional economic analysis', in S. Rose-Ackerman (ed.), *International Handbook on the Economics of Corruption*, Cheltenham: Edward Elgar.

Klitgaard, R. (1988) *Controlling Corruption*, Berkeley, CA: University of California Press.

Marwell, G. and Oliver, P. (1993) *The Critical Mass in Collective Action: A Micro-Social Theory*, New York: Cambridge University Press.

Michael, B. (2004) 'Explaining organizational change in international development: The role of complexity in anti-corruption work', *Journal of International Development*, 16: 1067–88.

Michael, B. and Bowser, D. (2009) 'The evolution of the anti-corruption industry in the third wave of anti-corruption work', *Proceedings from the Konstanz Anti-Corruption Conference*, pp. 1–13.

Miller, B. (1992) 'Collective action and rational choice: Place, community, and the limits to individual self-interest', *Economic Geography*, 68(1): 22–42.

Mungiu-Pippidi, A. (2006) 'Corruption: Diagnosis and treatment', *Journal of Democracy*, 17(3): 86–99.

Mungiu-Pippidi, A. (2011) 'Contextual choices in fighting corruption: Lessons learned', *NORAD*, Report 4/2011, July 2011, available at: www.norad.no/en/tools-and-publications/publications/publication?key=383808.

Olivier De Sardan, J. (1999) 'A moral economy of corruption in Africa?', *The Journal of Modern African Studies*, 37(1): 25–52.

Olson, M. (1965) *The Logic of Collective Action: Public Goods and the Theory of Group*, Cambridge, MA: Harvard University Press.

Olson, M. (1993) 'Dictatorship, democracy, and development', *American Political Science Review*, 87(3): 567–76.

Orbell, J. and Dawes, R. (1991) 'A "cognitive miser" theory of cooperators' advantage', *American Political Science Review*, 85(2): 515–28.

Ostrom, E. (1990) *Governing the Commons: The Evolution of Institutions for Collective Action*, New York: Cambridge University Press.

Ostrom, E. (1998) 'A behavioural approach to the rational choice theory of collective action', *Presidential Address, American Political Science Association, 1997: American Political Science Review*, 92(1): 1–22.

Ostrom, E. (2000) 'Collective action and the evolution of social norms', *Journal of Economic Perspectives*, 14: 137–58.

Ostrom, E. (2007) 'Collective action and local development processes', *Sociologica*, 3: 1–32.

Ostrom, E. (2010) 'Analyzing collective action', *Agricultural Economics*, 41: 155–66.

Ostrom, E., Gardner, R. and Walker, J. (1994) *Rules, Games, and Common-Pool Resources*, Ann Arbor, MI: University of Michigan Press.

Ostrom, E., Walker, J. and Gardner, R. (1992) 'Covenants with and without a sword: Self-governance is possible', *American Political Science Review*, 86(2): 404–17.

Persson, A., Rothstein, B. and Teorell, J. (2013) 'Why anti-corruption reforms fail: Systemic corruption as a collective action problem', *Governance*, 26(3): 449–71.

Poteete, A., Janssen, M. and Ostrom, E. (2010) *Working Together: Collective Action, the Commons and Multiple Methods in Practice*, Princeton, NJ: Princeton University Press.

Rao, S. (2013) 'Interventions for accountability and collective action', *GSDRC Helpdesk Research Report 904*, GSDRC, Birmingham: University of Birmingham, available at: www.gsdrc.org/docs/open/hdq904.pdf.

Rocha-Menocal, A. *et al.* (2015) 'Why corruption matters: Understanding causes, effects and how to address them', evidence paper on corruption, UK Department for International Development, available at: www.gov.uk/government/uploads/system/uploads/attachment= data/file/406346/corruption-evidence-paper-why-corruption-matters.pdf.

Rose-Ackerman, S. (1978) *Corruption: A Study in Political Economy*, New York: Academic Press.

Rosen, L. (2010) 'Understanding corruption', *The American Interest*, March/April, pp. 78–82.

Ross, S. (1973) 'The economic theory of agency: The principal's problem', *The American Economic Review*, 63(2): 134–9.

Rothstein, B. (2011) 'Anti-corruption: The indirect "big bang" approach', *Review of International Political Economy*, 18(2): 228–50.

Sampson, S. (2010) 'The anti-corruption industry: From movement to institution', *Global Crime*, 11(2): 261–78.

Schlager, E. (1995) 'Policy making and collective action: Defining coalitions within the advocacy coalition framework', *Policy Sciences*, 29(3): 243–70.

Seabright, P. (1993) 'Managing local commons: Theoretical issues in incentive design', *Journal of Economic Perspectives*, 7(4): 113–34.

Simon, H. (1955) 'A behavioural model of rational choice', *Quarterly Journal of Economics*, 69: 99–188.

Simon, H. (1957) *Models of Man*, New York: Wiley.

Simon, H. (1999) 'The potlach between political science and economics', in J. Alt, M. Levi and E. Ostrom (eds), *Competition and Cooperation: Conversations with Nobelists about Economics and Political Science* (pp. 112–19), New York: Russell Sage Foundation.

Transparency International (2009) *Integrity Pacts*, available at: http://archive.transparency.org/ layout/set/print/global_priorities/public_contracting/integrity_pacts (accessed 31 October 2014).

Ugur, M. and Dasgupta, N. (2011) 'Corruption and economic growth: A meta-analysis of the evidence on low income countries and beyond', MPRA Paper, no. 31226.

Walton, G. (2013) 'Is all corruption dysfunctional? Perceptions of corruption and its consequences in Papua New Guinea', *Public Administration and Development*, 33: 175–90.

World Bank Institute (2008) *Fighting Corruption through Collective Action: A Guide for Business*, available at: http://info.worldbank.org/etools/docs/antic/Whole_guide_Oct.pdf.

Yamagishi, T. and Cook, K. (1993) 'Generalized exchange and social dilemmas', *Social Psychology Quarterly*, 56(4): 235–48.

8

THE ETHICS OF PUBLIC OFFICIALS IN THE UNITED STATES

Strong, bent, broken?

Donald C. Menzel*

> 'If men were angels, no government would be necessary.'
>
> James Madison, The Federalist #51

Introduction

The ethical challenges facing elected and appointed public officials[1] and government employees are numerous, daunting, and evermore complex in the hyperconnected world of the Internet, blogs, tablets, and electronic communication. Is it any wonder that so many public officials fall off the ethical ladder as they move up in tenure or position of authority? No, but the question might be rephrased to wonder, "why do so many keep their balance?" The truth of the matter is that we do not know precisely how many men and women holding public office in America stay the ethical course, but it is reasonable to presume that the numbers are much greater than those we know about whose ethical worldview is ajar.

This chapter explores the ethicality of public officials in the United States with particular interest in probing for reasons, motivations, and circumstances that have led some to stray from and others to stay on the ethical pathway. But isn't it an oxymoron to speak of the "ethics of public officials," a subject that is often the butt of jokes and perhaps worse, public cynicism about who gets what, when, and how at the public trough? As one disgruntled citizen put it quite plainly in a letter-to-editor: "Government has long ceased to govern for the overall good and well-being of the general population and has instead become a cesspool of corruption based on self-enrichment and the buying and selling of access and favor" (Keller 2013).

There is certainly no end to disgruntled voices, media stories, and court dates for erstwhile officials who, as the infamous New York Tammy Hall politician State Senator George Washington Plunkitt put it in his day, "I seen my opportunities and I took 'em." Still, perhaps it is time to push beyond the "what's in it for me" perspective and explore more fully the ins and outs of those public officials whose ethics are strong, others whose ethics may be bent, and those whose ethics are broken.

The reader should note that the data in this chapter deal with two subjects seldom joined in the literature, corruption and ethics. Corruption can be defined as the misuse or abuse of one's public office for personal gain typically in the form of bribes, extortion, kickbacks, awards, and favors to friends. Corrupt behavior is generally illegal behavior as set forth in laws and regulations. Ethics may be defined as values and principles that guide right and wrong behavior (Menzel 2012). Another way of saying this is that corruption and ethics, while defined differently, are two sides of a common coin—behavior.

Let's begin by taking a look at some statistics about governmental bodies and public officials in the United States.

The big picture

Governing America is a complex enterprise that involves nearly 90,000 governmental units. There is one U.S. government, 50 state governments, and 89,476 local governments as of 2007 (U.S. Census Bureau 2012). Among local governments, there are 3,033 counties, 19,492 municipalities, 16,519 townships and towns, 13,051 school districts, and 37,381 special districts. The number of popularly elected officials is, of course, much larger. It is reasonable to estimate that the total number of elected officials exceeds 500,000. The last survey conducted by the Bureau of Census published in 1992 put the count at 513,200, or approximately one elected official for every 485 inhabitants. The numbers vary widely across the states depending on the population and governance history. The average number of state elected officials in 1992 was 376.6, ranging from Delaware with 80 to Pennsylvania with 1,200. Public employees (i.e., non-elected), of course, far outnumber elected officials in the United States. Federal government civilian employment in March 2011 numbered 2,854,251, while the 50 states employed 3,779,258 people and local government employees numbered 10,781,323.[2]

It should come as no surprise, then, with 500,000 elected officials holding public offices and more than 17 million individuals on federal, state, and local government payrolls, that some would fall off the ethical ladder in any given year. There are no precise statistics or survey data that inform us about the ethicality of elected officials and public employees, although there is no shortage of laws, rules, and guidelines that prescribe and proscribe the ethical behavior of those officials and employees. But, we do have some statistics that allow us to conjecture about the numbers.

The U.S. Justice Department's Public Integrity Section compiles annual data on public corruption convictions.[3] An analysis of this data for the period 2001–2010 finds that the most convictions are recorded by the more populous states, with Texas leading the way (696), followed by California (679), Florida (674), and New

York (589) (Maciag 2012). When the number of convictions is put on 100,000-population base, the picture shifts considerably, with the smaller states leading the pack. The first five spots are claimed by Louisiana (8.5 convictions/100,000 population), North Dakota (8.2), South Dakota (7.2), Alaska (6.8), and Kentucky (6.5). The picture changes some also when one compares states using the number of convictions per 10,000 employed in local, state, and federal government. Louisiana retains the top spot but several larger states—Pennsylvania, New Jersey, Ohio, and Florida—move into the top 10 (see Table 8.1). Those convicted of public corruption over this 10-year period are primarily local government employees, including elected officials, with 44 percent of the convictions, with the federal government collecting 22 percent, and state government 9 percent. Private citizens make up the remaining 25 percent. The aggregated data do not identify specific types of officials (elected, appointed, employee) prosecuted and convicted.

A different database can help in this regard—ethics complaints filed by Florida residents against local and state officials over the period 2001–2013. Table 8.2 shows the number of complaints filed against the type of elected officials and as a percentage of the total complaints.

A few legal and practical caveats are in order. First, filing an ethics complaint in Florida is a straightforward task that involves signing and completing a form provided by the Florida Commission on Ethics.[4] The complainant merely states the facts regardless of the source (e.g., newspapers, rumors, blogs, etc.). While ethics complaints against elected officials typically increase during an election cycle, Florida's ethics laws ban the filing of complaints within 30 days of an election.[5] Second, the alleged violation may or may not be legally sufficient, that is, fall within

TABLE 8.1 American states with most public corruption convictions/10,000 employees, 2001–2010

	2010 Government Employment	2001–2010 Public Corruption Convictions	Convictions/ 10,000 Employees
Louisiana	366,300	384	10.5
Kentucky	330,700	281	8.5
South Dakota	78,700	59	7.5
Delaware	63,800	46	7.2
Mississippi	249,000	178	7.1
Pennsylvania	761,200	542	7.1
Alabama	387,200	273	7.1
North Dakota	79,600	55	6.9
New Jersey	640,000	429	6.7
Montana	91,400	59	6.5
Ohio	780,200	495	6.3
Florida	1,112,300	674	6.1

Source: www.governing.com/blogs/by-the-numbers/state-public-corruption-convictions-data.html (accessed July 7, 2014).

TABLE 8.2 Ethics complaints filed against state/local elected officials in Florida, 2001–2013

	State	District	County	Municipal	Elected Total	Total # Complaints Filed/ % Elected	Dismissed Due to Lack of Legal Sufficiency/ % of Total Dismissed
2001	7	4	32	49	92	186/49	76/41
2002	5	13	40	67	125	187/67	79/42
2003	16	13	44	60	133	209/64	78/37
2004	14	17	50	64	145	243/60	114/47
2005	3	9	31	66	109	190/57	87/46
2006	14	16	36	71	137	288/48	189/66
2007	17	14	70	68	169	256/66	105/41
2008	9	13	35	47	104	167/62	84/50
2009	11	8	19	50	88	176/50	60/34
2010	16	16	28	62	122	190/64	79/42
2011	10	18	22	64	114	169/67	68/40
2012	76	16	43	67	202	296/68	123/42
2013	24	10	34	42	110	210/52	119/57
Totals/ % of total complaints	222/ 8	167/ 6	484/ 18	777/ 28	1650/ 60		

Note: Percentages are rounded to nearest whole number. Subtotals do not add to total complaints filed due to omission of a small number of cases classified as "appointed officers" for each type of government.

Source: Florida Commission on Ethics, *Annual Reports*, 2001–2013.

the statutory jurisdiction of the Commission. Thus, the first task of the Commission staff is to determine the legal sufficiency of the complaint. And, it should not be surprising, therefore, to learn that many complaints do not pass this first test. In fact, an analysis of the data in Table 8.2 shows that, on average, more than 4 out of 10 are summarily dismissed. This means that 6 out of 10 are subject to investigation to determine if there is "probable cause" that a violation of the state's ethics statutes may have occurred[6] (see Table 8.3).

To put all of this in perspective, it is helpful to note that the total number of state employees in Florida during the past decade ranged from 208,151 in 2002 to 170,261 in 2010.[8] The number of those employed by special districts, counties, and municipalities ranged from 685,418 in 2002 to 645,673 in 2009.[9] These numbers translate into 1.6 complaints per thousand population if we assume that the total number of government officials during this period is 850,000. Thus, the 913 complaints of possible unethical behavior by elected officials and the 447 complaints

TABLE 8.3 Ethics complaints filed against Florida (non-elected) public employees, 2001–2012[7]

	State	District	County	Municipal	Public Employees Total	Total # Complaints Filed/ % Employees
2001	43	3	7	421	74	186/40
2002	11	2	10	24	47	187/25
2003	7	9	8	22	46	209/22
2004	19	5	17	29	70	243/29
2005	7	4	12	39	62	190/33
2006	28	5	19	62	114	288/40
2007	18	7	25	23	73	256/29
2008	9	8	19	15	51	167/31
2009	30	3	18	19	70	176/40
2010	8	5	10	28	51	190/27
2011	7	2	9	15	33	169/20
2012	17	7	9	37	70	296/23
2013	29	3	17	20	69	210/33
Totals/ % of total complaints	233/ 8	63/ 2	180/ 6.5	333/ 12	809/ 29	2,767/ 29

Note: Percentages are rounded to nearest whole number. Subtotals do not add to total complaints filed due to omission of a small number of cases classified as "appointed officers" for each type of government.

Source: Florida Commission on Ethics, *Annual Reports*, 2001–2013.

against public employees, even if deemed violations, constitute a relatively small percentage of possible wrongdoing.

One more caveat—the Florida Commission on Ethics typically finds a small number of cases in any given year a violation of state law. And, it must be noted, that a violation of state law, while defined as an ethics violation, does not encompass a more inclusive meaning of unethical behavior. In other words, there is likely to be more unethical behavior than first meets the eye when focusing only on state ethics violations. The same caveat is relevant to the public corruption convictions data. Both data sets are based on and defined by law.

In sum, the public corruption and the Florida ethics complaint data can be interpreted to mean that while there is unethical behavior by public officials, it would be presumptuous to contend that all public officials are unethical. Does this mean that we should pay less attention to corrupt or unethical behavior? Of course not. Both are unacceptable behaviors and cost the taxpayers hundreds of millions of dollars. A recent study of corruption in Illinois estimated that the cost to the state's taxpayers amounted to $500 million a year (Simpson *et al.* 2012).

We turn our focus next to the ethicality (or lack thereof) of six public officials to illustrate in greater detail the spectrum of strong ethics, bent ethics, and broken ethics.

Public officials with strong ethics[10]

Local elected officials are certainly not immune to unethical behavior or corrupt misdeeds. Indeed, as the Florida Ethics Commission data suggests, city and county officials are at the top of the list of alleged errant behavior. Yet, some seem to have an immunity that has served them well in office.

Case #1: One such individual was city manager LeRoy F. Harlow (1914–1995), who served five communities in three different states. He "walked the talk" with an integrity philosophy that went something like "do not fear others or losing your job, just do the right thing . . . and do not do favors." With a B.S. degree in Industrial Engineering from Iowa State University in 1938 and an M.S. degree in Public Administration from the University of Minnesota in 1943, LeRoy Harlow moved West to become the first city manager of Sweet Home, Oregon, population 3,300— a war-boom logging and lumbering town that had the local FBI reputation as the "toughest town in Oregon" (Harlow 1977, p. 2).

His career start-up in Sweet Home was followed by city manager jobs in Albert Lea, Minnesota, a city that enjoyed a reputation as progressive and up-and-coming, Fargo, North Dakota, Richfield, Minnesota, and Daytona Beach, Florida, in 1952, where Harlow describes the climate as beautiful but the "political climate" as "anything but beautiful" (Harlow 1977, p. 226). In 1954, he departed Daytona Beach to work as a consultant and advisor from Connecticut to California for another 20 years. Upon his departure from Daytona Beach, the local newspaper (*Daytona Beach Morning Journal* 1954) described Harlow as "a dedicated man and believes every citizen is entitled to equal treatment and service from their City employees."

LeRoy F. Harlow understood that public service is an honorable profession. He knew that in his role as a city manager, he had a fiduciary responsibility to not only do things right, but to do the "right" thing. His motivation and integrity served him well for building a reputation for honesty and a career with many accomplishments.

Case #2: Another individual whose career spans a variety of local public service positions is Pam Iorio. Ms. Iorio was an elected Hillsborough County Commissioner (1985–1993) and City of Tampa Mayor (2003–2011). Elected at the age of 26 to the Hillsborough County Commission, she served eight years as a beacon of integrity followed by a 10-year stint as the elected Supervisor of Elections (1993–2003). She then moved on to serve as the mayor of Tampa (2003–2011). All were elected positions but with different slants—legislator as county commissioner, administrator as supervisor of elections, and chief executive as mayor.

No unethical or corrupt allegation has ever been made against her, a claim not honored by her predecessors in Hillsborough County. The county experienced a rash of corruption a few years before she took office, when an FBI sting resulted in three county commissioners led out of the courthouse in handcuffs and later convicted of bribes and extortion. And, before being elected Tampa's mayor, the city housing director was convicted of fraud and corruption in a sweetheart deal with a local builder who received more than $1 million in housing contracts in return for building a 4,200-square foot house that the director and his wife (a former girlfriend and subordinate in the housing department) purchased for the bargain-basement price of $105,000 (Menzel 2010). U.S. District Judge Richard A. Lazzara, upon sentencing the housing director to a five-year prison term, described the city government culture this way: "What strikes me about the LaBrakes' situation is that they were part of the culture that permeates Tampa government, where you do me a favor and I'll do you a favor, even though it violates the public trust" (Menzel 2012, p. 135).

So, as should be evident, Pam Iorio brings a most interesting background and set of experiences to explore the motives and circumstances for staying the ethical course. We will return to the Pam Iorio case after exploring several others. We turn next to two appointed Florida county administrators whose ethics were found wanting, although not broken.

Public officials with bent ethics[11]

Case #3: This case involves an administrator, Hillsborough County (Florida) Administrator Pat Bean (2003–2010),[12] who climbed the ladder of success over more than 30 years to become its chief executive.[13] Alas, Stephen K. Bailey's (1964) dictum that "the higher a person goes on the rungs of power and authority, the more wobbly the ethical ladder" became a reality for her.

What happened? The county established an independent auditor who, among other things, reported that the administrator had given herself and top aides pay rises at a time in which the county was experiencing significant fiscal stress with cutbacks and layoffs occurring. Moreover, the county's 8,000 employees were asked to take on more work to cope with the downsizing, a recipe for low morale and disgruntlement. The county had in place an unwritten policy to reward employees who engaged in innovative cost-saving measures, which included laying off subordinates. One of her top aides nominated her for a reward in recognition of the decision she made to layoff one of her assistant county administrators. Uncertain that she was eligible to participate in the program, she consulted the County Attorney, who told her that she was indeed eligible. Therefore, she accepted (some critics would say "gave" herself) a $2,000 annual salary increase that was determined by a set percentage of her $224,000 salary. However, she did not seek approval from the county commission that was unaware of the policy to adjust her salary. The county charter specifically authorizes the commission to set the pay of the administrator.

As events unfolded, including private exchanges between the auditor and individual members of the commission, the administrator began to suspect that the auditor was "out to get her." Consequently, she ordered one of her managers to collect all emails involving the auditor, commission, and county attorney relevant to the pay issue. The media began to follow the story and broke the "email snooping" news, as it was called. The administrator admitted that she had collected the email messages but, upon second thought, decided not to read them. The commission's trust in this claim rapidly deteriorated and motivated them to place the administrator, the county attorney, and the auditor on 90 days of paid administrative leave.

As the leave period moved along, the commission struggled with "what to do"—demote the administrator, fire her and the others with or without cause, wait out an investigation by the state law enforcement agency into whether or not email snooping violated the law and then decide what to do, or strike a deal with the administrator to resign. Firing the administrator without cause would let her walk with more than $500,000 in compensation and unpaid leave time. Consequently, the commission and the administrator, through their lawyers, attempted to work out a settlement. As the suspension approached its end, the administrator became more determined to find an arrangement that would let her receive $550,000 or more in severance and benefits. In the meantime, there was considerable stress and distress reported in the media about the ill effects that the situation was having on employee morale, job performance, and the public's negative perception of the imbroglio. The story ends with the auditor losing his job, the administrator fired unceremoniously with cause, and the county attorney reinstated.[14]

This case is replete with bent ethics, most of which are obvious. Perhaps a less obvious but ever so important breach was the matter of doing what was believed to be in the best interests of the community, and, of course, putting an end to the erosion of public trust and confidence in county government. While it was clearly in the best financial interests of the administrator to stay the course, did she also have an obligation to put the community interest ahead of her personal and professional interests? It would seem so. However, it is fair to say that she felt strongly that she had been victimized, especially by the auditor's reports and behavior. Also, her sense of fair treatment and justice was at stake, as well as her professional reputation that, together with, and independent of, fiscal considerations, made it very, very difficult to simply steal away in the night. Moreover, a 30-year-plus longevity of county employment meant that she was well known in the community and had many friends and colleagues.

It should be noted that the administrator was held in high regard during her six-year tenure as chief executive and years as HR director and assistant county administrator. She also had a reputation for promoting professional behavior among managers and employees.

Case #4: Another high-ranking county manager, Sarasota County (Florida) Administrator Jim Ley (1997–2011), found himself ethically blindsided and eventually forced to resign. First, some background on Sarasota County. The county is an affluent charter county located on the Gulf Coast about 70 miles south of Tampa-Hillsborough County. With a highly educated, older population of nearly 380,000 and four incorporated cities, including the well-known community of Venice, the county has enjoyed a strong record of good governance. A five-member county commission that appoints a professional administrator is responsible for overseeing county affairs.

Jim Ley served the county for 14 years, no small feat in local government management. During those years, he garnered the respect and admiration of the Board of County Commissioners, good government citizen groups, and the local media. He viewed himself as a person with high ethical standards and took pride in the organization's performance in getting the job done at an affordable price. He also took considerable pride in a progressive management style that delegates responsibility to top managers.

The county has a model code of ethics and the administrator trusted his management team to be exemplars in integrity and performance. He had every reason to feel comfortable with the ethical culture that pervaded the 2,000-member workforce until . . . all hell broke out! The local newspaper published a story about a 55-year-old project manager in the public works department for accepting $15,000 in cruises, hotel stays, gift cards, and other kickbacks from a company whose contract he helped supervise.

As the scandal unfolded, other misdeeds were alleged. County supervisors were reported to "piggyback" contracts (i.e., opt for the same deal another local government had with a company), thus allowing county administrators to avoid putting contracts out to bid. Procurement managers also practiced "change orders," where a contract is bid for specific terms only to be altered at points along the way, with extra work and pay added. The "change orders" practice would allow favored companies to come in at unrealistically low bids. Topping off the string of procurement problems was the fact that administrators and supervisors could use county-issued credit cards to purchase products that would ordinarily be put out to bid if they exceeded $10,000. In other words, credit cards could be used to "break" a payment into several parts whose sum would not exceed the $10,000 limit.

The administrator was shocked to learn of these practices. He said to himself, "Frankly, either I have failed personally or I feel abandoned by the entire management team, in the sense that my business and personal ethics appear to have not been translated into the culture of at least one operation." "What should I do?" he mused. "Should I clean house by firing a number of managers? Should I accept responsibility and resign? Should I fashion a memo to my top managers admonishing them to 'fix the problems or resign'?"[15]

Faced with an ever-widening probe by the local media, one commissioner urged the administrator to fix it. "Ultimately, he's accountable for his employees' action and we as a board are accountable for his actions and the public's trust. I would now suggest that all are in jeopardy."

The administrator took the commissioner's advice seriously and acted quickly by drafting a memo to his top managers that said, among other things:

> These last two weeks have been the most uncomfortable ones of my 36 year career in public service. I am appalled by what I learned as a result of the now named John Doe incident, and that in fact I keep learning as new stuff seems to be revealed to me every day.[16]

A month later, the administrator resigned. In his letter of resignation, he said: "I take responsibility as the leader of the organization when such things happen." A termination agreement was reached, which, one newspaper reporter declared, enabled the administrator to walk "with hugs and smiles" and with a severance payout of the lump sum equivalent to his annual salary and benefits for one year (estimated at $265,833).

Is this a case of "bent" or "broken" ethics? Jim Ley's professional ethics as evidenced by his admission of "I take responsibility" suggests "broken" would be in error. Nor does "bent ethics" accurately describe his ethics. Rather, this case points to the possibility that an experienced administrator can develop an "ethical blind spot." Bazerman and Tenbrunsel (2011, p. 5) call this "bounded ethicality"— a condition that occurs when individuals make decisions that harm others and when that harm is inconsistent with the decision-makers' conscious beliefs and preferences. Administrator Ley appears to have lost sight of the unethical and corrupting behaviors taking place on his watch.

Broken ethics[17]

Case #5: Congressman Charles B. Rangel is completing his 21st term in Congress, having first been elected to Congress in 1970 from the 13th Congressional district in New York City's Harlem. The 82-year-old Mr. Rangel, a flamboyant and congenial person, defeated an equally flamboyant Adam Clayton Powell in 1970 by 200 votes.[18] Mr. Rangel once wielded the gavel on the powerful Ways and Means Committee, a much-coveted post that his seniority enabled him to claim when Democrats reclaimed the House of Representatives in 2006.

In 2010, standing in the well of the House before Speaker Nancy Pelosi, Mr. Rangel heard her read House Resolution 1737: "Resolved, that one, Representative Charles B. Rangel of New York be censured." Chastised but not repentant, Mr. Rangel said:

> I am confident that when the history of this has been written, people will recognize that the vote for censure was a very, very, very political vote . . . I did not curse out the speaker. I did not have sex with minors. I did not steal money.
>
> (Kocieniewski 2010)

What were Mr. Rangel's ethical lapses? According to the Office of Congressional Ethics and following a public trial before an adjudicatory subcommittee, he was found guilty of 11 ethical violations that involved accepting rent-stabilized apartments in Manhattan and misusing his office to preserve a tax loophole worth half a billion dollars for an oil executive who pledged a donation for an educational center being built in Mr. Rangel's honor (Lipton and Kocieniewski 2010). He was also charged with failing to report or pay taxes on rental income from his beachfront Dominican villa. The full committee, with the concurrence of the House by a vote of 333 to 79, censured Mr. Rangel. Did Mr. Rangel suffer broken ethics? Yes, according to his congressional peers!

Next, we examine one of those "bad souls"—former Illinois Governor, now federal prison inmate #40892-424, Rod Blagojevich.

Case #6: Perhaps the most sensational, highly publicized case involving gubernatorial corruption belongs to Democrat Rod Blagojevich, who succeeded Republican Governor George Ryan in 2002. As the 40th Illinois governor, Mr. Blagojevich was the first Democrat to win the Illinois governor's seat in 25 years. He campaigned on a platform of government reform, including ethics reform (yes, you read that right). Seven years later (2009), he became the first governor in Illinois to be impeached (House vote 114–1) and removed (Senate vote 59–0) from office for abuse of power and corruption. Most controversial was his alleged effort to "sell" the Senate seat formerly held by President Obama. In his own words:

> I'm going to keep this Senate option for me a real possibility, you know, and therefore I can drive a hard bargain. You hear what I'm saying. And if I don't get what I want and I'm not satisfied with it, then I'll just take the Senate seat myself.
>
> (Davey 2008)

Following his removal from office, Mr. Blagojevich was indicted by a federal grand jury on racketeering and charged with 16 felonies, including racketeering conspiracy, wire fraud, extortion conspiracy, attempted extortion and making false statements to federal agents. The trial in the summer of 2010 resulted in a hung jury on 23 out of 24 counts against him with a single guilty finding of lying to federal agents. Federal prosecutors called for a second trial in May–June 2011, and this time Mr. Blagojevich was not so fortunate. He was convicted on 17 of 20 counts, including the charge that he conspired to sell the senate seat held by Barack Obama. "His abuse of the office of governor is more damaging than the abuse of any other office in the United States except president," U.S. District Judge James Zagel said in announcing Blagojevich's 14-year prison sentence (CBS Chicago 2012). The jury forewoman, a retired church employee from the Chicago suburbs, said: "There's a lot of bargaining that goes on behind the scenes . . . but I think in the instances when it is someone representing the people, it crosses the line." After seeing up close about six weeks of testimony, she added, "I told my husband that if he was running for politics, he would probably have to find a new wife" (Davey and Fitzsimmons 2011).

Motives, reasons, circumstances

The motives for wrongdoing are often recounted as money, power, greed, and, as John Dean of the famous Watergate scandal reminds us, unbridled blind ambition. Of course, some errant behavior occurs because of plain stupidity or ignorance. Other than this latter possibility, the "gotcha" spotlight typically shines on the individual—the "bad apple" in the barrel. Rod Blagojevich probably fits the bad apple mold very well, although the sordid history of Illinois politics supports the often self-proclaimed defense, "I'm not doing anything different than anyone else in Illinois politics."[19] Charlie Rangel is a somewhat more difficult character to type as a "bad apple," although his shenanigans certainly seemed to cross the line as his peers so judged. He may have deluded himself into believing that his office was personal property, not an atypical delusion of elected officials with long tenures, 42 years in his case. He certainly is a candidate for the "broken" category.

But what could be the motives for "right-doing"? Conventional ethics wisdom claims that there are "good" and "bad" apples in any organization. Of course, a bad apple in a good barrel may spoil the entire barrel. Consider the views of former Tampa Mayor Pam Iorio. She generally subscribes to the "bad and good apples" view of the ethics of public officials. Here is how she describes 26 years of interacting with elected officials and government employees of all sizes and shapes:

> There are two categories of people in public office. You have the people who kind of "get it" about public service – that it's an honor, it's a privilege – they are there to serve the public and to conduct themselves in a certain way. Now, they do it in varying degrees, some are really good at it and some are marginal at it, but their intentions are good. Maybe they can't articulate things really well. Maybe they don't always come up with the best ideas in the whole world but their intentions are good. Alright – ok so that's that spectrum – but then you see and I've seen it – people who get elected and have an honorable and elected title in front of their name and it makes up for a deficiency they have in their lives, either they have never been that successful or no one has ever thought that much of them or they have low self-esteem or a whole variety of things. No one has really looked at them or ever has – so getting elected fills a void in their life – now all of a sudden they are important in their view and they have never been important and then they view public service not as public service at all. Rather, it becomes something wholly personal to them as to how serving can benefit them.
>
> It's really all about themselves – how they can get attention – how they can get VIP treatment – how they can get phone calls returned – how they can have a parking space – how they can get free tickets to sporting events and how they can even get bribe money under the worse circumstances for their votes. You know they are blights on our political system and that kind of person you can tag them from the time they have been elected. I've seen it.
>
> (Iorio 2012)

Pam Iorio's experiences might seem to be the exception rather than rule given that she has stayed on the ethical path even though she encountered organizational environments rife with unethical and corrupt behavior. But is it the exception? How does she explain her immunity to the all-too-often-irresistible temptations of elected officials to benefit themselves? Here is her explanation:

I don't think I ever had ethical challenges. As a county commission legislator: I think the vow you make to yourself and your constituency is to gather as much information and make the best decision and vote your conscience at all times. Never succumb to vote a certain way because you want to please a donor or friend or vote a certain way because you want to get re-elected. Those are ethical lapses. As Supervisor of Elections, I always felt it was my job to have a non-partisan office and told everyone they could not engage in any political races of any sort. That we were the vote counters and there was no partisanship and everything was fair and square. So that was the tone I set there. Then as Mayor, I felt that one of the things – going back to my time as a Commissioner – was to always implement public policy based on reasoning and logic and facts. But the other component at that time was to build a team that was ethical.

(Iorio 2012)

While it might seem surprising, if not unbelievable, to hear an elected official say "I don't think I ever had ethical challenges," Ms. Iorio, in both public and private settings, always conveyed in words and body language that public service is an honorable profession. Thus, it is entirely believable that she did not experience ethical challenges. The Pam Iorios of elected officialdom are individuals who live lives of personal and public integrity, no easy task for sure. Yet, it does happen, perhaps much more than is recognized by an increasingly distrustful public. In her book *Straightforward Ways to Live & Lead* (2011, p. 116), she calls it a "centered" inner life, one in which a "successful leader strives to build a balanced life—not perfect, but centered." Neither money nor titles nor power nor influence measure a person's contribution to society; this is the "get it" she notes above. Her conception of public service is both admirable and more widely embraced by elected officials than the public credits. The words of Thomas Jefferson surely resonate as true today as when he uttered them: "When a man assumes a public trust he should consider himself a public property" (Raynor 1834, p. 356).

In essence, public officials with broken ethics can be thought of as individual with "bent and bad souls" (Lessig 2011, pp. 226–227). The ethics of the Rangels, Blagojvichs—and others such as Congressman Randy "Duke" Cunningham (R-California; 1991–2005), who took over $2.4 million in exchange for securing contracts from the Defense Department, and Congressman William J. Jefferson (D-Louisiana: 1991–2009), who received the longest prison sentence for corruption in the history of the United States Congress (13 years), are broken beyond repair.

Bad apples, bad barrels, or both?

But could the "bad apple" interpretation be in error? Might the problem be a "bad barrel?" Dennis F. Thompson's comprehensive study of *Ethics in Congress* (1995) contends that legislators in particular have mixed motives: "They act for the benefit of particular constituents, for the good of the whole district or state, for the good of the nation, and for their own interest in reelection or future political goals" (1995, p. 110). Some "motives may be more admirable than others, but none is illegitimate in itself and all are in some measure necessary in our democratic system," he asserts (1995, p. 110). Driven by mixed motives, lawmakers are not always able to perceive the "bright line" between right and wrong. Both Charlie Rangel and Rod Blagojevich perceived themselves to be acting as politicians with others' and their own interests at heart. Blagojevich also perceived his behavior as consistent with the political milieu in which he was embedded—a quid pro quo culture.

Thompson concludes that the corruption by members of Congress has become institutionalized. "It thrives," he claims, "in a political world where private greed mixes insidiously with the public good, where the difference between serving all citizens and serving supporters blurs, where public officials can evade responsibility for institutional failure" (1995, p. 166). Although a conclusion reached more than 15 years ago, it might well be repeated in the second decade of the new millennium.

Lawrence Lessig, in *Republic, Lost* (2011), is sympathetic to the view that ill deeds have become institutionalized in the U.S. Congress, although he describes the "bad barrel" in a different manner. The Randy "Duke" Cunningham crimes are rare, he asserts. Yet, venal and systematic corruption can emerge because of the dependency of elected officials on funding support from special interests and their lobbyists. It is not a quid pro quo relationship, but a much more sophisticated combination of access and good intentions subverted—"a corruption crafted by good souls. By decent men. And women" (2011, p. 7). And, he notes:

> Theorists of corruption don't typically talk much about decent souls. Their focus is upon criminals—the venally corrupt who bribe to buy privilege, or the systematically corrupt who make the people (or, better, the rich) dependent upon the government to ensure that the people (or better, the rich) protect the government.
>
> (2011, p. 8)

Nonetheless, the "bad apple" view lingers in the minds of the public and has historic linkages in both literature and fact. As Mark Twain once famously quipped about the U.S. Congress with tongue in cheek: "It could probably be shown by facts and figures that there is no distinctly Native American criminal class except Congress" (Twain 1897).

There is little question that public service in America has its share of bad apples, whether in the U.S. Congress, state capitals, or county courthouses. But it's also true that there are "good" apples, as cases in this chapter have illustrated. Separating "good/bad" apples from "good/bad" barrels, however, is no easy task, partly because of the challenge of self-policing.

Self-policing is hard work

The "new" corruption described by Thompson and Lessig cannot be curbed by the usual methods (i.e., laws, rules, commissions). Why? Partly because elected officials in legislative bodies such as Congress, state legislatures, and at the local level, city councils and county commissions, find it very difficult to police the behavior of themselves and one another. To be sure, there is no absence of self-policing efforts within and across state capitals, courthouses, and city halls. But it is hard work and often tricky. Sometimes it is even hard work to agree to a set of values or ethics that should be uppermost in the conduct of one's office.

Consider the case of North Mankato, Minnesota (population 13,394 in 2010). One of the five members of the city council urged her colleagues to adopt a "Statement of Values to promote and maintain the highest standards of conduct among elected officials, managers and employees of the city" (Fischenich 2012). The values consisted of a lengthy list developed by the League of Minnesota Cities (2012). Not so fast, her colleagues replied. After surveying the Statement of Values, one council member commented: "God is the only one I know of who could do all this stuff. And I wish he was on the council." To which the council member added: "to me, this [referring to the list of values] is wishful thinking." The City Attorney in turn asked the usual lawyerly question: "Is this a 'gotcha' kind of thing?" (Fischenich 2012).

If the usual methods cannot control the "new" corruption, what can? Lessig (2011, p. 323) believes that a "bad" barrel can be patched by greater citizen participation in governance. In fact, he calls "for a politics without politicians." Idealistic? Naïve? Perhaps. Should his call for action at the grassroots level be ignored, he warns, America may become a republic lost. But is the matter this dire? Citizen "watchdogs" do exist and often unleash their suspicions on wayward public officials, sometimes bringing the harsh spotlight of media attention on them, while at other times their aim is amiss. Good intentions, of course, do not always result in good outcomes.

Conclusion

At the outset of this chapter, it was recognized that the "new digital age" is upon us and with it is the empowerment of the individual to speak loudly and intensely via blogs and communication tools such as Twitter, Instagram, Facebook, YouTube, and more. The classic role of the "representative" official who mediates and ameliorates the clash of interests may slip into the shadows. Insofar as this may happen, the job of public officials, elected and appointed, may well become much more complex and ethically challenging than ever before in modern times. If a public official's job is not to broker clashing interests, what is his or her job?

The new digital age may well contribute to the further "hollowing out" of America. Stated differently, the shrinking of the state that has been underway for several decades has ushered in an era in which the borders between public and private have largely disappeared (Milward and Provan 2000). And with it, issues of accountability and ethics have grown larger and all-too-often more murky.

So it might be asked: Is the ethicality of public officials in America in jeopardy? Will the ethical voices of public officials become mute? After all, ethical muteness could offer protection from rampant, if not misguided, individualism. The findings outlined earlier in this chapter suggest that there are ethically minded public officials who act on their values. Of course, there are others whose ethics are bent, and a smaller number whose ethics are broken. There remains, however, a compelling need to take a close look at the motives of those who stay on the ethical path, as well as those who stray. And, perhaps more importantly, it may be time to recognize that there is a new game in town that is not driven by a quid pro quo culture that fosters unethical behavior, or worse, venal corruption. The Blagojevichs, Rangels, Cunninghams, and Jeffersons in American politics are not likely to disappear from the scene, but the means to deal with them do exist. Lessig's message and warning that corruption can be the unintended handiwork of good souls should not and cannot be ignored. Is it not the time to think about and guard against the venal aspects of the "new" corruption? So it would seem.

America may never become a nation of "Jimmy Carters," but we can aspire to be so. David Gergen, professor of public service leadership at the Kennedy School of Government and close advisor to four U.S. presidents, once delivered a talk about the behavior of presidents. When finished, a member of the audience stood up and said: "Mr. Gergen your talk was quite interesting but why didn't you say anything about Jimmy Carter?" Gergen stared into space as if to ask himself "why didn't I?" and replied, "as presidents go Jimmy Carter was a saint."

Notes

* Many thanks to Kay Menzel, Alan Lawton, and Zeger van der Wal for very helpful comments and edits. Also appreciated is Professor Ed Benton's "dogged" help in securing U.S. Bureau of Census statistics on Florida.
1 For purposes of this paper, the term public official is broadly construed to include individuals elected, appointed, and employed in governmental bodies in the United States.
2 See www2.census.gov/govs/apes/11fedfun.pdf.
3 The Justice Department data includes public employees for all levels of government, along with private citizens involved in corruption cases.
4 There are some constraints and risks involved in filing a complaint. Sworn complaints must be filed within five years of the alleged violation and, if deemed filed with malicious intent to injure the official's reputation or if the complainant knew that false statements are made, the complainant may be required to pay the attorney's fees for the person against whom the complaint is filed.
5 A complaint or referral under this part against a candidate in any general, special, or primary election may not be filed nor may any intention of filing such a complaint or referral be disclosed on the day of any such election or within the 30 days immediately preceding the date of the election, unless the complaint or referral is based upon personal information or information other than hearsay. Fl Statute 112.324.
6 Calculation for the number of legally sufficient complaints filed against non-elected Florida public officials: (.447 × 809=361.6 – subtract 362 from 809 = 447).
7 Among the six possible violations, there is no precise way to determine how many are directed at elected officials versus public-sector employees and other officials. However, we can make a guesstimate by dividing the number of complaints dismissed for legal sufficiency (1,211) by the total complaints (2,767) and then multiplying that number (.447) times the complaints filed against elected officials (1,650) to arrive at 737 complaints dismissed. Thus, 913 complaints against elected official were deemed legally sufficient to investigate the allegations. The equivalent statistic for Florida public employees is 447 complaints deemed legally sufficient.

8 See www2.census.gov/govs/apes/10stfl.txt.
9 See www2.census.gov/govs/apes/09locfl.txt.
10 This discussion is adapted in part from Cooper and Menzel (2013, Chapter 1) and Menzel (2012).
11 This discussion is adapted from Cooper and Menzel (2013, Chapter 1).
12 This discussion is adapted from Cooper and Menzel (2013, Chapter 1).
13 This case is drawn from newspaper accounts published in the *Tampa Tribune* and *St. Petersburg Times* in March–June 2010.
14 See www.tampabay.com/news/localgovernment/hillsborough-commissioners-fire-pat-bean-as-administrator-restore-county/1102741.
15 While this is the author's interpretation, Mr. Ley's admonishments to his staff clearly leads to this conclusion. See www.heraldtribune.com/article/20110408/ARTICLE/11040 9499/0/search.
16 See www.heraldtribune.com/article/20110408/ARTICLE/110409499/0/search.
17 This discussion is adapted in part from Menzel (2012).
18 Mr. Rangel is also a humorous, self-deprecating individual. He once remarked, "at my age I don't buy green bananas."
19 Four former Illinois governors have received prison sentences for crimes such as bribery, conspiracy, perjury, or income-tax charges: Otto Kerner, Jr. (D-1961–1968) three years, Dan Walker (D-1973–1977) seven years, George H. Ryan (R-1999–2003) six and a half years, and Rod Blagojevich (D-2003–2009) 14 years.

References

Bailey, S. (1964) "Ethics and the public service," *Public Administration Review*, 24: 234–243.

Bazerman, M.H. and Tenbrunsel, T.E. (2011) *Blind Spots: Why We Fail to Do What's Right and What to Do About It*, Princeton, NJ: Princeton University Press.

CBS Chicago (2012) "Rod Blogjevich sentenced to 14 years in prison," available at: http://chicago.cbslocal.com/2011/12/07/rod-blagojevich-sentenced-to-14-years-in-prison/ (accessed July 3, 2012).

Cooper, T. and Menzel, D.C. (2013) *Achieving Ethical Competence for Public Service Leadership*, Armonk, NY: M.E. Sharpe.

Davey, M. (2008) "Illinois governor arrested in inquiry into filling Obama's Senate seat," *New York Times*, December 9, available at: www.nytimes.com/2008/12/09/world/americas/09iht-10illinois.18524701.html?_r=1 (accessed July 3, 2012).

Davey, M. and Fitzsimmons, E.G. (2011) "Jury finds Blagojevich guilty of corruption," *New York Times*, June 28.

Daytona Beach Morning Journal (1954) Editorial.

Fischenich, M. (2012) "North Mankato City Council cool to 'values' proposal," available at: http://mankatofreepress.com/local/x1291711149/North-Mankato-City-Council-cool-to-Values-proposal (accessed June 26, 2012).

Florida Commission on Ethics, *Annual Reports*, 2001–2011.

Harlow, L.F. (1977) *Without Fear or Favor: Odyssey of a City Manager*, Provo, UT: Brigham Young University Press.

Iorio, P. (2011) *Straightforward: Ways to Live & Lead, Pam Iorio*, Tampa.

Iorio, P. (2012) Personal interview with D.C. Menzel DC, June 29.

Keller, L. (2013) "Politics is cesspool of corruption," *Tampa Bay Times*, March 27, 2013.

Kocieniewski, D. (2010) "Rangel Censured over Violations of Ethics Rules," *New York Times*, December 3.

League of Minnesota Cities (2012) *Ethics Resources*, available at: www.lmc.org/page/1/ethics-resources.jsp (accessed July 3, 2012).

Lessig, L. (2011) *Republic, Lost: How Money Corrupts Congress—and a Plan to Stop It*, New York: Hachette Book Group.

Lipton, E. and Kocieniewski, D. (2010) "Panel in House will try Rangel in ethics cases," *New York Times*, July 23.

Maciag, M. (2012) *Which States Have the Highest Public Corruption Convictions?*, March 23, available at: www.governing.com/blogs/by-the-numbers/state-public-corruption-convictions-data.html (accessed March 25, 2013).

Menzel, D.C. (2010) *Ethics Moments in Government: Cases and Controversies*, Boca Raton, FL: CRC Press.

Menzel, D.C. (2012) *Ethics Management for Public Administrators: Leading and Building Organizations of Integrity* (2nd ed.), Armonk, NY: M.E. Sharpe.

Milward, H.B. and Provan, K.G. (2000) "Governing the hollow state," *Journal of Public Administration Research and Theory*, 10(2): 359–79.

Raynor, B.L. (1834) *Life of Thomas Jefferson*, Boston, MA: Lilly, Wait, Colman, & Holden.

Simpson, D., Nowlan, J., Gradel, T.J., Zmuda, M.M., Sterrett, D. and Cantor, D. (2012) *Chicago Politics @ UIC*, available at: www.uic.edu/depts/pols/ChicagoPolitics/leading thepack.pdf (accessed July 3, 2012).

Thompson, D.F. (1995) *Ethics in Congress: From Individual to Institutional Corruption*, Washington, DC: The Brookings Institution.

Twain, M. (1897) *Following the Equator*, London: Chatto & Windus.

U.S. Census Bureau (1992) *1992 Census of Governments*, V. 2 Popularly Elected Officials.

U.S. Census Bureau (2012) *Statistical Abstract of the United States: 2012*, p. 267, available at: www2.census.gov/govs/apes/10stfl.txt (accessed July 3, 2012).

PART IV
Managing integrity

9

INSTITUTIONALIZING INTEGRITY MANAGEMENT

Challenges and solutions in times of financial crises and austerity measures

Alain Hoekstra

Introduction

Organizations pay more attention to ethics and integrity nowadays (Huberts *et al.* 2008).[1] The importance of integrity is usually formulated in terms of the enhancement of public trust (Lewis and Gilman 2005), the reinforcement of the constitutional state (Cowell *et al.* 2011), the improvement of economic growth, social stability and service delivery (Bossaert and Demmke 2005), and as a crucial aspect of good governance (Huberts 2014).

Although the significance of integrity seems undisputed, that has not always been the case. Integrity is still a relatively young policy area (Behnke and Maesschalck 2006) within public administration. Before the 1990s, technical implementation and efficiency issues dominated the agenda. Until then, there was relatively little interest for ethical considerations, and integrity policies consisted mostly of unwritten agreements and non-binding measures (Adams and Balfour 1998; Huberts 2005; Van Den Heuvel *et al.* 2010). This all changed in the early 1990s. Since then, integrity gradually received more and more attention, and climbed up the political, administrative and academic agendas. In the Netherlands, this is apparent from the development of all kinds of integrity-related legal requirements, standards, policy measures, guidelines, courses, instruments, research groups, special chairs, officers and agencies (Hoekstra 2012).

Instead of studying all these separate integrity initiatives, this chapter concentrates on *integrity management*, here defined as the sum of systematic and integrated efforts to promote integrity within public-sector organizations. *Institutionalization* is an important aspect of integrity management and relates to its sustainability. It addresses the question of how these concerted efforts are thoroughly secured, anchored, embedded or safeguarded within the organization.

Particular attention is paid to this specific aspect because, to date, this seems to be a weak link in the integrity management chain.

This is also the case in the Dutch public sector (Hoekstra and Kaptein 2012), which is used as an example throughout this chapter. According to Transparency International (2012), the Netherlands has a rather good reputation and is known as a relatively incorrupt country. Efforts in the field of integrity management can be characterized as long-lasting (Hoekstra and Kaptein 2014) and also, in an international context, the Dutch National Integrity Office is regularly pitched as 'good practice' (European Commission 2014a, 2014b). Nevertheless, integrity management in Dutch organizations is far from perfect since it suffers from several shortcomings. We will argue that these shortcomings, or challenges, are related to institutional weakness.

Austerity measures that, as a result of the global financial crisis, impact public service institutions amplify these challenges. The financial crisis seems to have a negative influence on the time, resources and attention organizations (can) spend on integrity management. Integrity policies that are not (already) formally insti-tutionalized become susceptible to (further) de-prioritization and neglect when resources become scarce. This may be imprudent since the risks of unethical behaviour seem to have increased as well because of the crisis. Combining both trends (higher risks and less priority for integrity management) provides the ingred-ients of a rather unbecoming and even poisonous cocktail. Because the Netherlands is not alone in these challenges (Demmke and Moilanen 2012), this article suggests some solutions for these deficiencies. They are partly based on Dutch experiences and research, and may serve as 'good practices' to inspire policymakers, managers and ethics officers in countries that experience similar problems.

The next section reflects on the before-mentioned challenges and their impact on ethical behaviour and integrity management. Thereafter, it is argued that institutionalization is problematic, but key to address these challenges. This is fol-lowed by prescriptions for how (internal and external) integrity networks can offer effective and cost-efficient solutions. The chapter closes with a summary and some implications.

Integrity management: some challenges

With regard to integrity management, several challenges can be distinguished. They occur in the Netherlands but they will, to some extent, be recognizable to other countries as well. They relate to the lack of coherence, implementation and balance (Karssing and Hoekstra 2004), as to the effects of austerity measures on integrity management. Since the latter seem to be the most current and urgent of challenges, they will get the most attention.

Coherence, implementation and balance: common challenges

By definition, integrity management requires an integrated, systematic and coherent approach. Integrity instruments and initiatives are more effective when they are part of a systematic style (Van Tankeren 2010). Although the importance of such a concerted approach seems almost a matter of course, this is not yet the case in many public organizations (Bowman 1990; Lawton *et al.* 2013). For instance, in the UK, 'reforms to the integrity management framework have been . . . prompted by specific scandals or events, rather than developed in a comprehensive and integrated manner' (Heywood 2012, p. 478). Integrity policies in Dutch public organizations are similarly incoherent and incomprehensive (Algemene Rekenkamer 2010; De Jong 2008). The fact that integrity is a multidisciplinary policy area (Huberts 2014), and various departments within an organization (e.g. HR, Audit, Legal, Finance, the Work Council) are responsible for certain aspects of integrity policies, contributes to this fragmentation (see Figure 9.1).

Second, integrity management suffers from implementation deficiencies. Integrity policies have repeatedly proven to be a somewhat paper issue that has not received a direct follow-up (Transparency International 2012; Van Den Heuvel and Huberts 2003). Various surveys, carried out by the Ministry of the Interior and Kingdom Relations and the National Integrity Office in the Netherlands, reveal that organizations encounter problems implementing integrity policies (Ministerie Van BZK 2004, 2008; National Integrity Office 2012a). This has led to public organizations not yet fully complying with the legal requirements of the Civil Service Act. International research also points out that integrity management does not suffer from a lack of rules or instruments, but from an implementation weakness (Demmke 2004, Demmke and Moilanen 2012; Herrmann 1997; OECD 2009).

Third, it appears to be difficult to find a balanced integrity management approach combining both compliance and integrity strategies (Paine 1994). Compliance strategies are based on rules and supervision, intended to prevent non-compliant behaviour. Integrity strategies are values-based, intended to promote ethical behaviour through awareness training. Although experts (Cooper 2006; Lawton *et al.* 2013; Van Blijswijk *et al.* 2004) consider a combination to be most effective, a balanced approach is mostly non-existent. Emphasis on one strategy or another shifts during time, as is evident from a historic meta-analysis (Hoekstra and Kaptein 2014). Within the public sector, close attention has been paid in recent years to the importance of culture, leadership, awareness, trust, exemplary behaviour, dilemma training, professional pride and similar 'softer controls'. These elements are mainly based on the, now popular, integrity strategy that has suppressed important compliance elements and 'harder controls': risk analysis, internal monitoring and reporting mechanisms, and enforcement (National Integrity Office 2012a). The OECD also recognizes this trend and argues therefore that: 'The balance should be maintained and one should . . . be aware of a too enthusiastic and radical switch towards the values-based approach' (OECD 2009, p. 13).

Influence of austerity measures on integrity management: new challenges

In addition to the aforementioned challenges, there are indications that austerity measures introduced in public organizations may result in higher integrity risks, while less resources are spent on integrity management. Indeed a dangerous combination, but this claim requires some caution. Since this is still an under-researched topic, there is little 'hard evidence' available. And although there exist contra-indications that refute the claim, a raft of worrisome signals seem to support it. These signals could at best be described as 'circumstantial evidence' since they are mostly of an indirect and diverse nature. This section will take a closer look into these signals, but starts with two contra-arguments.

In order to meet European budget standards, the Dutch government had to realize a reduction of €12.4 billion in 2013 (AEF 2014). According to some scholars and institutions, this decrease in public expenditure could have a mitigating effect on integrity risks. Less subsidies, for instance, imply less room for malpractice, and if thrift is the (new) standard, excessive spending will no longer be accepted (Bekker 2012). Others argue that employees may take fewer risks, and are less inclined to steal from their employers, when economic prospects seem weak. Employees are afraid of losing their jobs in an uncertain labour market (Achmea Rechtsbijstand 2013; Ethics Resource Center 2014).

On the other hand, several reports point out that austerity measures impose a risk on public-sector integrity. The National Integrity Office (2012b) conducted an inquiry that revealed that a quarter of the civil servants felt that unethical behaviour between colleagues had increased; a third witnessed more unethical conduct towards the employer; and the same amount of respondents expressed that integrity programmes within their organizations were under pressure because of the crisis. Although these three findings are based on rather small-scale research, other sources provide additional and supporting evidence.

Recent large-scale research confirms that unethical behaviour such as bullying, intimidation, harassment and discrimination are nowadays indeed the most serious problems in Dutch public organizations, presumably instigated by the crisis (De Graaf 2014; De Graaf and Strüwer 2014). The National Association for Confidential Integrity Councillors (2012) confirms the crisis' devastating effect on ethical behaviour and observes the work floor turning into an arena. Feelings such as anxiety, stress, frustration and job insecurity lead to an unpleasant, competitive and unsafe work environment where employees act out towards each other. Austerity measures thus negatively affect workplace behaviour and lead to demoralization (Demmke and Moilanen 2012).

But acting out also occurs in the relation between employees and their employers. Postponed promotions, not extending contracts, and lay-offs lead to personal financial problems (NIBUD 2009) as feelings of unfair treatment lead to rising labour disputes (ARAG Rechtsbijstandsverzekeraar 2012). Financial issues and a mental state of disappointment, vindictiveness and resentment could result in theft and abuse of company assets or other integrity breaches. Potential lay-off candidates are more likely to flirt with impropriety, and belt-tightening measures such as cutting management layers result in less managers to supervise more workers, whereas the increase of contingency workers – which are likely to feel less loyal to the organization – may lead to more integrity risks as well (Treviño and Nelson 2004). Not surprisingly, forensic consultants report that they are hired more often to investigate cases of misconduct (see, for instance, Ernst & Young 2011, 2012; PricewaterhouseCoopers 2009).

These same consultants also report that there has been a decline in the use of anti-fraud, anti-bribery prevention and control measures precisely in the period when incentives to act unethically have been the highest. This coincides with a warning sounded by the Dutch Court of Audit: '. . . the promotion and maintenance of a significant level of integrity management will come under pressure in the coming years as a result of financial targets and reconsiderations' (Algemene Rekenkamer 2010: 9). In 2012, an assessment of the Dutch National Integrity System, conducted by Transparency International, confirms this prophecy:

> organisations are no longer affording integrity the highest priority. From here it emerges that integrity is often still regarded as 'something extra' and not as a basic requirement for an organisation's good functioning. It is clear that such an attitude brings along great risks for ensuring integrity.
>
> (Transparency International 2012, p. 288)

From a more theoretical point of view, Treviño and Weaver (2003) suggest that organizational changes, such as restructuring, pose serious problems for ethics programmes. Since resources decrease, and organizations will tend to focus on their primary processes, it can be assumed that this will be at the expense of integrity management efforts.

Altogether, and despite some contra-indications, there seem to be enough reasons to be on high alert. Transparency International's (2010) observation, that corruption has increased in those countries that have been hit the hardest by the financial crisis, illustrates that integrity management is not a luxury, but something that requires permanent maintenance and continuity. In other words, institutionalization is key.

Institutionalization as an essential, but weak, link

The matter of institutionalization is, in this section, discussed and positioned as an overarching issue in terms of the identified challenges, and potential solutions. The assumption is that adequate institutionalization has a mitigating effect on these challenges. This section starts with an exploration of two institutionalization approaches. Then we will look into some arguments for the formal approach and suggest why it could overcome integrity management challenges.

Ethics literature points out that there are two approaches to instil integrity measures within organizations: informal and formal institutionalization (Brenner 1992). The nature of the informal approach is implicit, indirect and concerns less visible and tangible organizational aspects that, while affecting the ethical climate of the organization, are not primarily targeting ethics. This could include the behaviour of supervisors (leadership), the creation of shared values, fair remuneration, appraisal and promotion systems, and rewarding 'good' behaviour. The formal approach is, however, explicit, direct and visibly aimed at promoting ethical behaviour within organizations (Tenbrunsel et al. 2003). This includes the development of sustainable structures, standards and systems that support ethical behaviour in the organization (Cummings and Worley 2001; Sims 2003).

Although a balanced institutionalization approach is recommended (Rossouw and Van Vuuren 2004), advocates of the formal approach underline the importance of its visibility and clarity to employees and external stakeholders (Berman *et al.* 1994). Moreover:

> relying solely on informal mechanisms has inherent dangers. Without formal systems to safeguard ethical behaviour and clear standards against which employees can benchmark their actions, the same informal mechanisms that can contribute to a positive ethical climate may instead foster laxity and unethical decision making.
>
> (Pajo and McGhee 2003, p. 62)

Others emphasize that a formalized approach contributes to the effectiveness of integrity policies (Van Den Heuvel *et al.* 2010) and that it is both insufficient and unwise to merely call upon the conscience of employees and to rely on good intentions. Formalization prevents concern for integrity from becoming dependent on a few well-willing individuals: if they leave the company or retire, there will be a risk that the subject will get less attention (Conijn 2009).

Also, in the context of the above-mentioned (common and current) challenges, this formal- institutional approach seems appealing. When the risks are high, clear benchmarks, active control and support systems are important to prevent and detect wrongdoing. And since integrity programmes, after an enthusiastic start, tend to get overshadowed by many other everyday organizational issues, a more resilient and structured approach may be worthwhile. Integrity officers and entities are, furthermore, conducive to keeping these programmes going and can ensure a well-balanced, integrated approach. Moreover, formalized policies with clearly defined targets, assigned responsibilities and accompanying monitoring systems are better resistant to implementation pitfalls. Yet another reason for a formalized integrity management approach is that, in case employees are prosecuted because of suspected integrity breaches, judges nowadays take into account and review the organizations' deployed integrity activities. What the employer did to prevent the employee from turning into a 'bad apple' is then the central question to be answered. In the Netherlands, but all the more in the US (since the introduction of the Federal Sentencing Guidelines), this has become an important aspect of the court's verdict. Tangible structures, systems and documents specifically aimed at integrity management are helpful in that regard. Table 9.1 provides an overview of some of the characteristics of both institutionalization approaches.

But, unfortunately, institutionalization turns out to be a weak point of integrity management, as is asserted in a comparative EU study (Demmke and Moilanen 2012). This, however, is not an exclusive public-sector problem, since the private sector faces similar challenges (De Colle and Werhane 2008; Jose and Thibodeaux 1999; Singhapakdi and Vitell 2007). In Dutch government organizations, formal

TABLE 9.1 Approaches for institutionalizing integrity

Aspects	Formal	Informal
Policies	Specific policies, directly and explicitly aimed at fostering integrity	General policies with an indirect and implicit influence on the ethical climate
Products	Integrity structures, systems, procedures, norms and plans	Organizational culture, values, leadership, fair and just company procedures
Responsibility	Specific integrity officers are responsible in general, and they support line management to manage integrity in their units	Everyone is responsible for ethics, and individual line managers are responsible for ethical behaviour in their units
Objectivity	Ensures an objective and univocal companywide integrity management approach, based on coherent actions	Susceptible to subjective and ambiguous interpretations of individual managers, because of a decentralized approach
Visibility	Highly visible, and tangible, for both internal and external actors (employees, managers and external watchdogs); provides clear and accessible benchmarks for new personnel	Less visible, and tangible, for both internal and external actors (employees, managers and external watchdogs); new personnel is required to internalize the organization's culture
Accountability	Strong steering, monitoring and accountability mechanisms	Indirect steering and monitoring mechanisms, more difficult to account for
Pressure	Can quickly be organized and is thus a common response to external pressure, which calls for immediate action; pitfall: abused as symbolic action	Internalizing ethics in the organizational culture, requires long-term efforts; pitfall: certain extent of ambiguity and slowness

institutionalization has likewise remained an underexposed, under-researched and therefore weak aspect of integrity management, as an extensive analysis of reports points out (Algemene Rekenkamer 2005, 2010, 2014; Hoekstra and Kaptein 2012; Jongmans 2011; Olsthoorn 2010; Transparency International 2012; Van Den Heuvel *et al.* 2010; Van Emmerik *et al.* 2014; Van Tankeren 2010). These studies illustrate that too many public-sector organizations have not yet formulated, and laid down, their integrity policies in an inclusive formal document. Instead, bits and pieces are scattered over a diverse range of policy letters, papers, reports, notes, circulars or codes. Consequently, integrity policies are anything but coherent: there is plenty, but there hardly is an integrated approach. Moreover, integrity policies are seldom based on a deliberate vision, lack measurable goals, are hardly evaluated, and are not integrated in (standard) management reports. Neither is integrity management regarded as a separate policy domain, nor are specific integrity officers frequently designated.

By design or mistake?

How can this institutional weakness be explained: is it on purpose or just a slip-up? This is an intriguing but difficult question to answer. Some possible explanations for this flaw are:

- Highly decentralized state systems offer public bodies much liberty to give substance to integrity policies. In such states (as the Netherlands), integrity policies are often of a general nature. Public bodies have to comply with some basic requirements (such as having a code of ethics and a reporting system, administrating the oath of office, and conducting risk analysis), but if, and how, they actually *manage and organize* integrity is their own responsibility. Many organizations consider it to be sufficient to meet the basic criteria, but do not really aspire to a systematic, coherent and institutionalized integrity management approach.
- A 'looser' approach could be appealing because it is less restrictive and offers more opportunities to give other organizational goals priority: an organized and integrated integrity system is more likely to have (sometimes unwanted) consequences for the daily organizational goals and operations (Treviño and Weaver 2003).
- Integrity policies often have an incident-driven and symbolic character whereby more attention is paid to new measures than to the implementation and institutionalization of existing policies (Demmke and Moilanen 2012).
- Explicit and visible commitment to integrity management could be risky if expectations are not met (Kaptein and Wempe 2002), for instance if there turn out to be more problems than expected.
- A potential risk of institutionalizing integrity and appointing specific officers is that others within the organization could interpret this as a dismissal of their own ethical responsibilities (Maesschalck 2005).
- Institutionalization could be discarded as additional bureaucracy, an administrative burden and red tape that is undesirable and unnecessary, for which the capacity and resources are lacking (Lawton *et al.* 2013; Van Den Heuvel and Huberts 2003).

In short, the institutional dimension of integrity management is essential but weak. In the next section, we will explore possible solutions to this vexing problem.

Improving integrity management and institutionalization: potential solutions

Research on integrity management and institutionalization points out that there are several ways to organize integrity (Hoekstra and Kaptein 2012). Some organizations, for instance, create a central integrity office, whereas others decentralize the responsibility for integrity completely to line management. Yet another possibility is to work with internal and external networks. This option seems particularly attractive since it is cheaper, certainly for smaller organizations, to organize a network than to equip and run an integrity office. Certainly at times when budgets are under pressure, such offices are often dismantled. A decentralized integrity approach is often used by organizations showing no clear commitment to formalize and address integrity as an explicit issue. They 'manage' integrity in a reactive fashion based on incidents, or even demonstrate passiveness because integrity is not considered to be a matter of much concern. This approach is not a serious option at times when the risks are high and the identified integrity management challenges are to be addressed. Instead of a centralized or a decentralized approach, two relatively low-cost but effective network methods are introduced in the next section. Both are based on empirical studies conducted in the Dutch public sector (Hoekstra *et al.* 2014; National Integrity Office 2013).

Internal integrity networks: towards coordination and control

Integrity is a multidisciplinary theme that, in most organizations, is shaped by various functionaries and departments. Rossouw and Van Vuuren (2004) indicate these actors as 'key role players'. All of them give, based on their own professional backgrounds, content to (specific elements of). integrity programmes. Figure 9.1 provides an overview of the main actors that play a role in the implementation of integrity policies within Dutch government institutions. Table 9.2 provides a short explanation of the possible roles and tasks.

Naturally, the participants may differ by organization and by country. At the same time, it is likely that there will be many similarities. Owing to the multitude of actors, integrity policies may soon acquire an incoherent and fragmented character, which may also blur the view of the implementation. Therefore, it is useful to think in terms of an internal integrity network and to organize coordination between the various internal actors. This is critical to the successful implementation of integrity programmes, but requires an integrity officer positioned in the heart of the model:

> An organization which implements an ethics and compliance program without designating an individual to oversee it, risks the possibility that the function will fail for lack of leadership. Similarly, talking about the importance of ethics without creating a formal function to uphold and promote organizational standards may be perceived as hypocritical.
>
> (Ethics Resource Center 2007, pp. 13–14)

The creation of such a coordinating function is important (Driscoll and Hoffman 2000; Segon 2010; Treviño *et al.* 2014), as it: allows for synergies between instruments; allows for accumulation of expertise based on experiences; ensures continuity of ethics in the long term; and strongly signals that integrity is considered important within the organization (OECD 2009). The concept of internal integrity networks

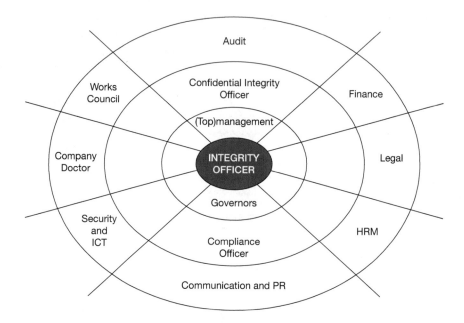

FIGURE 9.1 Main integrity actors

is also considered effective as it generates support throughout the organization and prevents integrity officers from becoming 'lone rangers': isolated individuals that are seen, and act, as the moral consciences of their organizations.

Preparing a formalized integrity plan, or document, is a powerful tool for integrity officers to be able to manage integrity in their networks. Establishing a joint vision on integrity, formulating clear objectives and activities, and defining and assigning responsibilities are some important elements of such a plan. Once established, a formalized plan will prevent integrity ambitions being watered down. Integrity plans also offer guidelines for monitoring integrity policies, resulting in a better grip on the implementation. And finally, as mentioned before: to be able to register a tangible integrity plan is helpful when it comes to lawsuits. The main elements for such an integrity plan are identified in Table 9.3.

External integrity networks: towards collaboration

Nevertheless, coordinating integrity policies and networks turns out to be a difficult, time-consuming and challenging job. Even more so since the integrity officer's function is usually not treated as a proper full-time job, but as an additional chore amidst many other responsibilities (Hoekstra and Kaptein 2012). Due to these internal struggles and limitations, many integrity officers indicate the need for sparring partners from outside their own organization who can support and inspire them. Certainly for those for whom the position is still new, this is even more crucial:

TABLE 9.2 Integrity Network Analysis

Category	Department/position	Integrity role
Management	Highest officer	Ultimately responsible for the agenda, implementation and enforcement of integrity policies for the entire organization.
	Management	Responsible for implementation of integrity policies and for promoting ethical behaviour within the organizational units for which they are responsible.
Integrity	Integrity officer Integrity coordinator Compliance officer Policy staff	It concerns a wide range of different types of officers who fulfil roles relating to: support, advice, design, engineering, operationalization, enforcement and coordination of integrity policies.
Staff services and officers	Audit	Setting up of the administrative organization and the internal control in a manner that promotes ethical behaviour.
	Finance	Taking care of vulnerable actions around purchasing, tenders, work budgets and expense claims in a responsible manner.
	Legal	Formulating administrative-legal policy and providing advice based on relevant legislation and the drafting of delegation and mandate regulations.
	HRM	Establishing procedures and providing advice concerning recruitment and selection, job descriptions, performance and assessment interviews, disciplinary research, sanctions and corporate culture.
	Communication/information	Communication concerning the importance of integrity and any integrity violations.
	Security, ICT	Setting up of the physical and ICT security from the point of view of integrity.
	Facility services	Responsible for purchasing, maintenance and the management of company resources.
	Confidential adviser	Advising and coaching of employees in the internal reporting process in the event of suspected integrity violations.
	Works council	Advising about the organization's proposed integrity policies.
	Company doctor	Safety net for employees who encounter problems (bullying, discrimination, intimidation, violence) through unethical behaviour of the organization or other employees.

TABLE 9.3 Main elements of an integrity plan

Elements	Orientation questions
1. Mission and vision	What is the importance of integrity for the organization? What does it mean? How are integrity ambitions and objectives defined? Which integrity strategies are chosen?
2. Policy and instruments	What are the basic integrity requirements (laws and regulations) the organization should comply with? To what extent does the organization adhere to these requirements? What additional policy measures does the organization have to take?
3. Results and activities	What concrete integrity activities does the organization have to take each year to ultimately achieve the desired results? In which sequence are these carried out?
4. Roles, tasks and positioning	Which specific officers and departments are involved in the implementation of integrity policies? For which tasks are the various actors responsible precisely? How are they positioned within the organization and relative to each other?
5. Coordination and coherence	How is coherence between various policy measures, instruments and activities ensured? Who is responsible for the internal coordination between the various actors?
6. Evauation and responsibility	How are policies and intended measures monitored, evaluated and improved? How is that reported? How is responsibility accounted for?
7. Resources	How much time and budget is required to implement integrity policies? What other resources are necessary?

we are unable, or only to a limited extent, to debate issues within our organization given that we are mostly a 'one-man band' . . . it is very good to be able to discuss with others what you are up against, or how they deal with it . . . in this way we learn from each other . . . and you are not left entirely to your own devices.[2]

However, there is hardly any scientific knowledge available about such forms of inter-organizational collaboration in the field of integrity management. A recent explorative study provides a first insight into this matter (Hoekstra *et al.* 2014). From in-depth interviews with 30 integrity officers, who work together with 'peers' from other organizations, four types of integrity partnerships (IPs) emerged. These partnerships contribute to the sustainable embedding of integrity because participating organizations are more inclined to keep it on their agendas since they do not want to remain behind their 'counterparts': 'a joint approach also generates pressure on each other, and if you say, "gosh, there's six parties . . . five of which are making that qualitative leap", then it's difficult for the sixth party to say, "I'm not taking part"'.

In addition, IPs offer the opportunity to learn from each other. Knowledge can be exchanged about the organization and implementation of well-balanced, and coherent, integrity policies.

Experiences and solutions can thus be shared regarding the challenges identified earlier in this chapter. But as we will see, most IPs also have certain efficiency advantages, offering promising solutions for integrity management in times of financial crises and austerity.

Further to the already mentioned exchange of knowledge, other IP types and functions are identified: in some IPs, integrity instruments are developed for common use; in others, organizations mutually share, or lend out, their integrity experts; and there exist IPs that represent a certain sector or branch, try to influence policymakers, regulatory authorities, or the media. These four forms of integrity collaboration are briefly explained below, albeit in a somewhat different sequence:

1   In the *Workshop*, organizations work together with similar organizations to develop practical integrity instruments, such as guidelines, formats, protocols, codes and 'toolkits'. Usually, Workshop IPs arise because different organizations require the same instrument at the same time. New legislation can, for example, be a reason for this. Individually, these organizations lack the time, expertise and resources to develop the necessary instruments on their own. Jointly, it appears that they can achieve this better, faster and cheaper.

2   When capacity and expertise is scarce, the *Pool* offers the solution. From this Pool of integrity professionals, organizations share investigators, trainers or policy advisers. Usually, this is carried out because individual organizations are too small to have such experts full-time on their payroll, but nevertheless now and then require their services. Contractual agreements with respect to authorization, management, finance and capacity agreements underpin the sharing and exchange of experts. The main advantages of the Pool are the diversity, flexibility and continuity that it offers. It increases the availability of professionals: 'Even if someone's on leave, there's always a point of contact. It is therefore almost guaranteed that the work gets done'.

3   In the *Forum*, integrity officers share knowledge, become acquainted with other experts and exchange experiences. This takes place 'offline' during meetings, workshops and lectures; however, professionals also find each other 'online' in network groups, in shared email contacts and via social media, such as in LinkedIn groups. The Forum thus offers the desired sparring partners. The Forum can be described as an informal and non-binding network where integrity officers contact each other to share inspiration and solutions for the problems they encounter in their own organizations.

4   In the *Megaphone*, organizations join forces to exercise influence or improve their sector's reputation. These IPs generally arise as a result of integrity violations with a large social impact. These violations lead to pressure from the government, regulatory authorities and the media. Megaphones attempt to voice their concerns, and exert collective counter-pressure towards regulatory authorities and policymakers to influence or divert impending legislation: 'governments come with lists, check marks and regulations . . . but that does not work. It does not connect. I'd therefore like the government to listen to

what our sector can and cannot do, and then to work together . . . instead of them once again coming up with irrational demands'. These IPs also represent the sector in the media and mostly act as a logical discussion partner for the national government. Where each individual organization lacks influence, they can accomplish this more effectively as a collective organization.

As indicated above, integrity management suffers from some persistent challenges. The most recent of challenges are the austerity measures that lead to both higher integrity risks and fewer resources spent on integrity management. Internal and external collaboration seem to provide both effective and cost-efficient solutions to overcome these challenges.

Conclusion

Although public-sector integrity management has increased in recent decades, there are still some serious problems to be addressed. Integrity management is still too incoherent and imbalanced, while implementation turns out to be laborious. In the meantime, integrity programmes are under pressure because of austerity measures, while the risks are going up: an increase of unethical behaviour between colleagues, and between employees and their employers, turns out to be a double-edged sword.

A formal, institutionalized integrity management approach is presented as a remedy for these challenges. It provides for a deliberate vision on integrity, clear targets, better coordination, support and monitoring systems, and assigned responsibilities to all key role players, just to mention some of the benefits. But alas, institutionalization turns out to be weak, sometimes arouses resistance, and can in general be considered as a neglected aspect of public integrity management. Government organizations should, however, be on high alert because of current integrity risks and should rapidly work on more sustainable integrity management systems to overcome these challenges. While the creation of full-fledged, centralized integrity offices seems both too expensive and bureaucratic, and a more decentralized approach is susceptible to ambiguity, integrity networks are proposed as potential intermediate solutions.

Integrity officers are the focal point of such networks. They are the organizations' engines of integrity management, they are responsible for coherent and well-balanced integrity plans, and they coordinate the activities of all internal integrity players. Because this integrity function is still quite new, and integrity officers sometimes feel isolated within their organizations, they have a strong urge to find some external support and advice. Collaboration with their peers, or counterparts, from other organizations is therefore considered to be necessary. In that case, an integrity functionary acts as a liaison officer between his or her own organization and external partners. Because of such collaborations, integrity officers will be better equipped to manage integrity in their own organizations, and to tackle the internal problems they may encounter. Although this may seem like a 'centralized' solution, it should be stressed that an integrity officer is above all a '*primus inter pares*', someone amidst other key role players with a supporting and harmonizing role, leaving responsibilities to whom they belong.

Inspired by both research and practice, the aim of this chapter is to take a step forward in thinking about integrity management. By now, it is sufficiently recognized that organizations have a responsibility to promote integrity, that the instruments that can be used to this effect are known, and that they are ideally a combination of compliance and integrity measures. Consequently, the many ongoing discussions about the usefulness of rules versus awareness have now become obsolete. The next phase in the thinking process should therefore focus more explicitly on the question how integrity management can be thoroughly embedded in public organizations. This assurance aspect of integrity management has received relatively little attention to date, while various studies illustrate that more work is needed in this area. The development of new concepts and methods, such as integrity networks, plans and partnerships, can support organizations and their integrity officers therein.

Although the methods outlined are based on present administrative practices, and network theory has quite a rich tradition in public administration, they are relatively new and unexplored concepts in integrity management literature. Therefore, presented network approaches need to be further researched and integrated in existing knowledge: leading to a new (intra- and inter-organizational) integrity management network approach. Since they are grounded in practice, and first experiences seem promising, these methods can – despite their newness – be applied in order to be further tested and improved.

Another area that certainly needs more research concerns the impact of austerity measures on ethical behaviour, and on integrity management in the public sector. The existing circumstantial evidence should be classified as alarming, but has to be examined in much greater detail. Recent developments, signalling that the financial crisis might be on its return in some countries, provide all the more reason not to wait with this kind of research since a relapse may be possible. More generally, we should improve resilience for future economic crises.

Notes

1   This chapter is partly based on Hoekstra (2012) and Hoekstra *et al.* (2014).
2   This quotation, and the following quotations, are from interviews reported in Hoekstra *et al.* (2014).

References

Achmea Rechtsbijstand (2013) *Meer arbeidszaken, minder ontslag op staande voet*, Zeist: Achmea Rechtsbijstand.
Adams, G.B. and Balfour, D.L. (1998) *Unmasking Administrative Evil*, London: Sage.
AEF (2014) *Integriteit in ontwikkeling: Implicaties van trends en ontwikkelingen voor de integriteit van het openbaar bestuur*, Utrecht: AEF.
Algemene Rekenkamer (2005) *Zorg voor integriteit: Een nulmeting naar integriteitszorg in 2004*, The Hague: Algemene Rekenkamer.

Algemene Rekenkamer (2010) *Stand van zaken integriteitszorg Rijk 2009*, The Hague: Algemene Rekenkamer.

Algemene Rekenkamer (2014) *Integriteit bij de Dienst Justitiële Inrichtingen*, The Hague: Algemene Rekenkamer.

ARAG Rechtsbijstandsverzekeraar (2012) *Meer conflicten doorbezuinigingen op ambtenaren.*

Behnke, N. and Maesschalck, J. (2006) 'Integrity systems at work: Theoretical and empirical foundations', *Public Administration Quarterly*, 30(3): 111–26.

Bekker, R. (2012) *De arbeidsverhoudingen in de publieke sector van bovenaf gezien*, Helicopterview nr. 6.

Berman, E., West, J. and Cava, A. (1994) 'Ethics management in municipal governments and large firms', *Administration & Society*, 26(2): 185–203.

Bossaert, D. and Demmke, C. (2005) *Main Challenges in the Field of Ethics and Integrity in the EU Member States*, Maastricht: European Institute of Public Administration.

Bowman, J.S. (1990) 'Ethics in government: A national survey of public administrators', *Public Administration Review*, May/June: 345–53.

Brenner, S.N. (1992) 'Ethics programs and their dimensions', *Journal of Business Ethics*, 11: 391–9.

Conijn, F. (2009) 'Henk Van Luijk, bedrijfsethicus; Ik doe graag een beroep op het geweten van mensen, maar dat schiet helaas niet op', *Het Financiële Dagblad*, 3 October.

Cooper, T. (2006) *The Responsible Administrator: An Approach to Ethics for the Administrative Role* (5th edn), San Francisco, CA: Jossey-Bass.

Cowell, R., Downe, J. and Morgan, K. (2011) 'The ethical framework for local government in England: Is it having any effect and why?', *Public Management Review*, 13(3): 433–57.

Cummings, T.G. and Worley, C.G. (2001) *Organizational Development & Change* (7th edn), Cincinnati, OH: South-Western Thompson Learning.

De Colle, S. and Werhane, P.H. (2008) 'Moral motivation across ethical theories: What can we learn for designing corporate ethics programs', *Journal of Business Ethics*, 81: 751–64.

De Graaf, F. and Strüwer, T. (2014) *Aard en omvang van integriteitsschendingen binnen de Nederlandse overheid*, Amsterdam: VU.

De Graaf, G. (2014) 'Ambtenaar lijkt minder integer na crisis', *Binnenlands Bestuur*, 25 April: 8–9.

De Jong, M. (2008) 'Integriteit en beleid: Klokkenluidersregeling remt integere bedrijfscultuur', *Overheidsmanagement*, 30 June: 21–5.

Demmke, C. (2004) *Working Towards Common Elements in the Field of Ethics and Integrity*, for the 43rd meeting of the directors-general of the public services of the member states of the European Union, Maastricht: European Institute of Public Administration.

Demmke, C. and Moilanen, T. (2012) *Effectiveness of Ethics and Good Governance in Central Administration of EU-27: Evaluating Reform Outcomes in the Context of the Financial Crisis*, Frankfurt: Peter Lang.

Driscoll, D.N. and Hoffman, W.M. (2000) *Ethics Matters: How to Implement Values-Driven Management*, Waltham, MA: Bentley College Center for Business Ethics.

Ernst & Young (2011) *European Fraud Survey: Recovery, Regulation and Integrity.*

Ernst & Young (2012) *Growing Beyond: A Place for Integrity.*

Ethics Resource Center (2007) *Leading Corporate Integrity: Defining the Role of the Chief Ethics & Compliance Officer*, Washington, DC: ERC.

Ethics Resource Center (2014) *National Business Ethics Survey*, Arlington, TX: ERC.

European Commission (2014a) *Report from the Commission to the Council and the European Parliament: Anti-Corruption Report*, Brussels: European Commission.

European Commission (2014b) *Civil Society Involvement in Drafting, Implementing and Assessing Anticorruption Policies: Best Practices Manual*, Brussels: European Commission.

Herrmann, F.M. (1997) 'Bricks without straw: The plight of governmental ethics agencies in the United States', *Public Integrity Annual*, 2: 13–22.

Heywood, P.M. (2012) 'Integrity management and the public service ethos in the UK: Patchwork quilt or threadbare blanket?', *International Review of Administrative Sciences*, 78(3): 474–93.

Hoekstra, A. (2012) 'Integriteitsmanagement en – organisatie: Het borgen van goede bedoelingen', in J.H.J. Van Den Heuvel, L.W.J.C. Huberts and E.R. Muller (eds), *Integriteit: Integriteit en integriteitsbeleid in Nederland* (pp. 239–63), Deventer: Kluwer.

Hoekstra, A. and Kaptein, M. (2012) 'The institutionalization of integrity in local government', *Public Integrity*, 15(1): 5–28.

Hoekstra, A. and Kaptein, M. (2014) 'Understanding integrity policy formation processes: A case study in the Netherlands of the conditions for change', *Public Integrity*, 16(3): 243–63.

Hoekstra, A., Talsma, J. and Kaptein, M. (2014) 'Interorganisational cooperation as strategy for managing integrity? An exploration and categorization of integrity partnerships', conference paper presented in September 2014 in Speijer, Germany: 12th workshop of the EGPA Study Group 'Quality and Integrity of Governance'.

Huberts, L.W.J.C. (2005) *Integriteit en integritisme in bestuur en samenleving: Wie de schoen pas*, Amsterdam: VU.

Huberts, L.W.J.C. (2014) *The Integrity of Governance*, Basingstoke: Palgrave Macmillan.

Huberts, L.W.J.C., Maesschalck, J. and Jurkiewicz, C.L. (2008) 'Global perspectives on good governance policies and research', in L.W.J.C. Huberts, J. Maesschalck and C.L. Jurkiewicz (eds), *Ethics and Integrity of Governance: Perspectives Across Frontiers* (pp. 239–60), Cheltenham: Edward Elgar.

Jongmans, E. (2011) *Integriteit bij waterschappen: Tussen sturing en ruimte*, Twente: TU.

Jose, A. and Thibodeaux, M.S. (1999) 'Institutionalization of ethics: The perspective of managers', *Journal of Business Ethics*, 22(2): 133–43.

Kaptein, M. and Wempe, J. (2002) *The Balanced Company: A Theory of Corporate Integrity*, Oxford: Oxford University Press.

Karssing, E.D. and Hoekstra, A. (2004) 'Integriteitsbeleid als evenwichtskunst', *Bestuurswetenschappen*, 3: 167–92.

Lawton, A., Rayner, J. and Lasthuizen, K. (2013) *Ethics and Management in the Public Sector*, London: Routledge.

Lewis, C.W. and Gilman, S.C. (2005) *The Ethics Challenge in Public Service: A Problem Solving Guide* (2nd edn), San Francisco, CA: Jossey-Bass.

Maesschalck, J. (2005) *Een ambtelijk integriteitsbeleid in de Vlaamse overheid*, Leuven: Steunpunt Bestuurlijk Organisatie Vlaanderen.

Ministerie Van BZK (2004) *Inventarisatie integriteitsbeleid openbaar bestuur en politie*, The Hague: BZK.

Ministerie Van BZK (2008) *Inventarisatie integriteitsbeleid openbaar bestuur en politie*, The Hague: BZK.

National Association for Confidential Integrity Councillors (2012) De vertrouwenspersoon, zeker nodig in crisistijd.

National Integrity Office (2012a) *Monitor Integriteit Openbaar Bestuur: Integriteitsbeleid en – beleving*, The Hague: BIOS.

National Integrity Office (2012b) *Invloed van de bezuinigingen op integriteit(sbeleid): Een verkennend onderzoek binnen de (semi-)publieke sector*, The Hague: BIOS.

National Integrity Office (2013) *Integriteit verankeren! Kwaliteit van het integriteitsbeleid in de publieke sector*, The Hague: BIOS.

NIBUD (2009) *Financiële problemen op de werkvloer: Een peiling naar activiteiten en informatiebehoeften van P&O'ers en salarisadministrateurs*, Utrecht: NIBUD.

OECD (2009) *Towards a Sound Integrity Framework: Instruments, Processes, Structures and Conditions for Implementation*, Paris: OECD Publications.

Olsthoorn, S. (2010) 'Integriteitsbeleid gemeenten onsamenhangend', *Binnenlands Bestuur*, 11 June: 17.

Paine, L.S. (1994) 'Managing for organisational integrity', *Harvard Business Review*, 72(2): 106–17.

Pajo, K. and McGhee, P. (2003) 'The institutionalization of business ethics: Are New Zealand organizations doing enough?', *Journal of the Australian and New Zealand Academy of Management*, 9(1): 52–65.

PricewaterhouseCoopers (2009) *Global Economic Crime Survey*.

Rossouw, G.J. and Van Vuuren, L. (2004) *Business Ethics* (3rd edn), Cape Town: Oxford University Press.

Segon, M. (2010) 'Managing organizational ethics: Professionalism, duty and HR practitioners', *Journal of Business Systems, Governance and Ethics*, 5(4): 13–25.

Sims, R.R. (2003) *Ethics and Corporate Responsibility: Why Giants Fall*, Westport, CT: Greenwood.

Singhapakdi, A. and Vitell, S.J. (2007) 'Institutionalization of ethics and its consequences: A survey of marketing professionals', *Journal of the Academy of Marketing Science*, 35: 284–94.

Tenbrunsel, A.E., Smith-Crowe, K. and Umphress, E.E. (2003) 'Building houses on rocks: The role of the ethical infrastructure in organizations', *Social Justice Research*, 16(3): 285–307.

Transparency International (2010) *Corruption Perceptions Index 2010*, Berlin: Transparency International.

Transparency International (2012) *National Integrity System Assessment Netherlands*, The Hague: Transparency International.

Treviño, L. and Nelson, K.A. (2004) *Managing Business Ethics: Straight Talk about How to Do It Right* (3rd edn), New York: John Wiley & Sons.

Treviño, L. and Weaver, G. (2003) *Managing Ethics in Business Organizations*, Stanford, CA: Stanford University Press.

Treviño, L.K., Den Nieuwenboer, N.A. Kreiner, G.E. and Bishop, D.G. (2014) 'Legitimating the legitimate: A grounded theory study of legitimacy work among ethics and compliance officers', *Organizational Behavior and Human Decision Processes*, 123: 186–205.

Van Blijswijk, J.A.M., Van Breukelen, R.C.J., Franklin, A.L., Raadschelders, J.C.N. and Slump, P. (2004) 'Beyond ethical codes: The management of integrity in the Netherlands Tax and Customs Administration', *Public Administration Review*, 64(6): 718–27.

Van Emmerik, M.L., Loof, J.P. and Schuurmans, Y.E. (2014) *Systeemwaarborgen voor de kernwaarden van de rechtspraak*, Research Memoranda Nr. 2, Jaargang 10, Raad voor de Rechtspraak, The Hague.

Van Den Heuvel, J.H.J. and Huberts, L.W.J.C. (2003) *Integriteitsbeleid van gemeenten*, Utrecht: Lemma.

Van Den Heuvel, J.H.J., Huberts, L.W.J.C., van der Wal, Z. and Steenbergen, K. (2010) *Integriteit van het lokaal bestuur: Raadsgriffiers en gemeentesecretarissen over integriteit*, The Hague: Boom Lemma Uitgevers.

Van Tankeren, M.H.M. (2010) *Het integriteitsbeleid van de Nederlandse politie: wat er is en wat ertoe doet*, Amsterdam: VU.

10

ETHICAL LEADERSHIP RESEARCH

Looking beyond the leader[1]

Leonie Heres

Introduction

Many organizations spend substantial portions of their budgets on developing and implementing values statements, codes of conduct, ethics training, and specialized ethics officers and integrity bureaus (e.g., Huberts *et al.* 2008; OECD 1996; Weaver *et al.* 1999). But even the best codes, policies, and training can only achieve so much. In fact, the long-term effects of such instruments may be negated or even become counterproductive if the organization's leaders do not support and reinforce it with ethical leadership.

An ever-growing body of research suggests ethical leadership is a key feature in building a strong ethical culture, and thereby preserving and strengthening the legitimacy, trust, and credibility needed for the governance of public institutions (e.g. Hassan *et al.* 2014; Lasthuizen 2008). In recent years, significant progress has been made in research on ethical leadership and its effects (see, for instance, Brown and Treviño 2006). Still, extant research does have an important caveat: it is predominantly leader-centered. Unlike studies on, for instance, servant or responsible leadership (Maak and Pless 2006; Sendjaya *et al.* 2008), those studying ethical leadership typically focus on a leader's characteristics and behavior and pay little attention to the role of stakeholders in the constitution and development of ethical leadership.

The apparent lack of attention to stakeholders is surprising when we consider that ethical leadership is by definition an ascribed and subjective phenomenon that exists only by virtue of the buy-in of such stakeholders (Bryman 1992). For one, it is the stakeholders that ultimately determine the 'relevant moral values and norms' that should guide the behavior of an ethical leader (cf. Heres 2014; Six *et al.* 2007). And without support from external stakeholders, leaders of public institutions may not be able to maintain their institutional integrity and legitimacy at all (Terry 2003).

Meanwhile, as internal stakeholders of ethical leadership, it is the followers who provide the terms and conditions for effective (ethical) leadership (Gini 2004; Hogg 2008). As a result, stakeholder perceptions of the leader's behavior, rather than the actual behavior of the leader, best predict the leader's influence on individual and organizational outcomes (Brown and Treviño 2006; Lord and Maher 1991; Moorman and Grover 2009). To advance our understanding of ethical leadership, we thus need to look beyond leaders and examine more in-depth the active and constitutive role of their internal and external stakeholders as well.

The aim of this chapter is to illustrate how a stakeholder-based perspective on organizational ethical leadership can further our understanding of what it means to be an ethical leader and how ethical leadership can help to effectively safeguard public values. To this end, the contemporary conceptualization of ethical leadership and where we currently stand with research in this field[2] are outlined. Next, the background and main results of a recent multi-study research project on follower expectations of ethical leadership are described (see Heres 2014). The chapter concludes with a discussion on the value and implications of broadening our scope from a leader-centered to a stakeholder-based perspective on ethical leadership.

Ethical leadership defined

Brown, Treviño and Harrison define ethical leadership as "the demonstration of normatively appropriate conduct through personal actions and interpersonal relationships, and the promotion of such conduct to followers through two-way communication, reinforcement, and decision-making" (Brown et al. 2005, p. 120). This definition suggests ethical leaders are not only moral persons, but moral managers as well (Treviño et al. 2000). While this definition is not without its limitations (see Heres 2014; Lawton and Páez 2014), it is undoubtedly the most widely adopted conceptualization to date.

As moral persons, ethical leaders are said to have strong moral character (Jurkiewicz 2006; Wright and Quick 2011) and a deeply held set of moral values (Storr 2004; Treviño et al. 2000; Van Wart 2005) that they uphold even in the face of significant external pressures or risks (Resick et al. 2011; Treviño et al. 2003; Yukl et al. 2013). Consistent with this, empirical studies associate ethical leadership with a multitude of moral traits and virtues such as integrity, trustworthiness, reliability, honesty, transparency, conscientiousness, and a concern for justice and fairness (e.g., Brown et al. 2005; Den Hartog and De Hoogh 2009; Frisch and Huppenbauer 2014; Yukl et al. 2013).

Ethical leaders furthermore recognize and reflect on the moral implications of their decisions and actions, the end goals they set, *and* the means they use to achieve these goals (Murphy and Enderle 1995; Treviño et al. 2003; Van Wart 2005). They look critically at an issue from multiple perspectives and take into consideration both the short- and long-term consequences that decisions have for all stakeholders (Dobel 1999; Frisch and Huppenbauer 2014; Resick et al. 2011). Indeed, ethical leaders' decisions and actions indicate an interest in others' well-being, as well as long-term sustainability and the broader common good (e.g., Eisenbeiss and Brodbeck 2014; Kalshoven *et al.* 2011; Treviño *et al.* 2003).

To advance organizational ethics, however, research suggests a more deliberate effort to foster ethical decisions and behavior of others is needed as well. First and foremost, such "moral management" includes the visible role modeling of ethical behavior (Brown *et al.* 2005). The behavior that followers observe in their leaders give strong moral cues (Cooper 2006; Menzel 2007) and set the ethical tone of an organization (Grojean *et al.* 2004; Treviño *et al.* 2003). In addition, ethical leaders reinforce ethical standards by holding others accountable for their moral conduct and applying rewards and discipline (Brown *et al.* 2005; Yukl *et al.* 2013). Reinforcement fulfills an important symbolic function as followers pay close attention to the behaviors that leaders reward and punish—even when they are not themselves involved (Cooper 2006; Lamboo *et al.* 2008; Treviño 1992).

Lastly, effective ethical leaders are said to engage followers in two-way communication about ethics and values (e.g., Brown *et al.* 2005; Kalshoven *et al.* 2011; Yukl *et al.* 2013). Through discussions, ethical leaders help clarify behavioral norms, expectations, and responsibilities (Kalshoven *et al.* 2011; Yukl *et al.* 2013). More importantly, the ethical leader also engages followers in an interactive dialogue that highlights the moral dimension of specific decisions and situations (De Hoogh and Den Hartog 2008), inspires followers to view issues from different perspectives, and motivates them to set their own interests aside for the sake of the greater good (Grojean *et al.* 2004; Resick *et al.* 2006).

Research developments and debates

Studies on ethical leadership found consistent support for the idea that ethical leaders play a critical role in reducing unethical behaviors such as fraud, theft, bullying, and misuse of organizational resources (e.g., Huberts *et al.* 2007; Lasthuizen 2008; Mayer *et al.* 2009). The extensive body of literature furthermore suggests many spillover effects of ethical leadership, both in terms of positive follower behavior and improved performance (e.g., Mayer *et al.* 2009; Toor and Ofori 2009; Walumbwa *et al.* 2011; Walumbwa *et al.* 2012)—although research on the latter is in its infancy (Lawton and Páez 2014).

In recent years, research seems to have shifted from "why does it matter?" to "how does it work?" (see also Lawton and Páez 2014). As such, scholars increasingly focus on identifying the *underlying mechanisms* at play (e.g., Avey *et al.* 2012; Kacmar *et al.* 2013), the *specific contingencies* of ethical leadership effectiveness (e.g., Avey *et al.* 2010; Kalshoven *et al.* 2013), and *antecedents* that help explain how ethical leaders develop (e.g., Brown and Treviño 2014; Jordan *et al.* 2013; Mayer *et al.* 2012).

In addition, scholars have begun to revisit the debate about the conceptualization and measurement of ethical leadership, raising various issues pertaining to: (1) the vagueness of the standards for "normatively appropriate behavior" that should guide an ethical leader's decisions and actions (cf. Eisenbeiss 2012; Frisch and Huppenbauer 2014; Giessner and Van Quaquebeke 2010; Tenbrunsel and Smith-Crowe 2008); (2) the need for a clear distinction between "normal," effective leadership and ethical leadership (see Kalshoven *et al.* 2011; Yukl *et al.* 2013); and (3) the dimensionality of the ethical leadership construct and its measures (Kalshoven *et al.* 2011; Yukl *et al.* 2013). Each of these issues has profound implications for our understanding of what it means to be an ethical leader and the way we study ethical leadership.

Ethical leadership from a stakeholder perspective: an empirical example

As indicated above, the literature on ethical leadership is predominantly leader-centered and typically neglects the role of stakeholders in the constitution and development of ethical leadership (see, however, Maak and Pless 2006; Resick *et al.* 2006; Resick *et al.* 2011; Van Den Akker *et al.* 2009). In its broadest sense, a stakeholder refers to "any group or individual who can affect or is affected by the achievement of the organization's objectives" (Freeman 1984, p. 46). An ethical leader should account for numerous stakeholders, including stakeholders both internal and external to the organization, proximal or distant, and individuals as well as groups, communities, organizations, institutions, societies, and even the natural environment and future generations (cf. Mitchell *et al.* 1997). As Mitchell *et al.* (1997) point out, identifying the most relevant among these stakeholders is a matter of assessing their power over the organization, as well as the legitimacy and urgency of their stake in the leader's decisions and actions.

Perhaps the most obvious and arguably also the most important stakeholders of the ethical leader are its (intended) followers. Given the leader's dependence on followers to achieve results and the leader's immediate effect on the lives of followers, followers' stake in the organization's ethical leadership is powerful, legitimate, and urgent indeed. Still, studies that examine ethical leadership from a follower perspective or critically examine the variance in follower perceptions of ethical leaders are scant (Brown and Mitchell 2010). While perceptions play an important role in whether or not an ethical leader is able to influence the behavior of its followers (Brown and Treviño 2006; Lord and Maher 1991; Moorman and Grover 2009), we thus know little about how and why followers differ in their interpretations of ethical leader behavior. In the words of Lord and Emrich (2000, p. 551): "if leadership, at least partly, resides in the minds of followers, then it is imperative to discover what followers are thinking."

To gain a better understanding of followers' perspectives on ethical leadership and of the variance in their perception of ethical leader behavior, a series of qualitative and quantitative studies on followers' own ideas about what ethical leadership should look like were conducted (see Heres 2014 for a more extensive overview of the research). First, using semi-structured interviews with 18 managers (Heres and Lasthuizen 2012) and a larger quasi-qualitative Q-method study among 59 working adults, all from a wide range of public- and private-sector organizations in the Netherlands, the similarities and differences in the assumptions, beliefs, and expectations of individuals towards ethical leadership were explored. Next, three cross-sectional survey studies among higher-educated working adults in the Netherlands (snowball sample, N = 355), members of the Netherlands Institute of Psychologists (N = 519), and employees of a large Dutch semi-public organization (N = 389) were conducted.

The results indicate that on a *general* level, followers' expectations of ethical leadership are rather similar and largely consistent with dominant academic conceptualizations. Supporting much of Brown *et al.*'s (2005) social learning perspective, nearly all respondents in both the qualitative and quantitative studies, for instance, considered personal integrity, role modeling ethical behavior, reinforcement of moral standards, and some form of communication about ethics to be key aspects of ethical leadership.

Ethical leadership as perceived by followers: five ideal-typical views

Yet, when we look more closely, respondents differed in the exact characteristics and behaviors that they expect of ethical leaders, and especially in how important they believe each of these characteristics and behaviors to be: while explicit, frequent, and value-based communication about ethics was very important to some, a substantial portion of the respondents believe it to be superfluous most of the time or at least do not consider it to be of particular importance.[3] And while some believed ethical leadership to revolve almost entirely around the person of the leader, others emphasized that ethical leadership was not possible without more proactive moral management. Synthesizing these results, the Q-study revealed five ideal-typical views on what followers believe ethical leadership should entail:

1   *The Safe Haven Creator:* an ethical leader is a leader who creates an environment in which there is room to make mistakes and followers feel safe to speak up if needed. The leader is open and honest about his or her decisions and actions, but explicit discussions about ethics and values are limited and ethical behavior is expected to be more or less self-evident.

2   *The Practicing Preacher:* an ethical leader is a leader who not only role models high ethical standards, but also engages in frequent two-way communication about ethics and dilemmas. The leader emphasizes values and principles over rules and procedures.

3   *The Moral Motivator:* an ethical leader is a charismatic leader who role models strong moral character, authenticity, self-reflection, and openness to criticism. The leader does not make ethics a priority within the organization, and leaves it up to followers to decide for themselves what is and what is not morally appropriate behavior.

4   *The Social Builder:* an ethical leader is a leader who emphasizes shared values and norms within the group and creates and maintains a good relationship

with followers. The leader always looks at situations from different perspectives, takes account of stakeholder and societal interests in decision-making, and shows moral courage, even if that comes at a cost to the organization.

5   *The Boundaries Setter:* an ethical leader is a leader who sets clear boundaries and rules to prevent unethical behavior, and maintains these boundaries in a strict but just way. The leader is loyal and fair to followers, but does not tolerate unethical behavior.

The survey data indicate that an individual's expectation of ethical leadership is typically a weighed mix of the five ideal-typical views mentioned above, although in most cases one or two of the views dominate. Across the three survey studies, the Safe Haven Creator was most widely endorsed, followed by the Practicing Preacher. Attributes described in the Moral Motivator and Social Builder view are somewhat less popular as the main focus of ethical leadership. However, the popularity of these views differed between the three samples, and their mean endorsement scores suggest that respondents did consider some of the attributes of the respective views as relevant "add-ons" to their preferred ethical leadership approach. The Boundaries Setter, finally, received considerably lower endorsement scores in all three samples and was the least endorsed view overall.

What do we take away from this? The apparent differences in follower expectations suggest that one particular set of ethical leadership characteristics and behaviors need not fit all. Indeed, subsequent analyses revealed that the variation in follower expectations of ethical leadership can be an important factor in the ethical leadership process. Consistent with research on leadership categorization theory (Lord and Maher 1991; Lord *et al.* 1984; Lord *et al.* 2001) and a previous study on expectations of ethical leadership (Van Den Akker *et al.* 2009), the quantitative research specifically suggested that followers' implicit assumptions, beliefs, and expectations act as a "lens" that shapes their perceptions of the characteristics and behaviors they observe in their leader: the more a leader's style of communication about ethics or reinforcement of norms deviated from what followers expect of ethical leadership, the less followers consider that leader to be an ethical leader. Sufficient alignment between follower expectations and leader practices is thus key to applying ethical leadership effectively. Moreover, this finding has important ramifications for how ethical leadership is measured.

Furthermore, the analyses showed that follower expectations of ethical leadership are at least in part related to the context in which they operate and the type of work that they do. For instance, the research indicated that task publicness (i.e., the extent to which followers' tasks are representative of public organizations, and as such impact the functioning of society) plays a role. Consistent with prior research by Heres and Lasthuizen (2012) and organizational publicness scholars (e.g., Bozeman 1987; Rainey and Bozeman 2000), followers with higher task publicness reported more frequent and more severe moral dilemmas. In other words, the publicness of the followers' tasks raises the moral task complexity that they experience. This in turn raises their expectations for ethical leadership: as evidenced by an increased endorsement of the Practicing Preacher and, to a lesser extent, the Social Builder, followers with higher moral task complexity expect a more proactive and explicit approach to ethical leadership than those whose work is less morally ambiguous. Meanwhile, followers' endorsement of the Safe Haven Creator, Moral Motivator, and Boundaries Setter remained consistent irrespective of both their demographic and structural work characteristics. This implies that when followers' moral task complexity increases, for instance due to the publicness of their work, it changes their expectations of ethical leadership, but only in the sense that they come to expect *additional* efforts on behalf of the leader.

In a similar vein, the study indicates that expectations of ethical leadership are related to the hierarchical level at which an individual operates. Similar to task publicness, one's hierarchical position raises the moral complexity of the tasks on hand and thereby one's ideas about what ethical leadership should entail. This result implies a more structural difference between leaders and followers in their understanding of ethical leadership. Importantly, leaders' own assumptions, beliefs, and expectations of ethical leadership are likely to form the basis for the behavior that they exhibit (Lord and Maher 1991), affect the quality of their relation with their followers (Engle and Lord 1997), and might also shape their expectations for their subordinates' ethical performance. As a result, they are also likely to have profound implications for our understanding of how and under which circumstances ethical leadership is more or less effective.

The value of stakeholder-based studies on ethical leadership

While the research discussed above focuses primarily on followers' perspectives on ethical leadership, many of its findings could apply to other stakeholders of the ethical leader as well. As such, the research highlights at least three important contributions that a stakeholder-based approach can make to current debates and developments in ethical leadership research. First, a stakeholder-based approach can shed light on a whole new set of previously ignored mechanisms, contingencies, and antecedents of ethical leadership. The aforementioned research example, for instance, identifies the discrepancies between follower expectations of ethical leadership as an important explanation of the variation in perceptions of ethical leadership. Similarly, a priori expectations of other stakeholders are likely to shape their interpretations of ethical leadership behavior. As such, the research points towards active management of and alignment with stakeholder expectations as a key factor in building a solid reputation for ethical leadership. Furthermore, given that differences in follower expectations are in part related to characteristics of their work, it provides an alternative or additional explanation for the varying effects of ethical leadership across different contexts (cf. Detert *et al.* 2007; Kacmar *et al.* 2013; Kalshoven *et al.* 2013): followers' work actually seems to shape their expectations of ethical leadership and could thereby make them either more or less responsive to the "textbook" approach. Finally, to the extent that leaders indeed take note of and anticipate stakeholders' needs and expectations for ethical leadership, a stakeholder-based approach can also help to explain variations in ethical leader behavior itself.

A second and perhaps more fundamental contribution of the stakeholder-based approach to ethical leadership research is its potential to advance and refine our ideas about how to conceptualize ethical leadership. For one, what constitutes the "normatively appropriate behavior" that ethical leaders should exhibit is ultimately determined by those who make up the social context in which a leader operates—stakeholders such as the leader's employees, suppliers, clients, the sector, and, ultimately, the (international) society at large (cf. Carroll and Buchholtz 2014; Six *et al.* 2007). Hence, from a stakeholder-based perspective, ethical leadership may be best conceived as a dynamic construct for which the moral standards vary by both time frame and entity (i.e., organization or group) under consideration (cf. Hunter 2012). As a consequence, while identifying a basic set of normative principles is crucial to giving more substantive meaning to "ethical leadership" (Eisenbeiss 2012; Giessner and Van Quaquebeke 2010; Tenbrunsel and Smith-Crowe 2008), a universalistic set of normative principles formulated by the academic community is unlikely to offer sufficient guidance to leaders in specific situations. Indeed, as Lawton and Paéz (2014, p. 7) note: "a discussion of the virtues cannot be separated from the context within which they are practiced [and] the exercise of different virtues will be appropriate to the different roles that leaders play." Hence, to define the ethics of ethical leadership it may be more useful to evaluate the moral standards that different groups of stakeholders set for leaders at a given point in time and examine how these standards are used in specific contexts to judge leader behavior.

As the data in the preceding section indicate, stakeholders hold specific and varying expectations not only of ethics and ethical behavior, but of ethical *leadership* as well. Stakeholder-based research can therefore also help to identify the distinctive characteristic necessary, and contributing attributes of the moral management side of ethical leadership. The FEEL model, derived from the results of the various studies on follower expectations of ethical leadership (Figure 10.1; see Heres 2014 for a more extensive discussion), for instance, suggests a baseline of minimum ethical leadership requirements that leaders should meet, regardless of their followers' personal characteristics or the structural characteristics of their work: when these baseline requirements are not met, the model suggests, leaders are less likely to build a strong reputation for ethical leadership. Contrary to dominant academic views on ethical leadership that emphasize communication about ethics or reinforcement (Brown *et al.* 2005), the FEEL model points out that followers first and foremost use aspects related to safety, approachability, learning from mistakes, and personal accountability to distinguish ethical leaders from ethically neutral leaders (Treviño *et al.* 2003). Furthermore, it implies that explicit and proactive discussions about ethics, values, and moral principles may be less relevant when followers' moral task complexity is low and their work is more straightforward.

In addition, the stakeholder-based perspective underscores the importance of both narrow *and* broad conceptualizations of ethical leadership to our understanding of what it means to be an ethical leader. As argued by Yukl *et al.* (2013), maintaining a clear conceptual and operational distinction between different leadership styles and associating the specific ethical leadership attributes with some sort of measure for ethical performance is essential to assessing its unique contribution to individual, group, and organizational ethics and effectiveness. At the same time, however, the results of the research outlined in this chapter indicate that practitioners themselves do not make such clear-cut distinctions. Stakeholders often have much broader definitions of the concept: some of the behaviors that respondents denoted as typical of ethical leaders (e.g., authenticity and charisma) are, for instance, excluded from most academic ethical leadership definitions

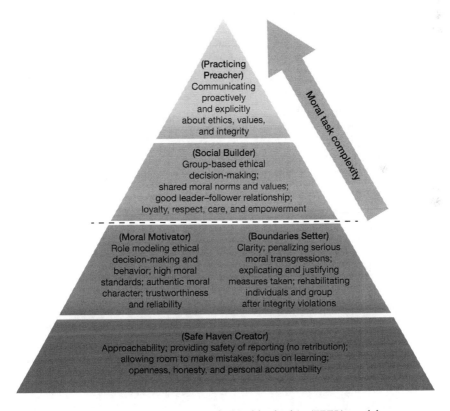

FIGURE 10.1 The follower expectations of ethical leadership (FEEL) model

Note: Attributes below the dashed line indicate the baseline expectations that followers typically have of ethical leadership, irrespective of their personal characteristics or characteristics of their work. The extent to which followers also expect attributes above the dashed line is more context-dependent and in part a function of the moral task complexity of their work.

Source: Reprinted with permission from Heres (2014).

(Brown and Treviño 2006; Yukl *et al.* 2013). Moreover, broader conceptualizations allow us to see that even though at a more general level ethical leadership has similar effects in public and private organizations (Hassan *et al.* 2013; Hassan *et al.* 2014), expectations and day-to-day practices of communication about ethics, values, and dilemmas may nevertheless differ across these sectors (Heres 2014; Heres and Lasthuizen 2012). The stakeholder perspective thus suggests that to gain a full understanding of what it means to be an ethical leader, we should take into account the variform universal nature of ethical leadership (cf. Bass 1997; Den Hartog *et al.* 1999; Heres and Lasthuizen 2012) and select either narrower or broader conceptualizations based on the aims of the research on hand.

A third contribution of the stakeholder-based approach is that it uncovers important methodological limitations *and* opportunities for the study of ethical leadership. First, as the research on follower expectations of ethical leadership indicates, perceptual measures of ethical leadership are prone to bias and capture not only the characteristics and behaviors of the leader, but the predispositions of the respondents (i.e., the stakeholders of ethical leaders) as well (see also Eden and Leviatan 1975; Engle and Lord 1997; Epitropaki and Martin 2005; Foti and Lord 1987; Nye and Forsyth 1991; Rush *et al.* 1977). Specifically, the results suggest that when filling out questionnaires, respondents in fact may be (partly) regenerating their implicit, a priori expectations of ethical leadership rather than critically reviewing a leader's actual behavior and traits (Rush and Russell 1988). Even more so, processes of pattern completion may be at play, in which respondents come to associate characteristics and behaviors with the leader that they did not actually observe, but which are prototypical of their ideas about what ethical leadership *should* look like (Lord and Emrich 2000; Shondrick *et al.* 2010).

This finding has important implications for the use and development of perceptual measures of ethical leadership—whether we are measuring perceptions of followers, or those of the leader's leader or constituents. Inclusion of more detailed, behavior-specific items seems especially necessary. Not only will this make perceptual measures less susceptible to bias (see Gioia and Sims 1985; Larson 1982), it also enables us to examine more in-depth the variation of ways in which managers exert ethical leadership in practice. Furthermore, the perceptual bias in ethical leadership measures argues in favor of more extensive, multidimensional measures as these will allow us to: (1) examine the relative effects of specific characteristics and behaviors on different sets of stakeholders and under varying circumstances; and (2) empirically explore the variation in the underlying measurement models and use such explorations to better understand how and why stakeholder perceptions of ethical leadership differ (Brown and Mitchell 2010).

Looking beyond the leader: an agenda for future research

The last 15 years have seen an enormous proliferation of theoretical and empirical research on ethical leadership. Yet, while progress in the field is impressive, much uncharted territory remains. Most notably, research has largely overlooked the fact that ethical leadership, like leadership in general, is an inherently relational construct that ultimately depends upon the buy-in of others (Bryman 1992). As argued in this chapter, research on the roles, expectations, and experiences of these "others"—the stakeholders of ethical leadership—can therefore have profound theoretical and practical implications for the further development of ethical leadership.

Focusing on the relational aspect of ethical leadership and examining the role of different groups of stakeholders of ethical leadership opens up many interesting avenues for further research. One such avenue for further research is to study the assumptions, beliefs, and expectations that the target leader's *own* leader has of ethical leadership. Indeed, the ethical leader's superiors are perhaps equally critical stakeholders as its followers are. The apparent variation in ethical leadership expectations and their association with one's hierarchical level (Heres 2014) suggests discrepancies between managers' own ideas about ethical leadership and those of their superiors are not unlikely. Moreover, research by Keller (2003) (see also Shondrick *et al.* 2010; Sy 2010) suggests managers' expectations may bias their perceptions of subordinates' behavior and performance. Expectations of ethical leadership may thus work both ways—upward and downward; research on the effects of higher management's expectations on evaluations of mid-level managers' ethical leadership and performance could thus add interesting contributions to the literature on both ethical leadership and performance more in general.

Likewise, it seems imperative to explicitly acknowledge the organization or the institution as a key stakeholder in the ethical leadership process: the mutual dependence between the leader and the organization as a whole, and the importance of ethical leadership to the reputation and perhaps even the very survival of the organization (Cooper 2001; Terry 2003; Worden 2003), makes the organization's stake in the ethical leader both legitimate and powerful. While no research to date has examined the organization's perspective on ethical leadership, organizational assumptions, beliefs, and expectations of ethical leadership are ingrained in many of the structural and cultural features of the organization: in its basic procedures, rules, and norms, in its ethics codes and its management development programs, but also in its performance and selection criteria (i.e., strategic HR practices) and how they are applied in practice. What expectations of ethical leadership do these structural and cultural features *really* convey, and how does this affect the ethical leadership that managers exhibit? And what happens when these expectations conflict with managers' own assumptions and beliefs about ethical leadership, or with those of its followers? Exploring questions such as these empirically may point towards antecedents of ethical leadership development, or potential moderators that further inform us about the conditional requirements for effective ethical leadership.

Finally, we should consider the role of external stakeholders as well. Ethical leadership in organizations never just takes place within the organization: it is always situated in a broader societal context that determines the most basic rules of the game. Whether it is the customers, suppliers, business partners, and shareholders in the private sector, or the clients, constituents, and politicians in the public sector, external stakeholders can have direct and tangible effects on how ethical leadership is understood and practiced. In the Netherlands and the UK, for example, societal demands for complete transparency on public managers' expense claims have led some leaders to engage in more proactive, frequent, and explicit communication about ethics in general and to discuss more openly their personal accountability. Similarly, the heated public debate about the appropriateness of both public and private managers' salaries seems to have raised expectations regarding ethical role modeling. Again, though, there is a dearth of empirical research that unravels, explains, substantiates, and nuances the role of external stakeholders on how ethical leadership is developed and perceived across contexts. To advance the field of ethical leadership, then, is to look beyond the ethical leader itself and explore the intricate interactions between the leader and its many stakeholders.

Notes

1   Sections of this chapter are based on Heres (2014).
2   For a more extensive review of the literature on ethical leadership, see Brown and Treviño (2006) and Heres (2014).
3   The precise endorsement of this aspect of ethical leadership differed across the various samples and studies. In the three quantitative studies, about 25–40 percent of the respondents scored items related to explicit and frequent communication about ethics and values as neutral (on a scale of 1 to 5 from not at all important to very important), while up to 20 percent considered it to be not important (at all). Moreover, across the three samples, 30–60 percent of the respondents indicated that it was (very) important that the leader does not talk about ethics too much.

References

Avey, J.B., Palanski, M.E., and Walumbwa, F.O. (2010) "When leadership goes unnoticed: The moderating role of follower self-esteem on the relationship between ethical leadership and follower behavior," *Journal of Business Ethics*, 98(4): 573–582.

Avey, J.B., Wernsing, T.S., and Palanski, M.E. (2012) "Exploring the process of ethical leadership: The mediating role of employee voice and psychological ownership," *Journal of Business Ethics*, 107(1): 21–34.

Bass, B.M. (1997) "Does the transactional-transformational leadership paradigm transcend organizational and national boundaries?" *American Psychologist*, 52(2): 130–139.

Bozeman, B. (1987) *All Organizations Are Public: Bridging Public and Private Organizational Theories*, Frederick, MD: Beard Books.

Brown, M.E. and Mitchell, M.S. (2010) "Ethical and unethical leadership: Exploring new avenues for future research," *Business Ethics Quarterly*, 20(4): 583–616.

Brown, M.E. and Treviño, L.K. (2006) "Ethical leadership: A review and future directions," *The Leadership Quarterly*, 17(6): 595–616.

Brown, M.E. and Treviño, L.K. (2014) "Do role models matter? An investigation of role modeling as an antecedent of perceived ethical leadership," *Journal of Business Ethics*, 122(4): 587–598.

Brown, M.E., Treviño, L.K., and Harrison, D.A. (2005) "Ethical leadership: A social learning perspective for construct development and testing," *Organizational Behavior and Human Decision Processes*, 97(2): 117–134.

Bryman, A. (1992) *Charisma and Leadership in Organizations*, London: Sage.

Carroll, A. and Buchholtz, A. (2014) *Business and Society: Ethics, Sustainability, and Stakeholder Management*, Melbourne: Cengage Learning.

Cooper, T.L. (Ed.) (2001) *Handbook of Administrative Ethics* (2nd ed.), New York: Marcel Dekker.

Cooper, T.L. (2006) *The Responsible Administrator: An Approach to Ethics for the Administrative Role* (5th ed.), San Francisco, CA: Jossey-Bass.

De Hoogh, A.H.B. and Den Hartog, D.N. (2008) "Ethical and despotic leadership, relationships with leader's social responsibility, top management team effectiveness and subordinates' optimism: A multi-method study," *The Leadership Quarterly*, 19(3): 297–311.

Den Hartog, D.N. and De Hoogh, A.H.B. (2009) "Empowering behaviour and leader fairness and integrity: Studying perceptions of ethical leader behaviour from a levels-of-analysis perspective," *European Journal of Work and Organizational Psychology*, 18(2): 199–230.

Den Hartog, D.N., House, R.J., Hanges, P.J., and Ruiz-Quintanilla, S.A. (1999) "Culture specific and cross-culturally generalizable implicit leadership theories: Are attributes of charismatic/transformational leadership universally endorsed?" *The Leadership Quarterly*, 10(2): 219–256.

Detert, J.R., Treviño, L.K., Burris, E.R., and Andiappan, M. (2007) "Managerial modes of influence and counterproductivity in organizations: A longitudinal business-unit-level investigation," *Journal of Applied Psychology*, 92(4): 993–1005.

Dobel, J.P. (1999) *Public Integrity*, Baltimore, MD, & London: Johns Hopkins University Press.

Eden, D. and Leviatan, U. (1975) "Implicit leadership theory as a determinant of factor structure underlying supervisory behavior scales," *Journal of Applied Psychology*, 60(6): 736–741.

Eisenbeiss, S.A. (2012) "Re-thinking ethical leadership: An interdisciplinary integrative approach," *The Leadership Quarterly*, 23(5): 791–808.

Eisenbeiss, S.A. and Brodbeck, F. (2014) "Ethical and unethical leadership: A cross-cultural and cross-sectoral analysis," *Journal of Business Ethics*, 122(2): 343–359.

Engle, E.M. and Lord, R.G. (1997) "Implicit theories, self-schemas, and leader-member exchange," *Academy of Management Journal*, 40(4): 988–1010.

Epitropaki, O. and Martin, R. (2005) "From ideal to real: A longitudinal study of the role of implicit leadership theories on leader-member exchanges and employee outcomes," *Journal of Applied Psychology*, 90(4): 659–676.

Foti, R.J. and Lord, R.G. (1987) "Prototypes and scripts: The effects of alternative methods of processing information on rating accuracy," *Organizational Behavior and Human Decision Processes*, 39(3): 318–340.

Freeman, R.E. (1984) *Strategic Management: A Stakeholder Approach*, Boston, MA: Pitman.

Frisch, C. and Huppenbauer, M. (2014) "New insights into ethical leadership: A qualitative investigation of the experiences of executive ethical leaders," *Journal of Business Ethics*, 23(1): 23–43.

Giessner, S. and Van Quaquebeke, N. (2010) "Using a relational models perspective to understand normatively appropriate conduct in ethical leadership," *Journal of Business Ethics*, 95(1): 43–55.

Gini, A. (2004) "Moral leadership and business ethics," in J.B. Ciulla (Ed.), *Ethics, The Heart of Leadership* (pp. 25–43), Westport, CT: Praeger.

Gioia, D.A. and Sims, H.P. (1985) "On avoiding the influence of implicit leadership theories in leader behavior descriptions," *Educational and Psychological Measurement*, 45(2): 217–243.

Grojean, M., Resick, C., Dickson, M., and Smith, D. (2004) "Leaders, values, and organizational climate: Examining leadership strategies for establishing an organizational climate regarding ethics," *Journal of Business Ethics*, 55(3): 223–241.

Hassan, S., Wright, B.E., and Yukl, G. (2014) "Does ethical leadership matter in government? Effects on organizational commitment, absenteeism, and willingness to report ethical problems," *Public Administration Review*, 74(3): 333–343.

Hassan, S., Mahsud, R., Yukl, G., and Prussia, G.E. (2013) "Ethical and empowering leadership and leader effectiveness," *Journal of Managerial Psychology*, 28(1–2): 133–146.

Heres, L. (2014) *One Style Fits All? The Content, Origins, and Effect of Follower Expectations of Ethical Leadership*, Amsterdam: VU University.

Heres, L. and Lasthuizen, K. (2012) "What's the difference? Ethical leadership in public, hybrid, and private organisations," *Journal of Change Management*, 12(4): 441–466.

Hogg, M.A. (2008) "Social identity processes and the empowerment of followers," in R.E. Riggio, I. Chaleff, and J. Lipman-Blumen (Eds.), *The Art of Followership* (pp. 267–276), San Francsico, CA: Jossey-Bass.

Huberts, L.W.J.C., Anechiarico, F. and Six, F.E. (Eds.) (2008) *Local Integrity Systems: World Cities Fighting Corruption and Safeguarding Integrity*, The Hague: BJu Legal Publishers.

Huberts, L.W.J.C., Kaptein, M., and Lasthuizen, K. (2007) "A study of the impact of three leadership styles on integrity violations committed by police officers," *Policing. An International Journal of Police Strategies & Management*, 30(4): 587–607.

Hunter, S. (2012) "(Un)ethical leadership and identity: What did we learn and where do we go from here?" *Journal of Business Ethics*, 107(1): 79–87.

Jordan, J., Brown, M.E., Treviño, L.K., and Finkelstein, S. (2013) "Someone to look up to: Executive–follower ethical reasoning and perceptions of ethical leadership," *Journal of Management*, 39(3): 660–683.

Jurkiewicz, C.L. (2006) "Soul food: Morrison and the transformative power of ethical leadership in the public sector," *Public Integrity*, 8(3): 245–256.

Kacmar, K.M., Andrews, M.C., Harris, K.J., and Tepper, B.J. (2013) "Ethical leadership and subordinate outcomes: The mediating role of organizational politics and the moderating role of political skill," *Journal of Business Ethics*, 115(1): 33–44.

Kalshoven, K., Den Hartog, D.N., and De Hoogh, A.H.B. (2011) "Ethical leadership at work questionnaire (ELW): Development and validation of a multidimensional measure," *The Leadership Quarterly*, 22(1): 51–69.

Kalshoven, K., Den Hartog, D.N., and De Hoogh, A.H.B. (2013) "Ethical leadership and followers' helping and initiative: The role of demonstrated responsibility and job autonomy," *European Journal of Work and Organizational Psychology*, 22(2): 165–181.

Keller, T. (2003) "Parental images as a guide to leadership sensemaking: An attachment perspective on implicit leadership theories," *The Leadership Quarterly* 14(2): 141–160.

Lamboo, M.E.D., Lasthuizen, K., and Huberts, L.W.J.C. (2008) "How to encourage ethical behavior: The impact of police leadership on police officers taking gratuities," in L.W.J.C. Huberts, C.L. Jurkiewicz, and J. Maesschalck (Eds.), *Ethics and Integrity of Governance: Perspectives across Frontiers* (pp. 159–177), Cheltenham: Edward Elgar.

Larson, J.R. (1982) "Cognitive mechanisms mediating the impact of implicit theories of leader behavior on leader behavior ratings," *Organizational Behavior and Human Performance*, 29(1): 129–140.

Lasthuizen, K.M. (2008) *Leading to Integrity: Empirical Research into the Effects of Leadership on Ethics and Integrity*, Enschede: Printpartners Ipskamp, available at: www.lasthuizen.com.

Lawton, A. and Páez, I. (2014) "Developing a framework for ethical leadership," *Journal of Business Ethics*: 1–11, doi: 10.1007/s10551-014-2244-2.

Lord, R.G. and Emrich, C.G. (2000) "Thinking outside the box by looking inside the box: Extending the cognitive revolution in leadership research," *The Leadership Quarterly*, 11(4): 551–579.

Lord, R.G. and Maher, K.J. (1991) *Leadership and Information Processing*, London: Routledge.

Lord, R.G., Foti, R.J., and De Vader, C.L. (1984) "A test of leadership categorization theory: Internal structure, information processing, and leadership perceptions," *Organizational Behavior and Human Performance*, 34(3): 343–378.

Lord, R.G., Brown, D.J., Harvey, J.L., and Hall, R.J. (2001) "Contextual constraints on prototype generation and their multilevel consequences for leadership perceptions," *The Leadership Quarterly*, 12(3): 311–338.

Maak, T. and Pless, N.M. (2006) "Responsible leadership in a stakeholder society: A relational perspective," *Journal of Business Ethics*, 66(1): 99–115.

Mayer, D.M., Aquino, K., Greenbaum, R.L., and Kuenzi, M. (2012) "Who displays ethical leadership, and why does it matter? An examination of antecedents and consequences of ethical leadership," *Academy of Management Journal*, 55(1): 151–171.

Mayer, D.M., Kuenzi, M., Greenbaum, R., Bardes, M., and Salvador, R. (2009) "How low does ethical leadership flow? Test of a trickle-down model," *Organizational Behavior and Human Decision Processes*, 108(1): 1–13.

Menzel, D.C. (2007) *Ethics Management for Public Administrators. Building Organizations of Integrity*, Armonk, NY, & London: M.E. Sharpe.

Mitchell, R.K., Agle, B.R., and Wood, D.J. (1997) "Toward a theory of stakeholder identification and salience: Defining the principle of who and what really counts," *The Academy of Management Review*, 22(4): 853–886.

Moorman, R.H. and Grover, S. (2009) "Why does leader integrity matter to followers? An uncertainty management-based explanation," *International Journal of Leadership Studies*, 5(2): 102–114.

Murphy, P.E. and Enderle, G. (1995) "Managerial ethical leadership: Examples do matter," *Business Ethics Quarterly*, 5(1): 117–128.

Nye, J.L. and Forsyth, D.R. (1991) "The effects of prototype-based biases on leadership appraisals: A test of leadership categorization theory," *Small Group Research*, 22(3): 360–379.

OECD (1996) *Ethics in the Public Service: Current Issues and Practice*, available at: www.oecd.org/dataoecd/59/24/1898992.pdf.

Rainey, H.G. and Bozeman, B (2000) "Comparing public and private organizations: Empirical research and the power of the a priori," *Journal of Public Administration Research and Theory*, 10(2): 447–470.

Resick, C.J., Hanges, P.J., Dickson, M.W., and Mitchelson, J.K. (2006) "A cross-cultural examination of the endorsement of ethical leadership," *Journal of Business Ethics*, 63(4): 345–359.

Resick, C.J., Martin, G.S., Keating, M.A., Dickson, M.W., Kwan, H.K., and Peng, C. (2011) "What ethical leadership means to me: Asian, American, and European perspectives," *Journal of Business Ethics*, 101(3): 435–457.

Rush, M.C. and Russell, J.E. (1988) "Leader prototypes and prototype-contingent consensus in leader behavior descriptions," *Journal of Experimental Social Psychology*, 24(1): 88–104.

Rush, M.C., Thomas, J.C., and Lord, R.G. (1977) "Implicit leadership theory: A potential threat to the validity of leader behavior questionnaires," *Organizational Behavior and Human Performance*, 20(1): 93–110.

Sendjaya, S., Sarros, J.C., and Santora, J.C. (2008) "Defining and measuring servant leadership behaviour in organizations," *Journal of Management Studies*, 45(2): 402–424.

Shondrick, S.J., Dinh, J.E., and Lord, R.G. (2010) "Developments in implicit leadership theory and cognitive science: Applications to improving measurement and understanding alternatives to hierarchical leadership," *The Leadership Quarterly*, 21(6): 959–978.

Six, F.E., Bakker, F.G.A., and Huberts, L.W.J.C. (2007) "Judging a corporate leader's integrity: An illustrated three-component model," *European Management Journal*, 25(3): 185–194.

Storr, L. (2004) "Leading with integrity: A qualitative research study," *Journal of Health Organization and Management*, 18(6): 415–434.

Sy, T. (2010) "What do you think of followers? Examining the content, structure, and consequences of implicit followership theories," *Organizational Behavior and Human Decision Processes*, 113(2): 73–84.

Tenbrunsel, A.E. and Smith-Crowe, K. (2008) "Ethical decision making: Where we've been and where we're going," *The Academy of Management Annals*, 2(1): 545–607.

Terry, L.D. (2003) *Leadership of Public Bureaucracies: The Administrator as Conservator* (2nd ed.), Armonk, NY, & London: M.E. Sharpe.

Toor, S.U.R. and Ofori, G. (2009) "Ethical leadership: Examining the relationships with full range leadership model, employee outcomes, and organizational culture," *Journal of Business Ethics*, 90(4): 533–547.

Treviño, L.K. (1992) "The social effects of punishment in organizations: A justice perspective," *Academy of Management Review*, 17(4): 647–676.

Treviño, L.K., Brown, M.E., and Hartman, L.P. (2003) "A qualitative investigation of perceived executive ethical leadership: Perceptions from inside and outside the executive suite," *Human Relations*, 56(1): 5–37.

Treviño, L.K., Hartman, L.P., and Brown, M.E. (2000) "Moral person and moral manager: How executives develop a reputation for ethical leadership," *California Management Review*, 42(4): 128–142.

Van Den Akker, L., Heres, L., Lasthuizen, K., and Six, F.E. (2009) "Ethical leadership and trust: It's all about meeting expectations," *International Journal of Leadership and Organizational Studies*, 5(2): 102–122.

Van Wart, M. (2005) *Dynamics of Leadership in Public Service. Theory and Practice*, Armonk, NY, & London: M.E. Sharpe.

Walumbwa, F.O., Mayer, D.M., Wang, P., Wang, H., Workman, K., and Christensen, A.L. (2011) "Linking ethical leadership to employee performance: The roles of leader-member exchange, self-efficacy, and organizational identification," *Organizational Behavior and Human Decision Processes*, 115(2): 204–213.

Walumbwa, F.O., Morrison, E.W., and Christensen, A.L. (2012) "Ethical leadership and group in-role performance: The mediating roles of group conscientiousness and group voice," *The Leadership Quarterly*, 23(5): 953–964.

Weaver, G.R., Treviño, L.K., and Cochran, P.L. (1999) "Corporate ethics practices in the mid-1990's: An empirical study of the Fortune 1000," *Journal of Business Ethics*, 18(3): 283–294.

Worden, S. (2003) "The role of integrity as a mediator in strategic leadership: A recipe for reputational capital," *Journal of Business Ethics*, 46(1): 31–44.

Wright, T.A. and Quick, J.C. (2011) "The role of character in ethical leadership research," *The Leadership Quarterly*, 22(5): 975–978.

Yukl, G., Mahsud, R., Hassan, S., and Prussia, G.E. (2013) "An improved measure of ethical leadership," *Journal of Leadership and Organizational Studies*, 20(1): 38–48.

11

THE LIMITS OF RULE GOVERNANCE

Paul M. Heywood and Jonathan Rose

Introduction

We are now approaching a point where corruption is seen as universally harmful. Old arguments about potential economic efficiencies resulting from corrupt acts have given way, in the face of new empirical and theoretical evidence, to an understanding that corruption is a burden on societies (see Rothstein 2011, Ch. 10). Corruption, or citizens' perceptions thereof, damages social trust (Rose 2014, pp. 65–7), reduces the ability of governments to deliver infrastructure (Golden and Picci 2005), damages citizens' health (Rothstein 2011, pp. 58–60; Vian 2008), and undermines the rational basis for tax paying (Rothstein 2000). Given such severe consequences, it is perhaps unsurprising that reducing corruption has become an important objective for governments, international institutions, third-sector agencies, and civil society more generally.

The regulation of corruption in public administration is often, and arguably increasingly, managed through formal rules, laws and codes (Evans 2012, p. 104). These formalized codes aim to ensure compliance with a minimum standard of integrity; they delineate the situations in which certain actions are prohibited, and regulate the processes by which non-prohibited actions ought to be conducted. This approach is based upon the fundamental logic that such rules can be used to create an environment in which corruption cannot occur, since they remove the space for corrupt acts. However, despite increasing efforts to prevent corruption, the task of reducing the level of corruption has seen only modest successes. Indeed, Heywood and Rose (2014, pp. 8–9) show that the average country score on Transparency International's Corruption Perceptions Index (CPI) has barely changed in a period of over a decade since the turn of the century; the same is true of the World Bank's Control of Corruption Index. If these results are not purely statistical artefacts caused by poor methodological choices, they are strongly indicative of a world in which corruption is not being addressed adequately.

Such findings pose a challenge to our understanding of the solution to the problem of corruption. Corruption – or, at any rate, the perception of corruption – is essentially as bad as it was over a decade ago despite a huge investment in regulations and codes (Evans 2012), along with an increasing focus on managerialist techniques to monitor and assess performance in the public sector (Kirkpatrick *et al.* 2005). On the standard assumptions of many policymakers, these innovations ought to have reduced the rate of corruption; it is a particularly troubling finding that, so far as we can tell, they are not working.

If corruption control is failing, the question that follows is why, and how can we begin to address such failures? This question is multifaceted, and speaks to a great variety of substantive topics within the debate about corruption. In this chapter, we focus upon the use (and abuse) of formal, compliance-based rules as a response to corruption. In particular, we question whether such formalized codes are capable of ensuring *high* standards of integrity, rather than functioning solely as a way to minimize corruption. We begin by contextualizing the discussion in terms of the important, but underappreciated, distinctions between anti-corruption approaches and pro-integrity approaches to public-sector regulation. It is argued that each of these conceptualizations of the ends of ethics speak to different conceptualizations of how ethics ought to be managed. This is discussed in light of the values-based and compliance-based traditions of ethical regulation, their underlying logics, and their implementation. We problematize the oft-chosen compliance-based approach to regulation by asking whether such policies are creating a malformed system of incentives, which in turn can unwittingly undermine integrity in practice. Finally, we present empirical data drawn from a survey of high-ranking civil servants in the UK, suggesting both an appetite for greater values-based policies, as well as their perceived utility.

The conclusion of this chapter is that formalized rules are at best a partial and imperfect mechanism through which to promote integrity within public life. While we would certainly not advocate the removal of such rules altogether, securing integrity through the enforcement of rules ought to be a last resort, rather than the primary tool.

The ends of public ethics: pro-integrity or anti-corruption?

The 'goal' of public ethics may seem obvious – to enforce ethical behaviour in the public sector. However, the meaning of 'ethical behaviour' is far less obvious than it might at first appear. To take one example, does ethical behaviour exist when there is no corruption, or does it require more than simply the absence of active malevolence? To phrase the question another way, do public ethics require non-corruption or public integrity? While it is true that the inverse of integrity is corruption, and so there is a temptation to see both corruption and integrity as two poles on the same continuum, it is far from apparent that the opposite of corruption is integrity (Rose and Heywood 2013, p. 151). Indeed, corruption and integrity can be very different concepts in practice, differing in both their scope and their application. To see why this is the case, consider the differing concepts of corruption and integrity.

The conceptualization of 'corruption' has not been an easy task. Despite centuries of effort, there remains no single definition of corruption that is accepted by all or most researchers or practitioners. However, some agreement has been reached about some of the core elements of 'corruption', as Philp (2006, p. 45) notes:

> There is some consensus in the literature that we have a case of corruption when: A public official (A), acting for personal gain, violates the norms of public office and harms the interests of the public (B) to benefit a third party (C) who rewards A for access to goods or services which C would not otherwise obtain.

This definition captures much of what we mean when we talk of corruption, although it has an exclusive focus upon the public sector. Indeed, on this definition, it is impossible for corruption to occur outside of public life, in turn denying the ability to classify clearly unethical business practices as corrupt. Especially given what we now know about unethical business practices in the financial sector, and the dramatic consequences of such behaviour, this may seem like a particularly glaring omission. This exclusive focus in turn follows a tradition dating back at least as far as Nye's influential definition of corruption as 'behavior which deviates from the formal duties of a public role because of private-regarding (personal, close family, private clique) pecuniary or status gains; or violates rules against the exercise of certain types of private-regarding influence' (1967, p. 419). Nonetheless, where the focus is upon *political* corruption explicitly, many currently used definitions of corruption can be subsumed under this conceptualization. Indeed, almost any action that is classed as (politically) corrupt using Transparency International's widely adopted definition, 'the abuse of entrusted power for private gain' (Transparency International 2011) will similarly be classed as corrupt by this definition.

Two features of Philp's three-part conceptualization of corruption are particularly important for the present discussion: (1) that corruption exists only in specific behaviours. Corrupt acts are therefore *acts* in the strong sense, in that they require some positive action, or an active choice of inaction. Corruption is not merely laziness, or recklessness, or incompetence; instead, it is the active choice to cause harm in exchange for a benefit of some kind. (2) That the absence of corruption – the state in which 'a public official (A), *not* acting for personal gain, does *not* violate the norms of public office or harm the interests of the public (B) to benefit a third party (C)' – does not necessarily represent a state of high integrity. Indeed, this non-corrupt state could be defined as minimally moral, in the sense that it represents the absolute minimum standard to which we should hold public officials.

Conceptual evaluations of integrity are far less common than those dealing with corruption. Nonetheless, some features of integrity are common to most definitions. Integrity is far less focused on specific acts, and instead is more concerned with the overall *approach* to governance. Of course, integrity is indeed about not being corrupt and not violating the law. However, more importantly, integrity is about going *beyond* such minimal morality. Integrity is about being open and fair in the process of governance, and about citizens being treated impartially by the state (Agnafors 2013; Rothstein 2011, p. 443; Rose 2014; Tyler 1994, 2000). What count as 'fair' processes, or 'impartial' treatment, are in turn difficult questions. However, there seems to be some consensus that processes are fair when they are open to participation and open about the criteria used in decision-making (see Rose 2014, pp. 10–11; Tyler 2000). Impartiality is usually understood in terms of disregarding personal factors about citizens when administering government services, except to the extent that such considerations are mandated by law (see Rothstein 2011).

In short, integrity is far more concerned with a reflexive self-conscious approach to ethics. This obviously moves integrity a significant distance away from the 'minimally moral' state delineated by a strict anti-corruption approach. Integrity is not merely about adhering to mandated codes at specific moments; it is an ever-present duty to consider the interests of and rights of citizens, and the pursuit of ethical governance in support of those interests and rights. In turn, this shows two important features of integrity that differ substantially from the conceptualization of corruption discussed above: (1) integrity is not only about specific behaviours. Although it is a requirement of integrity for any specific acts to be non-corrupt, integrity does not require 'acts', per se. (2) A state with integrity represents a state of 'thick' morality (Agnafors 2013, pp. 437–8), and as such necessarily implies non-corruption. Of course, the practicalities of governance, along with the requirements for thousands of individual people to work within government institutions, means that it is impossible to reach such an idealized 'integrity' state, in much the same way that even in very corrupt countries not all public officials are corrupt all the time.

The dissimilarities between corruption and integrity, and the fact that an absence of corruption does not guarantee the presence of integrity, are of practical significance. Indeed, this suggests that real-world regulation of behaviour via prescriptive rules alone will not guarantee integrity, since such regulation can potentially prevent corrupt actions, but likely cannot guarantee any personal commitment to ethics. Despite this, anti-corruption policies (rather than pro-integrity policies) are still the most favoured political vehicle for regulatory change. In practice, this is usually manifested in a choice of compliance-based regulation over values-based regulation.

The two worlds of public service ethics: values and compliance

The practical regulation of public-sector ethics has often been conceptualized in terms of two traditions: a values-based approach to regulation, and a compliance-based approach to regulation (Bies 2014; Maesschalck 2004; Paine 1994; Roberts 2009; Scott and Leung 2012). Each of these two traditions places a different emphasis upon the regulation of integrity: in the case of the values-based tradition, an emphasis is placed upon the personal values of public servants, whereas compliance-based approaches focus on direct and specific regulation of behaviour. Not only do these approaches have a different fundamental logic; they are also enacted differently, and have very different strengths and weaknesses in their practical effects.

The compliance-based tradition

The compliance-based tradition places the emphasis for ethical regulation upon formalized rules, codes and the law. Compliance-based regulations seek to delineate exactly what can and cannot be done by public servants, and the procedures that must be followed when conducting such actions. There is often an emphasis upon detecting and punishing violations of the rules (Paine 1994, p. 106), something that serves both to deter potential violations in future as well as normative ends. Moreover, under the compliance tradition, it is thought that if a sufficient system of (formal) regulations can be developed, corruption will become very difficult, since there is little 'space' for corrupt acts to occur. Personal discretion is therefore seen as a threat to the integrity of the institution, as it provides such 'space' for corrupt acts (Scott and Leung 2012, p. 40). The caution with which discretion is treated under the compliance tradition is well founded. Indeed, Langseth *et al.* (1997, p. 3), writing at the beginning of the important and significant *National Integrity System* project, argue that discretionary power is a necessary condition of corruption. Of course, as Langseth *et al.* also acknowledge (1997, pp. 12–13), it is neither practical nor possible to completely eliminate discretion. Langseth *et al.* recommend addressing this problem by either creating rival sources of power within bureaucracies, such that citizens could seek to interact with a wider pool of officials in the hope that some of them are not corrupt, or – preferably – by 'keeping the areas for discretion narrowly defined and by providing clear, public guidelines for the exercise of this discretion' (1997, p. 13). The latter suggestion, in particular, closely follows the compliance-based tradition.

To see the underlying logic of the compliance tradition, consider public ethics under the (impossible) condition of perfect compliance-based rules. Perfect rules optimally delineate between acceptable and unacceptable actions, and they provide a comprehensive set of processes under which those actions should be performed; discretion is not needed, as the rules already reflect the best (however defined) approach in every situation. In effect, anti-corruption reaches its zenith, and corruption falls to maximally low levels. Under this system, there is no need to trust any employee, since the actions of the most malicious and corrupt official will be indistinguishable from those of a perfectly ethical one (see also Bies 2014, p. 231; Lewicki *et al.* 1998, pp. 446–7; Tyler 2014, pp. 273–4). In place of trust, which simultaneously supposes a vulnerability to harm (Levi and Stoker 2000, p. 476), the regulations seek to provide certainty and regularity. A (greater) regularity of outcomes exists even for real-world, non-perfect, compliance-regulation, and is in turn one of the key advantages of compliance-based systems (Scott and Leung 2012, p. 40).

However, in ensuring regularity of outcomes, such systems also strip integrity from the discourse of public ethics (see Paine 1994, p. 106; Roberts 2009). The ends of public ethics thus become the adherence to the rules. As was noted above, this approach is good at ensuring non-corruption, at least when functioning adequately, but poor at ensuring integrity. This is particularly a problem in times of societal change, where challenging ethical situations emerge faster than regulations can be adapted, thereby providing both the opportunity and the means for unethical behaviour (Pendse 2012). Moreover, it is poorly suited to addressing the increasing fragmentation of public service delivery as agencification, contracting out and public–private partnerships have blurred traditional demarcations and lines of accountability. In a situation in which those responsible for public service have not been inculcated with integrity values, it becomes almost impossible to ensure a consistently ethical response. However, research on the economics of incentives suggests that compliance-based systems may face serious problems even outside of such changes.

Compliance-based systems work with the idea of incentives. As we have seen, people can be expected to adhere to the rules within a compliance-based system regardless of their fundamental nature; the rules seek to abstract away the need for notions such as trust by effectively creating a system of incentives such that compliance is (usually) the optimal choice. Unfortunately, once the need for ethics has been abstracted away, the reliance upon the incentive system becomes problematic. It has been well demonstrated that incentive schemes are difficult to design, and even punitive incentive schemes can be problematic. Indeed, a punishment is merely another factor to include in any decision calculus. Outside of a moral relationship, the refrain is merely that 'a fine is a price' (Gneezy and Rustichini 2000); if in any circumstance the personal costs of action under the condition of being punished are less than the returns from that action, carrying out the action makes sense (see also Braithwaite and Makkai 1991; Tyler 2014, pp. 270–1). Moreover, even where the individual costs of punishment are greater than the potential reward from a single corrupt act, a non-risk-averse actor will still engage in corruption whenever their subjective assessment of the probability of being caught is such that, on average, they gain by engaging in corruption (on the effect of punishment severity, see Goel and Rich 1989, p. 273). This is a serious weakness, one that potentially allows corruption to gain a foothold in the public service. Indeed, such an approach leads to an unsustainable 'arms race' between potentially corrupt officials, along with their potential corruptors, and regulators, which is clearly unsustainable in the long term. Moreover, precisely because this approach undermines trust in public servants, it also has the potential to undermine public servants' trust in their management systems (Tyler 2014, p. 273).

With such seemingly negative consequences, it might be questioned why compliance systems have proved so popular. The reason for their popularity, however, depends on at least three factors, none of which is particularly relevant to the goal of increasing organizational integrity. First, while compliance measures can be both expensive and time-consuming to administer (Scott and Leung 2012, p. 40), they are relatively easy to implement, and their existence is unambiguous. These factors make compliance-based policies an especially useful response for policymakers to individual ethical breaches, as they provide an easy way to satisfy the public's desire that 'something must be done'. Second, such measures can provide legal protection for senior managers, effectively offering a form of indemnity for those in charge (see Paine 1994). While this rationale is stronger for private companies, that lack any immunity connected to being part of a state, the effect is still notable even in the public sector. Indeed, managers and state officials may still bear some liability, either personally or through the administration as a whole, in the absence of such regulations. Moreover, the push towards such regulation in the private sector will have consequential effects both through the general development of managerial norms, which can function across sectors, and through societal expectations of the appropriate form of regulation. The public begin to question why, if compliance regulations are effectively a legal requirement for private business, they are not required for public-sector organizations. Finally, compliance-based methods are a good way to fight corruption because they have an act-focused approach. As was discussed above, this makes compliance-based policies a poor way to promote integrity, but this is rarely conceptualized as problematic in public discourse. Indeed, numerous organizations – not least Transparency International and the World Bank – have taken the fight against corruption as a substantive end in its own right. This shifts the emphasis away from integrity-enhancing policies towards compliance policies, because the latter are seen as particularly useful for fighting corruption.

The values-based tradition

The values-based tradition places an emphasis upon the individual public servant making ethical choices in his or her work. Public servants are conceptualized as reflexive evaluators of the ethical situation in which they find themselves, and are expected to 'have a moral code that enables them to determine appropriate courses of action within the norms and values prescribed by their organizations' (Scott and Leung 2012, p. 39). Thus, a values-based system has a sizeable role for personal discretion, although it is often expected that this discretion will be utilized in conjunction with discussions with management and colleagues (Blijswijk *et al.* 2004). The individual's moral code is expected to operate in conjunction with the law, but the moral code will provide contextualizing information that allows the public servant not only to adhere to the letter of the law, but to do so in a way that maximizes public integrity. This is especially necessary in situations in which laws and regulations provide no firm guidance on the appropriate course of action.

It was noted above that one weakness of compliance-based approaches is that even perfect compliance-based regulation cannot guarantee integrity when new situations emerge in which regulations have yet to be developed. These emerging situations pose much less of a threat under a values-based system, as the values inculcated within public servants provide an ostensibly universal framework for deciding upon the ethical course of action. Moreover, and of particular importance, such values provide the motivation for pursuing the ethical course of action, a motivation that can be conspicuously absent in a compliance-based situation. Indeed, it has long been an objection to compliance-based measures that they existed primarily to provide a legal protection to senior managers (see above; see also Paine 1994), a rationale that de-prioritizes actual ethics in favour of token adherence for its own sake.

The fundamental logic of values-based measures sits in stark contrast to such utilitarian considerations, being based primarily upon trust (Bies 2014, p. 231; see also Lewicki et al. 1998). A clear example can be seen in the case of the Netherlands Tax and Customs Administration, who consciously developed a values-based integrity programme. In a case study of the development of this values-based programme, Blijswijk et al. (2004, pp. 721–2) note:

> The second prong of the integrity program inculcated the organization's basic values and integrity rules while also fostering the individual's professional responsibility and occupational values. This second prong assumed that employees are responsible and sensible. It depended highly on the capacity of each individual civil servant to make judgment calls on ethical matters and matters of integrity in upholding organizational values independently and autonomously.

Here, the trust placed in officials is demonstrated by providing space for personal autonomy. Importantly, there is also the potential for abuse by the regulated officials, a situation reflecting the inherent vulnerability in trust relationships (Levi and Stoker 2000, p. 476). Of course, this vulnerability is also a key weakness of values-based approaches; undoubtedly, it is one of the central weaknesses that compliance-based systems seek to address. As a result, despite the promises offered by values-based pro-integrity regulations, there are practical situations in which values-based regulations may not be the optimal choice. One clear example of a situation in which values-based regulations will not be helpful is when public officials themselves are not trustworthy. Under such a circumstance, it is probable that placing trust in the officials, and thus making the public at large vulnerable to the officials, will simply result in increased corruption. Indeed, this is the point that Langseth et al. were referring to when they warned of the ability of discretionary power to enable corruption (1997, p. 3).

Notwithstanding such potential limitations, promoting integrity offers the potential of instrumental benefits, relative to compliance-based measures. Theoretically, such an approach to regulation ought to be fast, efficient and economical; a values-based system can in theory offer significant efficiencies by reducing time spent on bureaucratic administration of both the rules themselves, and investigations into compliance with the rules (Scott and Leung 2012, p. 40; see also Anechiarico and Jacobs 1996). A particularly clear example of this can be seen in the regulatory changes to the UK Members of Parliament expenses system following the MPs' expenses scandal of 2009. The expenses regime moved from a primarily values-based system, which was efficient but open to abuse, to a compliance-based system that has dramatically reduced abuse while greatly increasing costs. Indeed, in 2011, a year into the operation of the new system, the cost of administration exceeded the cost of the claim itself in 38 per cent of cases (Public Accounts Committee 2011, p. 9; for a detailed description of the process of validation, see National Audit Office 2011, p. 32).

However, regardless of such proposed benefits, the risks discussed above highlight that the values-based approach might not be particularly appropriate for the substantive goal of anti-corruption, unlike compliance-based measures that excel at anti-corruption. In turn, though, the key advantage of values-based systems is that they can offer the promise of promoting integrity, something with which compliance systems inherently struggle. Such a distinction highlights the importance of considering the substantive goal of regulation: is the objective to reduce corruption or to promote integrity? As has been discussed above in detail, each substantive objective leads to a different ideal form of regulation. However, the trade-offs are more complex than they at first appear, and directly speak to the limits of (compliance-based) rule governance for the maintenance of probity.

The limit of rule governance

So far, we have discussed compliance-based and values-based approaches to regulation, and have shown that each reinforces a different conceptualization of the substantive ends of regulation (anti-corruption or pro-integrity, respectively). This has been presented in terms of trade-offs and choices, where the choice is dictated both by practicalities on the ground (including whether officials are trustworthy), and by philosophic conceptions of the ends of ethical regulations. Moreover, because practical regulation will not perfectly adhere to a single archetype (see Scott and Leung 2012, p. 40), it might be supposed that regulators will have essentially a free hand to develop whatever system of regulation they desire, encompassing both values and compliance. However, such a choice is in reality less free than it might appear. Indeed, there are various situations in which compliance-based regulations not only cease to be productive, but can become actively counterproductive. Moreover, a mix of values- and compliance-based measures risks undermining the values, while leaving inadequate rules-based regulations in place.

As has been noted, compliance-based regulations usually rely on the prospect of punishment as the principal means to deter corrupt or unethical behaviour. This can result in encouraging rational utility maximizers to engage in unethical behaviour, should the opportunity arise, whenever the expected cost of punishment is less than the potential reward. However, given that real-world regulation is almost always a mixture of values-based and compliance-based regulations, it may be questioned whether such self-conscious ethics-free utility maximization is likely to occur in practice. This is a question of whether the existence of some values-based policies, or some element of values-based regulation within a wider compliance framework, will be sufficient to prevent the hollowing out of ethics from public-sector work. If such utility-maximizing behaviour is unlikely to occur in practice with even a moderate level of values-based regulation, then there is no cost to implementing compliance policies whenever it appears right to do so. However, if compliance-based policies themselves undermine integrity values, then there is always a cost to the implementation of compliance-based measures.

In order to understand what the consequences for values are of the introduction of a compliance system, it is again helpful to consider the policies as representing a view of trustworthiness of public officials. Bies (2014, pp. 231–2), applying the trust/distrust typology of Lewicki *et al.* (1998), argues for the importance of understanding the trust relationship encompassed in differing forms of integrity management as not merely occurring within a unidimensional space, but instead as representing a two-dimensional typology.

Under this typology, the trust and distrust expressed by differing forms of ethical regulation can be understood as reflecting varying combinations of trust and distrust (Bies 2014, pp. 231–2; Lewicki *et al.* 1998, p. 445; see Table 11.1). As conceptualized through the regulatory approaches discussed here, the values-based policy represents the 'high trust and low distrust' quadrant, and the compliance-based model represents the 'low trust and high distrust' quadrant. The other two quadrants reflect mixes of these ideal types. The 'low trust and low distrust' quadrant is indicative of 'bounded, arms-length transactions', where relationships are weak and intermittent (Lewicki *et al.* 1998, pp. 445–6). This model is unlikely to be found in practice as it is inherently unstable; as interactions between people deepen, beliefs about the other, as well as group dynamics, lead to the establishment of regulatory expectations and procedures, even if only informally (see also Lewicki *et al.* 1998, p. 446). The 'high trust and high distrust' can be thought of as a 'trust but verify' model (Bies 2014, p. 231). This is a hybrid system that sits between

TABLE 11.1 Integrating trust and distrust*

High Trust	*'Values-based'*	High Trust	Mixed model
Low Distrust		High Distrust	
Low Trust	Mixed model	Low Trust	*'Compliance-based'*
Low Distrust		High Distrust	

* Characterized as follows:
High Trust: Hope, Faith, Confidence, Assurance, Initiative
Low Trust: No Hope, No Faith, No Confidence, Passivity, Hesitance
High Distrust: Fear, Scepticism, Cynicism, Wariness, Vigilance
Low Distrust: No Fear, No Scepticism, No Cynicism, Low Monitoring, No Vigilance

Source: Based on Lewicki *et al.* (1998, p. 445).

values-based and compliance-based policies, and can emerge either as part of a conscious plan or instead as a consequence of increasingly adding compliance-based policies to a values-based system, or vice versa. Thus, moving from a values-based system to a compliance-based system almost inherently requires going through the intermediary step of the 'high trust and high distrust' system.

However, when conceptualized in terms of the Lewicki *et al.* (1998) model, it becomes apparent that increasingly adding compliance-based policies to a values-based system is not a neutral act; it is instead actively asserting increasing levels of distrust. Importantly, this is the case regardless of changes in the underlying level of 'trust' (as opposed to distrust) vested in officials. Under such circumstances, many of the negative effects of high distrust can still emerge. This is not only in terms of the potentially very significant cost of maintaining institutions of distrust (such things as regulatory agencies and compliance procedures), but also in terms of the effect upon individual values. All things being equal, distrust will beget distrust, which in turn weakens the values-based motivations for engaging in self-regulation, and particularly in ethically reflexive self-regulation (Tyler 2014, p. 273).

Tyler (2014, pp. 288–9) relates the problem of relying upon compliance policies to the problem of law enforcement interrogations. In both regulation and interrogation, authorities have the potential to work from a position of trust, appealing to the personal values and integrity of suspects, or to work from a position of distrust, focusing upon coercion and incentives. As Tyler (2014, p. 289) notes:

> With both deterrence and coercion, the core problem is similar: by embarking on a force-based strategy, authorities undermine their rapport with the people involved, who come to mistrust and even hate the authorities, to develop oppositional consciousness, and to resist and undermine those authorities. Any hope for cooperation or collaboration is undermined by feelings of distrust and anger and by motives of concealment and misdirection.

Importantly, this is not simply about the abstract overarching question of whether a system should be values-based or compliance-based; it also applies to situations in which degrees of coercive policies are introduced. Research by Alison *et al.* (2013, p. 426) on police interviews of terrorists found that 'even minimal instances of [coercive or hostile interactions from police] profoundly and significantly reduced [interview] yield and increased suspect resistance'. It therefore appears that the addition of even small levels of distrust, including those manifest in compliance policies, are enough seriously to undermine the opportunities afforded by a values-based system.

The perceived utility of values-based and compliance-based policies

Thus far, it has been seen that there are conceptual and empirical reasons to believe that compliance-based policies will rarely be helpful additions to regulation in situations where public officials are not very corrupt. However, thus far there has been very little consideration of the perceptions of public officials themselves, and we therefore have little information about whether the reasoning set out above might be shared by the very people who would be best placed to comment on the various approaches to regulation.

In order to examine the perceptions of public officials, we conducted a survey of 196 high-ranking UK civil servants in early 2013 via the Internet.[1] The survey questions were drawn from *A Comparative Survey of the Public Sector Values of Hong Kong's Senior Civil Servants, 1994 and 2011* (Brewer *et al.* 2012) and exclusively targeted civil servants at Grade 7 and above.[2] Civil servants at these grades represent the top 38,030 employees, out of a total staff of 463,810 people, and are considered senior and upper management (Office for National Statistics 2012).[3] The target group thus represent the top 8 per cent of all civil servants in the UK. Permission to conduct the survey was granted by the office of the head of the civil service, who then disseminated the survey to permanent secretaries, very senior civil servants responsible for managing entire divisions. At the insistence of the office of the head of the civil service, individual permanent secretaries were responsible for deciding whether to send the survey to civil servants within their section. As we had no contact with individual permanent secretaries, we are unable to know which permanent secretaries sent out the survey. The sample is therefore closer to an opportunity sample, and thus a response rate cannot be calculated. However, assuming that the reason for permanent secretaries to not send out the survey is not conditional upon the substantive variables of interest here, the nature of the sample is not especially problematic.

Of our survey respondents, who are by definition at Grades 7 and above, about 80 per cent were at Grades 7 and 6, and about 20 per cent are formally members of the senior civil service. In the civil service as a whole, the ratio is around 13 per cent senior civil servants to 87 per cent at Grades 7 and 6 (Office for National Statistics 2012). Thus, among our respondents, there is a moderate bias towards more senior members of staff. The median age of senior civil servants, in the civil service as a whole, is 49 (Office for National Statistics 2012); in our sample, the median age is 48. The median age of civil servants working at Grades 7 and 6, in the civil service as a whole, is 46 (Office for National Statistics 2012); in our sample, the median is 45. This is not a meaningful difference, and so the age profile of our sample closely matches that of the population of civil servants at Grades 7 and above. Of all civil servants at Grade 7 and above, 60 per cent are male (Office for National Statistics 2012); among survey respondents, 55 per cent were male, showing a slight bias towards female respondents. Of our survey respondents, 95 per cent worked within a government department, 3.1 per cent worked within a non-departmental public body, and 2.1 per cent worked outside of this structure.

We asked respondents to evaluate the utility of five potential policy responses that aim to curb unethical behaviour. The policies represent either predominately values-based or predominately compliance-based responses to unethical behaviour; this allows us both to evaluate the specific policies suggested, and to draw conclusions about how useful each of these responses are perceived to be in general. The policies evaluated were: stricter hierarchical supervision (compliance), develop training programmes to cultivate a stronger sense of morality among public officials (values), adopt more legislation to regulate and punish unethical behaviour in the public sector (compliance), introduce a more detailed code of administrative ethics to guide bureaucratic actions and decisions (mainly values-based), and create a moral climate in the public sector through exemplary political and administrative leadership (values). The results are shown in Table 11.2 below.

As can be seen in Table 11.2, the perceived usefulness of the wholly compliance-based policy suggestions was low. Fewer than 30 per cent of high-ranking civil servants considered either stricter hierarchical supervision or adopting more legislation to regulate behaviour to be a useful response to unethical behaviour. The suggestion to introduce a more detailed code of administrative ethics was seen as being useful by slightly fewer than 50 per cent of respondents. The more explicitly values-based policy suggestions received even greater support. The suggestion to develop training programmes to cultivate a stronger sense of morality among public officials was seen as useful by over 67 per cent of respondents. Finally, the suggestion to create a moral climate in the public sector through exemplary political and administrative leadership was seen as useful by nearly the whole sample. Indeed, over 75 per cent of the sample considered this final proposal to be 'very useful'.

TABLE 11.2 The perceived usefulness of policy responses aimed at reducing unethical behaviour

The following list contains some suggestions which have been proposed for improving ethical behaviour and decision-making among public officials. How useful do you think they are?

	Very useful (%)	Useful (%)	Not very useful (%)	Not at all useful (%)
Stricter hierarchical supervision	5.3	19.6	54.1	21.1
Develop training programmes to cultivate a stronger sense of morality among public officials	17.6	49.7	24.4	8.3
Adopt more legislation to regulate and punish unethical behaviour in the public sector	7.2	20.6	46.4	25.8
Introduce a more detailed code of administrative ethics to guide bureaucratic actions and decisions	4.6	41.8	43.3	10.3
Create a moral climate in the public sector through exemplary polticial and administrative leadership	75.4	21.5	1.5	1.5

Although this is just one survey of senior civil servants, and can therefore at best be indicative only, the sum total of these results does suggest a strong endorsement of the values-based approach to ethical regulation, and a corresponding suspicion of the compliance-based approach. Importantly, this finding cannot simply be disregarded as reflecting frustration or a desire for change in any direction; the results show a consistent and coherent favouring of values-based policies. What we cannot comment on is whether this represents concern about compliance-based policies altogether, or simply a reaction to the ever-increasing tendency to use compliance to regulate ethics. However, regardless of the specific cause, given that the institutional situation is similar in many countries, this finding may well be more generally applicable to other countries with similar ethical regulatory systems.

Conclusion

This chapter has critically examined the two main traditions underlying contemporary public sector ethical regulation – the values-based tradition and the compliance-based tradition. The main thrust of the argument here is that compliance strategies may not only cease to be productive, they could conceivably become counterproductive in certain circumstances. The purpose of this chapter is not to argue that there is never a need to use compliance-based strategies; on the contrary, in situations where officials are not trustworthy, such a strategy is likely to be necessary. Indeed, because compliance reforms excel at anti-corruption, they are useful in situations where reaching a state of minimal integrity is a positive move. Instead, the purpose of this chapter is to highlight that assuming bad faith on the part of public officials, and thus strongly regulating behaviour through compliance policies, could in turn prompt acts of bad faith, even among those officials who otherwise would not have engaged in such action. There is a significant potential risk of creating an 'us–versus–them' attitude among groups of officials whose work is stripped of an ethical discourse, which in turn can create the space for conflicts of interest between group loyalties and obligations to the law.

This chapter has also presented empirical data, albeit small-scale, to show that, in the United Kingdom at least, there appears to be a strong appetite for greater use of values-based policies among senior public officials. Given that we would expect results to be more positive if the people who are subject to new policies see those policies as appropriate, this is an important endorsement. Of course, this should not be a surprising finding; a values-based approach shows trust in officials and treats them as professionals. However, it seems it may be possible that the ethical values upon which the values-based system relies could conceivably be undermined by compliance systems, making a transition back to a values-based system more difficult (Tyler 2014, p. 289). Yet, the fact that introducing more values-based policies is difficult is not a reason to avoid it, especially given the potential longer-term benefits.

Ultimately, however, practical decisions about forms of regulation are likely to be decided by concerns other than integrity, efficiency or value. As has been noted, compliance-based regulations offer a greater degree of immunity for the people who craft legislation (see, for example, Paine 1994), and they can be implemented more quickly and with more public visibility than can values-based systems. These may prove to be irresistible benefits for those who are tasked with creating regulatory systems.

Notes

1   The survey was conducted as part of a project funded by the Economic and Social Research Council and the Hong Kong Research Grants Council (RES-000-22-44070).
2   In the UK civil service, grades represent divisions in seniority and responsibilities, rather than substantive differences in the roles. Thus, two people at the same grade may have a job dealing with similar substantive issues, or they may not. Grades are organized such that Grade 7 is less senior than Grade 6, which in turn is less senior than what is now formally called the senior civil service. The senior civil service was previously separated into Grades 5, 4, 3, 2 and 1, with Grade 1 being the most senior. The senior civil service can be differentiated into dozens of separate classifications, which were not probed here.
3   Although note that the statistics compiled by the Office for National Statistics (ONS) do not include civil servants in non-departmental public bodies, which our data do include. However, given the very small percentages of respondents who work in non-departmental public bodies in our sample (3.1 per cent), the ONS statistics still provide a useful comparison.

References

Agnafors, M. (2013) 'Quality of government toward a more complex definition', *American Political Science Review*, 107(3): 433–445.
Alison, L.J., Alison, E., Noone, G., Elntib, S. and Christiansen, P. (2013) 'Why tough tactics fail and rapport gets results: Observing rapport-based interpersonal techniques (ORBIT) to generate useful information from terrorists', *Psychology, Public Policy, and Law*, 19(4): 411–31.
Anechiarico, F. and Jacobs, J. (1996) *The Pursuit of Absolute Integrity: How Corruption Control Makes Government Ineffective*, Chicago, IL: University of Chicago Press.
Bies, R.J. (2014) 'Reducing criminal wrongdoing within business organizations: The practical and political skills of integrity', *Am. Crim. L. Rev.*, 51: 225–317.
Blijswijk, J., Breukelen, R., Franklin, A., Raadschelders, J. and Slump, P. (2004) 'Beyond ethical codes: The management of integrity in the Netherlands Tax and Customs Administration', *Public Administration Review*, 64(6): 718–27.
Braithwaite, J. and Makkai, T. (1991) 'Testing an expected utility model of corporate deterrence', *Law and Society Review*, 25: 7–40.
Brewer, B., Leung, J.Y. and Scott, I. (2012) *A Comparative Survey of the Public Sector Values of Hong Kong's Senior Civil Servants, 1994 and 2011*, Hong Kong: Department of Public and Social Administration, City University of Hong Kong.
Evans, M. (2012) 'Beyond the integrity paradox: Towards "good enough" governance?', *Policy Studies*, 33(1): 97–113.
Gneezy, U. and Rustichini, A. (2000) 'A fine is a price', *Journal of Legal Studies*, 29(1): 1–17.
Goel, R.K. and Rich, D.P. (1989) 'On the economic incentives for taking bribes', *Public Choice*, 61(3): 269–75.
Golden, M.A. and Picci, L. (2005) 'Proposal for a new measure of corruption, illustrated with Italian data', *Economics & Politics*, 17(1): 37–75.

Heywood, P.M. and Rose, J. (2014) '"Close but no cigar": The measurement of corruption', *Journal of Public Policy*, 34(3): 507–29.

Kirkpatrick, I., Ackroyd, S. and Walker, R. (2005) *The New Managerialism and Public Service Professions*, Basingstoke: Palgrave Macmillan.

Langseth, P., Stapenhurst, R. and Pope, J. (1997) *The Role of a National Integrity System in Fighting Corruption*, EDI working papers, Washington, DC: World Bank.

Levi, M. and Stoker, L. (2000) 'Political trust and trustworthiness', *Annual Review of Political Science*, 3(1): 475–507.

Lewicki, R.J., McAllister, D.J. and Bies, R.J. (1998) 'Trust and distrust: New relationships and realities', *Academy of Management Review*, 23(3): 438–58.

Maesschalck, J. (2004) 'Approaches to ethics management in the public sector: A proposed extension of the compliance-integrity continuum', *Public Integrity*, 7(1): 20–41.

National Audit Office (2011) *Independent Parliamentary Standards Authority: The Payment of MPs' Expenses*, HC 1273, London: The Stationery Office.

Nye, J.S. (1967) 'Corruption and political development: A cross-benefit analysis', *American Political Science Review*, 61(June): 417–27.

Office for National Statistics (2012) *Civil Service Statistics, 2012*, available at: www.ons.gov.uk/ons/dcp171778_284549.pdf.

Paine, L.S. (1994) 'Managing for organizational integrity', *Harvard Business Review*, 72(2): 106–17.

Pendse, S.G. (2012) 'Ethical hazards: A motive, means, and opportunity approach to curbing corporate unethical behavior', *Journal of Business Ethics*, 107(3): 265–79.

Philp, M. (2006) 'Corruption definition and measurement', in C. Sampford, A. Shacklock, C. Connors and F. Gatlung (eds), *Measuring Corruption* (pp. 45–79), London: Ashgate.

Public Accounts Committee (2011) *Independent Parliamentary Standards Authority*, HC 1426, London: The Stationery Office.

Roberts, R. (2009) 'The rise of compliance-based ethics management', *Public Integrity*, 11(3): 261–78.

Rose, J. (2014) *The Public Understanding of Political Integrity: The Case for Probity Perceptions*, Basingstoke: Palgrave Macmillan.

Rose, J. and Heywood, P.M. (2013) 'Political science approaches to integrity and corruption', *Human Affairs*, 23(2): 148–59.

Rothstein, B. (2000) 'Trust, social dilemmas and collective memories', *Journal of Theoretical Politics*, 12(4): 477–501.

Rothstein, B. (2011) *The Quality of Government: Corruption, Social Trust, and Inequality in International Perspective*, Chicago, IL: University of Chicago Press.

Scott, I. and Leung, J.Y. (2012) 'Integrity management in post-1997 Hong Kong: Challenges for a rule-based system', *Crime, Law and Social Change*, 58(1): 39–52.

Transparency International (2011) *What is the Corruption Perceptions Index*, available at: www.transparency.org/cpi2011/in_detail/#myAnchor3.

Tyler, T. (1994) 'Governing amid diversity: The effect of fair decision-making procedures on the legitimacy of government', *Law & Society Review*, 28(4): 809–32.

Tyler, T. (2000) 'Social justice: Outcome and procedure', *International Journal of Psychology*, 35(2): 117–25.

Tyler, T.R. (2014) 'Reducing corporate criminality: The role of values', *Am. Crim. L. Rev.*, 51: 267–317.

Vian, T. (2008) 'Review of corruption in the health sector: Theory, methods and interventions', *Health Policy and Planning*, 23(2): 83–94.

12

RESEARCHING AND IMPROVING THE EFFECTIVENESS OF ETHICS TRAINING

Jeroen Maesschalck and Annelies De Schrijver

Introduction

Ethics training certainly has been one of the most popular instruments of integrity management in organizations. Likewise, in many professional educational programmes, ethics courses are taught to prepare students for real-life professional ethical decision-making (Delaney and Sockell 1992; Menzel 1997; Ritter 2006). In spite of (or perhaps because of) all this enthusiasm, genuine evaluation research of these courses has been scarce (Van Montfort *et al.* 2013; Yoder and Denhart 2001). Those studies that do exist generate conflicting findings. Weber (1990, p. 183) attributes these mixed results to differences in the measurement instruments, methods of data analysis, and research populations. At the same time, there is also significant conceptual confusion. There are substantial differences in the types of training evaluated and there is no agreed-upon conceptual framework to specify these differences. Moreover, the outputs and the outcomes that are measured differ substantially. As a result, hypotheses about the impact of training on those outputs and outcomes are often difficult to falsify or corroborate. This chapter first briefly reviews the empirical literature on the effectiveness of ethics training and then proposes a conceptualization of both ethics training and its expected outcomes.

The effectiveness of ethics training in professional context

Before considering the effectiveness of ethics training, it is important to address the often implicit assumption behind it: that it is at all possible to teach ethics in a professional context. While several authors suggest that this is an unsettled debate (Adams *et al.* 1999; Cragg 1997; Ritter 2006; Yoder and Denhart 2001), our review of the academic literature did not identify strongly pronounced proponents nor opponents. Most consulted authors agree that while character development and value internalization can be considered completed in adulthood (Campbell *et al.* 2007; Cragg 1997; Williams and Dewett 2005), professional education and training are still good occasions to develop one's own vision about professional ethical issues (e.g. Parks 1993, cited in Adams *et al.* 1999). This nuanced view is reflected in recommendations about both the training's target audience and its objective. First, many seem to assume that ethics training is only valuable for people already inclined to take ethics seriously (Cragg 1997). Second, although ethics training by itself is not strong enough to change deeply rooted ethical values, it is able to make participants more competent in dealing with the ethical dimensions of the professional environment they (will) work in. Typically, ethics training would then contain discussions of the organization or profession's normative framework, as well as exercises in practical ethical decision-making (Adams *et al.* 1999; Maesschalck 2005; Ritter 2006).

Having thus delineated the target audience and the objectives, we can now turn to findings concerning the effectiveness of ethics training. An obvious first stop for such findings is Waples *et al.*'s (2008) meta-analysis of 25 studies on the effectiveness of business ethics instruction for college students and professionals. While generally concluding that business ethics training is 'at best minimally effective in enhancing ethics among students and business people' (p. 146), they also point at some moderators that were found to increase effectiveness. For example, courses that are 'shorter in length (i.e., span no more than 30 days time in total), and delivered in the mold of a weekend seminar/workshop format are, for the most part, more effective' (p. 147). As for the actual instruction, they concluded that the case-based approach and the combination of multiple teaching activities increase effectiveness. They also observed the effectiveness of 'instructional programs designed to foster critical thought processes, geared toward understanding of the problem at hand – in the appropriate context – and then dissecting the thought and behavior process leading to the resolution of the problem' (p. 147). While this meta-analysis thus offers useful conclusions, its authors also point at some limitations. The analysis was hindered by the vagueness in many studies about the training goals and by the limited information in many studies about the contents of the training. For those reasons, their analysis is inevitably limited to very general conclusions. This chapter will, instead, focus on a number of specific studies, not only in the private, but also in the public sector, using them to explore and illustrate the theoretical framework we propose. We will now introduce these studies organized around three often-used research designs.[1]

A first frequently used research design for the evaluation of ethics training is the comparison between participants and non-participants. In these studies, professionals are asked whether they were taught ethics during a degree programme (e.g. master of business administration, master of public administration) and/or in other professional training (e.g. company training). Those who were, even if it had been many years ago, are then compared with those who were not. In several studies, differences between both groups in moral attitudes and cognitive moral development are found and attributed to the ethics training (Delaney and Sockell

1992; Green and Weber 1997; Luthar *et al.* 1997). Yet, Peppas and Diskin (2001) find no significant differences, while Lowry (2003) and Sparks and Hunt (1998) find negative effects on participants' moral sensitivity.

In the second research design, respondents who once participated in ethics training are asked to indicate to what extent they believe the training affected them. Again, they might have followed the training many years before the study. Respondents of Eynon *et al.* (1997) are rather positive, while those of Menzel (1997) are rather negative. While these studies offer valuable insights, their use in evaluating ethics training is limited, because various types of ethics training are addressed within one study.

More useful for the evaluation of ethics training are those designs where one type of training is evaluated through a pretest-posttest design (often with experimental and control groups). Several studies show a positive effect of the ethics training on participants' moral sensitivity (Gautschi and Jones 1998; Myyry and Helkama 2002; Wu 2003), moral reasoning (Glenn 1992; Loe and Weeks 2000; O'Leary 2009; Schlaefli *et al.* 1985), moral values (Weber and Glyptis 2000; Wu 2003), cognitive flexibility (Carlson and Burke 1998), and autonomous problem-solving (Kavathatzopoulos 1994). However, other studies using this same design could not find any effect on participants' ethical orientation (DeMoss and McCann 1997) and moral attitudes (Wynd and Mager 1989). Yet other studies report mixed results. Van Montfort *et al.* (2013) only find a short-term positive effect of one of two studied ethics training types on participants' moral sensitivity and moral reasoning. The other type of training they investigated had no impact. Richards (1999) also reports only short-term effects. In her study, Ritter (2006) only found a positive effect of the evaluated ethics training on female participants, while Abdolmohammadi and Reeves (2000) obtained the opposite result: only a positive effect on male participants. Nguyen *et al.* (2008) only observed progress in participants' ethical perceptions in one of the three studied dilemmas.

The literature on ethics training is not only diverse in terms of methodology; there is also significant conceptual variation. The independent variable, ethics training, is under-theorized. While the actual contents of the studied trainings differ substantially across the studies, the literature offers no agreed-upon conceptual framework to specify these differences. Likewise, the conceptualization of the dependent variable also has its problems. Authors are not always clear about the objectives of the ethics training, which results in various conceptualizations of the dependent variable in evaluation studies. Examples of objectives used in the literature include transferring knowledge about the organization's code of ethics (Carlson and Burke 1998), introducing moral philosophical theories and values (Carlson and Burke 1998; Strong and Hoffman 1990), raising awareness and sensitivity for ethical issues (Carlson and Burke 1998; Loeb 1991; Sims and Sims 1991; Strong and Hoffman 1990), strengthening analytical and critical ethical decision-making skills (Carlson and Burke 1998; Kavathatzopoulos 1994; Loeb 1991; Sims and Sims 1991; Strong and Hoffman 1990), raising awareness for consequences for others (Weber 2007), stimulating moral imagination (Carlson and Burke 1998;

Menzel 1997), and showing participants how to deal with ambiguity and different opinions (Carlson and Burke 1998; Loeb 1991).

In sum, some problems in the existing literature on ethics training have to do with measurement difficulties, but many can be ascribed to the limited degree of theorizing on the topic. Specifications of the independent variable (ethics training) and dependent variable (intended effects) are often vague, resulting in equally vague hypotheses, difficult to falsify or corroborate. The following section hopes to address these theoretical concerns by proposing a conceptualization of both the independent and the dependent variables that is broad enough to encompass various types of training and of training effects, but still specific enough to allow for clear conceptualizations and falsifiable hypotheses.

The dependent variable: ethical competence

As illustrated above, the literature offers various objectives of ethics training that could serve as dependent variables in evaluation studies, but no overall framework that could be used across studies. In search for such a general framework, it is useful to look beyond ethics training at the broader literature on training evaluation. Probably the most widely used framework in that literature is the 'four-level evaluation model' of Kirkpatrick (1959, 1994). While often presented as a general evaluation model, it is in fact better characterized as a 'taxonomy of outcomes' (Holton 1996, p. 5), and hence a way of operationalizing the dependent variable of training evaluation. Although widely used, Kirkpatrick's model has also been criticized and adapted versions have been proposed (e.g. Alliger *et al.* 1997; Alvarez *et al.* 2004; Holton 1996). We first briefly present Kirkpatrick's model, taking on board some of those more recent insights. We then turn to our operationalization of the dependent variable 'ethical competence' (i.e. the necessary knowledge, skills and attitudes (KSAs) of an ethically competent employee) (De Schrijver and Maesschalck 2013, p. 36).

Kirkpatrick distinguishes between what he calls four 'levels', but would probably better be described as four (types of) dependent variables: reactions, learning, behaviour and results. We briefly address each in turn. 'Reactions' are the trainees' immediate responses to the training. Alliger *et al.* (1997, pp. 344–5) distinguish between affective reactions and utility reactions. Interestingly, their meta-analysis showed that affective reactions did not have any impact upon learning: it is not because trainees like the training that they also learn (Alliger *et al.* 1997). It did show an impact of the utilitarian reactions: when trainees reported that they found the training useful and relevant to their job, they were indeed more likely to learn. The second level, 'learning', refers to knowledge, skills and attitudes (KSAs) acquired as a consequence of the training. Various other taxonomies, sometimes more complicated than the KSA triad, have been used. Alvarez *et al.* (2004, pp. 395–7), for example, made a threefold distinction that significantly differs from the traditional KSA triad: posttraining attitudes (e.g. adopting the attitudes intended by the training, strengthening motivation, strengthening organizational commitment), cognitive learning (e.g. acquisition of knowledge, situated problem-solving) and training performance (i.e. the ability to perform newly acquired skills at the end of training). Kirkpatrick's third level was originally termed 'behaviour', but more recent models use other terms. Alvarez *et al.* (2004, p. 397) use 'transfer performance', thus emphasizing that this third level only refers to performance/behaviour on the job. They situate behaviour exhibited during the training ('training performance') in level two. Thus, 'transfer performance' is about the transfer of acquired KSAs to actual daily life on the job. In the context of ethics training, this would, for example, mean that ethical reasoning skills are actually used on the job in real-life dilemmas or that employees know and apply the contents of the ethics code in daily practice. The fourth dependent variable, 'results', refers to the achievement of the final outcomes of the training. In the case of sales training, these could be increased sales. In the context of ethics training, these could mean that the organization better deals with ethical dilemmas or that clients indeed perceive the organization as more ethical.

Returning to ethics training, it is clear that an extensive development of all four levels would be beyond the scope of this chapter. Instead, we focus on the level that we think would be most useful to understand given the current state of the research: level two, 'learning'. The first level (reactions) is relatively easy to conceptualize. Indeed, many studies already report on the extent to which participants liked the ethics training and whether they found it useful, and the interpretation of these results is usually fairly straightforward. That is very different for the second level, which could certainly use a more theorized classification of the many ways in which this level is operationalized. Moreover, several models (e.g. Alvarez *et al.* 2004) hypothesize that 'learning' is an intermediary variable that in turn (partly) impacts behaviour on the job ('transfer performance') and results. Any research agenda investigating the causal chain from 'learning' over performance to results will therefore have to start with an operationalization of 'learning'.

Now we can turn to the actual conceptualization of 'ethical competence'. Drawing from the literature on administrative and business ethics, De Schrijver and Maesschalck (2013) argue that ethical competence should not be considered a one-dimensional concept, but instead consists of 12 components. Table 12.1 represents these in 12 cells defined by two dimensions. The columns refer, respectively, to knowledge, skills and attitudes (KSAs) that ethics training might aim to impact. The rows refer to four sub-competencies. Inspiration for these sub-competencies was drawn from Rest's (1986) four component model, which identifies four processes preceding ethical behaviour: moral awareness, moral judgement, moral motivation and moral character. As Table 12.1 below shows, this list was complemented by the sub-competence 'rule abidance' because legality is an important value in public administration. Also, 'moral motivation' and 'moral character' were merged because Rest's (1986) conceptualization of moral motivation refers only to a skill and that of moral character only to an attitude.

TABLE 12.1 Ethical competence framework of De Schrijver and Maesschalck (2013, p. 37)

	Knowledge	Skill	Attitudes
Rule abidance	Law, ethics code, rules and procedures (1)	Applying rules (2)	Importance of rules (3)
Moral sensitivity	Position in the organization and society (4)	Defining a situation as an ethical one; seeing different solutions (5)	Empathy; perspective taking (6)
Moral reasoning	Moral arguments: rules; consequences for others; consequences for oneself (7)	Using different moral arguments: rules; consequences for others; consequences for oneself (8)	Attitude of flexibility: not only rules; not only consequences for others; not only consequences for oneself (9)
Moral motivation and character	Rules and consequences for others are more important than consequences for oneself (10)	Priority to rules and consequences for others in what you choose to do (11)	Autonomy; ego strength (12)

We discuss each of the respective KSAs of each of the four sub-competencies.[2]

The first sub-competence is 'rule abidance'. As for knowledge, an ethically competent employee should know the rules, procedural guidelines and code(s) of ethics that are applicable to him or her (cell 1). Knowing is not enough, however. He or she should also have the skill to apply them in specific situations (cell 2). Yet, knowledge and skills are only relevant when there is a genuine willingness to apply them. That is what cell 3 refers to: a positive attitude towards rules. The second sub-competence is 'moral sensitivity', which refers to a sensitivity for ethical issues. In terms of knowledge, this means that a public servant should understand his or her position in both society and his or her organization or profession, as well as the responsibilities implied by that position (cell 4). A police officer, for example, should be aware of his or her exemplary function. Cell 5 refers to the skill not only to sense when a moral dilemma is at stake, but also to think of possible solutions and to understand their possible consequences in the short and long term. However, those skills can only be applied if the ethically competent employee has the ability to empathize and take the perspective of others, as depicted in cell 6. The third sub-competence, 'moral reasoning', again has knowledge, skill and attitude components. As for knowledge, cell 7 indicates that an ethically competent employee must be familiar with three different types of moral arguments: (1) arguments that refer to rules and procedures; (2) arguments that refer to consequences of actions for others; and (3) arguments that refer to consequences of actions for oneself. Cell 8 then refers to the skill to actually use these arguments in a specific moral dilemma. Yet, knowledge and skill are only useful if they are supported by a matching attitude (cell 9): flexibility or 'the willingness to accept that there is never only one solution for a problem' (De Schrijver and Maesschalck 2013, p. 40). 'Moral motivation and character' is the fourth sub-competence. As for knowledge, it implies an understanding that, among the three types of moral arguments, those referring to rules and consequences for others should be considered more important than the egoistic considerations (cell 10). Cell 11 then refers to the actual skill of doing that, and cell 12 refers to attitudinal aspects necessary for that: autonomy and ego strength. Autonomy refers to the ability to make a decision independently from others' expectations and judgements, while ego strength refers to the moral courage needed when making a difficult decision (De Schrijver and Maesschalck 2013).

Admittedly, the resulting framework with 12 cells based on two dimensions is complex. Yet, as De Schrijver and Maesschalck (2013) show, this reflects complexity in the literature. Moreover, De Schrijver's (2014) study offers empirical support for the need for such complexity. Her longitudinal study among trainee police officers in Belgium not only confirmed the existence of 12 separate dimensions; it also showed that patterns over time on these dimensions diverge significantly, with some dimensions increasing, some decreasing and some remaining constant.

Hence, we argue that these 12 cells of ethical competence can be used as a map of objectives ethics training can hope to achieve. Training could aim to affect only one cell. For example, a traditional lecture on the ethics code might be limited to impacting cell 1. It could also aim at improving specific rows or columns. Training in ethical decision-making, for example, might focus on the skills column. Perhaps it could even be more ambitious, aiming at more than one column or row.

It is interesting now to use this framework to conceptualize and compare the stated objectives of the training programmes studied in the pretest-posttest evaluation studies mentioned above. Many of the training programmes in those studies seem to focus on skills (i.e. the middle column in Table 12.1). The training evaluated by Van Montfort et al. (2013) and the one evaluated by Kavathatzopoulos (1994) indeed focus on the skills specified in cell 5 (seeing different solutions), cell 8 (using different moral arguments) and cell 11 (giving priority to rules and consequences). The training studied by Ritter (2006) aimed at impacting those same three cells by improving participants' cognitive competence. In addition to that, it also aimed at improving participants' moral understanding, which in our framework would be the knowledge component of the second sub-competence (cell 4). The training studied by Myyry and Helkama (2002) aims at the same four objectives as Ritter (2006): cells 4, 5, 8 and 11. In other studies, the stated objectives of the training are less clear (e.g. Carlson and Burke 1998; Gautschi and Jones 1998; Loe and Weeks 2000; Richards 1999; Wu 2003; Wynd and Mager 1989).

Interestingly, those stated objectives of the training programmes did not always coincide with the actual dependent variables that were measured in the empirical study. For example, from the four objectives Ritter (2006) describes, only two are actually measured as dependent variables: moral sensitivity (cell 5) and moral reasoning (cell 8).

The independent variable: types of ethics training

A conceptual framework for the evaluation of ethics training, of course, also needs a nuanced operationalization of its main independent variable.

A brief look at the practice-oriented literature reveals a very broad range of types of ethics training, thus rendering it very difficult for trainers to make an informed choice and for researchers to develop a cumulative understanding of what works. Unfortunately, the academic literature is also of limited use in this respect. Many studies are not very specific on the contents of the ethics training, and those studies that are are often difficult to compare. Hence, if the aim is to develop a cumulative research agenda that provides really useful information, a framework will be necessary that is generic but still sufficiently specific as well. The first step towards such a framework will be to identify the dimensions along which these types of training vary.

One such dimension is drawn from the well-known rules-based vs. values-based (or compliance vs. integrity) distinction for ethics management more generally (Maesschalck 2005; Paine 1994). The 'rules-based' approach emphasizes the importance of formal and detailed rules and procedures, and assumes that individual employees need extrinsic pressure to behave ethically. A typical format for a rules-based integrity training would be a classroom setting, where the trainer would be talking most of the time, explaining what is expected from the organizational members according to the laws, rules and codes, and what the consequences will be if one does not follow these directions. The 'values-based' approach focuses on guidance and positive incentives, assuming that individual employees are intrinsically motivated to behave ethically. A case in point would be a training in which the trainees do most of the thinking and talking and the trainer is merely a facilitator, stimulating discussion, provoking thinking, playing the devil's advocate. The assumption is that only when both approaches are judiciously combined, an integrity training programme will have the desired effect of improving the ethical competence of employees. This distinction offers a useful way to conceptualize ethics training, but is still very general. In order to really understand what works in ethics training, more fine-grained dimensions will be necessary.

There are many dimensions along which ethics training can vary, depending on aspects such as the background and affiliation of the trainer, the duration and the frequency of the training sessions, or the actual substance as well as the instructional methods used (e.g. Waples *et al.* 2008). Even minor variations along these dimensions might significantly impact the effectiveness of the training (O'Leary 2009). Hence, any comprehensive theory about the impact of ethics training will have to take all dimensions into account. Yet, in the context of this contribution, the focus will be on the latter two: the substance of the training and the instructional methods used.

In terms of substance, one might distinguish between four possible perspectives that could be emphasized in an ethics training (Maesschalck 2012). First, training might focus on formal ethics guidelines as formulated in various types of legal instruments, such as laws, codes of ethics, contracts, etc. Second, ethics training could also focus on values. Which values are relevant for the trainees' professional context? What should be done when values conflict with each other, as they do by definition in ethical dilemmas? Is there perhaps a hierarchy among those values? Discussions of values could be addressed both deductively and inductively. As for the former, trainees could be presented with a list of applicable values that are then applied on specific situations. An inductive approach could start with an open discussion where trainees are asked to list relevant values and to develop shared definitions. The training would then also have to address possible discrepancies between those values and the formal values prescribed by the organization. Third, the training could also focus on specific moral philosophical approaches. Of course, the two previously mentioned approaches also imply certain moral philosophical choices, but they remain implicit. Yet, techniques and concepts from moral philosophy might be enlightening, and might help to ask critical questions relevant for practice. There are several ways in which moral philosophy can be used in ethics training. One could develop and use philosophical definitions of terms such as 'ethics', 'integrity', 'morality', 'values', etc. One could also explicitly refer to (simplified versions) of important moral philosophies, such as utilitarianism, deontology and virtue ethics, and the conflicting solutions they offer. Fourth, ethics training might also focus specifically on ethical decision-making. These types of training typically attempt to combine elements of the previous three types. They would typically rely on a specific step-by-step decision-making model that is either inductively developed during the training or deductively taught at the outset of the training (Cooper 2012; Gortner 1991; Karssing 2001; Maesschalck 2004; Van Luijk 2000).

Again, this fourfold distinction can now be applied on the ethics training programs in the pretest-posttest studies mentioned above, with some programmes combining several dimensions. First, several of the studied training programmes indeed address formal ethics guidelines. O'Leary (2009), for example, describes how the training programme studied by him introduces trainees into the code of ethics of the accounting profession. Participants in Ritter's (2006) training are also introduced into 'ethical guidelines for decision-making provided by the Academy of Management'. The trainings discussed in three other studies (Gautschi and Jones 1998; Myyry and Helkama 2002; Richards 1999) emphasize values and would hence fit in the second category. Myyry and Helkama (2002), for example, describe a training where principles of procedural justice and values are introduced so as to stimulate trainees to use them in their discussions of cases. Third, the training programmes evaluated by O'Leary (2009), Myyry and Helkama (2002) and Richards (1999) all refer to moral philosophy. Richards (1999), for example, describes ethics training where participants are required to read a chapter about ethical principles, followed by a lecture and a discussion about those principles, and completed with a discussion of cases applying those principles. The fourth perspective is ethical decision-making. Among the studies under review, only O'Leary (2009) reports that a step-by-step model for ethical decision-making was used in the training he evaluates. Other authors also mention ethical decision-making as a training objective, but do not report the use of an explicit ethical decision-making model. Again, some studies could not be mentioned in this review as the specific perspectives of the studied training are not discussed (e.g. Carlson and Burke 1998; Loe and Weeks 2000; Van Montfort et al. 2013; Wu 2003; Wynd and Mager 1989).

Training programmes not only vary in the type of substance they offer, but also in the instructional methods they apply. Three frequently used techniques are lectures, open discussions and discussions on specific cases (Maesschalck 2012). First, in a lecture, the trainer offers a theoretical exposition and participants are expected to listen. The principal objective is to transfer knowledge, although some assume that this technique might also help to train skills. Second, in open discussions, the trainer's role is that of a facilitator and participants are expected to do the talking. In these discussions, participants, for example, search for definitions of morally relevant concepts or engage in other types of philosophical dialogue (e.g. Kessel et al. 2003). Third, ethics training could also involve discussions of actual cases. In this context, 'cases' refers to specific situations where an ethically relevant decision should be made. The actual label used to refer to this case could vary depending on the substance of the course (e.g. 'legal puzzle' or 'ethical dilemma'). The cases could be either hypothetical or prepared by the trainees. While the latter option might increase the training's relevance, it might also be experienced as threatening. For the actual case discussions, there are many specific techniques that could be applied and combined, including role play and group discussions of the case.

Applying this classification on the training programmes described in the pretest-posttest evaluation studies mentioned above, it appears that most programmes combine all three instructional methods (Gautschi and Jones 1998; Kavathatzopoulos 1994; Loe and Weeks 2000; Myyry and Helkama 2002; O'Leary 2009; Richards 1999; Ritter 2006; Van Montfort et al. 2013). Some studies do not contain sufficient information to specify this (Carlson and Burke 1998; Wu 2003; Wynd and Mager 1989).

Of course, the choice for a particular instructional method is not entirely independent from the choice for substantive perspectives. Some substantive perspectives are more naturally combined with some particular instructional methods than others. For a training programme that emphasizes formal ethics regulations, for example, one might tend towards lectures, while for ethical decision-making training programs one might tend towards cases. Yet, these links are not as natural as may appear. Formal ethics regulations could also be taught using cases, and ethical decision-making could also be explained in lectures. With some creativity, any substantive approach might be combined with any of the instructional methods. Moreover, the listed types are not exhaustive, so the possibilities are much richer.

Conclusion

This chapter suggested specific ways to operationalize both the independent and the dependent variables in ethics training research. It showed how these operationalizations can be used to analyze existing empirical studies. In the future, the framework could be a useful source of inspiration to design ethics training programmes and to specify their intended outcomes. It also offers a generic conceptual framework that can be used for the evaluation of very different ethics training programmes with various training objectives. Most ambitiously, this framework might, in the long run, offer the language for an empirically grounded theory about the impact of ethics training on ethical competence. Such a theory could then rely on research that shows whether particular types of ethics training are associated with particular aspects of ethical competence. One might, for example, expect that particular types of substance of ethics training are associated with particular sub-competencies. Training programmes that focus on formal ethics regulations, for example, might be better at improving the first sub-competence, 'rule abidance', while programmes emphasizing ethical decision-making might be better at stimulating the third and fourth sub-competences. Likewise, the different didactic approaches could also differentially impact ethical competence. Traditional lectures, for example, might be more effective at strengthening knowledge, while the use of cases might be better at improving skills. The latter is suggested by a significant literature about the effects of 'active', 'cooperative' and 'problem-based' learning (e.g. Prince 2004; Slavin 1996). A particularly interesting literature that could inspire such research is the research tradition about the impact of training (usually in the context of secondary or higher education) on what is called 'critical thinking skills'. While the theoretical literature (e.g. Ennis 1989, as used in Abrami *et al.* 2008, pp. 1105–6) suggests that instructional methods differentially impact critical thinking, empirical research nuances these expectations. For example, the impact of collaborative learning (Abrami *et al.* 2008, p. 1119) on critical thinking was found to be relatively minor. It would be interesting to see whether research about the impact of instructional methods on ethical competence would generate similar results, evaluating the impact of different instructional methods on what is called 'critical thinking skills' (e.g. Johnson and Mighten 2005; Prince 2004; Tynjälä 1998).

While this chapter indeed offered two useful building blocks, there is, of course, significant scope for further expansion of the framework. For example, future research might move on to the next step in the causal chain and look at how an individual's ethical competence relates to his or her actual behaviour on the job ('transfer performance'). Alvarez *et al.*'s (2004) integrated model on training more generally indeed suggests such a link, but also identifies individual and organizational characteristics that might complicate this impact. In the context of ethics training, relevant individual characteristics could be age (Waples *et al.* 2008, pp. 141–2) or an individual's learning style (e.g., Coffield *et al.* 2004). For the operationalization of organizational characteristics, it would be useful to turn to the ethics management literature and its hypotheses about the impact of organizational factors (e.g., leadership, culture or codes) on ethical behaviour (e.g., Maesschalck and Bertok 2009).

A research agenda using the framework proposed in this chapter would offer at least two major benefits. First, it would generate theory-driven and empirically grounded understanding of what works in ethics training and why. It offers a language that allows for cumulative research of very different types of ethics training in significant detail. Second, such a research agenda would also help to understand what is not effective or what might in fact generate the opposite effect of what is intended. As for the latter, the proposed operationalizations of the independent and dependent variables indeed offer a map to conceptualize unintended effects. Suppose, for example, that a particular ethics training programme would emphasize the contents of formal ethics guidelines. One would expect that this stimulates the trainees to study the rules and thus increase his or her level of ethical competence in cell 1. That is not the only possible pathway, however. It is also possible that the training might in fact decrease ethical competence. A training that empha- sizes rules might in fact deter trainees to such an extent that it undermines the second sub-competence, 'moral sensitivity', which by definition implies that one understands that ethics is more than simply obeying rules. Such a systematic investigation of the unintended and often undesirable side effects might offer an important and evidence-based complement to the unconditional enthusiasm about ethics training that is not uncommon among actors in what has been labelled the 'ethics industry' (Huberts 2014, p. ix).

Notes

1 The literature discussed in the remainder of this section is drawn from De Schrijver (2014, pp. 52–5).
2 This description of the framework strongly draws from De Schrijver (2014, p. 41) and De Schrijver and Maesschalck (2013, p. 42).

References

Abdolmohammadi, M.J. and Reeves, F.M. (2000) 'Effects of education and intervention on business students' ethical cognition: A cross sectional and longitudinal study', *Teaching Business Ethics*, 4(3): 269–84.
Abrami, Ph. C., Bernard, R.M., Borokhovski, E., Wade, A., Surkes, M.A., Tamin, R. and Zhang, D. (2008) 'Instructional interventions affecting critical thinking skills and dispositions: A stage 1 meta-analysis', *Review of Educational Research*, 78(4): 1102–34.
Adams, J.S., Tashchian, A. and Shore, T.H. (1999) 'Frequency, recall and usefulness of undergraduate ethics education', *Teaching Business Ethics*, 3(3): 241–53.
Alliger, G.M., Tannenbaum, S.I., Bennett, W., Jr., Traver, H. and Shotland, A. (1997) 'A meta-analysis of the relations among training criteria', *Personnel Psychology*, 50(2): 341–58.
Alvarez, K., Salas, E., and Garofano, C.M. (2004) "An integrated model of training evaluation and effectiveness," *Human Resource Review*, 3(4): 385–416.
Campbell, A.V., Chin, J. and Voo, T-C. (2007) 'How can we know that ethics education produces ethical doctors?', *Medical Teacher*, 29(5): 431–6.

Carlson, P.J. and Burke, F. (1998) 'Lessons learned from ethics in the classroom: Exploring student growth in flexibility, complexity and comprehension', *Journal of Business Ethics*, 17(11): 1179–87.

Coffield, F., Moseley, D., Hall, E. and Ecclestone, K. (2004) *Learning Styles and Pedagogy in Post-16 Learning: A Systematic and Critical Review*, London: LSRC Reference, Learning & Skills Research Centre.

Cooper, T. (2012) *The Responsible Administrator: An Approach to Ethics for the Administrative Role* (6th edn), San Francisco, CA: John Wiley & Sons.

Cragg, G.R. (1997) 'Teaching business ethics: The role of ethics in business and in business education', *Journal of Business Ethics*, 16(3): 231–45.

De Schrijver, A. (2014) *De weg naar politionele integriteit: Een longitudinaal onderzoek naar de ontwikkeling van ethische competentie bij aspirant-inspecteurs*, The Hague: Boom.

De Schrijver, A. and Maesschalck, J. (2013) 'A new definition and conceptualization of ethical competence', in D.C. Menzel and T.L. Cooper (eds), *Achieving Ethical Competence for Public Service Leadership* (pp. 29–51), Armonk, NY: M.E. Sharpe.

Delaney, J.T. and Sockell, D. (1992) 'Do company ethics training programs make a difference? An empirical analysis', *Journal of Business Ethics*, 11(9): 719–27.

DeMoss, M.A. and McCann, G.K. (1997) 'Without a care in the world: The business ethics course and its exclusion of a care perspective', *Journal of Business Ethics*, 16(4): 435–43.

Ennis, R.H. (1989) 'Critical thinking and subject specificity: Clarification and needed research', *Educational Researcher*, 18(3): 4–10.

Eynon, G., Hill, N.T. and Stevens, K.T. (1997) 'Factors that influence the moral reasoning abilities of accountants: Implications for universities and the profession', *Journal of Business Ethics*, 16(12–13): 1297–309.

Gautschi, F.H.I. and Jones, T.M. (1998) 'Enhancing the ability of business students to recognize ethical issues: An empirical assessment of the effectiveness of a course in business ethics', *Journal of Business Ethics*, 17(2): 205–16.

Glenn, J.R. (1992) 'Can a business and society course affect the ethical judgment of future managers?', *Journal of Business Ethics*, 11(3): 217–23.

Gortner, H. (1991) 'How public managers view their environment: Balancing organizational demands, political realities, and personal values', in J.S. Bowman (ed.), *Ethical Frontiers in Public Management: Seeking New Strategies for Resolving Ethical Dilemmas* (pp. 34–63), San Francisco, CA: Jossey-Bass.

Green, S. and Weber, J. (1997) 'Influencing ethical development: Exposing students to the AICPA code of conduct', *Journal of Business Ethics*, 16(8): 777–90.

Holton, E.F., III (1996) 'The flawed four-level evaluation model', *Human Resource Development Quarterly*, 7(1): 5–21.

Huberts, L. (2014) *The Integrity of Governance: What It Is, What We Know, What Is Done and Where to Go*, Basingstoke: Palgrave Macmillan.

Johnson, J.P. and Mighten, A. (2005) 'A comparison of teaching strategies: Lecture notes combined with structured group discussion versus lecture only', *Journal of Nursing Education*, 44(7): 319–22.

Karssing, E.D. (2001) *Morele Competenties in Organisaties*, Assen: Van Gorcum.

Kavathatzopoulos, I. (1994) 'Training professional managers in decision-making about real life business problems: The acquisition of the autonomous problem-solving skill', *Journal of Business Ethics*, 13(5): 379–86.

Kessel, J., Boers, E. and Mostert, P. (2003) *Vrije ruimte: Filosoferen in organisaties*, The Hague: Boom.

Kirkpatrick, D.L. (1959) 'Techniques for evaluation of training programs', *Journal of American Society of Training Directors*, 13: 21–6.

Kirkpatrick, D.L. (1994) *Evaluating Training Programs: The Four Levels*, San Francisco, CA: Berret-Koehler.

Loe, T.W. and Weeks, W.A. (2000) 'An experimental investigation of efforts to improve sales students' moral reasoning', *The Journal of Personal Selling & Sales Management*, 20(4): 243–51.

Loeb, S.E. (1991) 'The evaluation of "outcomes" of accounting ethics education', *Journal of Business Ethics*, 10(2): 77–84.

Lowry, D. (2003) 'An investigation of student moral awareness and associated factors in two cohorts of an undergraduate business degree in a British university: Implications for business ethics curriculum design', *Journal of Business Ethics*, 48(1): 7–19.

Luthar, H.K., Dibattista, R.A. and Gautschi, T. (1997) 'Perception of what the ethical climate is and what it should be: The role of gender, academic status, and ethical education', *Journal of Business Ethics*, 16(2): 205–17.

Maesschalck, J. (2004) 'Een aanpak voor dilemmatrainingen: een stappenmodel voor ethische besluitvorming', *Vlaams Tijdschrift voor Overheidsmanagement*, 9(4): 7–19.

Maesschalck, J. (2005) *Een ambtelijk integriteitsbeleid in de Vlaamse Overheid*, Leuven: Steunpunt Bestuurlijke Organisatie Vlaanderen.

Maesschalck, J. (2012) 'Integriteitstrainingen', in J.H.J. Van Den Heuvel, L.W.J.C. Huberts and E.R. Muller (eds), *Integriteit: Integriteit en integer en integriteitsbeleid in Nederland* (pp. 325–47), Deventer: Kluwer.

Maesschalck, J. and Bertok, J. (2009) *Towards a Sound Integrity Management Framework: Instruments, Structures and Conditions for Implementation*, Paris: OECD.

Menzel, D.C. (1997) 'Teaching ethics and values: A survey of graduate public affairs and administration programs in the U.S.', *Political Science and Politics*, 30(3): 518–24.

Myyry, L. and Helkama, K. (2002) 'The role of value priorities and professional ethics training in moral sensitivity', *Journal of Moral Education*, 31(1): 35–50.

Nguyen, N.T., Basuray, M.T., Smith, W.P., Kopka, D. and McCulloh, D.N. (2008) 'Ethics perception: Does teaching make a difference?', *Journal of Education for Business*, 84(2): 66–75.

O'Leary, C. (2009) 'An empirical analysis of the positive impact of ethics teaching on accounting students', *Accounting Education: An International Journal*, 18(4–5): 505–20.

Paine, L.S. (1994) 'Managing for oganizational integrity', *Harvard Business Review*, 72(2): 106–17.

Peppas, S.C. and Diskin, B.A. (2001) 'College courses in ethics: Do they really make a difference?', *International Journal of Educational Management*, 15(7): 347–53.

Prince, M. (2004) 'Does active learning work? A review of the research', *Journal of Engineering Education*, 93(3): 223–31.

Rest, J.R. (1986) *Moral Development: Advance in Theory and Research*, New York: Praeger.

Richards, C. (1999) 'The transient effects of limited ethics training', *Journal of Education for Business*, 74(6): 332–4.

Ritter, B.A. (2006) 'Can business ethics be trained? A study of the ethical decision-making process in business students', *Journal of Business Ethics*, 68(2): 153–64.

Schlaefli, A., Rest, J.R. and Thoma, S.J. (1985) 'Does moral education improve moral judgment? A meta-analysis of intervention studies using the Defining Issues Test', *Review of Educational Research*, 55(3): 319–52.

Sims, R.R. and Sims, S. (1991) 'Increasing applied business ethics courses in business school curricula', *Journal of Business Ethics*, 10(3): 211–19.

Slavin, R.E. (1996) 'Research on cooperative learning and achievement: What we know, what we need to know', *Contemporary Educational Psychology*, 21(1): 43–69.

Sparks, J.H. and Hunt, S.D. (1998) 'Marketing researcher ethical sensitivity: Conceptualization, measurement, and exploratory investigation', *Journal of Marketing*, 62(2): 92–109.

Strong, V.K. and Hoffman, A.N. (1990) 'There is relevance in the classroom: Analysis of present methods of teaching business ethics', *Journal of Business Ethics*, 9(7): 603–7.

Tynjälä, P. (1998) 'Traditional studying for examination versus constructivist learning tasks: Do learning outcomes differ?', *Studies in Higher Education*, 23(2): 173–89.

Van Luijk, H. (2000) *Integer en verantwoord in beroep en bedrijf*, Amsterdam: Boom.

Van Montfort, A., Beck, L. and Twijnstra, A. (2013) 'Can integrity be taught in public organizations? The effectiveness of integrity-training programs for municipal officials', *Public Integrity*, 15(2): 117–32.

Waples, E.P., Antes, A.L., Murphy, S.T., Connelly, S. and Mumford, M.D. (2009) 'A meta-analytic investigation of business ethics instruction', *Journal of Business Ethics*, 87: 133–50.

Weber, J. (1990) 'Measuring the impact of teaching ethics to future managers: A review, assessment, and recommendations', *Journal of Business Ethics*, 9(3): 183–90.

Weber, J.A. (2007) 'Business ethics training: Insights from learning theory', *Journal of Business Ethics*, 70(1): 61–85.

Weber, J. and Glyptis, S. (2000) 'Measuring the impact of a business ethics course and community service experience on students' values and opinions', *Teaching Business Ethics*, 4(4): 341–58.

Williams, S.D. and Dewett, T. (2005) 'Yes, you can teach business ethics: A review and research agenda', *Journal of Leadership and Organizational Studies*, 12(2): 109–20.

Wu, C-F. (2003) 'A study of the adjustment of ethical recognition and ethical decision-making of managers-to-be across the Taiwan strait before and after receiving a business ethics education', *Journal of Business Ethics*, 45(4): 291–307.

Wynd, W.R. and Mager, J. (1989) 'The business and society course: Does it change students' attitudes?' *Journal of Business Ethics*, 8(6): 487–91.

Yoder, D.E. and Denhart, K.G. (2001) 'Ethics education in public administration and affairs: Preparing graduates for workplace moral dilemmas', in T. Cooper (ed.), *Handbook of Administrative Ethics* (pp. 59–77), New York: Dekker.

PART V
Ethics across boundaries

13

PUBLIC SERVICE MOTIVATION IN A COMPLEX PUBLIC SECTOR

Alan Lawton and Julie Rayner

Introduction

The institutional context of public service delivery has, increasingly, become complex. Public- and private-sector organizations, as well as the third sector, collaborate and work in partnership with each other, as evident in a range of policy areas, from urban renewal to education. Public officials now have to engage with others, horizontally, in different types of organizations, and not just hierarchically within their own organizations. Indeed, for some officials, the institutional location of their work has shifted from public to private, or partnership, organizations. Such a dynamic in the institutional setting of public service delivery may render traditional goals, values and processes problematic. It may also provide new opportunities. Boundaries between different types of organizations that deliver public services become blurred as do the differences between policy formulation and implementation, and between public and private interests.

In such a changing environment, traditional notions of a public service ethos underpinning public sector delivery and the commitment through public service motivation (PSM) are contested. One big question is: how can private and semi-public-sector organizations, and those who work within them, have the same commitment to the public interest as traditional public-sector organizations? Scholars have argued that a key problem for partnerships and networks is how to reconcile individual interests with those of the network or partnership as a whole.

This chapter underscores the need for researchers to develop a better understanding not only of sectoral differences, but also whether or how PSM impacts performance of individuals in collaborative and networked contexts. Thus, a key research question becomes, 'What might PSM look like in a complex and fragmented public service arena?' We respond to this by examining the literatures on public service networks through the prism of PSM and develop five propositions. We conclude with suggestions for a future research agenda.

Background and framing of the problem

The core purpose of the public sector is to serve the public interest and to provide citizens with an adequate level of welfare, agreed upon through the political process, which would not otherwise be provided. In contrast, private-sector organizations, operating in the market, pursue different ends, which do not appear to correspond well with the altruistic value foundations of PSM (Kjeldsen and Jacobsen 2012). Their survival depends on their ability to make a profit, and the services they provide are not in the interests of the general public, but are targeted at specific customers. However, delivering public services through different organizations working together is now commonplace. It is usual to find public-, private- and third-sector organizations sharing in the production of economic development, health and social care, or environmental sustainability, and there is nothing new in the idea of partnerships and collaboration. Business strategists have also studied inter-organizational collaborations (Håkansson and Snehota 1989; Ring and Van De Ven 1992; Snow et al. 1992), as have organizational theorists (Boje and Whetten 1981).

Sociologists have examined the 'networked society', and within public administration much has been written about policy networks (Rhodes and Marsh 1992), delivery networks (Lawless and Moore 1989) and sector-specific networks (Ferlie and Pettigrew 1996; Hudson 1987). More recently, there has been an explosion in research on networks, partnerships and collaboration, and its 'family member' governance, in and across public service organizations. There is also an abundance of literature on the reasons for such close working relationships (Head 2008), what forms they might take (Austin and Seitanidi 2012a, 2012b; Klijn 2008), how they are managed (Kickert et al. 1997), or how effective they are (Mandell and Keast 2008; Skelcher and Sullivan 2008).

Irrespective of the form they take (e.g. partnerships or loose networks), sharing goals and values and building trust are considered to be key ingredients in their success. However, despite the wealth of research that has been undertaken over recent decades, the impact on the values, behaviour and motivation of public officials who have engaged with partners from different sectors has been under-examined (Davies 2009). Different stakeholders rarely agree on one common goal (Boyne 2003). At the same time, there is emerging evidence of some convergence of norms, values and motivations among public and private providers of similar services (e.g. Van Steden et al. 2015).

A consistent theme in public administration research is the alleged differences between individuals employed in public and private sectors (e.g. Boyne 2002; Houston 2000, 2006; Nalbandian and Edwards 1983; Newstrom et al. 1976; Perry and Rainey 1988; Taylor 2010; Wittmer 1991). This differentiation is often attributed to the values and beliefs associated with a PSM or with a public service ethos such that some individuals are highly attracted and motivated by public service work (Horton 2008; Rayner *et al.* 2011). A key issue becomes to what extent the changing context of public service delivery influences the motivation of public officials as they are exposed to private-sector sets of values (see van der Wal *et al.* 2008). Similarly, to what extent do those individuals working within private-sector organizations involved in the delivery of public services adopt some of the attitudes and behaviours of their public-sector counterparts? Without doubt, the concepts of work motivation and performance are different in the two sectors, and yet inconsistent findings have been reported from the many studies that have investigated sectoral differences in PSM (Rainey 2009).

We should seek to find explanations and develop theories of effective collaboration between traditional public servants and their network partners; the former who are believed to be motivated by public interest rather than a narrow economic self-interest associated with the private sector (van der Wal and Oosterbaan 2013). The focus of the debate has been the grounding of PSM in a commitment to public service values in tension with business-like values and market-style reforms experienced over recent decades in the public sector (Perry and Hondeghem 2008). And yet absolute agreement in, and clarity of, key concepts has been found wanting: 'Despite an extensive body of quantitative research, it is still not clear what being public service motivated exactly means, and hence what behavioural consequences can be expected from somebody scoring high on PSM' (Schott *et al.* 2014, p. 2). This is particularly relevant as PSM is now considered to be a central variable in creating high-performance organizations and can be used in managing people to this end. Hence, we need to investigate whether PSM is fragmented or, alternatively, whether there is a spillover to private-sector employees uniting networked organizations towards a strong sense of PSM. It is now time to shed light on the reality for networked organizations and assess the levels and behavioural effects of PSM existing in such partnerships.

The dimensions of public service motivation

The PSM literature contains a number of definitions of the concept; it was originally defined by Perry and Wise (1990) as 'an individual's predisposition to respond to motives grounded primarily or uniquely in public institutions and organizations' (p. 368). This view was later contested as it was demonstrated that PSM transcends the public sector (Brewer and Selden 1998). Moreover, Rainey and Steinbauer (1999, p. 23) define PSM as 'a general altruistic motivation to serve the interests of the community of people, a state and nation, or humankind'. They note that it has been part of public administration discourse for some time and, central to this discourse, are discussions of ethical and equitable behaviours (Frederickson 1997). A more recent definition is broader still, and incorporates 'the belief, values and attitudes that go beyond self-interest and organizational interest, that concern the interest of a larger political entity and that motivate individuals to act accordingly whenever appropriate' (Vandenabeele 2007, p. 547). At the same time, 'publicness' is not confined to government organizations (Bozeman 2007). This multitude of definitions will, in part, be due to PSM being a 'fuzzy concept', and that individual interpretation of what it means to serve the public interest needs to be considered to fully understand it and its behavioural consequences (Schott *et al.* 2014).

There are also a variety of measures of PSM. These range from Perry's original 24-item, multidimensional instrument to the popular global five-item measure, to the commonly used one-item measure. Perry's dimensions contain 'commitment to the public interest' (CPI), 'compassion' (COM), 'self-sacrifice' and 'attraction to policymaking' (APM). Kim and Vandenabeele (2010) renamed the CPI dimension 'commitment to public values' as it is founded in loyalty, impartiality and a duty to serve the interests of government and society. The APM dimension is the most problematic as research has found a weak correlation between APM and a recently validated five-item version of Perry's original scale (Wright *et al.* 2013). There is also an implicit contradiction of the altruistic motive, as it is more individual and private as opposed to emphasizing serving society. However, it is argued that participation in policy process can be viewed as a way to do good for as many people as possible (Kim and Vandenabeele 2010).

The public interest dimension is founded in the duty to serve the interests of government and society. As Kjeldsen (2012, p. 59) points out, 'when someone is occupied with the provision of public services it is normatively appropriate to do what is considered best for society as a whole'. Indeed, PSM differs in meaning and in relation to culture (Kim *et al.* 2013), and consensus on the operationalization of PSM appears to be missing (Perry *et al.* 2010).

The issue of whether PSM is prevalent in the private sector has been underplayed despite empirical evidence showing spillover effects from PSM into the public realm (e.g. Houston 2000, 2006). Only recently is it becoming increasingly recognized that it exists in private-sector organizations as evident through civic participation and pro-social behaviour. So if we take the broader definition offered by Brewer and Selden (1998, p. 417), 'The motivational force that induces individuals to perform meaningful . . . public, community, and social service', we observe that PSM is linked to the delivery of public goods and services, and not necessarily linked to a sector. This is important to investigate further as PSM is now assumed to be a route to improved performance, and the public sector is increasingly challenged by the private sector in the delivery of public services. Thus, the question raised is whether private employees are equally public service motivated (Kjeldsen 2012), particularly as different levels of PSM can be related to professionalism and occupation irrespective of sector (Andersen and Pedersen 2012), as well as a range of other variables, including pro-social attitudes, agreeableness, gender, education and religion.

Evidence of public service motivation

Over the decades, PSM research has developed in such a way that it can be described as comprising three 'waves': definition and measurement, assessing and confirming construct validity, and learning from past research and overcoming shortcomings (Perry 2014). In particular, the volume of research on PSM has increased significantly in the last five years, and studies have produced confirmation of a range of positive attitudes and behaviours and a body of empirical evidence (Ritz *et al.* 2013). Although mainly generated in the US, more recent research extends throughout Europe and China (e.g. Bellé 2013; Bellé and Ongaro 2014; Liu *et al.* 2013; Liu *et al.* 2014; van der Wal forthcoming). There is a growing agenda that it should be nurtured, as, importantly, it is manifest in both attitudes and behaviours (Schott and Pronk 2014). For example, PSM is linked to forms of self-sacrifice such as whistle blowing; leads to high performance, higher job satisfaction, increased commitment and a decreased tendency to leave the job; places less value on extrinsic reward motivators such as high income and short work hours and more value on altruistic behaviour and public service activity; and is predictive of organizational citizenship behaviour (e.g. Brewer and Selden 1998; Buelens and Van Den Broeck 2007; Camilleri 2006; Crewson 1997; Houston 2000, 2006; Kim 2006, 2008; Naff and Crum 1999; Pandey *et al.* 2008; Taylor 2007; Taylor and Taylor 2010). Meta-analysis of PSM and performance research concluded that the relationship is positive, but effect sizes are small (Warren and Chen 2013).

The public sector versus private sector distinction is not helpful in explaining differences in commitment (Steinhaus and Perry 1996), as:

> we do not know whether the reported positive association between PSM and public sector employment is actually due to the employment sector or maybe rather due to the nature of public service work (which can be carried out in other sectors).
>
> (Kjeldsen and Jacobsen 2012, p. 2)

Nevertheless, public-sector workers do report greater PSM and tend to value meaningful public service more highly than private-sector employees (Perry *et al.* 2010; Steijn 2008). Recently, Bellé and Ongaro (2014) found that self-reported levels of three dimensions of PSM, CPI, COM and SS are on average higher for public relative to private employees. The fourth dimension – attraction to policy-making (APM) – did not provide a differentiated result for this aspect of PSM. This effect was described as 'not surprising' (p. 392), as it has been explained previously by Wright *et al.* (2012, p. 210) as 'a rational or self-interested motive that is less value or mission specific'. The assumption that PSM levels are broadly the same across the sectors has been discussed by Bellé and Ongaro (2014), where health care in Italy was subjected more to New Public Management (NPM) reform than other fields (e.g. law enforcement or general government). They point out that 'reforms inspired by NPM doctrines may have a more normalizing effect on the public sector, making it more like a commercial sector' (p. 386). However, this has never been directly elaborated through the theoretical lens of PSM.

More recent debate focuses on the stability of PSM; it is questioned whether it is a trait (a stable characteristic across situations over time of an individual) or a state (a transient characteristic, variable across situations). The trait/state debate views and assumptions are usually implicit and need to be scrutinized 'front and centre' (Perry 2014, p. 43). In support of this, Andersen et al. (2014) highlight recent evidence that PSM is a dynamic rather than stable trait or disposition (e.g. Bellé 2013; Kjeldsen and Jacobsen 2012). The implications are that managers can increase the level of PSM among their employees through a variety of mechanisms such as attraction, selection and design of job packages, and also they can do more to avoid PSM being crowded out by the use of incentives and command systems. Further, transformational leadership can be used by managers in organizations without severe value conflicts to increase individual levels of PSM, which in turn should increase performance (Krogsgaard et al. 2013).

Given the growth in collaborative networks, the focus of research should not be on such distinctions between different sectors, which, it is argued by Rainey (1997), are oversimplifications and stereotypes. Rather, we need to be concerned with identifying and analysing commonalities among such networks, as well as in hybrid organizational forms relating to dimensions of PSM and to those features that might lead to differences in PSM. For example, do individuals in different partner organizations have different conceptions of the public interest that emphasize concerns for service to the 'customer' rather than more classical conceptions such as the 'patriotism of benevolence' (Frederickson and Hart 1985; Staats 1988)? In investigating if ownership matters to employee motivation when occupation is controlled for, Andersen and Pedersen (2013) found that although employees in both sectors have pro-social motivation, those in the public sector were more motivated to work for the public interest, whereas those in the private sector were more motivated towards helping individual users of services. It is, however, not known if we can assume that if motivation differs between contexts, or whether this will be the same globally. As reminders of the 'noble calling' (Pattakos 2004) are issued, the context of public service delivery and the concept of public service have changed. Yet, Frederickson (2007) poses the question: 'When will people sing an anthem to a contractor, wear the uniform of a network, or pledge allegiance to non-jurisdictional forms of governance? Probably not soon' (p. 291).

Reward preferences are of specific interest as these differ for public and private managers, and particularly on two items: engaging in meaningful public service, and doing work that is helpful to other people (Rainey 1982). Clearly, longitudinal empirical evidence is needed in this arena, particularly as debate surrounds the stability or changeability of PSM. For example, Brewer (2008, p. 149) argues that: 'organizational socialization is an important mechanism for transmitting a 'public institutional logic' and seeding public service motivation in the individual. Organizational socialization may quicken an individual's sense of public service and inculcate public service-related virtues and norms'. Whether a network or partnership can develop such an institutional logic is a moot point.

Collaboration and public service networks

For the purposes of this chapter, we use a generic concept of networks to describe the different ways in which organizations work with each other, whether in policy networks, public–private partnerships or any other type of relationship. Such networks can be described as 'structures of interdependence involving multiple organizations, or parts thereof, where one unit is not merely the formal subordinate of the others in some larger hierarchical arrangement' (O'Toole 1997, p. 45). A useful background to governance and networks is provided by Klijn (2008) identifying different types: policy networks, service delivery networks and governing networks. We might also add professional networks, and area networks. One example of the latter was Local Strategic Partnerships in the UK that involved the coming together of different agencies, public, private and third sector, in a geographical area to jointly deliver services across a range of policy areas. In an early contribution to the discussion, Rhodes (1990) distinguishes between highly integrated policy communities, professional networks, intergovernmental networks, producer networks and loosely integrated issue networks, characterized by a limited degree of interdependence among a large number of members. An early definition of a partnership is offered by Kernaghan (1993, p. 61): 'a relationship involving the sharing of power, work, support and/or information with others for the achievement of joint goals and/or mutual benefits'. Key questions are: why have networks and what purposes do they fulfil? It is argued that network arrangements can, for example, address 'messy' problems (Waddock 1991), or the so-called 'wicked issues' (Courtney 2001), that they encourage the dispersal of power, and that they are more efficient and effective in delivering public services (Head 2008; O'Toole 1997).

The question of 'why collaborate?' can be answered in different ways (Austin and Seitanidi 2012a) and will affect the attitudes and behaviours of collaborating partners. If the main reason is to comply with top-down legislation in order to secure funding, then the motivation to engage with the network may be different than if the network is driven more by bottom-up considerations in order to address common community problems that cannot be addressed by one agency working alone. Klijn (1997) suggests that there are three important characteristics of networks. First, they exist because of interdependencies between actors; second, they consist of a variety of actors each with their own goals; third, they consist of relations of a more or less lasting nature between actors.

De Bruijn and Ringeling (1997) examine networks as a single entity that can be held accountable, which protects individual rights, promotes public value, and provides political and democratic legitimation. The role, however, as guardian of the public interest is unclear, as 'The public interest is difficult to identify in a quasi-network context in which subsidiary interests are constantly being put forward' (p. 159). Not just that, but it is where values are contested. Partnerships and networks are dynamic, often lack coherence, and involve competing sets of values (Davies 2009). If values are contested, then the notion of the public interest becomes problematic. Thus, Agranoff and McGuire (2001) suggest that 'In general, one can argue that the public sector's responsibility for affecting the public interest is compromised and limited by the use of networks' (p. 310).

In focusing upon networks, then, the unit of analysis needs to shift from the individual and the particular organization to the network as a whole. In so doing, it must be recognized that we can only touch upon key issues of structure and agency that have engaged social theorists over time (Cook and Whitmeyer 1992). The focal point of interactions between network members themselves also needs to be considered (Kickert et al. 1997).

Public officials play a dual role in networks. First, they are one of the actors themselves seeking to maximize their own interests and, second, they want to ensure that all essential values are represented. The key question then becomes: to what extent has the public interest become fragmented? Kickert et al. (1997) argue that finding a common purpose is one of the main tasks of network management and suggest that networks are condemned to fail where there is a neglect of common interests. Social–cognitive theory and goal-setting theory might be useful, as they provide mechanisms for the transmission or organization common purpose and values to an individual level (Perry and Vandenabeele 2008).

A common interest

In her work on collaboration, Huxham (1996) distinguishes between self-interest motivation, which recognizes that organizations cannot go it alone, and what she terms moral motivation, which recognizes that 'wicked issues' require a joined-up approach. She suggests that there are a number of different dimensions to the rationale for collaboration, and these include information exchange that enhances the capacity of the collaborating organizations, conflict resolution between organizations by creating a shared vision, and the fostering of participation and thereby changing the power relations between organizations. Clearly, a key issue is the extent to which individual members of a network are willing and able to put aside their individual interests in the interests of the network as a whole (Keast et al. 2004). How do individuals self-organize to solve collective problems? This is a recurring question in public administration and beyond (Ostrom 1990).

The extent to which the difficulties that organizations have in working with each other may result from a variety of perspectives: first, the history between the organizations; if it is the case that in the past, separate health and social care organizations, for example, have not worked well together and have a history of conflict, it will take more than legislative fiat to ensure cooperation. Second, diverse values and organizational cultures may make cooperation difficult. Schofield (1997) points to the different values of health and social care, and Hardy et al. (1990)

argue for the UK case that there is little agreement between the NHS and personal social services in what constitutes community care. Third, differences in understanding the nature of the problem as theories about how to deal with social problems vary from, say, a policing perspective as opposed to a social work perspective (Sink 1996). Fourth, professional territories and jealousies often occur within the same organization (see Bate 2000, discussed below). Not only that, but each network may favour one dominant professional group over another, and therefore it is likely that the functional/service area will have an impact upon whose values prevail. In networks that rely on technical expertise to deliver goals, it is likely that one group will rule. For example, economic development networks may be dominated by business, crime reduction by police, and health care by the medical profession. If networks involve the exercise of power, as they must do in order to achieve outcomes, then it is likely that the most powerful group will have its values dominating the agenda. The challenge is to persuade the network partners that their view of the world makes most sense. Fifth, different organizational arrangements, including structure, information technology systems, rules for decision-making and accountability mechanisms. It is a difficult for organizations to give up degrees of freedom or autonomy in order to secure needed resources, but as Cropper (1996) argues: 'The discovery and articulation of shared beliefs and values about conduct can, however, help to promote a sense of inclusion, of predictability or dependability and of unequivocality fundamental prerequisites for continuing motivation and commitment' (p. 96).

Still, for political theorists, the public interest is not an end state, but a process, and in constituting a process, it allows citizens to engage with each other. It is through this process that collective values are worked through rather than defining these in advance (Honohan 2002). Thus, the public interest is pluralistic, balancing different values and interests (Lewis 2006). It is impartial, and as such does not identify with particular interests, nor is it the same as local or community interests.

Public interest results from a dialogue within which different voices or interests can be heard, and public officials have a duty to help citizens articulate their interests (Denhardt and Denhardt 2007). As we know, however, this dialogue is flawed insofar as some interests have louder voices than others and some are excluded altogether. The public interest, then, can never be static, but will respond to different interests. Clearly, to move from self-interest, either of the individual or the organization, to network interests will not happen overnight. Agranoff and McGuire (2001) report: 'Over time each work group found that individual and organizational positions receded in favour of new group understanding' (p. 304). The environment for interests is a negotiated one (De Bruijn and Dicke 2006), and the public interest, from one perspective, arises out of shared interests and values (Denhardt and Denhardt 2007). It is claimed that 'As interpretations of the "public interest" vary depending on the roles people occupy in society, so does the meaning of public service motivation' (Schott et al. 2014, p. 1). Thus, if the very concept of the public interest itself is contested, then to assume that public officials have a monopoly of the term may be problematic. The public interest may be served best by fostering the interests of individual clients or users, or groups of clients and users, and a private- or third-sector organization may be committed to, and have expertise in, the delivery of public services to such individuals and groups.

This leads us to reflect on whether public interest can or should be determined in advance and to our first proposition:

> **Proposition 1: The public interest is contested between different individuals and organizations, and this contestation is intensified in a network.**

Types of network

There are different types of relationships, and the literature, generally, relies on a threefold taxonomy (Mandell and Keast 2008). The first is cooperation, which involves short-term voluntary participation where members do not lose their organizational identity, and individual goals or objectives are not merged into collective goals. Second is coordination, which entails joint planning and programmes (Head 2008). Third is collaboration, which requires long-term, robust, multi-stakeholder relationships, relying on commitments by all parties, and where joint new roles and functions, underpinned by shared norms and values, are created. Collaboration involves interdependence, shared norms and values (Thomson *et al.* 2007).

The different types can be mapped on to a continuum from loose- to close-knit ties, with the supposition that the closer the collaboration, the more sharing is involved. Different intensities will require different stages of relationship building, and motivation may change over time depending upon the development of the network/partnership. This view fits well with the notion that PSM is a state, rather than a trait, as discussed earlier. Additionally, the nature of the relationships will require different forms of commitment, or psychological ties to bind employees to the network. For example, information sharing requires less commitment than the joint delivery of public services. In turn, this requires less commitment than the working together in the articulation of a common interest and a desire to make a difference to the community. Whether or not networks manage to elicit such commitment from their members depends on a number of different factors (e.g. the network culture, the effectiveness of socialization within the network and the extent to which the network meets the members' expectations).

One of the consequences for those who have developed strong ties to the network but find that their expectations may not be met will be frustration and disillusionment. Agencies need to provide individuals with the opportunity to act upon their PSM in practice to avoid employees becoming frustrated (Steen and Rutgers 2011) or leaving (Giauque *et al.* 2013). We need to establish the type of psychological ties that predominate within such networks. Are they based on investments that have been made by various parties within the network? Or are they based on a shared commitment to important network values? These are important distinctions, as the former relates to a calculated exchange relationship (Becker 1960), whereas the latter represents a much deeper psychological tie. The two types of commitment may be in tension with each other, particularly as commitment among public-sector employees has been identified as a way to fulfil a PSM (Downs 1967; Romzek 1990).

Collaboration is described as:

> a process in which autonomous or semi-autonomous actors interact through formal or informal negotiation, jointly creating rules and structures governing their relationships and ways to act or decide on the issues that brought them together; it is a process involving shared norms and mutually beneficial interactions.
>
> (Thomson *et al.* 2007, p. 25)

Of course, not all values can be expected to be of equal importance within organizations, and given the dynamics associated with networks, as expected, there is considerable complexity and ambiguity (Huxham and Vangen 2000). One could say that where you stand depends on where you sit within the network in terms of roles, seniority and type of member. Thomson *et al.* (2007) recognize the tension between organizational self-interest and collective interest, and identified five key dimensions in measuring collaboration. The most problematic dimension was organizational autonomy, and they argue that a future research agenda needs to get a better understanding of the relationship between the individual and collective interests of the collaborating parties.

There are a myriad of questions to be asked here, and from a multidisciplinary perspective, such as: What is the link between PSM and job performance in these networks? How are the incentive and reward programmes different between organizations in the network, and in what ways do they impact? For example, individual incentive programmes may be a feature in private-sector organizations within the network; however, reward strategies of this nature are claimed to be less effective or even counterproductive in an environment characterized with high PSM. The explanation as to why there may have been negative consequences, for example, of monetary incentives on PSM (Georgellis *et al.* 2011; Giauque *et al.* 2013; Jacobsen *et al.* 2014) has been attributed to crowding out theory (Frey and Jegen 2001). What are the normative implications of PSM within these networks? What is the evidence of pro-social behaviours, and how do they help the efficient and effective delivery of public services? What are the implications for the more traditional public-sector employees regarding person–organization fit (Kim 2012)?

PSM is complex and its dimensions nuanced, particularly as neither public or private employees are homogeneous groups. It is timely to investigate to what extent they are evident where networks are concerned. Our area of interest is to investigate areas of motivation that are concerned with the goals of these networks and the reasons why individuals within them choose to pursue these goals. Although previous research has identified many types of employee commitment, the public–sector research has focused primarily on commitment to the organization (Wright 2004). We wish to look at this more closely and examine the nature of commitment towards the network, its mission, and PSM. The perception of importance of an organization's mission increases employee work motivation in the public sector (Wright 2008). Furthermore, employees who perceive that an organization's values and goals match their own have been found to be more satisfied, perform better, and are less likely to leave an organization (Kjeldsen and Jacobsen 2012). Naturally, person–organization fit can be achieved by attracting applicants with appropriate characteristics or by influencing applicants once they are employed (Cable and Parsons 2001). So is motivation and commitment in a network different than in a single organization? It is now well established that commitment is a multi-dimensional construct (e.g. Meyer and Allen 1997). A framework of analysis that offers a comprehensive measurement of this commitment construct shows that it is a psychological state with at least three separable components (Allen and Meyer 1990). These motives are, first, 'affective', reflecting a desire and concern of an individual wanting to belong or remain. Second, 'normative', perceived as an obligation to remain because individuals feel they should. This is consistent with social exchange theory, which explains that employees reciprocate favourable treatment with greater commitment and performance (Blau 1964), and may also develop from investments into an organization or through socialization (Wiener 1982). Third, 'continuance', based on a need to belong due to sunk costs or lack of alternative (Becker 1960). The three forms of commitment are not mutually exclusive, can be experienced to varying degrees, and are conceptually and operationally different (Meyer and Allen 1991, 1997). This leads us to our second and third propositions.

> **Proposition 2: The type of network affects the commitment of individuals and the motivation to pursue common goals.**
>
> **Proposition 3: There will be a positive relationship between public service motivation and individual identification within the network.**

These propositions offer many challenges, as they require study and measurement of internal processes beliefs and attitudes. Nevertheless, as Wright (2008) suggests, just because they are difficult to measure should not prevent us from trying. A starting point is to define the terms and find reliable and valid ways to measure the constructs of interest to collaboration within a complex public service. We now discuss these below.

Network relationships

A key feature of networks is the underpinning values, and these include trust, cooperation, altruism, loyalty, solidarity, and involve essentially relationships between equal social agents (Hudson 2004). At a very simple level, networking takes place between individuals on a person-to person basis rather than organization to organization (Himmelman 1996), and where information is exchanged for mutual benefit (Walker *et al.* 2007), whereas for Mandell and Keast (2008), 'it is not the formal requirements that keeps a network together, but, rather the ability to build mutual goodwill and commitment among the participants' (p. 721). Exchange theorists see social structure as a configuration of social relations and positions (Cook and Whitmeyer 1992). Here, the actor is motivated by interests or rewards, and the interactions consist of exchange of valued items (Levine and White 1961). From this perspective, interests are not fixed in advance, but are modified in action.

In addition, Rainey and Steinbauer (1999, p. 206) drew on expectancy theory to define mission valence as an employee's 'affective orientations toward particular outcomes' associated with an organization's mission. Mission valence can be viewed as an employee's perceptions of the attractiveness or salience of an organization's purpose or social contribution. Yet, our argument is that networks involve relationships, not just individual motivations, and these will involve expectations of the behaviour of others (Koppenjan 2008). Motivation, in this sense, then cannot be isolated from relationships with others. Relations are typically horizontal in such networks, rather than vertical, and the concept of 'making a difference' is not clear-cut in a world of contested performance outcomes. Andersen and Pedersen (2013, p. 845) ask 'whether individuals expect private employment to allow them to help specific users of public services more than public employment'.

Proposition 4: Public service motivation is positively related to the extent that mission valence is perceived by network members.

Network position and role

It is considered that the position that an organization takes in a network will be a function of its power, based upon control of resources, legitimacy, legal status, knowledge, and its importance to the network (Keast *et al.* 2004; Milward and Provan 2000). Typically, a local authority will be a lead player in any network involving local regeneration. Himmelman (2001), for example, distinguishes between collaborative 'betterment' and collaborative empowerment to explore these issues. Betterment is the norm and would involve large and influential organizations setting the agenda; policy is formulated by the elite and implemented by others; there is central control over administration and governance and there is a focus on institutionally related professions. In contrast, empowerment is characterized by power sharing, common values, transparency and bottom-up decision-making. To move from betterment to empowerment is very difficult to achieve, and 'This kind of transformation must encourage and respect a diversity of values and beliefs and strongly promote shared power to achieve common purpose' (p. 31). In an early work, Boje and Whetten (1981) measure the relationship between network centrality and influence, and Milward and Provan (2000, 2003) argue that network effectiveness will depend upon network stability and network structure in terms of control and centralized integration. Clearly, there are challenges for managers in working across organizational boundaries rather than in hierarchical organizations. Specifically, different skills are required, including negotiation, facilitating, brokering and bargaining, and an enhanced requirement to listen (Head 2008; Williams 2002). Similarly, Ferlie and Pettigrew (1996) identify interpersonal and communication skills, and also add the tolerance of high levels of ambiguity and uncertainty and the capacity to learn quickly. Himmelman (1996) examines management behaviours in networks and identifies different roles that are classified as convenor, catalyst, conduit, advocate, community organizer, funder, technical assistance provider, capacity builder, partner and facilitator.

There are five key areas where managers will have to manage: first, across jurisdictions as organizations have legitimate interests and expect to have their autonomy respected. Different definitions of the proper remit of public services activities are held by different agencies. Management under such circumstances requires the ability to balance both the goals of the individual organization and those of the network as a whole (Kickert and Koppenjan 1997). The manager needs to recognize that members of a network in the public services may represent separate and distinct and legal entities with different systems of accountability. Second, they are required to manage different stakeholders. For example, common interests need to be identified, and should be perceived as being more important than conflicting interests. Third, they need to manage stakeholder interests, which involves enforcing commitments across organizational boundaries. Fourth, it is necessary to manage implementation, and this will require a common base of information, standards and monitoring to overcome differences in organizational design and structure. Finally, it is vital they manage the exchanges, which means respecting confidences and building trust (see Rose and Lawton 1999). However, the degree of sharing of values and goals is contested. Termeer and Koppenjan (1997, p. 86) argue that:

> Attempts to ensure that all actors have the same perceptions are unnecessary, undesirable and doomed to failure. They are unnecessary because actors can cooperate without shared perceptions or consensus of common goals and are undesirable because they lead to the suppression of legitimate aspirations. Such efforts prevent a variety of actors accomplishing their objectives, which will in turn, discourage them from investing their resources in joint actions.

The tasks that managers have as part of a network will require new skills and a new articulation of the managerial role. This leads us to our next proposition.

Proposition 5: The more central the individual or organization role in the network, the higher the public service motivation.

Having identified our propositions, we now discuss a method to facilitate this research and provide an overall rationale for its use. We recognize that the dynamic nature of networks and the constructs of interest within them often result in a dearth of suitably validated measures. Also there may be no single best way to evaluate them. We propose that case study research is used here to establish construct validity, to sharpen definitions and inform the process of operationalization; although often exploratory in nature, it is appropriate when the field is underdeveloped, or if existing research does not address the particular research question (Gerring 2004; Yin 2013). One of the challenges to case study research is to demonstrate to positivist researchers that it can add to theory. Case study research provides for a better grounding of construct measures, thus helping to shape hypotheses and providing a road map for building theory (Eisenhardt 1989). As Eisenhardt and Graebner (2007) argue:

> with inductive theory building from cases producing new theory from data and deductive theory testing completing the cycle by using data to test theory. Moreover, since it is a theory-building approach that is deeply embedded in rich empirical data, building theory from cases is likely to produce theory that is accurate, interesting and testable. Thus, it is a natural complement to mainstream deductive research.
>
> (pp. 25–6)

The choice of networks to gather data will depend upon different criteria, including the length of time that a network has been in existence, how extensive is its membership, what is the purpose of the network, what type of network it is, and who provides the resources. There is a need for the development of analytical tools to dissect the attitudes and behaviours of those working in collaboration to deliver public services. Data collection should also involve individuals who play different roles in the networks, including board members, network managers, organizational representatives and network funders.

We propose a two-stage approach to further this research: the first entails clarifying constructs, sharpening propositions in an iterative process involving key stakeholders in a selection of different networks. The second stage requires a pool of items to develop measures to test our propositions.

Conclusions

This chapter has reviewed the relevant literature on public service networks through the prism of PSM and questioned what this would look like in networked organizations. Consideration has been given to the dimensions of PSM, and in such an environment it is likely that the public interest concept is contested, that goals are often ambiguous and that shared values are difficult to achieve. Therefore, meanings need to be investigated, concepts sharpened and relationships analysed to reveal whether the dimensions of PSM may be eroded or spill over to individuals employed in the private sector. Values commonly held by individuals employed within traditional public and private sectors need to be empirically tested to measure whether there is any impact and shift in values over time and, if so, establish the dominant influential direction within such collaborations.

We have summarized our theoretical arguments in the form of five propositions and now, to take the agenda forward, advocate the collection of both qualitative and quantitative data to provide empirical evidence in support of some or all of these assumptions. Initial research questions are thus:

1 *Does the complexity of public service delivery have a positive or negative effect on public service motivation of involved public- and private-sector actors?*
2 *Does the complexity of public service delivery make the concept of the public interest more ambiguous?*

This research is timely and will add to our understanding of PSM in a complex public sector. Thus, the aim of case study research is to gain knowledge that will help develop the basis of elements of theory to explain the function of PSM within networks. For researchers, it will enhance understanding of PSM in a dynamic environment, allowing us to examine both individual agency and organizational context. For policymakers, it should examine the assumptions that are made about delivering common goals through shared values. If public interest is seen as emerging from a process, then officials have a duty to create the space for deliberative engagement. For many, this will be problematic, as it will involve giving up power and professional status. However, PSM could be the vehicle that delivers high performance in networks by taking out of the equation sectoral differences and recognizing that it can be found in different organizations by different individuals and at different times.

References

Agranoff, R. and Mcguire, M. (2001) 'Big questions in public network management research', *Journal of Public Administration Research and Theory*, 11(3): 295–326.

Allen, N.J. and Meyer, J.P. (1990) 'Measurement and antecedents of affective continuance and normative commitment to the organization', *Journal of Occupational Psychology*, 63: 1–18.

Andersen, L.B. and Pedersen, L.H. (2012) 'Public service motivation and professionalism', *International Journal of Public Administration*, 35(1): 46–57.

Andersen, L.B. and Pedersen, L.H. (2013) 'Does ownership matter for employee motivation when occupation is controlled for?', *International Journal of Public Administration*, 36(12): 840–56.

Andersen, L.B., Heinesen, E. and Pedersen, L.H. (2014) 'How does public service motivation among teachers affect student performance in schools?', *Journal of Public Administration Research and Theory*, 24(3): 651–71.

Austin, J.E. and Seitanidi, M.M. (2012a) 'Collaborative value creation: A review of partnering between nonprofits and businesses. Part I: Value creation spectrum and collaboration stages', *Nonprofit and Voluntary Sector Quarterly*, 41(5): 726–58.

Austin, J.E. and Seitanidi, M.M. (2012b) 'Collaborative value creation: A review of partnering between nonprofits and businesses. Part 2: Partnership processes and outcomes', *Nonprofit and Voluntary Sector Quarterly*, 41(6): 929–68.

Bate, P. (2000) 'Changing the culture of a hospital: From hierarchy to networked community', *Public Administration*, 78: 485–512.

Becker, H.S. (1960) 'Notes on the concept of commitment', *American Journal of Sociology*, 66: 32–42.

Bellé, N. (2013) 'Experimental evidence on the relationship between public service motivation and job performance', *Public Administration Review*, 73(1): 143–53.

Bellé, N. and Ongaro, E. (2014) 'NPM, administrative reforms and public service motivation: Improving the dialogue between research agendas', *International Review of Administrative Sciences*, 80(2): 382–400.

Blau, P.M. (1964) *Exchange and Power in Social Life*, New York: Wiley.

Boje, D.M. and Whetten, D.A. (1981) 'Effects of organizational strategies and contextual constraints on centrality and attributions of influence in interorganizational networks', *Administrative Science Quarterly*, 26: 378–95.

Boyne, G.A. (2002) 'Public and private management: What's the difference?', *Journal of Management Studies*, 39(1): 97–122.

Boyne, G.A. (2003) 'What is public service improvement?', *Public Administration*, 81(2): 211–27.

Bozeman, B. (2007) *Public Values and Public Interest: Counterbalancing Economic Individualism*, Washington, DC: Georgetown University Press.

Brewer, G. (2008) 'Employee and organizational performance', in J.L. Perry and A. Hondeghem (eds), *Motivation in Public Management: The Call of Public Services* (pp. 136–56), Oxford: Oxford University Press.

Brewer, G.A. and Selden, S.C. (1998) 'Whistle blowers in the federal civil service: New evidence of the public service ethic', *Journal of Public Administration Research and Theory*, 8(3): 413–40.

Buelens, M. and Van Den Broeck, H. (2007) 'An analysis of differences in work motivation between public and private sector organizations', *Public Administration Review*, 67(1): 65–7.

Cable, D.M. and Parsons, C.K. (2001) 'Socialization tactics and person–organization fit', *Personnel Psychology*, 54(1): 1–23.

Camilleri, E. (2006) 'Towards developing an organizational commitment: Public service motivation model for the Maltese public service employees', *Public Policy And Administration*, 21(1): 63–83.

Cook, K.S. and Whitmeyer, J.M. (1992) 'Two approaches to social structure: Exchange theory and network analysis', *Annual Review of Sociology*, 18: 109–27.

Courtney, J.F. (2001) 'Decision making and knowledge management in inquiring organizations: Towards a new decision-making paradigm in DSS', *Decision Support Systems*, 31: 17–38.

Crewson, P.E. (1997) 'Public service motivation: Building empirical evidence of incidence and effect', *Journal of Public Administration Research and Theory*, 7(4): 499–518.

Cropper, S. (1996) 'Collaborative working and the issue of sustainability', in C. Huxham (ed.), *Creating Collaborative Advantage* (pp. 80–100), London: Sage.

Davies, J.S. (2009) 'The limits of joined-up government: Towards a political analysis', *Public Administration*, 87(1): 80–96.

De Bruijn, H. and Dicke, W. (2006) 'Strategies for safeguarding public values in liberalized utility sectors', *Public Administration*, 84(3): 717–35.

De Bruijn, J.A. and Ringeling, A.B. (1997) 'Normative notes: Perspectives on networks', in J.M. Kickert, E-H. Klijn and J. Koppenjan (eds), *Managing Complex Networks: Strategies for the Public Sector* (pp. 35–61), London: Sage.

Denhardt, J.V. and Denhardt, R.B. (2007) *The New Public Service: Serving not Steering*, New York: M.E. Sharpe.

Downs, A. (1967) *Inside Bureaucracy*, Boston, MA: Little-Brown.

Eisenhardt, K.M. (1989) 'Building theories from case study research', *The Academy of Management Review*, 14(24): 532–50.

Eisenhardt, K.M. and Graebner, M.E. (2007) 'Theory building from cases: Opportunities and challenges', *Academy of Management Journal*, 50(1): 25–32.

Ferlie, E. and Pettigrew, A. (1996) 'Managing through networks: Some issues and implications for the NHS', *British Journal of Management*, 7 (March special issue): S81–S99.

Frederickson, H.G. (1997) *The Spirit of Public Administration*, San Francisco, CA: Jossey-Bass.

Frederickson, H.G. (2007) 'Whatever happened to public administration? Governance, governance, everywhere', in E. Ferlie, L. Lynn and C. Pollitt (eds), *The Oxford Handbook of Public Management* (pp. 282–304), Oxford: Oxford University Press.

Frederickson, H.G. and Hart, D.K. (1985) 'The public service and the patriotism of benevolence', *Public Administration Review*, 45: 547–53.

Frey, B.S. and Jegen, R. (2001) 'Motivation crowding theory', *Journal of Economic Surveys*, 15(5): 589–611.

Georgellis, Y., Iossa, E. and Tabvuma, V. (2011) 'Crowding out intrinsic motivation in the public sector', *Journal of Public Administration Research and Theory*, 21(3): 473–93.

Gerring, J. (2004) 'What is a Case Study and what is it good for?', *The American Political Science Review*, 98(2): 341–54.

Giauque, D., Anderfuhren-Biget, S. and Varone, F. (2013) 'HRM practices, intrinsic motivators, and organizational performance in the public sector', *Public Personnel Management*, 42(2): 123–50.

Håkansson, H. and Snehota, I. (1989) 'No Business is an island: The network concept of business strategy', *Scandinavian Journal of Management*, 4(3): 187–200.

Hardy, B., Wistow, G. and Rhodes, R.A.W. (1990) 'Policy networks and the implementation of community care policy for people with mental handicaps', *Journal of Social Policy*, 19(2): 141–68.

Head, B. (2008) 'Assessing network-based collaborations: Effectiveness for whom?', *Public Management Review*, 10(6): 733–49.

Himmelman, A.T. (1996) 'On the theory and practice of transformational collaboration: From social service to social justice', in C. Huxham (ed.), *Creating Collaborative Advantage*, London: Sage.

Himmelman, A.T. (2001) 'On coalitions and the transformation of power relations: Collaborative betterment and collaborative empowerment', *American Journal of Community Psychology*, 29(2): 277–84.

Honohan, I. (2002) *Civic Republicanism*, London: Routledge.

Horton, S. (2008) 'History and persistence of an ideal', in J.L. Perry and A. Hondeghem (eds), *Motivation in Public Management: The Call of Public Services* (pp. 17–32), Oxford: Oxford University Press.

Houston, D.J. (2000) 'Public service motivation: A multivariate test', *Journal of Public Administration Research and Theory*, 4: 713–24.

Houston, D.J. (2006) 'Walking the walk of public service motivation: Employees and charitable gifts of time, blood, and money', *Journal of Public Administration Research and Theory*, 16: 67–86.

Hudson, B. (1987) 'Collaboration in social welfare: A framework for analysis', *Policy and Politics*, 15(3): 175–82.

Hudson, B. (2004) 'Analysing network partnerships: Benson re-visited', *Public Management Review*, 6(1): 75–94.

Huxham, C. (1996) 'Collaboration and collaborative advantage', in C. Huxham (ed.), *Creating Collaborative Advantage* (pp. 1–18), London: Sage.

Huxham, C. and Vangen, S. (2000) 'Ambiguity, complexity and dynamics in the membership of collaboration', *Human Relations*, 53(6): 771–806.

Jacobsen, C.B., Hvitved, J. and Andersen, L.B. (2014) 'Command and motivation: How the perception of external interventions relates to intrinsic motivation and public service motivation', *Public Administration*, 92(4): 790–806.

Keast, R., Mandell, M., Brown, K. and Woodcock, G. (2004) 'Network structures: Working differently and changing expectations', *Public Administration Review*, 64(3): 363–71.

Kernaghan, K. (1993) 'Partnership and public administration: Conceptual and practical considerations', *Canadian Public Administration*, 36(1): 57–76.

Kickert, W.J.M. and Koppenjan, J. (1997) 'Public management and network management: An overview', in W.J.M. Kickert, E-H. Klijn and J. Koppenjan (eds), *Managing Complex Networks: Strategies for the Public Sector* (pp. 35–61), London: Sage.

Kickert, W.J.M., Klijn, E.H. and Koppenjan, J. (eds) (1997) *Managing Complex Networks: Strategies for the Public Sector*, London: Sage.

Kim, S. (2006) 'Public service motivation and organizational citizenship behavior in Korea', *International Journal of Manpower*, 27(8): 722–40.

Kim, S. (2008) 'Revising Perry's measurement scale in public service motivation', *American Review of Public Administration*, 39(2): 149–63.

Kim, S. (2012) 'Does person-organization fit matter in the public sector? Testing the mediating effect of person-organization fit in the relationship between public service motivation and work attitudes', *Public Administration Review*, 72(6): 830–40.

Kim, S. and Vandenabeele, W. (2010) 'A strategy for building public service motivation research internationally', *Public Administration Review*, 70(5): 701–9.

Kim, S., Vandenabeele, W., Wright, B.E., Andersen, L.B., Cerase, F.P., Christensen, R.K., Desmarais, C., Koumenta, M., Leisink, P., Liu, B., Palidauskaite, J., Pedersen, L.H., Perry, J.L., Ritz, A., Taylor, J. and De Vivo, P. (2013) 'Investigating the structure and meaning of public service motivation across populations: Developing an international instrument and addressing issues of measurement invariance', *Journal of Public Administration Research and Theory*, 23(1): 79–102.

Kjeldsen, A.M. (2012) 'Sector and occupational differences in public service motivation: A qualitative study', *International Journal of Public Administration*, 35(1): 58–69.

Kjeldsen, A.M. and Jacobsen, C.B. (2012) 'Public service motivation and employment sector: Attraction or socialization?', *Journal of Public Administration Research and Theory*, doi: 10.1093/jopart/mus039.

Klijn, E.H. (1997) 'Policy networks: An overview', in W.J.M. Kickert, E-H. Klijn and J. Koppenjan (eds), *Managing Complex Networks: Strategies for the Public Sector* (pp. 14–34), London: Sage.

Klijn, E.H. (2008) 'Governance and governance networks in Europe: An assessment of ten years of research on the theme', *Public Management Review*, 10(4): 505–25.

Koppenjan, J. (2008) 'Creating a playing field for assessing the effectiveness of network collaboration by performance measures', *Public Management Review*, 10(6): 699–714.

Krogsgaard, J.A., Thomsen, P. and Andersen, L.B. (2013) 'Only if we agree? How value conflict moderates the relationship between transformational leadership and public service motivation', paper presented at the IRSPM conference, Prague, Czech Republic, 10–12 April.

Lawless, M.W. and Moore, R.A. (1989) 'Interorganizational systems in public service delivery: A new application of the dynamic network framework', *Human Relations*, 42(12): 1167–84.

Levine, S. and White, P.E. (1961) 'Exchange as a conceptual framework for the study of interorganizational relationships', *Administrative Science Quarterly*, 5(4): 583–601.

Lewis, C. (2006) 'In pursuit of the public interest', *Public Administration Review*, 55(5): 694–701.

Liu, B., Tang, T.L.P. and Yang, K. (2013) 'When does public service motivation fuel the job satisfaction fire? The joint moderation of person-organization fit and needs-supplies fit', *Public Management Review*, doi: 10.1080/14719037.2013.867068.

Liu, B., Yang, K. and Yu, W. (2014) 'Work-related stressors and health-related outcomes in public service: Examining the role of public service motivation', *The American Review of Public Administration*, doi: 10.1177/0275074014524298.

Mandell, M.P. and Keast, R. (2008) 'Evaluating the effectiveness of interorganizational relations through networks: Developing a framework for revised performance measures', *Public Management Review*, 10(6): 715–31.

Meyer, J.P. and Allen, N.J. (1991) 'A three component conceptualization of organizational commitment', *Human Resource Management Review*, 1: 61–89.

Meyer, J.P. and Allen, N.J. (1997) *Commitment in the Workplace: Theory, Research, and Application*, Thousand Oaks, CA: Sage.

Milward, H.B. and Provan, K.G. (2000) 'Governing the hollow state', *Journal of Public Administration Research and Theory*, 10(2): 359–79.

Milward, H.B. and Provan, K.G. (2003) 'Managing the hollow state', *Public Management Review*, 5(1): 1–18.

Naff, K.C. and Crum, J. (1999) 'Working for America: Does public service motivation make a difference?', *Review of Public Personnel Administration*, 19(4): 5–16.

Nalbandian, J. and Edwards, J.T. (1983) 'The values of public administrators: A comparison with lawyers, social workers, and business administrators', *Review of Public Personnel Administrators*, 4: 114–27.

Newstrom, J.W., Reif, W.E. and Monczka, R.M. (1976) 'Motivating the public employee: Fact v fiction', *Public Personnel Management*, 5: 67–72.

O'Toole, L.J., Jr. (1997) 'Treating networks seriously: Practical and research-based agendas in public administration', *Public Administration Review*, 57(1): 45–52.

Ostrom, E. (1990) *Governing the Commons: The Evolution of Institutions for Collective Action*, Cambridge: Cambridge University Press.

Pandey, S.K., Wright, B.E. and Moynihan, D.P. (2008) 'Public service motivation and interpersonal citizenship behavior in public organizations: Testing a preliminary model', *International Public Management Journal*, 11(1): 89–108.

Pattakos, A.N. (2004) 'The search for meaning in government service', *Public Administration Review*, 64(1): 106–12.

Perry, J.L. (2014) 'The motivational bases of public service: Foundations for a third wave of research', *Asia Pacific Journal of Public Administration*, 36(1): 34–47.

Perry, J.L. and Hondeghem, A. (eds) (2008) *Motivation in Public Management: The Call of Public Services*, Oxford: Oxford University Press.

Perry, J.L. and Rainey, H.G. (1988) 'The public-private distinction in organizational theory', *Academy of Management Review*, 13(2): 182–201.

Perry, J.L. and Vandenabeele, W. (2008) 'Behavioral dynamics: Institutions, identities, and self-regulation', in J.L. Perry and A. Hondeghem (eds), *Motivation in Public Management: The Call of Public Service* (pp. 56–79), Oxford: Oxford University Press.

Perry, J.L. and Wise, L.R. (1990) 'The motivational bases of public service', *Public Administration Review*, 50(3): 367–73.

Perry, J.L., Hondeghem, A. and Wise, L.R. (2010) 'Revisiting the motivational bases of public service: Twenty years of research and an agenda for the future', *Public Administration Review*, 70(5): 681–90.

Rainey, H.G. (1982) 'Reward preferences among public and private managers: In search of the service ethic', *The American Review of Public Administration*, 16(4): 288–302.

Rainey, H.G. (1997) *Understanding and Managing Public Organizations*, San Francisco, CA: Jossey-Bass.

Rainey, H.G. (2009) *Understanding and Managing Public Organizations* (3rd edn), Hoboken, NJ: John Wiley & Sons.

Rainey, H.G. and Steinbauer, P. (1999) 'Galloping elephants: Developing elements of a theory of effective government organizations', *Journal of Public Administration Research and Theory*, 9(2): 1–32.

Rayner, J., Williams, H.M., Lawton, A. and Allinson, C.W. (2011) 'Public service ethos: Developing a generic measure', *Journal of Public Administration Research and Theory*, 21(1): 27–51.

Rhodes, R.A.W. (1990) 'Policy networks: A British perspective', *Journal of Theoretical Politics*, 2(3): 293–317.

Rhodes, R.A.W. and Marsh, D. (1992) 'New directions in the study of policy networks', *European Journal of Political Research*, 21(1–2): 181–205.

Ring, P.S. and Van De Ven, A.H. (1992) 'Structuring cooperative relationships between organizations', *Strategic Management Journal*, 13: 483–98.

Ritz, A., Brewer, G.A. and Newman, O. (2013) 'Public service motivation: A systematic literature review', presented at the Public Management Research Conference, University of Wisconsin, Madison, WI, 17 June.

Romzek, B. (1990) 'Employee investment and commitment: The ties that bind', *Public Administration Review*, May/June: 374–81.

Rose, A. and Lawton, A. (1999) *Public Services Management*, Harlow: Pearson Education.

Schofield, J. (1997) 'Working together: Differing perspectives and persuasions amongst health and social care authorities', *Health Services Management Research*, 10: 163–72.

Schott, C. and Pronk, J.L.J. (2014) 'Investigating and explaining organizational antecedents of public service motivation', *Evidence-Based HRM: A Global Forum for Empirical Scholarship*, 2(1): 28–56.

Schott, C., Van Kleef, D.D. and Steen, T. (2014) 'What does it mean and imply to be public service motivated?', *The American Review of Public Administration*, doi: 10.1177/02750740 14533589.

Sink, D. (1996) 'Five obstacles to community-based collaboration and some thoughts on overcoming them', in C. Huxham (ed.), *Creating Collaborative Advantage* (pp. 101–9), London: Sage.

Skelcher, C. and Sullivan, H. (2008) 'Theory-driven approaches to analysing collaborative performance', *Public Management Review*, 10(6): 751–77.

Snow, C.C., Miles, R.E. and Coleman, H.J., Jr. (1992) 'Managing 21st century network organizations', *Organizational Dynamics*, 20(3): 5–20.

Staats, E. (1988) 'Public service and the public interest', *Public Administration Review*, 48: 601–5.

Steen, T.P. and Rutgers, M.R. (2011) 'The double-edged sword: Public service motivation, the oath of office and the backlash of an instrumental approach', *Public Management Review*, 13(3): 343–61.

Steijn, B. (2008) 'Person-environment fit and public service motivation', *International Journal of Public Management*, 11(1): 13–27.

Steinhaus, C. and Perry, J.L. (1996) 'Organizational commitment: Does sector matter?', *Public Productivity and Management Review*, 19(3): 278–88.

Taylor, J. (2007) 'The impact of public service motives on work outcomes in Australia: A comparative multi-dimensional analysis', *Public Administration*, 85(4): 931–59.

Taylor, J. (2010) 'Public service motivation, civic attitudes and actions of public, nonprofit and private sector employees', *Public Administration*, 88(4): 1083–110.

Taylor, J. and Taylor, R. (2010) 'Working hard for more money or working hard to make a difference? Efficiency wages, public service motivation, and effort', *Review of Public Personnel Administration*, 1: 1–20.

Termeer, C.J.A.M. and Koppenjan, J.F.M. (1997) 'Managing perceptions in networks', in W.J.M. Kickert, E-H. Klijn and J. Koppenjan (eds), *Managing Complex Networks: Strategies for the Public Sector* (pp. 79–98), London: Sage.

Thomson, A.M., Perry, J.L. and Miller, T.K. (2007) 'Conceptualising and measuring collaboration', *Journal of Public Administration Research and Theory*, 19: 23–56.

Vandenabeele, W. (2007) 'Toward a public administration theory of public service motivation: An institutional approach', *Public Administration Review*, 9(4): 545–56.

van der Wal, Z. (forthcoming) '"All quiet on the western front?" A systematic literature review of public service motivation scholarship in non-western contexts', *Asia Pacific Journal of Public Administration*.

van der Wal, Z. and Oosterbaan, A. (2013) 'Government or business? Identifying determinants of MPA and MBA students' career preferences', *Public Personnel Management*, 42(2): 239–58.

van der Wal, Z., De Graaf, G. and Lasthuizen, K. (2008) 'What's valued most? Similarities and differences between the organizational values of the public and private sector', *Public Administration*, 86(5): 465–82.

Van Steden, R., van der Wal, Z. and Lasthuizen, K. (2015) 'Overlapping values, mutual prejudices: Empirical research into the ethos of police officers and private security guards', *Administration & Society*, 47(3): 220–43.

Waddock, S. (1991) 'A typology of social partnership organizations', *Administration & Society*, 22(4): 480–515.

Walker, R.M., O'Toole, L.J., Jr. and Meier, K.J. (2007) 'It's where you are that matters: The networking behaviour of English local government officers', *Public Administration*, 85(3): 739–56.

Warren, D.C. and Chen, L. (2013) 'The relationship between public service motivation and performance', in E.J. Ringquist (ed.), *Meta-Analysis for Public Management and Policy* (pp. 442–73), San Francisco, CA: Jossey-Bass.

Wiener, Y. (1982) 'Commitment in organizations: A normative view', *Academy of Management Review*, 7: 418–28.

Williams, P. (2002) 'The competent boundary spanner', *Public Administration*, 80(1): 103–24.

Wittmer, D. (1991) 'Serving the people or serving for pay: Reward preferences among government, hybrid sector, and business managers', *Public Productivity and Management Review*, 144: 369–83.

Wright, B.E. (2004) 'The role of work context in work motivation: A public sector application of goal and social cognitive theories', *Journal of Public Administration Research and Theory*, 14(1): 59–78.

Wright, B.E. (2008) 'Methodological challenges associated with public service motivation research', in J.L. Perry and A. Hondeghem (eds), *Motivation in Public Management: The Call of Public Services*, Oxford: Oxford University Press.

Wright, B.E., Christensen, R.K. and Pandey, S.K. (2013) 'Measuring public service motivation: Exploring the equivalence of existing global measures', *International Public Management Journal*, 16(2): 197–223.

Wright, B.E., Moynihan, D.P. and Pandey, S.K. (2012) 'Pulling the levers: Transformational leadership, public service motivation, and mission valence', *Public Administration Review*, 72(2): 206–15.

Yin, R.K. (2013) *Case Study Research: Design and Methods* (5th edn), Thousand Oaks, CA: Sage.

14

WHAT DOES WORKING IN PUBLIC SERVICES MEAN?

Describing the public service ethos in practice

Steven Parker

Introduction

The literature on the public service ethos (PSE) has waxed and waned in fashion over recent years, with periodic bursts of academic interest. Descriptions of the PSE are usually associated with acting in the public interest by those employed in public services. There has been a positioning between commentators who see the PSE as something that is to be preserved, by those who argue for a new PSE (Stoker and Aldridge 2002), as well as explaining the loss of a public service ethic (Elcock 2014). Furthermore, innovative ways of planning and providing public services have developed in recent years, including commissioning (Bovaird *et al.* 2014) and co-production with citizens (LARCI 2010). This has further complicated the identification and location of a public service ethos. However, there has been little empirical research on the PSE, especially in comparison with the field of public service motivation (Rayner *et al.* 2011).

The aim of this chapter is to describe the different ways that the PSE can be theorized, but importantly what this means for practitioners in public services. The chapter contributes findings from a case study of a strategic partnership board on their understanding of the PSE, demonstrating that it remains a viable topic of study that continues to have meaning for staff working in public services, despite assaults on it as a concept. The chapter is structured as follows. First, it defines the PSE. Second, it describes the PSE in practice under the three headings of: (1) the meaning of the PSE; (2) motivation for working in public services; and (3) public service values. Third, it proposes a theory of the micro, macro and applied PSE to help understand its complexity. Finally, it concludes by summarizing the chapter and setting out ideas for future research.

Defining the public service ethos

It is difficult, and perhaps impossible, to provide a single account of the PSE. An established description of it is as 'long-established values and rules providing a benchmark for public servants and their institutions' (Public Administration Select Committee 2002), suggesting a responsibility for public officers to do what is right and good, and acting unselfishly while doing so. Furthermore, public officials are required to apply principles and standards to their actions (Kernaghan 1993), ensuring rules are enforced in an impartial and disinterested way (Plant 2003). The PSE is traditionally thought to play a role in ensuring the probity and impartiality of public officials, but with an obligation to serve people whose market power left them reliant on the state (Needham 2007). Such descriptions emphasize how public servants use 'public duty' to inform their decision-making and set their own interests aside (O'Toole 2006).

Rayner *et al.* (2011) state that research identifying the essence of PSE suggests four key ideas: first, that the PSE exists; second, that it is distinctive; third, that professionals who work in the public sector have a belief system that motivates them; and finally, that the public interest is an important feature of the PSE. Three theoretical dimensions are suggested: public service belief on why individuals are motivated to work for public services; public service practice on values, processes and practices that support motivation; and public interest on how individuals act in the interests of all.

Reflecting a concern with individual motivation, Perry (1997) has researched the antecedents of Public Service Motivation (PSM), detailing a number of influences informing it. These included the influence of family and parental background, political belief, religion, identifying oneself with a particular profession and an individual's demographic characteristics. Perry suggests that an individual's PSM developed from exposure to a range of experiences, some related to childhood, others associated with religion, as well as those linked to professional life. Close to 280 studies have been published on PSM in many different countries, making it one of, if not the most, studied topics in public administration today.

Although the PSE can be described positively, it has, conversely, been linked with bureaucratic processes that undermine it (Pratchett and Wingfield 1996). It is questioned if values associated with the PSE are merely rhetorical, used to defend decisions that are not in the best interests of the public (Plant 2003). Needham (2007) describes four approaches to assist understanding of the PSE. The first approach is that the PSE signals sympathy and understanding for public service workers, such as the commitment of teachers and nurses. This perspective can be aligned with the descriptions of the PSE as something that is principled and to be lauded. This links to Needham's second approach, with the PSE used as a talisman against radical change, with union leaders arguing the incompatibility of a distinct public sector with profit making and private-sector involvement. Third, it is also thought that the PSE can be strengthened by private-sector involvement, an approach to the delivery of public services that has grown in recent decades. Fourth, Needham suggests that, in practice, the PSE can be interpreted as negative and obstructive, and therefore needs to be challenged. The motivations and behaviour of public servants are described in public choice theory, which argues that public officials are, in reality, self-interested *agents* (Crouch 2011; Le Grand 2003), and that professionals and suppliers of public services are utility 'maximizers'. It can be asserted that the whole notion of PSE goes against public choice perspectives, and this counter-movement points to the origins of PSM as a concept (Perry and Wise 1990).

Such positions have informed, and have been informed by, the modernization of public services, an approach that has vigorously challenged the delivery of traditional public services (Martin *et al.* 2004). It is additionally argued that public services can be provided by the private and voluntary sectors, in lieu of the public sector, to improve efficiency (Stoker 2006). Whereas the 'traditional PSE' is associated with public administration, public service 'modernization' is related to the theory of New Public Management (NPM), an approach adopted by governments to transform public services since the 1980s. NPM is described as a move to disaggregation and competition in service delivery; the introduction of private-sector management techniques; disciplined resource management; 'hands-on' management; measuring performance; and greater emphasis on output (Hood 1995; Lawton *et al.* 2013). It is suggested that such reforms will improve public services by challenging the traditional PSE (Needham 2007).

Additionally, the PSE is described as a set of values guiding the behaviour of public servants, with individuals subscribing to an ethos that promotes the public rather than private interests (Lawton *et al.* 2013). Defining what a value is can be problematic, and identifying how they are meaningful for staff in specific settings, such as the public sector, is challenging (van der Wal 2011). A values-based approach to investigating the PSE continues to hold a key position, with the PSE described as an inventory of attributes, for instance those used to study local government officers (Pratchett and Wingfield 1996). Values selected by Pratchett and Wingfield for their research were accountability, bureaucratic behaviour, the public interest, motivation and loyalty. Their work has been cited as a basis for further research on the PSE by Lawton (1998), Hebson *et al.* (2003), Needham (2006) and Stackman *et al.* (2006).

The transition from 'traditional' to 'modern' public services throws into question whether a golden age for public service delivery ever existed (Lawton 1998). Although a major motivation for change is the perception, as well as the reality, of failings in public services, whatever the shortcomings of public services, there is something 'necessary, special and distinctive' about them (Public Administration Select Committee 2002). Needham notes that while the boundaries between the public and private sectors are increasingly 'porous', the idea of a distinct PSE remains popular (Needham 2007).

To conclude, theories of the PSE arise from research, public policy, society and the economy. Perhaps the best solution is to accept that the term has multiple meanings, which are influenced by constant change, including pressure from economics, politics and ideology. Although often taken for granted as a term, it is questionable whether it is possible to define the PSE (Lawton 2005), characterized by elasticity in its use (Needham 2007). On the PSE and modernization, Lawton remarks that it is inevitable that as public officials engage with other organizations, this will expose them to different practices. Although reforms have occurred, with different definitions of the PSE it is difficult to prove or disprove the effects of any changes (Lawton 1998).

Informed by a study of the role and meaning of the PSE for managers in UK public services, this chapter focuses on the meaning of the ethos 'on the ground' for public-sector practitioners. The discussion reports findings from research on a multi-agency strategic board in a UK city responsible for planning services for disabled children.

The public service ethos in practice

Discussions of the PSE have tended to focus on theoretical perspectives with a deficit in empirical research (Lawton *et al.* 2013). Furthermore, there has been a tendency to research 'officers' in public organizations, for example in local government, but without distinguishing between different professions and roles in public services. This chapter draws upon case study research to explore this further.

A case study approach was used, including documentary analysis, a board observation and semi-structured interviews. Board participants work in local government, health services and the voluntary sector, with the majority having undertaken professional training before moving into management. The partnership board was one among a range of other collaborative fora responsible for local governance in a city in the Midlands of England. Although it was responsible for services for disabled children, it reported to wider professional and governance networks. This included formal partnership boards, such as the local strategic Children's Trust board, and individual organizational and parent-led boards.

The board consisted of 28 members, of which 20 were interviewed on their choice of career, the board and working in partnership. Interviewees included local authority, health service, education, and voluntary sector representatives. One parent of a disabled child who attended the board was also interviewed. In addition, a board meeting was observed at the council offices, where 15 members attended, including local authority, health service, education and voluntary sector representatives, and two parents of disabled children. Lastly, documents informing the work of the board were analysed, including reports, agendas and minutes.

The discussion is organized under three headings of: (1) the meaning of the PSE; (2) motivation for working in public services; and (3) public service values.

The meaning of the PSE

The majority of participants had heard of the PSE, but reflecting its fragmented meaning several said they would have difficulty defining it. One way of describing it was as a personal ethos or calling for public-sector workers. It was asserted:

I think for the most part people want to make a difference and people do want to go home at the end of the day feeling they've done something worthwhile.

This comment indicated that a sense of personal ethos potentially contributed to why people chose to work in public services. This was contrasted with a comment about the private sector by another contributor, who said:

I do think there is an ethos within public service about working to improve the lot of the community. I must say I think it is different from private industry.

As well as illustrating personal beliefs, this quote articulated the possibility of a shared understanding of the PSE in public services. One participant believed such a 'global' PSE existed, pointing out:

I'm not sure that necessarily there are differences between different areas of public services or between different levels within the public sector. I think if you go and talk to operational people, once you get past all the baggage about pay and grading and all of the policies and all of that lot, once you get past that I think there is a common view of the public sector.

In contrast to this view, another participant thought the PSE varied in different parts of the public sector with no overarching ethos. These variations were shaped by the diversity of policy and performance arising from central and local government requirements for health, education or social services.

It was stated the PSE may be stronger or weaker in different parts of the same organization. It was suggested employees from children and young people's services in the council were more committed to the PSE because of their professional background. However, it was noted:

When I talk to other people who work for the city council in other directorates, then I get the feeling from them as well that they're actually working for the public good . . . So I think it is fairly common, but then perhaps I just happen to know people who share the same values so it's difficult to say really.

Differences in professional backgrounds were thought to influence how the PSE was understood. For example, an educational participant believed there were differences in how social services and schools worked with children and young people:

I look at the way social services have to work with kids and it's the nature of their job, I think, that they have to work in different ways to the way we work with kids. And that's often to do with the lack of continuity I think.

This suggested the PSE is shaped by how need is defined and services delivered by different professions. Social workers worked to a high threshold of need, often in situations of family crisis, but it was thought teachers provided services in a more predictable or consistent way. Both professions were committed to children and young people, but their perceptions of the public interest differed.

One participant wondered if, when senior managers referred to such values, the PSE would continue to have an influence on their role as a senior manager. However, it was stated that the PSE was probably stronger for front-line staff and lower management. Nevertheless, it seemed the PSE could have a strategic function for senior management, as articulated by a participant who wanted to have a:

strategic impact on the way residential or community services were going . . . I always feel that local authorities pay a lot of money for the services they're getting and I want to see that the money's being paid [spent] well, not only internally but also externally.

Another definition of the PSE offered by a participant focused on the need for honesty with service users about the limitations of resources available. This meant a social worker telling a service user about financial support:

I'm a public servant so I have to account for how I spend it (money) and at the moment with the current financial situation . . . I'm actually saying well I'm sorry, you'd want me to do all this but unfortunately I have to meet the needs of your circumstances and it's those gaps that I have to support you with, the others I can't and that's very hard.

Using resources effectively was implied by a board member who thought the PSE was changing as public services became increasingly business-like. Moreover, there were private-sector practices that could be applied in the public sector, including project management principles and attention to value for money. Furthermore, this participant believed the private sector had also learned lessons from public services, particularly the need for developing a clearer focus on client need.

The PSE was additionally thought to link with democratic processes. When asked about the PSE, one board member said he:

immediately thought of local authorities and things delivered through a locally, a democratically elected body.

His perception was that the PSE had always been related to the role of elected politicians, because of a local electoral 'feedback loop' between service providers and elected members. He wondered whether providing health services, primarily determined by central government, was part of the local democratic framework, and, if so, he questioned how the Primary Care Trust (PCT) would perceive the council being the foremost exponent of the PSE.

Motivation for working in public services

As well as describing the PSE, participants remarked on their motivation to work in public services. Personal, professional and political influences were identified.

Background was influential for many participants. For example, one participant emphasized coming from a family committed to championing equality and trade union involvement. Another interviewee felt his own values linked to an upbringing of serving the community, which he saw as a formative influence. As a young person, he had joined the Scouts, an organization he described as having a public service element. The use of the term community was also used by a local authority participant, who stated her commitment to improving the well-being, health and quality of life of the local population.

For a health participant, family background influenced an interest in social issues, with attendance at medical school the manifestation of her caring perspective and political outlook. This led to her working in:

> community paediatrics which is different from being a hospital doctor dealing with ill children, which is perhaps where the public bit comes in, and children's public health, and wanting to act for children as a group rather than just as individuals.

One interviewee stated his own problems with dyslexia at school were influential in choosing to work with disabled children. He noted:

> that if you get the right support at the right time and you are encouraged to take the opportunities then you can actually exceed what other people think you can do. You can acheive your potential. And that is really why I do the job that I do.

A council manager said contributing to society was central to his beliefs:

> I do remember when I was at university . . . I could go down that (business) route and make loads of money or I could go into public service and I know I won't make loads of money in public service. So why did I do that? I think probably it was about personal values really, about equity and responsibility of the more vulnerable people in society and all that kind of thing really. And also some negativity about, you know, this was in the eighties when all the money-making stuff was everything, and I was a bit anti all of that kind of thing, and not wanting to be hugely materialistic about things or needing loads of money.

In addition, subtle differences were identified between the wish to work in public services and choice of profession. When asked why she preferred to work in the public sector, a health representative asked if I meant 'Why did I choose to be a doctor?' This calling to profession was identified by a participant from a teaching background, who remarked:

> I chose to teach . . . I don't think I ever saw myself as coming into public service, I saw myself as a teacher.

Profession and training was thought a 'springboard' for moving into senior management within public services. An early interest in strategy for one participant originated from membership of a multidisciplinary social work team. This established a commitment to integrated working, which she continued to apply:

> I could see quite quickly that working with individual clients is okay and it gives you a certain level of satisfaction, but actually if you want to make a big difference then you have to be at a senior management level.

One participant stated she had previously been employed in the private sector, before moving into public services. Commenting on a move from retail work to working in a library, she said this had not been a calling, but an opportunity:

> No, it wasn't a calling. And I didn't quite stumble, because I made an active approach, I actually saw the job advertised – the first job advertised – in the newspaper . . . I thought, you know, 'I could do that job; I've got the basic skills, I've got the knowledge, I read, I know a book from a CD'.

Finally, a local authority manager said his religious faith had informed his choice to train as a social worker, and:

> I then had that (faith) overlaid with what I think we would all call academically Christian Socialist and the RM Titmuss work and Ann Oakley and various other work like that.

The connection between religion and a 'calling' to work in public services was related to attending church and a moral upbringing. Although no longer religious, this participant remained committed to social work and social justice.

As the research site was a partnership board, motivation was largely associated with partnership working, not only as a desire to undertake rewarding work, but the need to collaborate with other professionals to improve services. Hudson (1987) states that public officers can be *directed* to collaborate by government, but participants in this study did not state that they had been forced to go to board meetings with attendance accepted as a requirement of the job. Furthermore, the established view of the PSE and motivation is that individuals do not enter public service out of self-interest or personal utility maximization (John and Johnson 2008; Plant 2003; Pratchett and Wingfield 1996). However, Le Grand (2003) suggests that public officers are not always motivated by altruism and the public interest, and although it was stated that board members might wish to advance their careers, this was not identified as a significant issue by participants. Interview data pointed to a high level of cooperation, but it also stated that officers would not 'go into something strategic' unless benefit was to be found there for one's organization.

Public service values

Values are stated as central to public administration and policy, as reflected in recent literature on good governance in public services (De Graaf and van der Wal 2010). For the PSE, an important relationship between values and public services exists to inform the practice of officers, as well as being used as a tool for empirical research. However, defining what a 'public service value' is can be problematic, as can identifying how they are meaningful for staff in specific public-sector settings. Furthermore, in his discussions of organizational ethics, van der Wal states that both differences and similarities in the values of public- and private-sector organizational values can be found (van der Wal 2011). Discussions can also be identified on the need to share and integrate values in joint working (Goodwin 2013), and the relationship between the PSE and codes and standards of behaviour for public officers (Heywood 2012). Recent work by Cooke *et al.* (2013) examines accountability in the professions of teaching, medicine and law, but where they discuss professional accountability individually, the research discussed in this chapter locates it within a multi-agency partnership seeing asymmetrical accountability (Fenwick *et al.* 2012). This adds to the complexity of the discussion, but it is the case that this complexity characterizes the delivery of public services more and more.

There have been attempts to identify agreed values and standards of behaviour for public officials (Committee on Standards in Public Life 2013; Nolan 1995). It has been suggested that the activities of public servants should be informed by the Nolan Committee's 'seven principles of public life' of selflessness, integrity, objectivity, accountability, openness, honesty and leadership (Nolan 1995). Public Administration Select Committee (2002) identified the need for an updated PSE to help inform accountability, as well as moving from an 'unwritten traditional ethos' to clearer and more explicit values reflecting the upholding of an ethos by public staff. However, the diversity of actors and their contexts calls into question how far it is possible to design standards of behaviour with common meanings across diverse settings (Pratchett 2000), while at the same time avoiding introducing a catechism culture (Barberis 2001). While it is possible to be relatively clear about the normative understandings of values, they remain contested concepts open to interpretation (Pratchett 2000). Pratchett remarks that staff from separate agencies define public life differently, with values interpreted and informed by the legal context of each profession, as well as the diverse backgrounds of the actors involved.

The values used in the research reported here were taken from previous work by Pratchett and Wingfield (1996) and Plant (2003). Participants were asked to comment on their understanding of core public values. The values that generated the most discussion were accountability, bureaucratic behaviour and public interest. Values having less resonance with participants were loyalty, professionalism, impartiality and judgement. Interviewees provided a small amount of data on trust, surprising given the emphasis on it as a key value in the wider literature (Davies 2011; Lawton 2005; Plant 2003; Rhodes 2007).

As a PSE value, the standard description of accountability might be thought of as being accountable to one's employing agency or profession. Furthermore, as suggested by Pratchett and Wingfield (1996), local authority employees are accountable to the political structures within which they work. In the context of the case study discussed here, accountability in practice saw public officers being accountable for a range of issues and to a number of different people:

> Yeah, I mean I think accountability is one of the key ones (values) because that's what we've kind of been working towards, about having somebody with responsibility in the city for disability and reporting upwards within the structure, as well as downwards towards practitioners as well.

However, it was unclear whether board members had a shared understanding of accountability. This was understandable in terms of the confusion about local governance reflected in participants' comments. One local authority member thought that she was first accountable to her employer, rather than the board, but went on to question how non-council agencies could be accountable to a council-led board. That the participants attended a multi-agency partnership board added to this complexity, with different accountabilities stated to the board itself, to the local Children's Trust board, employer, profession, government department and disabled children.

Participants gave examples of other sites of governance the board linked with, such as the local health care trust, as well as central government, suggesting that a hierarchy of accountability existed. This set the context within which services were commissioned, information managed and performance measured, by reporting to the board and the board in turn reporting to the Children's Trust Board.

However, the interpretation of accountability could differ. For example, one participant did not think there was a hierarchy of accountability between his joint employers, the voluntary sector and the council. He saw authority as horizontal, implying that he was equally critical or loyal to both agencies. Offering an example of multiple accountabilities, he added:

> Through the (voluntary body) as champion I'm accountable to the (voluntary body), but obviously then as a joint partner I'm accountable to the board and City for making the post work.

While considering the lines of accountability for NHS participants, a council employee thought they were accountable to the PCT and even the Department of Health. Therefore, different lines of accountability were thought to exist compared to one single line of accountability to the Children's Trust. For another participant, multi-agency board members were accountable to the central Department for Education.

Regarding political accountability, although the lead councillor for children and young people did not attend the board, he requested regular updates. Additionally, strategic management was interested in the work of the board and a school participant thought this helped to focus the board on how it evidenced accountability.

A health participant commented that she was ultimately accountable to the General Medical Council. However, a different health member saw accountability as not only to her profession, but to patients too. Illustrating multiple accountabilities, she added that as a manager and board member, she also represented her organization. Finally, a parent representative considered she was accountable for taking information back to other parents.

With a focus on service users and citizens, some interviewees thought the board was primarily accountable to disabled children and parents. The children's champion said he was ultimately accountable to children and young people.

In sum, analysis suggested a more complex picture of accountability and governance than just one of hierarchy, with participants being accountable for a range of issues and to different groups.

On bureaucractic behaviour as a value, research participants voiced both negative and positive views. They stated it could undermine the board's work, but also acknowledged that it played an important role. This built on Pratchett and Wingfield's (1996) observations that some public officers see the PSE positively, while others associate it with red tape, encouraging inefficiency, obstructive behaviour and 'petty bureaucracy'. Several interviewees thought that the bureaucratic processes linked to the board from the participating agencies were useful. For example, agreeing a policy on disabled children had been straightforward, with processes described as responsive and supportive of getting things done as quickly as possible. However, it was also stated that the amount of paperwork could slow things down, some of it using jargon and terminology that not everyone understood. It was stated that some organizations wanted board papers to be presented in specific ways, and if this did not happen these papers would be thought less important. Conversely, bureaucratic behaviours could improve accountability as it provided an audit trail about how decisions had been made and how public money had been spent.

Several perspectives on the relationship between the public interest and the board were identified. These included improving public services, local councillors representing citizens, involving service users in planning, and providing value for money for taxpayers. Several participants emphasized that, in this context, the public interest related to disabled children. For example, at its inception, it had endeavoured to ensure the needs of disabled children were reflected by how it planned outcomes and the policy context underpinning it. A public interest focus on disabled children at the board was described as them:

> having the same opportunities that non-disabled children have, and for us to ensure that they have the access and entitlement to services. What we want to try and do is eradicate some of the barriers that they face to accessing those entitlements, and that any resources that we have are directed to enable disabled children to achieve their outcomes.

In addition, it was noted:

> in this case we're saying the bit of the public that we're acting in the interest of is disabled children, so that focus must be the top.

For the public interest, distinct meanings were identified for different professions in the case study. This is because different philosophies of how the public are cared for exist, such as the approach of a cure-oriented medical professional contrasted to a health visitor's public health role (Daly 2004). This was identified in how differences in professional backgrounds were thought to influence how the PSE was understood. For example, an educational participant believed there were differences in how social services and schools worked with children and young people.

Discussion of these public values suggests public officers work within a commonly understood vocabulary, as if there was an agreed civil contract between public staff and the state. However, it is debatable whether such a 'contract' exists as a static inventory, and it seems that PSE values can be broadened out to include others. In addition to what might be thought of as core public values, participants were asked to identify additional values they thought relevant for the PSE. Some of these can be described as 'traditional' values, including honesty and fairness, as well as social justice and equality. But although participants expressed allegiance to the traditional PSE, values with an association to public service modernization were advanced, pointing to the influence of management techniques from the business sector. Value for money was thought to be a prerequisite for strategic managers, associated with the public interest and being mindful about using taxes appropriately. Being 'evidence-based' was stated as important (Sheldon and Chilvers 2000), associated with public accountability, as well as policymaking keeping pace with a changing and complex society (Reid 2003), two issues central to the work of the board. Lastly, having a 'customer'-focused approach, in contrast to using the term service users or citizens. This has been described by government as 'personalizing' services, offering choice, being courteous and helping to improve service delivery (Brereton and Temple 1999; Needham 2006).

Discussion

Descriptions of the PSE have been dominated by theoretical models describing it in a binary way, best exemplified by the theory of New Public Management (Hood 1995; Lawton *et al.* 2013), with a focus on a transition from the 'traditional' to 'modern' delivery of public services. However, this creates the impression that the PSE can only be theorized in a binary way. The discussion that follows shows the potential for the PSE to be theorized differently, demonstrated by a discussion of the micro, macro and applied PSE.

The micro, macro and applied PSE

The research pointed to a theory of the micro, macro and applied PSE, informed by previous research on pro-social behaviour, described as 'a broad category of acts that are defined by some significant segments of society and/or one's social group as generally beneficial to other people' (Penner *et al.* 2005). The *micro PSE* links to the personal and biographical meaning of the PSE, and something that might be deeply held for the individual. In addition, the *macro PSE* articulates wider or shared conceptions of the PSE for professionals, organizations and groupings such as strategic boards. The *applied PSE* reflects discussion about service delivery, seeing the values of public service manifested in service delivery or changes to the environment. The three perspectives assist an understanding of the PSE described as difficult to articulate (Lawton 2005), as well as informing its relationship with partnership working.

First, the *micro PSE* describes a personal meaning, commitment and motivation to working in public services taken to the board by its members. The micro PSE focuses on the biographical origins of this perspective, as well as an individual's choice to work in the public sector. The micro PSE sees biography and background as important for public service workers (Perry 1997; Perry and Wise 1990) and the findings closely link to such research on the antecedents of PSM. Furthermore, the 'calling' or 'coming' to public service has been identified in previous research on the origins of care workers' and social workers' backgrounds and choice of career (Brannen *et al.* 2007; Cree and Davis 2007).

The findings suggested that the motivation to work in public services linked to personal, professional, political and religious influences, as identified in the work of Perry (1997). The interviewee who stated that his own problems with dyslexia at school were influential in choice of career suggests that an event in one's own life might be formative in wishing to help future generations, indicating that an act of ommission in an individual's biography can become an act of commission by using it to help others. Moreover, research participants' own understanding of the PSE contrasted with depictions of 'loyal' officers working within public institutions. For instance, one participant said she 'enjoyed' the PSE, interpreted as the satisfaction obtained by applying a deeply held ethic to her work (Hoggett *et al.* 2006). The use of such an emotional word was important as it contrasted with the image of the stereotyped officer placing rationality over emotion as 'a marginal mode of experience to be minimized in routine organizational life' (Putnam and Mumby 1993).

With senior managers as the focus of the research, the *micro PSE* also linked to research on the relationship between change and continuity for identity and career (Brannen *et al.* 2007). This reflects how a personal motivation and conviction to work in public services can continue for senior managers, even if they have not recently performed front-line duties. One participant thought the PSE was probably stronger for front-line workers, early career staff and lower management, when compared with senior managers. A senior manager interviewed thought his values had not changed, but the responsibilities of being a manager might require strategic rather than client-centred approaches to delivering services. It seemed that although the PSE was interpreted in different ways because of different responsibilities, it could still be called the PSE.

In sum, the micro PSE contributes to a more nuanced understanding of public staff, than the stereotyped portrayal of an officer in a public organization, therefore countering the 'absence of individuals in most recent social and political theory' (Hoggett *et al.* 2006). It provides a different perspective to the PSE described as something impersonal or solely the domain of large public organizations and institutions, discussed next as the *macro PSE*.

Second, the *macro PSE* describes a 'wider' or 'shared' PSE for public servants and the relationship of the *macro PSE* with the board as a distinct group. The macro perspective was articulated as a wider or shared manifestation of the PSE, suggesting it was something perceived as broad, bound by defined structures or through a set of shared values. This built on similar views of the PSE described as 'long-established values and rules providing a benchmark for public servants and their institutions' (Public Administration Select Committee 2002). This portrays a common understanding of the PSE by public servants, but the findings discussed here identified different views, suggesting that, in reality, the picture was more complex. For example, the findings suggest that the PSE is articulated as 'shared and institutionalized' in the public sector but at the same time acknowledges that it varies within different parts of it. However, it would be impossible to define where these macro boundaries lay, or the exact correspondence between the *macro* and the *micro PSE*, with difficulties delineating what is personal, organizational and professional. Kernaghan (1993) stated that public officials apply principles and standards to their actions, but this seems to suggest that officials only follow agreed values.

In addition to definitions of the *macro PSE* for the wider body of public servants and their institutions, there was also the macro perspective of the board as an institution in its own right. At the time of the research, the board had been established for several years, with several health and local government representatives attending it since its inception. At the time of the research reported here, participants were mostly managers in public service organizations representing health, education, social care, careers and the voluntary sector. As well as holding senior positions in their own organizations, many participants were professionally qualified as doctors, teachers, social workers and careers advisors. Consequentially, at the macro level of the board, a culture of cooperation was identified benefitting from the continued attendance of the same representatives over time. However, although positive views of professional relationships were reported, the challenge was to capture the ambiguities, tensions and conflicts between the different values and professions that could be identified there. For example, examples of unhelpful boundaries between social care and medical staff were stated, with disparities between the medical and social models of disability, as well as differences in opinion about how to define need. Another element of professionalism and partnership working was agreeing definitions with different terminology and jargon having the potential to impede the activity of being a public servant.

Finally, the *applied PSE* refers to how the PSE is employed in practice. Describing the PSE as something that can be applied sounds odd, but is best described as implementing the public interest. This understanding is informed by the description of pro-social behaviour as one person helping another at an interpersonal level, with the motivation to support others applied in a specific practice, for example by means of empathy (Penner *et al.* 2005).

A key focus for the applied perspective is the association between the PSE, partnership working and the pursuit of positive 'outcomes'. The relationship between the *applied* PSE and outcomes can be informed by 'change outcomes', for example improvements to an individual's physical and emotional health; and 'maintenance outcomes' to prevent or delay a deterioration in the health, well-being or quality of life of an individual (Dickinson 2008). However, where the concept of the applied PSE is more tangible is in relation to Dickinson's description of 'service process outcomes' related to how a service is delivered. Whereas such a focus on service might be thought to be targeted at individual children, the findings suggested the public interest might be manifested in practice by means of providing clubs and play schemes. This links to Lawton's observation that although described as an abstract ideal, the public interest can be realized in 'concrete' decisions (Lawton *et al.* 2013), indicating that the PSE is not just a theoretical notion, but can be manifested in service delivery. The key example of this for the applied PSE was the description in the research findings of providing accessible toilets for disabled children in the city centre. These new facilities were described as being larger and better equipped than standard accessible toilets for disabled children, and it was stated that they would improve social inclusion.

Conclusion

Informed by empirical research, this chapter has described what the PSE means for practitioners in public services, as well as describing the different ways that the PSE can be theorized. It shows that the PSE continues to have meaning for staff in public services, despite assaults on it as concept. However, the chapter confirms that theorizing and describing the PSE remains challenging, and it is clear that theories of the PSE remain current and will continue to be subject to debate for many years to come.

The chapter has discussed how the PSE has continued resonance, as described in previous literature (John and Johnson 2008; Pratchett and Wingfield 1996). Although the fieldwork suggested that participants had not previously reflected on its meaning, the PSE was described in a way that indicated participants were sympathetic to its aims and values. This was seen by the *micro, macro* and *applied PSE* revealing the complexity inherent in the PSE and its meaning and significance for participants. This framework complements our current understanding of the PSE, demonstrating its resilience, as well as providing theory for future research. This view corresponds with emerging literature on the multidimensional PSE by Rayner *et al.* (2011), identifying *public service belief*, on why individuals are motivated by the ethos; *public service practice*, about delivering services in accordance with it; and *public interest* on the ends individuals perceive the PSE to endorse. The description of the *micro* PSE can additionally be considered in the light of Salminen and Mäntysalo (2013), who note how participants inform their practice with a variety of experiences, and although public staff might be thought to be homogeneous, they have different understandings of the PSE.

Research continues on values and the relationship between the PSE and codes and standards of behaviour for public officers (Heywood 2012). However, suggesting values is highly subjective, raising questions about whether certain values have ascendancy over others. This links to the association between the macro and the micro PSE, and delineating what is personal, organizational and professional. Although it could be presumed that public officers share a set of values, as if there was an unspoken allegiance to them, it is debatable whether this really exists, and their own value base cannot be overlooked.

Future research should investigate how the PSE is applied in practice, as well as identifying case studies. This will provide tangible examples of public service practice that can be researched empirically. The chapter has also shown the importance of values for public officers, and it is suggested that further research is required on the relationship between the individual values of public officers and the relationship with institutional codes and standards of behaviour.

References

Barberis, P. (2001) 'Civil society: Virtue, trust – implications for the public service ethos in the age of modernity', *Public Policy and Administration*, 16(3): 111–26.

Bovaird, T., Briggs, I. and Willis, M. (2014) 'Strategic commissioning in the UK: Service improvement cycle or just going round in circles?', *Local Government Studies*, 40(4): 533–9.

Brannen, J., Statham, J., Mooney, A. and Brockmann, M. (2007) *Coming to Care*, Bristol: Policy Press.

Brereton, M. and Temple, M. (1999) 'The new public service ethos: An ethical environment for governance', *Public Administration*, 77(3): 455–74.

Committee on Standards in Public Life (2013) *Standards Matter*, London: The Stationery Office.

Cooke, S., Badini, L. and Jones, D. (2013) *Autonomy, Accountability and Professional Behaviour in Teaching, Medicine and Law* (seminar paper), University of Birmingham: The Jubilee Centre for Character and Values, Birmingham.

Cree, V.E. and Davis, A. (2007) *Social Work: Voices from the Inside*, London: Routledge.

Crouch, C. (2011) *The Strange Non-Death of Neo-Liberalism*, Cambridge: Polity Press.

Daly, G. (2004) 'Understanding the barriers to multi-professional collaboration', *Nursing Times*, 100(9): 78–9.

Davies, J. (2011) *Challenging Governance Theory*, Bristol: Policy Press.

De Graaf, G. and van der Wal, Z. (2010) 'Managing conflicting public values: Governing with integrity and effectiveness', *The American Review of Public Administration*, 40(2): 623–30.

Dickinson, H. (2008) *Evaluating Outcomes in Health and Social Care*, Bristol: Policy Press.

Elcock, H. (2014) 'What the Greeks taught us and we British have forgotten', *Public Policy and Administration*, 29(3): 241–56.

Fenwick, J., Miller, K. and McTavish, D. (2012) 'Co-governance or meta-bureaucracy? Perspectives of local governance "partnership" in England and Scotland', *Policy and Politics*, 40(3): 405–22.

Goodwin, N. (2013) 'Taking integrated care forward: The need for shared values', *International Journal of Integrated Care*, April–June, 13.

Hebson, G., Grimshaw, D. and Marchington, M. (2003) 'PPPs and the changing public sector ethos: Case-study evidence from the health and local authority sectors', *Work, Employment and Society*, 17(3): 481–501.

Heywood, P. (2012) 'Integrity management and the public service ethos in the UK: Patchwork quilt or threadbare blanket?', *International Review of Administrative Sciences*, 78(3): 474–93.

Hoggett, P., Beedell, P., Jimenez, L., Mayo, M. and Miller, C. (2006) 'Identity, life history and commitment to welfare', *Journal of Social Policy*, 35(4): 689–704.

Hood, C. (1995) 'The "New Public Management" in the 1980s: Variations on a theme', *Accounting, Organizations and Society*, 20(2/3): 95–109.

Hudson, B. (1987) 'Collaboration in social welfare: A framework for analysis', *Policy and Politics*, 15(3): 175–82.

John, P. and Johnson, M. (2008) 'Is there still a public service ethos?', in A. Park, J. Curtice, K. Thomson, M. Phillips, M. Johnson and E. Clay (eds), *British Social Attitudes (24th Report)* (pp. 105–23), London: Sage/National Centre for Social Research.

Kernaghan, K. (1993) 'Promoting public service ethics: The codification option', in R.A. Chapman (ed.), *Ethics in Public Service* (pp. 15–31), Edinburgh: Edinburgh University Press.

LARCI (2010) *Co-Production: A Series of Commissioned Reports*, Swindon: ESRC.

Lawton, A. (1998) *Ethical Management for the Public Services*, Buckingham: Open University Press.

Lawton, A. (2005) 'Public service ethics in a changing world', *Futures*, 37: 231–43.

Lawton, A., Rayner, J. and Lasthuizen, K. (2013) *Ethics and Management in the Public Sector*, London: Routledge.

Le Grand, J. (2003) *Motivation, Agency and Public Policy*, Oxford: Oxford University Press.

Martin, G.P., Phelps, K. and Katbamna, S. (2004) 'Human motivation and professional practice: Of knights, knaves and social workers', *Social Policy and Administration*, 38(5): 470–87.

Needham, C. (2006) 'Customer care and the public service ethos', *Public Administration*, 84(4): 845–60.

Needham, C. (2007) 'A declining public service ethos?', in P. Dibben, G. Wood, I. Roper and P. James (eds), *Modernising Work in Public Services: Redefining Roles and Relationships in Britain's Changing Workplace*, Basingstoke: Palgrave.

Nolan, Lord (1995) *Summary of the Nolan Committee's First Report on Standards in Public Life*, available at: www.archive.official-documents.co.uk/document/parlment/nolan/nolan. htm (accessed 30 June 2010).

O'Toole, B. (2006) *The Ideal of Public Service: Reflections on the Higher Civil Service in Britain*, London: Routledge.

Penner, L.A., Dovidio, J.F., Piliavin, J.A. and Schroeder, D.A. (2005) 'Pro-social behaviour: Multilevel perspectives', *Annual Review of Psychology*, 56: 365–92.

Perry, J. (1997) 'Antecedents of public service motivation', *Journal of Public Administration Research and Theory*, 7(2): 181–97.

Perry, J.L. and Wise, L.R. (1990) 'The motivational bases of public service', *Public Administration Review*, 50(3): 367–73.

Plant, R. (2003) 'A public service ethic and political accountability', *Parliamentary Affairs*, 56: 560–79.

Pratchett, L. (2000) 'The inherently unethical nature of public service ethics', in R.A. Chapman (ed.), *Ethics in Public Service for the New Millennium*, Aldershot: Ashgate.

Pratchett, L. and Wingfield, M. (1996) 'Petty bureaucracy and woolly-minded liberalism? The changing ethos of local government officers', *Public Administration*, 74(4): 639–56.

Public Administration Select Committee (2002) *The Public Service Ethos: Seventh Report of Session 2001–2*, London: The Stationery Office.

Putnam, L. and Mumby, D. (1993) 'Organisations, emotion and the myth of rationality', in S. Fineman (ed.), *Emotion and Organisations* (pp. 36–57), London: Sage.

Rayner, J., Williams, H.M., Lawton, A. and Allison, C.W. (2011) 'Public service ethos: Developing a generic measure', *Journal of Public Administration Research and Theory*, 21(1): 27–51.

Reid, F. (2003) *Evidence-Based Policy: Where Is the Evidence for It?*, Working Paper, School for Policy Studies, University of Bristol.

Rhodes, R.A.W. (2007) 'Understanding governance: Ten years on', *Organization Studies*, 28(8): 1243–64.

Salminen, A. and Mäntysalo, V. (2013) 'Exploring the public service ethos: Ethical profiles of regional and local managers in the Finnish public administration', *Public Integrity*, 15(2): 167–85.

Sheldon, B. and Chilvers, R. (2000) *Evidence-Based Social Care: A Study of Prospects and Problems*, Lyme Regis: Russell House.

Stackman, R.W., Connor, P.W. and Becker, B.W. (2006) 'Sectoral ethos: An investigation of the personal values systems of female and male managers in the public and private sectors', *Journal of Public Administration Research and Theory*, 16(4): 577–97.

Stoker, G. (2006) 'Public value management: A new narrative for networked governance?', *The American Review of Public Administration*, 36(1): 41–57.

Stoker, G. and Aldridge, R. (2002) *Advancing a New Public Service Ethos*, London: New Local Government Network.

van der Wal, Z. (2011) 'The content and context of organizational ethics', *Public Administration*, 89(2): 644–60.

15

CONFLICTS OF INTEREST AND ETHICAL DECISION-MAKING

Mainland China and Hong Kong comparisons

Ting Gong and Ian Scott*

Introduction

Conflicts of interest represent a particular form of ethical dilemma in which personal interests could actually or potentially bias the outcome of a decision or an action. One widely used definition views conflicts of interest as situations in which 'a public official has private-capacity interests which *could* improperly influence the performance of their official duties and responsibilities' (OECD 2005, p. 7) (emphasis in original). Most governments formally regard such conflicts as incompatible with ethical decision-making, and use rules and moral suasion to try to ensure that private interests are, as far as possible, excluded from the decision-making process. If there is suspicion that personal interests might be involved in a decision, value considerations about the integrity and fairness of the government may be triggered and public reactions could have political consequences well beyond the intrinsic importance of the issue.

Although governments usually emphasize strongly the necessity of avoiding conflicts of interest in decision-making, the distinction between private and public interests in practice is not always so easily and firmly drawn (Denhardt and Gilman 2005). Not all conflicts of interest represent corruption or even unethical behaviour, and some conflicts in public life are probably unavoidable. At least three situations can be identified: those where conflicts may exist but which are not considered sufficiently important to prohibit the official from making a decision; those that represent unethical behaviour but which may be tolerated and may not warrant prosecution; and those that violate express rules or norms governing such behaviour and involve the subversion of the public interest for private gain. Although any of these instances might be far more complex to categorize in practice, this does enable us to construct a simple continuum that stretches from the least to most serious conflicts of interest (Gong and Ren 2013). Procedures and sanctions are usually also expected to match the offence. In the first instance of mild conflicts, the official might proceed to make a decision or undertake some other activity subject to declaring an interest (although what is an interest is itself a separate and difficult definitional issue). In the second, where behaviour is unethical but not of a serious nature, the offender might expect a warning or some other form of punishment. In the third instance, which represents corruption, the official would be liable to criminal prosecution.

At this point, however, other dimensions of the definitional problem come into play. Conflicts of interest are perceptions; they exist in the eye of the beholder (Stark 2000, pp. 1–5). Because they are omnipresent with changing forms and characteristics under different organizational settings, rules can rarely be devised that cover all situations. In consequence, governments must constantly grapple with the problem of whether a conflict of interest is present, real or potential, and, if so, what punishment is appropriate for the offender. A particular difficulty is establishing *mens rea* – that is, whether the offender had a 'guilty mind' – and of dealing with the problem of the culpability of a person who had no perception that a conflict of interest existed.

Faced with the complexities of making the punishment fit the crime and of trying to reduce serious conflicts of interest, governments, including those in mainland China and Hong Kong, have adopted a range of measures. First, there are 'blunderbuss offences' (such as, for example, misconduct in public office in Hong Kong), which could cover many different types of conflict of interest and which could lead to prosecution. Second, there are specific internal rules and regulations, rendering an official liable to disciplinary action if they are breached. Third, value-based integrity management programmes, which place a greater burden of responsibility for identifying the conflict on the individual, have been introduced in some countries, including mainland China and Hong Kong (Huberts *et al.* 2008; OECD 2000). We argue that a value-based approach is necessary because the pervasiveness, uncertainty, diversity and increasing frequency of conflicts of interest mean that rule-based approaches are unlikely to cover the multiplicity of cases in which a conflict may arise. The success of value-based integrity management, however, is heavily dependent on values that are shared, widely understood and sensitively interpreted throughout the public sector. Governments, consequently, need to play a proactive role in supporting and entrenching desired values. We examine some initiatives in mainland China and Hong Kong later in the chapter.

Classifying conflicts of interest

To provide greater analytical clarity, we seek to classify conflicts of interest using the social and organizational relationships of the public official as the determining feature. By definition, conflicts of interest involve more than one 'interest'. These interests stem from personal and public relationships both within and outside the office. Different types of relationships consequently lead to different kinds of conflicts between private and public interests. From the perspective of the public official, we define his or her social and organizational relationships as:

- societal (relationships with family and friends);
- intra-organizational (relationships with colleagues in the workplace);
- inter-organizational (relationships with clients or parties involved or potentially interested in dealing with the government); and
- ultra-organizational (relationships with other private organizations once the official leaves the organization).

We assume that any official is bound to have the first two types of relationships and that many senior officials will also be involved in their work in negotiations with the private sector and with potential new employers once they leave the government.[1] In classifying typical patterns of conflicts of interest associated with these relationships, we also draw on experiences in mainland China and Hong Kong for examples of the types of conflicts of interest that are summarized in Table 15.1. In mainland China, while there is no official definition or classification of conflicts of interest, a document promulgated by the Central Committee of the Chinese Communist Party (CCP) in 2010, *The Code of Ethical Conduct of Leading Cadres*, identified 52 kinds of misconduct and unacceptable behaviour, which was derived from numerous cases.

In Hong Kong, the classification is derived from an analysis of 39 cases prosecuted under the common law offence of misconduct in public office between 1998 and 2010 (Leung and Scott 2012), two highly publicized cases involving senior civil servants and post-public employment, several instances in which high-level officials were accused of position-related consumption, and cases in which Legislative Councillors received benefits or failed to declare their interests when debating proposed legislation. In addition, we draw on interviews with 32 ethics officers in the Hong Kong government, which focused on their roles and problems in dealing with conflicts of interest.

This classification enables us to focus on comparative differences and similarities in the identification and treatment of conflicts of interest on the mainland and in Hong Kong. We do not claim that it is representative of all conflicts of interest. An accepted bribe, for example, also represents a conflict of interest and may be prosecuted under the laws of the land. In such cases, however, the *mens rea* and *acteus rea* (the 'guilty act') may well be sufficiently clear to warrant conviction. In the conflicts of interest with which we are concerned, the offenders may also be prosecuted, but in many cases, there may be doubt about their motives, about whether unethical behaviour deserves a custodial sentence, or indeed whether there was a conflict in the first place.

In the following sections, we analyse the reasons for the emergence of conflicts of interest as serious issues in mainland China and Hong Kong, and the means that have been adopted to deal with them. Using results from an administrative ethics survey administered to 355 senior civil servants in Hong Kong and to 366 senior civil servants in mainland China, we also assess whether civil servants themselves perceive that there are potential conflicts between their personal values and those of the organization. We then compare the four types of relationships listed in Table 15.1. Finally, we examine the measures taken to reduce conflicts of interest and enhance ethical decision-making through value-based integrity management programmes.

TABLE 15.1 Conflicts of interest and organizational relationships

Relationship	Types of conflict of interest	Examples of unacceptable behaviour	Possible remedies
Societal	Preferential treatment	Subverting the recruitment or tendering process to favour a relative or friend.	Strict separation of public and private interests backed by sanctions and reinforced by value training on why the separation is necessary.
Intra-organizational	'Blind spots'; position-related consumption	Ignoring unethical or corrupt behaviour on the part of a colleague; abuse of office through excessive position-related expenditure.	Value-based training on organizational commitments; tighter controls and independent monitoring of position-related expenditure.
Inter-organizational	'Sweeteners'; promises of deferred advantages; bribes	Accepting gifts or entertainment or meals from a government client or potential client; agreeing to join a private organization in a related employment field at some future date.	Rules governing acceptance of gifts or entertainment or meals. Value-based training on the dangers of 'sweeteners', particularly deferred advantages.
Ultra-organizational	Joining a private organization in a related field soon after ceasing to be a public employee	Using privileged information in the interests of a private organization; lobbying a department in which the former official was an employee.	Rules on the 'sanitization' period and value-based training in pre-retirement or pre-resignation seminars on the organizational expectations of the employee.

Source: Based on the sources listed in the paragraphs above and on Independent Commission Against Corruption (n.d.) *Reference Package on Conflict of Interest for Managers in the Civil Service*, Hong Kong: ICAC; The Central Committee of the Chinese Communist Party (2010) *The Code of Ethical Conduct of Leading Cadres of the Communist Party of China*.

Conflicts of interest in mainland China and Hong Kong

Concern over conflicts of interest has been growing in both mainland China and in Hong Kong over the past two decades. An increasing number of political scandals have resulted in calls for greater control over, and scrutiny of, the actions of public officials. On the mainland, in recent years, there has been a dramatic increase in corruption cases involving senior government officials (Wedeman 2004), with the sums in question continuing to soar (Yang 2004). The Chinese government is confronted with mounting challenges in dealing with the proliferation of corruption. It must also tackle various new and emerging forms of official misconduct. For example, predatory public managers take advantage of the restructuring of state enterprises to enrich themselves; government officials act as 'insiders' in economic transactions for rent-seeking; and local officials engage in lavish spending of public funds for personal pleasure and special perks. Worse yet, many of these activities have been carried out under the guise of normal market transactions or routine official functions, which obscure their illicit or unethical nature (Gong and Zhou 2014; Ko and Weng 2012).

The changing forms and characteristics of corruption challenge traditional ways of tackling it. For many years, the Chinese government launched top-down, periodic and tempestuous organizational campaigns to detect and punish corrupt party and government officials. During the 1980s and 1990s, for example, the government launched at least four massive nationwide anti-corruption drives, which were followed by numerous small-scale organizational clean-ups conducted sporadically and swiftly by anti-corruption agencies. With a relatively clear definition of corruption as the illegal exchange between public power and personal gain, and when corruption mainly takes the form of bribe giving and bribe taking, it may not be too difficult to identify and sanction corrupt activities. This explains partially why the government deemed it necessary to carry out anti-corruption political campaigns in order to decontaminate party and state organizations.

The effectiveness of the top-down campaign-style anti-corruption enforcement is largely a failure as far as mainland China is concerned. Despite the government's decades-long endeavours, corruption continued to proliferate, seemingly unchecked. Consequently, from the mid 2000s onwards, the government recalibrated its anti-corruption efforts to emphasize rule-based integrity management. Approximately 90 central official documents have been issued in the past 10 years, exceeding the combined total of the two previous decades (Gong and Ren 2013). The new ethical rules and regulations are extensive yet detailed, covering various kinds of corruption and many other types of misconduct. For example, government officials are prohibited from engaging in profit-making activities, making preferential arrangements for their children or relatives to profiteer in the market, concurrently holding positions in business organizations or reimbursing personal expenses through these organizations, making stock transactions with public funds, accepting honoraria, gifts or gift vouchers in connection with public duties, and using public funds for lavish consumption and extravagant entertainment (The Central

Committee of the Chinese Communist Party 2010). Some of these activities were traditionally 'grey areas' and did not necessarily break the law. In most cases, however, conflicts of interest are obviously involved, which, if not handled appropriately, may easily develop into corruption.

Hong Kong, by comparison, has successfully reduced corruption in the civil service to minimal levels. The Independent Commission Against Corruption (ICAC), established in 1974, initially focused on the public sector and was given strong powers to prosecute, prevent and change community attitudes to corruption. In the colonial period, the predominant pattern of corruption was bribery. Where it could be shown that an advantage had been obtained, prosecutions were lodged under *The Prevention of Bribery Ordinance*. Shortly before 1997, however, the ICAC became concerned that it was becoming more difficult to prove that an advantage had been received; other forms of corruption, such as deferred advantages and serious conflicts of interest, were becoming more prevalent. In response to these problems, in 1998, the ICAC began to supplement *The Prevention of Bribery Ordinance* by prosecuting under the broader remit of the common law offence of misconduct in public office (McWalters 2010, pp. 673–715). In collaboration with the government's Civil Service Bureau, it also introduced an ethical enhancement programme designed to focus on the core values of the civil service and to increase inter alia awareness of conflict of interest issues. The ethics regime of the Hong Kong civil service is thus a mixture of a rule-based and value-based system.

In Hong Kong, there are significant differences between the ethical rules and regulations that apply to civil servants and the somewhat weaker controls that pertain to the Chief Executive, political appointees, and members of the Executive and Legislative Councils. Although the Codes governing conflicts of interest are similar for both civil servants and political appointees, the sanctions applied to political appointees are less extensive than those that apply to civil servants (Chief Executive's Office 2012; Civil Service Bureau 2009). Civil servants are subject to a range of penalties, from warnings to fines, to dismissal, to prosecution, all of which can be adjusted to fit the severity of the offence (Independent Review Committee 2012, pp. 33–4). Political appointees, like civil servants, can be prosecuted under *The Prevention of Bribery Ordinance* and can be charged with the offence of misconduct in public office, but there are few evident intermediary sanctions short of prosecution.

The monitoring of conflicts of interest is also less developed in the case of political appointees. In the civil service, any potential conflict of interest must be reported to the immediate supervisor, who then deals with the matter; in the case of political appointees and Executive Councillors, it is formally the Chief Executive who must deal with such issues. The rules and procedures governing the Chief Executive and Legislative Councillors are even looser. Two critical provisions of *The Prevention of Bribery Ordinance* do not apply to the Chief Executive, and he is not obliged to adhere to the *Code for Officials under the Political Appointment System*, although the last two Chief Executives have done so voluntarily. Principal Officials are required to disclose their interests, but they have not always shown sensitivity to potential conflicts. In 2003, for example, the then Financial Secretary, Anthony Leung Kam-chung, purchased a car shortly before he was about to raise registration tax on vehicles (Legislative Council, Panel on Constitutional Affairs 2003). He did not disclose an interest and did not resign until several months after the incident was revealed.

The requirement that Legislative Councillors should disclose their interests is also vague, especially in relation to property; transgressions, at best, are only mildly sanctioned (Legislative Council 2006, 2013). Common practice is that a Legislative Councillor involved in a conflict of interest or failure to disclose an interest apologizes and makes a charitable donation in compensation. Somewhat paradoxically, but perhaps because of these differing sets of rules and expectations, Hong Kong has both a generally clean civil service, highly conscious of potential unethical behaviour, and a political system that has been constantly racked by scandals over conflicts of interest.

The most striking difference between mainland China and Hong Kong lies in the perception of what constitutes a conflict of interest. On the mainland, for example, it is not uncommon for officials to use government resources for private purposes on the grounds that this facilitates the broader objective of serving the public interest or at least does no harm to the public. To illustrate: many local governments have built expensive buildings with luxurious internal decorations and officials often use government vehicles for personal purposes. In Hong Kong, where there is a more rigorous separation of public and private interests, it would be regarded as a conflict of interest if government transport was used by civil servants for private purposes. Exposing conflicts of interest also occurs in very different settings in Hong Kong and on the mainland. The media in Hong Kong is quick to seize upon potential scandals, and many conflicts of interest have been revealed as a result of investigative reporting. On the mainland, by contrast, the revelation of scandals and conflicts of interest usually only occurs *ex post facto* after the downfall of the official.

The values and attitudes of public officials in mainland China and Hong Kong towards conflicts of interest also vary. In 2011 and 2012, we conducted an administrative ethics survey in both places to determine whether senior civil servants felt any conflicts of interest between their own personal well-being and the public interest, between loyalty to colleagues and their superiors, or between their personal well-being and obligations to the law.[2] In the Hong Kong case, although important isolated cases still surface, there is little evidence to suggest that conflicts of interest pose a major problem within the civil service (as opposed to the wider political system). A firmly embedded rule-based system, focused value-based programmes designed to increase ethical awareness, and an organizational environment in which the separation of public from private interests is well understood appear to have been sufficient to reduce the likelihood of serious conflicts arising. Most respondents in Hong Kong reported that conflicts of interest never happened or very infrequently happened between their personal well-being and the public interest (92 per cent); between personal well-being and loyalty to their organization (88 per cent); and between their well-being and obligations to the law (97 per cent). They believed their superiors were as ethical as they were.

By contrast, on the mainland, where the rules governing the civil service are less firmly embedded, the potential for conflicts of interest seems greater. More mainland respondents than their Hong Kong counterparts reported that conflicts of interest frequently or occasionally happened between their personal well-being and the public interest (20 per cent versus 8 per cent); between personal well-being and loyalty to their organizations (27 per cent versus 12 per cent); and between personal well-being and obligations to the law (16 per cent versus 3 per cent). They were not as certain as the Hong Kong respondents that their superiors were as ethical as they were. There were also differences in responses to conflict between personal well-being and loyalty to the organization, with only 12 per cent of Hong Kong respondents reporting that it happened frequently or occasionally, but some 26 per cent of mainland respondents perceiving there to be conflicts. The survey results provide us with a snapshot of attitudes towards ethics and organizational behaviour in two very different civil services. In order to explore further, however, examples of particular types of conflicts of interest are analysed to extend the comparison.

Relationships with relatives and friends

Often attributed to the Confucian emphasis on family and interpersonal relationships, there is a strong Chinese cultural tradition that those with connections or positions of authority are expected to help family members and friends, and that there should be reciprocity in the exchange of gifts and products. This tradition has been referred to as *guanxi*. For a public official, it may translate into expectations of recruitment to government positions or to preferential treatment for contracts, goods and services. Formally, both the Hong Kong and mainland civil services recruit on grounds of merit, and consequently there should be no conflicts of interest. Practices are nevertheless quite different in the two places.

In mainland China, pulling *guanxi* is still important in various areas of the civil service. In terms of recruitment and promotion, some candidates receive favourable considerations because of family backgrounds or personal connections. A case in point is the rapid promotion of a 25-year-old girl from a clerical position to the head of a township within three years in Shandong province. The case drew the attention of social media and consequently this woman and her father, who was the deputy director of the Organization Department at the next higher level of the government, resigned under pressure on the same day in April 2013. A preliminary investigation did not reveal any evidence of misconduct, although the case caused considerable suspicion of the role of her father in the promotion.[3] There was no involvement of bribery or other legal transgression, nor did the father directly promote the daughter. In cases such as this, there does not seem to have been a very clear line between public and private interests. Conflicts of interest are concealed because there is no evidence of personal gain, an illicit act, or an exchange of favours.

In Hong Kong, there are long-established regulations in place to ensure that recruitment to the civil service is by merit, defined as the best person for the position. Monitoring organizations, the Public Service Commission and the ICAC, make certain that departments follow procedures. Lapses that are identified do not usually relate to conflicts of interest or corruption. There have been occasional cases, however, where public officials have implied that government contracts would be awarded to companies if they employed family or friends. Political appointees in Hong Kong also do not meet the criterion of recruitment by merit. They are not elected or endorsed by the Legislative Council nor required to possess certain credentials to hold office. However, they constitute a minute proportion of public officials, only 32 in 2012.

Although corruption offences in the civil service in Hong Kong are rare, one of the most common forms has been awarding government contracts to relatives and friends. For example, of 43 public officials prosecuted for misconduct in public office between 1998 and 2010, 17 (of whom 11 were convicted) involved offences relating to contracts and procurement (Leung and Scott 2012, p. 10). In *HKSAR v Shum Kwok Sher*, the accused, who was the government's Chief Property Manager, was convicted of awarding contracts worth HK$150 million to companies in which his family members had a financial interest. The judgment provided the legal basis for subsequent prosecutions, defining misconduct in public office as situations in which public officials wilfully neglected or failed to perform their duties with seriously detrimental consequences.

Incidents similar to the *Shum Kwok Sher* case have taken place quite frequently in mainland China. The transformation from central planning to a market economy resulted in the outsourcing of many public works and services. Conflicts of interest, as well as information asymmetry, adverse selection and moral hazards, are well-known problems associated with public–private partnerships, stemming from the lack of oversight and control over collaborative contracts and weakened accountability mechanisms (Rosenbloom and Gong 2013). In addition to directly awarding contracts to relatives or friends, the misconduct of government officials has taken other forms. For example, a project may be awarded to the institution with which the spouse of an official is affiliated; businesspeople may provide the relatives of an official with benefits (such as job opportunities or housing) after receiving favourable treatment.

In dealing with conflicts of interest that favour family or friends, the critical factor is the extent to which there is a separation of public and private interests. In Hong Kong, this separation is strongly enforced, and transgressions, although not widely prevalent, are prosecuted if discovered. On the mainland, the widespread acceptance of *guanxi* means that the separation of public and private interests cannot be easily sustained, and there are, in consequence, many cases in which relatives and friends benefit from connections within government.

Relationships within the organization

In this section, we deal with conflicts of interest that relate mainly to abuse of position-related consumption, although we should note that in the Hong Kong case, the ICAC also strongly emphasizes that abuse of office (and a conflict of interest) may occur when persistent misconduct by colleagues is ignored (ICAC n.d. –*Reference Package*).

Position-related consumption has resulted in some major scandals involving high-level politicians in both places. In Hong Kong, in February 2012, the then Chief Executive, Donald Tsang Kam-yuen, admitted accepting travel on private jets and yachts, attending lavish banquets organized by friends in business, and renting a residence at sub-market prices for use after he left office (Independent Review Committee 2012, p. 1). While Tsang apologized for his behaviour to the Legislative Council, he denied any impropriety and said that the residence had been rented by his wife. He appointed an independent review committee to consider improvements in procedures relating to conflicts of interest, and asked the Audit Commission to investigate a charge that he had overspent on accommodation on duty visits (Audit Commission 2012; Independent Review Committee 2012). The Committee suggested changes to the code governing political appointments and also recommended that Sections 3 and 8 of *The Prevention of Bribery Ordinance*, which relate to accepting an advantage, should be applied to the Chief Executive. The incoming Chief Executive accepted the recommendations and minor changes were made immediately. However, *The Prevention of Bribery Ordinance* has still not been amended to include the Chief Executive. When the scandal broke, the ICAC also announced that it would conduct an investigation, but to date there has been no public report on its findings. Dissatisfied with Tsang's explanation of his conduct, some Legislative Council members tabled a motion to impeach him, but the motion could not be debated before he left office. The Tsang case raised serious questions about the integrity of the incumbent of the highest political office in Hong Kong and pointed to flaws in the legal and institutional arrangements designed to ensure accountability on issues relating to conflict of interest.

Another important case of position-related consumption concerned the former Commissioner of the ICAC, Timothy Tong Hing-ming. In May 2013, the Chief Executive set up another independent review committee to examine claims that Tong had sanctioned excessive levels of expenditure on entertainment and gifts and that there were irregularities in arrangements for the 35 duty visits that he undertook during his five years in office. The Committee found that 37 per cent of the 206 lunches hosted during the period had exceeded official expenditure limits; that some official gifts were too expensive; that some duty visits had not been properly approved; and that, in some cases, no quotes had been obtained for air fares (Independent Review Committee 2013, pp. 25, 34, 40). The Committee recommended that the ICAC should pay more attention to the official guidelines and that it should be more frugal in its use of public money. The ICAC launched a criminal investigation into Tong's conduct and the Legislative Council set up a

Select Committee. The Council's Public Accounts Committee also set up an enquiry and, in November 2013, published a report that was highly critical of Tong's behaviour (Public Accounts Committee 2013).

Tong himself did not appear to benefit much from the excessive expenditure and there is some question of whether his actions represent a conflict of interest. As he told the Select Committee, 'overspending is not a sin' (Chong 2014). The Public Accounts Committee, however, saw a conflict between his public duty and his violations of the rules, particularly since the integrity of the ICAC was involved (Public Accounts Committee 2013, p. 76). In both the Tsang and Tong cases, the reporting bodies focused mainly on improving the existing rules rather than introducing new rules or stressing value considerations. However, despite the relatively minor infractions involved in these cases, the impact on the values embodied in Hong Kong institutions has been significant. In the Tsang case, the integrity issue related not only to the person holding the office, but to the office of Chief Executive itself. In the Tong case, there was an impact on the credibility of the ICAC; corruption complaints dropped by 36 per cent after the issue became public (Public Accounts Committee 2013, p. 81).

While in Hong Kong misconduct concerning position-related consumption appears as isolated cases involving high-level officials, in mainland China such misbehaviour is prevalent and has in some institutions even been routinized as a part of organizational life. Three types of position-related consumption are especially prominent: using official vehicles for purposes other than public duties; lavish banqueting with public money; and overseas sightseeing in the name of business trips. What has triggered public criticism and the leadership's concern is the huge public expenditure and conflicts of interest involved in these activities. According to official estimates, the total public spending in the central government on these three types of consumption reached ¥9.4 billion (approximately $1.5 billion) in 2010 and 2011 (Li 2012). In local government, the situation was even worse because units had to host visits from higher-level officials. When external audits or inspections were conducted, the auditors and inspectors (often government officials themselves) were provided with extravagant meals, expensive gifts and luxurious accommodation. In 2012, Mr Feng Feien, a member of the Chinese People's Political Consultative Committee, submitted a proposal to the central government, suggesting that excessive position-related consumption be treated as breaching the law. He estimated that, with local governments included, the public spending on banqueting alone had reached ¥300 billion (approximately $46 billion) a year.[4]

Position-related consumption is a grey area where it is often difficult to distinguish between necessary and excessive spending and to separate duty-required consumption from private activities. As a result, in both Hong Kong and mainland China, the rules regulating position-related consumption are insufficiently clear. In Hong Kong, the implementation of the regulations for high-level officials seems to be too loose, while in mainland China the abuse of position-related consumption has taken place at all levels of the government and in ways that defy simple remedies.

Relationships with other organizations

In this section, we look particularly at 'sweeteners', which are sometimes given to officials by private companies seeking to win contracts. These kinds of conflicts typically arise in situations where the company seeks a benefit. It may be, however, that the company does not seek to corrupt the official but merely to establish good working relationships, usually through providing various forms of entertainment. On the mainland, this is sometimes seen as an integral part of good business practice; in Hong Kong, civil servants who accept frequent offers of hospitality from companies outside formal business transactions face dismissal, even if there is no evidence of corruption.

The ICAC has focused on the relationships between civil servants and contractors at all points in the procurement process. There are elaborate procedures governing the tendering process that are designed to ensure that no single company is given preferential treatment (Corruption Prevention Department n.d., pp. 5–8). Once a large contract has been signed, ICAC officers meet with both senior civil servants and the contractors to explain their ethical obligations. Proper procedures are also outlined in numerous publications and seminars and there is extensive advice to civil service managers on avoiding such 'sweeteners' as frequent and lavish entertainment; gambling with contractors for high financial stakes; personal favours; and borrowing money (ICAC n.d. – *Ethics in Practice*, p. 25). The ICAC also warns contractors against attempts to subvert the tendering process or government monitoring of the quality of goods and services they deliver. These methods seem to have been largely successful, although there are still occasional transgressions in the tendering process, where contracts have been awarded to companies run by family or friends.

There are fewer controls over 'sweeteners' for politicians. The Legislative Council has a Committee on Members' Interests, but its disclosure requirements are vague and much weaker than those in Western parliamentary systems. Its advisory guidelines, for example, contain the provision that a member should not 'seek to influence another person to further the Members' private interests', but it does not provide advice on what the member should do when offered a 'sweetener' (Committee on Members' Interests 2009). There have been such cases. In August 2013, seven Legislative Councillors and an Executive Councillor accepted a six-day trip to Paris for themselves and a companion from Cathay Pacific Airlines. At the time, the company had an interest in two controversial issues under government consideration, the granting of a licence to a budget carrier and the construction of a third airport runway (Chong 2013). Two of the invited members were on the Airport Authority Board. The visit, according to the company, was to inspect a new aircraft that it had purchased. On their return from Paris, the delegation was faced with calls to explain the potential conflict of interest. The company, somewhat disingenuously, argued that the government rather than the Legislative Councillors would make the decisions on the controversial issues. Some members of the delegation accepted that there could be perceptions of a conflict of interest and paid the cost of the trip to charities, but others saw no conflict and did not.

On the mainland, the government's role in economic affairs is more limited than in the past. However, individual officials remain connected with private enterprises in various capacities – legally or illegally. Government procurement serves as an example where 'sweeteners' are often used by firms in their effort to set up *guanxi* networks with government officials despite numerous formal anti-bribery rules. Several types of officials are pursued by businesspeople: those from the purchasing institutions who decide on specific items and what procurement methods to use, those who oversee procurement and may turn a blind eye to irregular bidding activities, and those who hold higher-level positions in government and can therefore influence procurement decisions. Competition in the bidding system is often a competition for connections (*guanxi*). Few firms succeed in winning public contracts without providing benefits to officials in the first place (Gong and Zhou 2014). 'Sweeteners', however, may take various forms in the process along the road to outright bribery. Advantages may be offered, for instance, in tangible ways such as consulting fees or instant gifts, but may also happen in disguised forms such as free shares in companies, stamps for stamp collectors, or benefits to a third-party beneficiary designated by the official. The possibilities are endless, and this makes it difficult to develop clear rules for 'sweeteners' by distinguishing what is legal from what is illegal.

Relationships after leaving the organization

Deferred advantages – in particular, offering a public official employment at a later date in the private sector for favours granted – have increasingly become ethical problems for governments. Prescribing rules to cover such conflicts requires finding a balance between the right to work and the contributions that experienced officials can make, on the one hand, and concerns about the use of privileged information, lobbying and the consequences of perceptions of 'jobs for favours', on the other. In Hong Kong, the possibility of conflicts of interest resulting from post-public employment sparked two major political debates.

In the first case, in 2004, a former senior civil servant was asked to explain her conduct in supporting the bid of her parent company for multimillion-dollar contracts for a proposed new cultural centre. She had previously worked in a department with cultural responsibilities. The implication was that she was lobbying. She defended herself vigorously, pointing out that she had not worked in the department for five years and that she had complied with the post-public employment rules. Eventually, the government accepted that she did not have a conflict of interest, but warned her not to engage in lobbying activities in the future. The debate triggered considerable public interest and the government slightly strengthened the rules on post-public employment.

The problems with the rules, however, were illustrated in a second case, which caused even more public concern. When in office, a former Director of Housing, Leung Chin-man, had been involved in the sale of flats to a developer. The view at that time was that the 'premium' received by the government on the sale was 'ludicrous' (Legislative Council 2010, p. 235). Leung subsequently retired and, after the 'sanitization' period expired, was offered, and accepted, a highly paid position with the company with which he had previously been dealing. There was an immediate public outcry. The appointment was seen as reward for past services and as damaging to public confidence in the conduct of former officials (Legislative Council 2010, p. 235). A review committee recommended further changes to the rules and a Legislative Council Select Committee was set up to investigate the issue (Legislative Council 2010; Review Committee 2009). Leung did not take up the position.

In mainland China, conflicts of interest in the post-retirement arrangements of government officials did not receive much attention until 2010 when *The Code of Ethical Conduct of Leading Cadres* was adopted. In the 1980s, government officials could work for any private enterprise immediately after leaving public office. Later in the early 1990s, conflicts of interest took another form with many governmental officials concurrently holding positions in social organizations or private firms to make income for their institutions or themselves. The policy permitted this practice because public institutions were encouraged to make earnings to help alleviate the burden of the state coffers. The profit-making activities of government officials brought ample opportunities for corruption. The central government finally decided to shut down all businesses affiliated with government departments and carried out several major 'clean-up' campaigns. *The Civil Servant Law of the People's Republic of China* promulgated in 2005 makes it clear that civil servants may not participate in any profit-making activity or hold a concurrent post in any profit-making organization. The law also stipulates that no government officials are permitted to take a post in a profit-making organization that is directly related to their former official duties within a two-year period following the cessation of their active service. For senior officials, the restriction is for three years. In practice, however, how to decide whether a post is 'directly related' remains difficult.

In both places, there have been difficulties in devising rules that maintain public integrity but which also allow civil servants to take up post-public employment opportunities. In Hong Kong, there have been long-standing rules against bringing the public service 'into disrepute', but there are few sanctions against those who do, other than to face criticism in the media and the Legislative Council. On the mainland, the interpretation of the rules and weak mechanisms for the public exposure of transgressors probably means that rules are honoured more in the breach than in practice.

Value-based measures and conflicts of interest

These kinds of conflicts of interest have led to concerns that the rules alone are insufficient to effect control. Consequently, there has been increasing interest in supplementing the rules by more value-based approaches. The burden of responsibility for determining a conflict of interest would then shift to the individual official rather than mechanical reference to the rules. The role of government in supporting such a value-based approach, however, cannot be restricted to exhortations or vague generalizations. Programmes and systems have to be designed to convey and reinforce shared values throughout the public service. The government must also ensure that sanctions will be applied if standards are not met. Rules and values are complementary in this sense, with values providing the moral compass that the rules ideally should reflect.

In Hong Kong, the inception of a value-based approach dates from 1998 when the core values of the civil service were promulgated. They were defined as: commitment to the rule of law; honesty and integrity; accountability for decisions and actions; political neutrality; impartiality in the execution of public functions and dedication; and professionalism and diligence in serving the community. Training programmes were changed to incorporate these values and publicity on the dangers of conflicts of interest was also stepped up. In 2006, the government appointed an Ethics Officer at a very senior level in every department. The Ethics Officer was required to monitor both the effectiveness of the anti-corruption rules and value-based considerations relating to ethical standards and training programmes. Smaller departments deliver the programmes using ICAC and the Civil Service Bureau training materials, sometimes drawing on personnel from those bodies (Independent Commission Against Corruption n.d. – *Reference Package*). In larger departments, such as the Police, which have their own training capacity, programmes tend to be more individually tailored to suit their needs. There is some evidence that the more decentralization to the department in this regard, the more effective the ethics programmes tend to be (Brewer *et al.* forthcoming). Most departmental training programmes, whether in small or in large departments, now include material on core values and ethical concerns and are reinforced at every step on the career ladder. In 2009, the meaning of the core values was further developed in the Civil Service Code.

Our administrative ethics survey confirms that there is wide awareness of potential conflicts of interest at the senior and middle levels of the Hong Kong civil service, and that civil servants understand that they are personally responsible for any violations of standards. For example, under the Civil Service Code, civil servants must bring any potential conflicts of interest to the attention of their superiors. Members of promotion boards are required to disclose any relationships with candidates. Participating in committees of outside organizations, once a matter of routine, is now more carefully considered. Matters that might previously have been of minor concern – such as, for example, a travel company offering discounts to civil servants – now receive much more attention. In the Police Force, the stress on values has become a central focus of its training programmes. At the apex of the system, the ICAC and the Civil Service Bureau serve as final arbiters on whether a conflict identified in a bureau or department is in fact a conflict or simply a situation that can be tolerated. Both corruption cases and disciplinary cases relating to ethical issues have dropped sharply over the past decades; the integrity of the civil service, as distinct from the rest of the political system, has increased markedly.

In mainland China, the Civil Servant Law requires all public officials to observe as core values: the rule of law, professionalism, diligence in serving people, loyalty to public duty, honesty and integrity, and safeguarding state security. The Central Commission for Discipline Inspection, the top anti-corruption agency in mainland China, has issued an ethics handbook detailing these values and the guidelines for government officials to observe. In 2010, the Central Discipline Inspection and Supervision Academy was established in Beijing as the leading institution in integrity training and education. Its major mission is to provide regular short-term training for government officials. Many value-based measures have also been introduced in order to tackle potential or actual conflicts of interest. It is worth noting, however, that in departing from the previous top-down one-size-fits-all approach to integrity management, the central government has placed more emphasis on local innovation in promoting ethical values in recent years, which has led to various local ethics initiatives. In some localities, for instance, self-learning integrity programmes have been introduced to engage government officials in exercises to help them find solutions to ethical dilemmas. In a county in Southern China, some 2,500 Party members and civil servants receive regular newsletters, praising those who honestly and diligently perform their duties and promoting famous integrity sayings. Special training programmes have also been developed by local governments for different types of officials: for senior officials, junior civil servants and ethics officers, respectively. There have even been special training programmes designed for the spouses of senior officials in some government organizations in order to raise their ethical awareness. Although the Chinese government seems committed to controlling corruption and has recalibrated its anti-corruption strategies to encourage local integrity initiatives, conflict-of-interest regulation in mainland China is still a centrally guided process and is 'managed' through the Party's cadre system. It is contingent upon the definition of conflict of interest by the centre and what measures it deems appropriate, which may or may not reflect the evolving scope and complexity of the issues at stake.

Despite these efforts to improve integrity, there is still a tendency, as reactions to the various scandals in both mainland China and Hong Kong show, to assume that strengthening the rules will solve any ethical problems. Rules are clearly important, but the difficulty with conflicts of interest is that rules cannot cover every situation. A supporting ambience of shared values is critical to avoid the assumption that what is not prohibited is permitted. Without such an ambience, the danger is that, although rules might be observed, loopholes or the uniqueness of the case might still result in unethical behaviour.

Conclusion

We have examined patterns of conflicts of interest with the aim of identifying common themes and approaches to controlling them. In the Hong Kong case, controls on conflicts of interest in the civil service appear to have worked successfully, using a combination of a rule-based and a value-based approach. There are also examples, however, from the political system of political appointees and Legislative Councillors who are governed by much looser sets of rules and who do not display a consistent value orientation towards integrity. On the mainland, there is even less sensitivity to conflicts of interest, although many attempts have been made to improve the rules and to introduce value-based elements.

Approaches to controlling conflicts of interest in both places have been focused on producing compliance with the rules and of introducing new rules if necessary. In some instances, such as the rules governing the ethical standards of Hong Kong Legislative Councillors, introducing credible and effective rules would be a desirable first step. A supplemental focus on values nonetheless seems necessary for integrity management systems to work well over time. In post-public employment, for example, in both mainland China and Hong Kong, the rules were observed but perceived unethical behaviour still occurred. The benefit of a focus on values is that they provide a reference point, shared by colleagues, which might even make the specific rules redundant. In contrast, if rules become the first point of reference, the assumption is often that they are all that matter. Yet, if value-based integrity management is to be successful, it cannot remain simply at the level of extolling virtues and condemning vices. Governments need to put concrete programmes in place, say what they mean by those values, and provide training and numerous examples of appropriate and inappropriate behaviour.

The classification of various types of conflicts of interest also suggests ways in which values and rules might work together to improve controls. In relationships between civil servants and society, the value that matters is that the rigid distinction between public and private interests should be maintained. The Hong Kong civil service has been largely successful in conveying that value to its employees, even if violations do occasionally occur. Respondents to the Hong Kong administrative ethics survey, for example, in contrast to those on the mainland, revealed that they do not normally discuss work issues in the family. Distance and separation between public and social activity has been achieved, with corresponding benefits to the integrity of the organization.

In intra-organizational relationships, position-related consumption in both places has had detrimental effects on the integrity of political institutions. If the rules are not in place, infringements could well occur, but the broader value question is the sort of accountability that can be expected of high-level officials. A first step may be to tighten the rules while also considering how the value of accountability can be better realized through the political system. In mainland China, 'sweeteners' have been a frequent feature of government/private-sector interactions and there is little evidence to suggest that the weak current controls are effective. In Hong Kong, infringements are less common, especially in the civil service, where the need to avoid contact with private contractors outside the workplace is frequently stressed. Politicians tempted to accept 'sweeteners' may also be aware that a vigilant media enjoys nothing more than a prominent figure who has accepted what appears to be an illicit favour.

Finally, in ultra-organizational relationships, the important consideration is whether accepting post-public employment positions may bring the civil service or the executive into disrepute. While what amounts to disrepute is an organizational issue, it is also a matter that a public official should personally consider before making a decision. In an important sense, this also relates to the effectiveness of controls over the conflict of interest issue. An informed and sensitive public official who cannot claim ignorance of the values of his or her organization is less likely to make ethical mistakes than one who simply goes by the rule book.

Notes

★ The authors gratefully acknowledge the support of the Research Grant Council of Hong Kong and City University of Hong Kong (CityU11402814;7004097). The research was also supported by the National Social Science Fund of China (No. 13 and 20011). We would also like to thank Deng Lijun and Xiao Hanyu for providing research assistance.

1 Strictly speaking, our 'societal' category could fall within 'ultra-organizational' relationships. However, since this is a prevalent form of conflicts of interest, we have treated societal relationships separately.
2 In Hong Kong, the survey instrument was originally used in 1994 by Lui and Cooper (1997) and replicated in 2011–2012 (Brewer et al. 2013). The composition of the sample and the nature of the questionnaire are described in greater detail in Scott and Gong (2014).
3 See http://news.xinhuanet.com/yuqing/2013-04/24/c_124624145.htm (accessed 14 February 2013).
4 See http://news.163.com/12/0303/09/7RLNL6TR00014AEE.html (accessed 15 February 2014).

References

Audit Commission (2012) *Chief Executive's Office: Hotel Accommodation for the Chief Executive's Duty Visits outside Hong Kong*, available at: www.aud.hk.

Brewer, B., Leung, J.Y.H. and Scott, I. (2013) 'Values in perspective: Administrative ethics and the Hong Kong public servant re-visited', *Administration & Society*, DOI: 10.117/009539971349742.

Brewer, B., Leung, J.Y.H. and Scott, I. (forthcoming) 'Value-based integrity management and bureaucratic organizations: Changing the mix', *International Public Administration Journal*.

Chief Executive's Office (2012) *Code for Officials under the Political Appointment System*, available at: www.cmab.gov.hk/en/issues/PAO/Code 1.7.2012.pdf.

Chong, T. (2013) 'Lawmakers face criticism after Cathay junket to France', *South China Morning Post*, 22 August.

Chong, T. (2014) 'Overspending "was not a sin", Timothy Tong Hing-ming tells select committee', *South China Morning Post*, 26 January.

Civil Service Bureau (2009) *Civil Service Code*, available at: www.csb.gov.hk.

Committee on Members' Interests (2009) *Advisory Guidelines on Matters of Ethics in Relation to the Conduct of Members of the Legislative Council of the Hong Kong Special Administrative Region in Their Capacity as Such*, available at: www.legco.gov.hk.

Corruption Prevention Department (n.d.) *Best Practice Checklist: Procurement*, Hong Kong: ICAC.

Denhardt, K. and Gilman, S. (2005) 'In search of virtue: Why ethics policies spawn unintended consequences', in H.G. Frederickson and R.K. Ghere (eds), *Ethics in Public Management* (pp. 259–73), New York: M.E. Sharpe.

Gong, T. and Ren, J. (2013) 'Hard rules and soft constraints: Regulating conflicts of interest in China', *Journal of Contemporary China*, 22(79): 1–17.

Gong, T. and Zhou, N. (2014) 'Corruption and marketization: Formal and informal rules in Chinese public procurement', *Regulation and Governance*, doi: 10.1111/rego.12054f.

Huberts, L.W.J.C., Maesschack, J. and Jurkiewicz, C.L. (eds) (2008) *Ethics and Integrity of Governance: Perspectives across Frontiers*, Cheltenham & Northampton, MA: Edward Elgar.

Independent Commission Against Corruption (n.d.) *Reference Package on Conflict of Interest for Managers in the Civil Service*, Hong Kong: ICAC.

Independent Commission Against Corruption (n.d.) *Ethics in Practice: A Practical Guide for Managers of Public Bodies*, Hong Kong: ICAC.

Independent Review Committee (2012) *Report of the Independent Review Committee into the Prevention and Handling of Potential Conflicts of Interest*, available at: www.irc.gov.hk/eng/report/report.html.

Independent Review Committee (2013) *Report of the Independent Review Committee on ICAC's Regulatory Systems and Procedures for Handling Official Entertainment, Gifts and Duty Visits*, available at: www.gov.hk/en/theme/irc-icac/pdf/irc-icac-report.pdf.

Ko, K. and Weng, C. (2012) 'Structural changes in Chinese corruption', *The China Quarterly*, 211: 718–40.

Legislative Council (2006) *Guidelines on Registration of Interests*, available at: www.legco.gov.hk.

Legislative Council (2010) *Report of the Select Committee to Inquire into Matters Relating to the Post-Service Work of Mr Leung Chin-man*, available at: www.legco.gov.hk.

Legislative Council (2013) *Register of Members' Interests*, available at: www.legco.gov.hk.

Legislative Council, Panel on Constitutional Affairs (2003) *Minutes of a Meeting Held on the 17th March*, available at: www.legco.gov.hk.

Leung, J.Y.H. and Scott, I. (2012) *Misconduct in Public Office: An Analysis of Hong Kong Cases*, Hong Kong: Department of Public and Social Administration, City University of Hong Kong.

Li, Q.F. (2012) *Zhongguo fanfuchanglian jianshebaogao (Report on Combatting Corruption and Upholding Integrity in China)*, No. 2, Beijing: Social Sciences Academic Press.

Lui, T.T. and Cooper, T.L. (1997) 'Values in flux: Administrative ethics and the Hong Kong public servant', *Administration & Society*, 29(3): 301–24.

McWalters, I. (2010) *Bribery and Corruption Law in Hong Kong* (2nd edn), Hong Kong: LexisNexis.

OECD (2000) *Trust in Government: Ethics Measures in OECD Countries*, Paris: OECD.

OECD (2005) *OECD Guidelines for Managing Conflict of Interest in the Public Sector*, Paris: OECD.

Public Accounts Committee (2013) P.A.C. Report 60A, available at: www.legco.gov.hk/yr12-13/english/pac/reports/pac_rpt_60a.htm.

Review Committee (2009) *Report on Review of Post-Service Work for Directorate Civil Servants*, Hong Kong: Government Logistics Department.

Rosenbloom, D. and Gong, T. (2013) 'Preventing corruption in the age of collaborative governance', *Public Performance & Management Review*, 36(4): 543–60.

Scott, I. and Gong, T. (2014) 'Administrative values in the mainland Chinese and Hong Kong public services: A comparative analysis', *Asian Pacific Journal of Public Administration*, 36: 22–33.

Stark, A. (2000) *Conflict of Interest in American Public Life*, Cambridge, MA: Harvard University Press.

Wedeman, A. (2004) 'The intensification of corruption in China', *The China Quarterly*, 180: 895–921.

Yang, D. (2004) *Remaking the Chinese Leviathan: Market Transition and the Politics of Governance in China*, Stanford, CA: Stanford University Press.

PART VI

Expanding ethical policy domains

16

ETHICAL DECISIONS AND THE GREAT MORAL CHALLENGE OF OUR TIME

Ken Coghill

Introduction

Climate change was described as 'the great moral challenge of our generation' by the then future Prime Minister of Australia, Kevin Rudd, in March 2007. The seriousness of that challenge continues to grow, and with it comes ever-greater significance in the ethical bases of decisions made by public officials from the most to the least powerful.

Decisions by heads of government, members of legislatures and officials appointed to exercise discretionary powers all contribute to whether mankind's impact places our survival at increasing risk. Even the smallest, most incremental impact, adverse or beneficial, has ethics at its base.

However, these damaging decisions arise from a rejection of responsibility for protecting and preserving the very environment on which we are dependent. In some cultures, it is unethical to damage their environment. The dominant culture rejects that obstacle to 'progress'.

Addressing the greatest moral challenge of our time requires re-conceptualizing 'progress' as a vision based on ethical decision-making rather than jeopardizing mankind's survival.

As the title suggests, this chapter will deal with the emerging ethical issues confronting public officials developing and implementing policies in response to climate change. It will first deal with conventional approaches with their limitations and then discuss the potential to learn from ancient traditions.

When this issue burst to public attention in 1972, there seemed to be all the time needed and more to address the predicament posed by the limits to growth as identified by Meadows and published for a receptive worldwide readership that year (Meadows 1972). For most readers, it was their first exposure to the scientific evidence of threats ranging from the depletion of non-renewable oil and other minerals used by mankind to adverse, human-induced impacts on the climate. As Rolston observed soon after, the topography of the 'ecological frontier' and its associated ethics was 'largely uncharted; to cross it will require the daring, and caution, of a community of scientists and ethicists who can together map both the ecosystem and the ethical grammar appropriate for it' (Rolston 1975, p. 109).

In the years that followed, the focus remained overwhelmingly on the science and technical responses to the mounting evidence. Even the Catholic Church was muted in relation to ethical questions in the Holy See's *Address on Development and Ecology* at the United Nations (Holy See 2006).

Forty years after Meadow's revelations, we find that some of the most dire impacts predicted by the evidence are already proving to have been underestimates. True, some have not materialized. For example, aggregate oil reserves are not yet exhausted, and so there is not yet a crisis in the availability of transport fuels. However, new oil discoveries have only partly offset the loss of supply from depleted reserves. The decline in aggregate known reserves and continuing high demand have driven prices up, notwithstanding some fall-back since mid 2014. Energy efficiency policy measures were introduced in the 1970s, but as a response to the large 'oil shock' price increases initiated by oil exporting nations in 1973 and the second crisis due to Iran's suspension of oil exports in 1979.

Concern about the potential for climate change moved slowly. In 1988, the Intergovernmental Panel on Climate Change (IPCC) was established by the United Nations Environment Programme (UNEP) and the World Meteorological Organization (WMO) to provide the world with a clear scientific view on the current state of knowledge in climate change and its potential environmental and socio-economic impacts. The UN General Assembly endorsed the action by WMO and UNEP in jointly establishing the IPCC. It has become the leading international body for the assessment of climate change.

The next significant step was the United Nations Conference on Environment and Development (UNCED), attended by many heads of government in 1992 – the Rio Summit. A major outcome was the United Nations Framework Convention on Climate Change (UNFCCC). Most countries have become signatories ('parties') and there have been annual Conferences of the Parties (COP) since 1995.

In 1997, a legally binding agreement, the Kyoto Protocol treaty, was negotiated to come into force in 2005. Industrialized countries undertook to reduce their collective emissions of greenhouse gases by 5.2 per cent compared to the year 1990. Individual countries' targets varied, some being permitted increases. The treaty was scheduled to expire in 2012, with the expectation that a more comprehensive treaty would be negotiated to succeed it. The new treaty was planned to be agreed at COP15 in December 2009, in Denmark. In the lead-up to COP15, there was widespread hope that that objective would be met. The technical arguments for effective action were given a moral perspective by Australia's Kevin Rudd, then Leader of the Opposition and soon to become Prime Minister, who made the statement that we opened the chapter with. Rudd was speaking in relation to moral values that he would seek to apply if elected to government, and indeed which he stated should be 'beyond politics' in Australia (i.e. should be held in common by the nation's major political parties) (Rudd 2007). He was referring to public-sector ethics – the theme of this volume.

In more recent times, many other leaders have emphasized overwhelming significance of threats posed by climate change and anthropogenic factors driving it. At the United Nations Climate Summit 2014, the Chairman, UN General Secretary Ban Ki-moon, stated in his opening address that as a consequence of climate change, 'the dreams of people throughout the world hang in the balance. Climate change threatens hard-won peace, prosperity, and opportunity for billions of people. Today we must set the world on a new course' (Ban Ki-moon 2014a).

He went on to claim that climate change is the defining issue of our age. The world's most powerful political leader, US President Obama, in an address to the Climate Summit, which dwelt on a responsibility to act, said:

> For all the immediate challenges that we gather to address this week – terrorism, instability, inequality, disease – there's one issue that will define the contours of this century more dramatically than any other, and that is the urgent and growing threat of a changing climate.
>
> (Obama 2014)

UK Prime Minister Cameron echoed President Obama's acceptance of responsibility to act (Cameron 2014). The Holy See (i.e. Catholic Church) emphasized the moral dimension, stating:

> the Holy See has often stressed that there is a moral imperative to act, for we all bear the responsibility to protect and to value creation for the good of this and future generations. Pope Francis, from the beginning of his Pontificate, has underlined the importance of 'protecting our environment, which all too often, instead of using for the good, we exploit greedily, to one another's detriment'.
>
> (Parolin 2014)

The widespread embrace of Ban Ki-moon's concerns was reflected in his summary of the Summit's outcomes, that a comprehensive global vision on climate change emerged from the statements of leaders at the Summit: 'World leaders agreed that climate change is a defining issue of our time and that bold action is needed today to reduce emissions and build resilience and that they would lead this effort' (Ban Ki-moon 2014b).

Ban Ki-moon's summary confirmed that there is acceptance by the over-whelming majority of political leaders of the world's public sectors that climate change is a great challenge – one that should not be ignored, irrespective of other major challenges that compete for attention and resources.

The speeches by political leaders and the summary also confirmed that the issue at stake is not the level of awareness among political leaders (with few exceptions). Likewise, Gallup's worldwide survey of public opinion found that 61 per cent of adults were aware of climate change in 2007–2008; it was regarded as a very or somewhat serious threat by 41 per cent overall, 67 per cent in the Americas and 50 per cent in Europe (Pugliese and Ray 2009).

At stake is the basis and nature of actions by public-sector decision-makers in the face of widespread awareness of the problem. It is the moral dimension of climate change policy and its implications for ethical decision-making that is examined in this chapter, including the place of public-sector ethics within the broader canvas of sociopolitical governance at all levels – from the local to the global.

Public-sector ethics and integrity

Public-sector ethics are among the key normative factors affecting the efficiency and effectiveness of societies from the most local of polities to those at the global level. Ethical behaviour facilitates trust between social actors, whether that be the local resident and a public official who exercises authority affecting his or her life (e.g. water supply) or a nation state and the United Nations Security Council (e.g. when territorial integrity is threatened). There is reduced risk that those in authority will use their power to bias their choices of action according to inducements, currying favour or personal relationships. Higher levels of trust reduce the time, effort and emotional stress required to secure decisions and actions that are fair, reasonable and consistent with the law. Borrowing a term from economics, this can be described as reducing the transaction costs of an activity involving the public sector.

Consistent with higher levels of trust is a reliance on well-established evidence. Trust is undermined where one or more actors participating in an activity withholds or misrepresents pertinent facts or analysis required to establish the evidence base for a policy decision, implementation or evaluation. A sound evidence base provides a set of relevant facts that the social actors can debate, respecting and having regard to the values that each holds, and reach compromise or full agreement.

At the same time, public-sector ethics forms a central feature of National Integrity Systems. The concept of a National Integrity System (NIS) has been recognized as a valuable way of developing and evaluating measures to reduce risks of corruption and acting to curb it. According to Transparency International, the NIS

> assessment approach provides a framework which anti-corruption organisations can use to analyse both the extent and causes of corruption in a given country as well as the effectiveness of national anti-corruption efforts. This analysis is undertaken via a consultative approach, involving the key anti-corruption agents in government, civil society, the business community and other relevant sectors with a view to building momentum, political will and civic pressure for relevant reform initiatives.
>
> The assessment makes use of the concept of the National Integrity System (NIS), which has been developed and promoted by TI as part of its holistic approach to countering corruption. The NIS consists of the principle

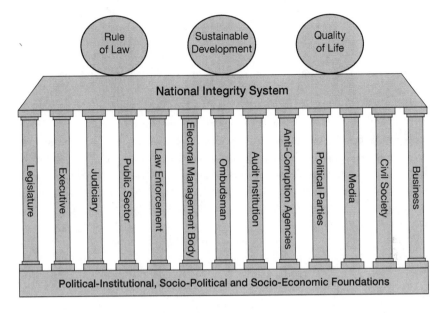

FIGURE 16.1 National Integrity System

institutions and actors that contribute to integrity, transparency and accountability in a society.

A well-functioning NIS provides effective safeguards against corruption as part of the larger struggle against abuse of power, malfeasance, and misappropriation in all its forms. However, when these institutions are characterised by a lack of appropriate regulations and by unaccountable behaviour, corruption is likely to thrive with negative ripple effects for the societal goals of equitable growth, sustainable development and social cohesion. Strengthening the NIS promotes better governance across all aspects of society, and, ultimately, contributes to a more just society overall, as depicted in the NIS Temple.

(Transparency International 2009)

Thus, although the NIS approach is a much broader concept than public-sector ethics, the latter forms an integral part of an NIS. However, the NIS has a strong but limiting orientation to the public sector. These ethical considerations are not internal to the public sector, it being one of the three social sectors involved in the integrated governance of contemporary societies.

Integrated governance

The three sectors are not distinct from one another; the functions of actors in each sector overlap to varying extents, so that a state actor may be involved in the delivery of certain services in the market (e.g. child care in some societies), or a civil society organization may regulate standards applying to market actors supplying professional services (e.g. accounting standards). The interrelationships between the social sectors in the governance of communities are increasingly widely recognized. Governance functions as a complex evolving system (Mitleton-Kelly 2003), represented in Figure 16.2.

The sectors vary between polities and over time in the relative size and strength sector. Thus, the UK state sector has far fewer nationalized industries now than in the 1950s, but the British National Health Service has a much greater role than any US parallel. The US government nationalized huge businesses in its economy after the 2008 crisis, but has reduced its holdings as quickly as possible.

In the schematic representation in Figure 16.2, each arrow indicates the multi-stranded relationships between sectors or between a sector and the general community. For example, the state sector provides legal infrastructure (regulation) to the market sector and services to market actors (downward arrow), and the market actors contribute tax revenues, policy requests and contractual services to the state sector (upward arrow). High standards of public-sector ethics enable those relationships to operate with low transaction costs and consistent with the intentions, policies and priorities of the Executive Government as authorized by the Legislature and upheld by the Courts.

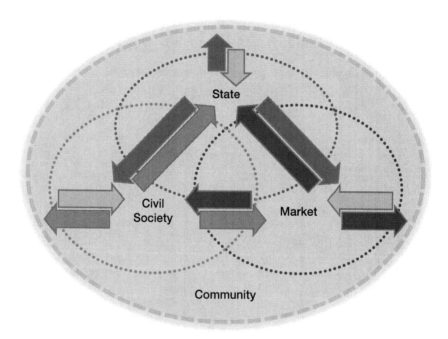

FIGURE 16.2 Sociopolitical governance – the social sectors embedded in the community

Public office as public trust

In this volume concerning public-sector ethics, we focus on 'public officials', but just who do we mean? In this context, the term 'public officer' is regarded as synonymous with public official. R.S. French, Chief Justice of the High Court of Australia, relying on the authority of the Oxford Dictionary, finds that a public officer occupies 'a position of trust, authority, or service under constituted authority' (2011, p. 11). French includes members of parliament and hence ministers among public officers. Accordingly, the public sector includes all persons elected or appointed to serve the polity in some capacity.

The responsibilities of the public officer flow from the public trust concept. Again, French provides authority on the nature and consequences of the concept. The concept of a public office as a public trust arises, French argues, from ancient principles of equity in which the duties of trustees are defined. According to these principles, if one holds property as its legal owner, but does so for the benefit of another person, one is a trustee for that person. As such a trustee, one has fiduciary obligations to that person who is the beneficiary (French 2011). The implications of this are spelled out by Worthington, who states:

> (e)quity insists that beneficiaries are entitled to the single-minded loyalty of their trustees, or, more generally, that principals are entitled to the single-minded loyalty of their fiduciaries. Put starkly, the fiduciary duty of loyalty requires fiduciaries to put their principals' interests ahead of their own; it requires fiduciaries to act altruistically . . . The duty demands a general denial of self-interest: the fiduciary role proscribes certain perfectly legitimate activities unless the principal consents to the fiduciary's involvement. The fiduciary's personal autonomy is correspondingly constrained.
>
> (Worthington 2003, p. 121, cited in French 2011, p. 8)

While these principles are commonly applied to non-public actors, 'there are clear and obvious parallels (with) the requirements of proper decision-making by, and the standards of conduct imposed on, persons in the public sector' (Finn 2012, p. 31). Thus, applying this to the public sector, the public officer must have a single-minded commitment to serving the public interest and must put that ahead of other interests at all times, not only ahead of his or her personal interests, but those of any other entity whose interests may compete or conflict with the public interest. In exercising whatever public power is associated with the responsibilities of a public office, the public officer must act not only within the formal provisions of the law, but is expected to act ethically (French 2011).

Notwithstanding that 'the most fundamental of fiduciary relations in our society is that which exists between the community (the people) and the State and its agencies that serve the community' (Finn 2012, p. 31), the extent to which those principles have been accepted into the operation of the law varies between jurisdictions. Some common law countries, especially the US, have given it real effect, while others, such as Australia, have thus far largely resisted doing so. Finn (2012) attributes the US experience to popular sovereignty, which was established by the American Revolution. However, in the United Kingdom, and by extension its sometime colonies, the idea began to develop from the seventeenth century. In Australia, it finds expression in reports of inquiries in corrupt practices by public officials and legislation addressing the investigation and prosecution of corrupt conduct. For example, 'corrupt conduct' includes 'conduct of a public official that constitutes or involves a breach of public trust' (Independent Commission Against Corruption Act 1988 (NSW), cited in Sampford 2012, p. 33).

Smith has questioned whether the fiduciary obligations or public officials are a 'political metaphor', as argued by French (Smith 2014). In doing so, he draws attention to a recent English decision (*Magill v Porter* (2002)), which confirms the responsibilities of public officials:

> (s)tatutory power conferred for public purposes is conferred as it were upon trust not absolutely – that is to say, it can validly be used only in the right and proper way which Parliament when conferring it is presumed to have intended . . . It follows from the proposition, that public powers are conferred as if upon trust, that those who exercise powers in a manner inconsistent with the public purpose for which the powers conferred betray that trust and so misconduct themselves.
>
> (quoted in Macknay 2012, p. 12)

However, for the purposes of this volume, it is sufficient that a public trust is seen as imposing 'a moral or political obligation' (Finn 2012, p. 34) on public officials in the exercise of public power such as a public trust. Except to note that Australian Chief Justice French has found that 'echoes of the concept of fiduciary obligation are to be found in the standards which the law imposes upon the exercise of official power by admin decision-makers' (French 2011, p. 34), it is not necessary here to examine the interpretation and application of the law affecting public trust and fiduciary duties.

The idea that public trust is applicable to the atmosphere, and hence climate change, derives from ancient Justinian code doctrine of res communes (Feaver 2012) and later common law. These 'recognised that there were certain things that were ownerless or in which the public collectively had rights' (Finn 2012, p. 36).

The exercise of public power extends throughout the chain of decision-making, management and administration. At the decision-making level, it must first include recognition of the values leading to a matter being selected as relevant to the public interest. In the case of climate change, there is overwhelming agreement that its potential impact on virtually every national community dictates that policy action is in the public interest. This agreement is reflected in the United Nations Framework Convention on Climate Change (UNFCCC), through which almost every nation state has committed itself to act to curb climate change, including Article 3, Principle 3:

The Parties should take precautionary measures to anticipate, prevent or minimize the causes of climate change and mitigate its adverse effects. Where there are threats of serious or irreversible damage, lack of full scientific certainty should not be used as a reason for postponing such measures, taking into account that policies and measures to deal with climate change should be cost-effective so as to ensure global benefits at the lowest possible cost. To achieve this, such policies and measures should take into account different socio-economic contexts, be comprehensive, cover all relevant sources, sinks and reservoirs of greenhouse gases and adaptation, and comprise all economic sectors. Efforts to address climate change may be carried out cooperatively by interested Parties.

(United Nations Framework Convention of
Climate Change 2012)

National governments having committed themselves to these principles of action, it follows logically that their public officials should be aiming to implement those principles. Climate change having been accepted as requiring policy action, the values that will be applied to it should be identified. This in itself raises public-sector ethics as an issue. Climate change is neither affecting all national communities in the same way or to the same extent, nor all sections of each community uniformly, as recognized in the above principle. Importantly, it recognizes the need to act expeditiously, even in the absence of 'full scientific certainty' (United Nations Framework Convention of Climate Change 2012). This necessarily involves relying on the best available information; to ignore that information or to reject it is to repudiate the fiduciary obligation to subordinate the public officials' own interests, in this case a claim to superior reasoning, below the collective wisdom of those accepted by the polity as most expert in climate science and related disciplines. The claim to superior reasoning is commonly expressed as claims that short-term economic interests should prevail. As such, it misses the point made by Sampford that mankind, and thus public officials, must pursue long-term interests if there is to be a long-term future for human civilization (Sampford 2012). In any event, the US experience indicates 'that there does not have to be a conflict between a sound environment and strong economic growth' (Obama 2014).

It was out of concern for the long term that Wood developed the concept of Atmospheric Trust Litigation (ATL) and worked with Our Children's Trust in all US states in seeking to force recognition of the responsibility of public officials to act to protect the public trust in respect of the ownerless atmosphere (Our Children's Trust 2014; Wood 2012). The nature and actions sought by these writs varied from state to state depending on state constitutional and other considerations. At the time of writing, these individual writs have had varied success. Among the more successful to date is the case in Oregon, in which the plaintiffs are seeking a declaration that the State of Oregon and its governor 'have violated their duties to uphold the public trust and protect the State's atmosphere as well as the water, land, fishery, and wildlife resources from the impacts of climate change'. The Court upheld their appeal against dismissal of their litigation (Court of Appeals of the State of Oregon 2014). In some other US states, the plaintiffs are seeking the establishment by the respective State Administration of a science-based Climate Recovery Plan (Our Children's Trust 2014). The aim in each case is to have the relevant public officials recognize their fiduciary duties and protect the public trust in the instance of the atmosphere.

Responsibilities to global community

Another approach that complements ATL is advocated by Fox-Decent (2012). He argues for a human right to a healthy environment, in particular a healthy atmosphere, making the link between excess carbon dioxide in the atmosphere and health impacts ranging from the immediate effects of the higher incidence of extreme weather events (e.g. heat waves) to threats to food supplies. Here, 'human rights are conceived as norms arising from a fiduciary relationship that exists between states (or state-like actors) and the citizens and non-citizens subject to their power'. Importantly, he notes that 'fiduciary theory explains why every state owes a cosmopolitan duty to extra-territorial non-citizens' (Fox-Decent 2012, pp. 253–4). The latter point is recognition that the atmosphere is boundary-less and that, irrespective of its source, carbon dioxide emissions rapidly spread throughout the earth's thin layer of air. Accordingly, the public official's responsibilities relevant to climate change are not limited to any particular geographic territory, but extend to all publics throughout the world.

A more radical concept is expressed in a number of national statutes. It entrenches legal rights of the earth's natural environment in law, providing the opportunity for (human) litigation to seek protection for parts of the nation's natural environment from potential or actual harm (Morales Ayma 2011). Examples of these new types of constitutional law include *Ley de Derechos de la Madre Tierra* (Framework Law on Mother Earth and Integral Development for Living Well), introduced first in Ecuador and later in Bolivia (Bolivia 2011; Celsias 2011).

A slightly different approach is taken by Germany, which adopted an amendment to its Basic Law (constitution), to provide that:

> Mindful also of its responsibility toward future generations, the state shall protect the natural bases of life by legislation and, in accordance with law and justice, by executive and judicial action, all within the framework of the constitutional order.
>
> (Federal Republic of Germany 1994)

The Federal Agency for Nature Conservation (Federal Agency for Nature Conservation Federal Republic of Germany 2014) states that it is their ethical duty to conserve and safeguard biodiversity, for reasons of social and intergenerational equity. The leading role that Germany has taken to reduce carbon dioxide emissions may well reflect this provision.

Feaver has speculated that litigation aided by the equitable rule that imposes a duty upon all nation states to preserve 'common property of mankind' may establish a breach of international law. He draws attention to clarification of the legal status of the atmosphere as falling within the scope of 'common heritage property' by UN General Assembly Resolution 43/53 in 1988 (Feaver 2012).

These views are consistent with those of one of the leading legal authorities of our time, Weeramantry, of the International Court of Justice. In 1997, he argued:

> The protection of the environment is likewise a vital part of contemporary human rights doctrine, for it is a sine qua non for numerous human rights such as the right to health and the right to life itself. It is scarcely necessary to elaborate on this, as damage to the environment can impair and undermine all the human rights spoken of in the Universal Declaration and other human rights instruments.
>
> (Weeramantry 1997)

It may also be argued that international law protecting human rights, identified by Weeramantry, while essentially anthropocentric, nonetheless confirms a responsibility to act to protect the environment with similar effect to the Law of Mother Earth. While Weeramantry's views have yet to attract majority support among justices, they point to a possible direction in which courts may move. The potential identified by Feaver for successful international litigation adds to the ethical responsibility of public officials to exercise their fiduciary obligations and protect this global public trust, thereby reducing both compensatory and climatic risks to their polity.

However, the values articulated to support the most favoured policy responses (e.g. emissions trading schemes – ETS) fail to reflect the depth of understanding identified by Sampford (2012) as being required. Sampford bases his argument for a different policy response on a deeper argument, that the very nature of what constitutes the 'good life' should be reviewed as it relies on an unsustainable level of exploitation and consumption of finite resources, including those that are ownerless or in which the public collectively has rights.

Sampford questions beliefs and values that are deeply engrained in the thinking of populations and political decision-makers in wealthy industrialized societies. These assume a materialist view of progress, in which change in the form of new material goods, new fashions and new services is not only desirable, but inevitable. That does not have to be so; indeed, these values are not universal.

Perspectives from theology

Major religions have ethical traditions that long pre-date the contemporary 'progressive' era. It is useful to consider them and their potential relevance to the great moral challenge of climate change.

Christian traditions have featured fiercely contested views, but in recent years have increasingly accepted that the Earth's resources are not simply God's gift to be uncritically exploited and despoiled. In 2006, the Holy See representative at the United Nations said:

> that an 'ecological conversion' is needed for sustainable development to take place . . . Even in the context of its fast transition and mutation, our economy continues to rest basically upon its relation to nature. Its indispensable substratum is soil, water and climate; and it is becoming rapidly ever clearer that if these, the world's life-support systems, are spoiled or destroyed irreparably, there will be no viable economy for any of us. Therefore, rather than being external or marginal to the economy, environmental concerns have to be understood by policy-makers as the basis upon which all economic – and even human – activity rests.
>
> (Holy See 2006)

This reflected arguments that have developed over many decades, canvassed by, for example, Nash (1989). These have led to rejection of the extreme view that 'nature as enemy, the alien force, to be conquered and broken to man's will' (Dwyer 1973, cited in Nash 1989, p. 120). Baer led a breakthrough in reconciling Christian tradition with environmental concerns when he argued that because 'the world belongs to God . . . no member of His world can "dictate the destiny" of any other member', and so mankind's rights are limited and subject to God's authority (Nash 1989, pp. 100–1). Furthermore, God was pleased with the world He had created, including the interrelationships between its many elements. For some, this led to the concept of mankind's stewardship of the natural world – a stewardship responsibility that was not utilitarian, but accepted nature as having intrinsic value (Nash 1989).

In the Islamic tradition, the Quran can be depicted 'as the tree of sustainability' just as 'a tree is visible through its roots, stems, branches, leaves, fruits and seeds', according to Marinova *et al.* (2008). They indicate that Sharia laws provide general guidance on the practise of sustainability of the natural environment, informed by Sufism's guidance on sustainability ethics (Marinova *et al.* 2008).

In the Buddhist tradition, the concept of 'eco-sangha' provides an 'earth-centred interpretation of the Four Noble Truths', in which the suffering of the entire planet and its beings is due to profound and complex causes 'arising from our deep interconnectedness'. Rev. Don Castro of Seattle Betsuin Buddhist Temple asserts that 'to be a Buddhist is automatically to be an ecologist and a conservationist' (Castro 2010).

While these teachings provide some guidance, it is not clear in what way they significantly inform or advance thinking on public-sector ethics in relation to addressing climate change.

The 'caring for country' ethic

Could it be that the beliefs and values on which to base governance for sustainability are here with us now, albeit hidden by the dominance of the view that progress equates to increasing consumption of non-renewable resources? It may be that insights into relevant beliefs and values are to be found embedded in places as diverse as the little-known legal concept of usufructuary rights and certain subsistence cultures.

A dictionary definition describes usufructuary rights as:

> the right of enjoying a thing, the property of which is vested in another, and to draw from the same all the profit, utility and advantage which it may produce, *provided it be without altering the substance of the thing.*
> (The Lectric Law Library 2014) (emphasis added)

These rights resonate with the concept of sustainability, which is at the heart of many approaches to curbing climate change. There are surprising parallels between the contemporary idea of sustainability, the little-used term usufructuary rights and seemingly diverse traditional belief and practices.

Ancient traditional conceptions of a responsibility to protect a healthy environment that are preserved in the value systems of many indigenous societies have parallels in contemporary and emerging approaches. According to some traditional value systems, the object of life in these communities is to preserve that natural environment upon which they depend for their survival. Thus, traditional Australian Aboriginal culture – probably the world's oldest continuous culture – is founded on 'caring for country' (Coghill and Samaratunge 2013). By this is meant maintaining the landscape with its plants and animals in their current state rather than 'improving', developing or otherwise changing the natural environment (Davis 2009).

A description of a fictional Aboriginal woman's place in the world illustrates the point:

> Nambiyin has always considered herself literally part of her environment; her existence has meaning, and she has personal and group identity, in reference to the land. She has no concept of owning the land, but she knows deep responsibilities towards it, payable even with death if the spirits think it necessary. The land feeds her and her children, but she does not so much consider it a 'resource' as part of her being ... In Nambiyin's world view, culture and environment are inseparable. Landscape forms are the reference point – and she believes the point of origin – for all cultural beliefs and behaviour. The landscape is also a cultural one – every landform, plant and animal is named and has cultural meaning. History, the stories of the Ancestors, ties culture and environment together.
>
> For such Aboriginal people, quality of life comes from appreciating one's country, and a lively religious and social life. Material possessions are not essential to enjoy life.
> (Ross 1992, pp. 149–50)

Many other ancient, indigenous cultures enjoy a similar relationship with the natural environment. These value systems challenge the very basis of the values that have brought climate change upon us (Coghill and Samaratunge 2013). The belief systems of many such indigenous communities living traditional lives are fundamentally based on notions of sustaining the ecosystem within which they live and of which they accept that they are an integral part.

Numerous examples of indigenous communities whose belief systems, values and practices are oriented to living sustainably were documented by Kemf (1993). Wade Davis has reported the way Aboriginal Australians explained it:

> In the (Australian) Aboriginal universe . . . There is no notion of linear progression, no goal of improvement, no idealisation of the possibility of change. To the contrary, the entire logos of the Dreaming is stasis, constancy, balance, and consistency. The entire purpose of humanity is not to improve anything. It is to engage in the ritual and ceremonial activities deemed to be essential for the maintenance of the world precisely as it was at the moment of creation.
>
> (Davis 2009)

In a telling example, McNeely recounts how conservation of forests in the Himalayas failed when traditional shinga nawas (forest guards) were replaced with centralized regulation and administration. As a result, the traditional system was reinstated (McNeely 1993, pp. 249–57).

In another example, the sustainability of Bali's irrigated agriculture has likewise been shown to be a product of ritual, in that case orchestrated through temples (Lansing 1987).

This view of the world is increasingly recognized by the 'developed' world. For example, the value of one traditional Australian Aboriginal practice has been confirmed by science as reducing carbon dioxide emissions. The active management of savannah landscape in Northern Australia by deliberately igniting early dry season fires reduces carbon dioxide emissions by lowering fuel loads and thus the intensity of dry season wild fires (often ignited by lightning strikes) and much larger carbon dioxide emissions later in the year. It is ritual that maintains the world. That practice was proposed by the Australian Government as part of its Carbon Farming Initiative Commentary on the exposure draft Regulations that dealt with the positive and negative lists of activities under the Carbon Farming Initiative August 2011.

In each of these cases, mankind's governance of the ecosystem relied on acceptance by members of the society that they had a responsibility to maintain that society's common interest in maintaining the health of the environment in which their community was embedded. Here, community and society are distinguished according to Nancy (i.e. the community is the population occupying a geographic area; the society of the organization of that community through informal and formal rules and cultural practices) (Nancy 1991).

In one sense, this regard for the natural environment is to accord rights to the environment in a manner somewhat analogous to the Law of Mother Earth. It is to say that mankind will do more than simply deny itself the right to modify, exploit or destroy non-human components of the overall environment. Rather, mankind's governance will incorporate beliefs, values and practices that conserve the features and qualities of that environment. This conservation of the environment will be established as a duty of the society and its members.

It is only a short step from that cultural basis for sustainability to its more formal incorporation in theology, legal principles and statutory provisions. Indeed, it is close to the judicial thinking articulated by Weeramantry (above) and the possibility of successful litigation foreshadowed by Feaver (above).

Elected officials

The above discussion applies to all public officials, including that peculiar category of public official – politicians (i.e. members of parliament – legislators, lawmakers – and local government mayors and councillors).

However, advances in public-sector ethics will, as ever, be subject to the extent and nature of leadership demonstrated by politicians. As discussed above, the record is very mixed. Germany is a leader among developed nation states, with a strong constitutional provision and a record of effective progress towards a low carbon economy. The Law of Mother Earth in each of Ecuador and Bolivia suggests an innovative approach with potential to orientate the nations towards sustainable futures. China has demonstrated the potential for a one-party state to remarkably rapidly reorientate its economic structures towards greater sustainability (Jotzo 2014).

However, politicians have generally found it difficult to accept and apply the primacy of a fiduciary obligation to the polity and to protecting the public trust. They find it difficult to subordinate partisan political interests to the public interest. This, though, reflects the incentives to which politicians are subject as a consequence of the structure of electoral systems and political cultures – both matters beyond the scope of this chapter, except in one respect: that is to note the potential for extending the representative democratic model.

Deliberative democracy and participative democracy models have shown considerable promise in facilitating the resolution of wicked problems (for discussion of forms of citizen participations, see Arnstein 1969; Roberts 2004). In a recent example, superior social outcomes in Brazilian cities that have applied Participatory Budgeting have been reported by Touchton and Wampler (2014). Public-sector ethics obliges politicians to have regard to the relative success of these models, as there appears to be considerable opportunity to achieve greater progress in addressing climate change by supporting and facilitating widespread deliberative democracy and participative democracy practices within local communities.

The example of participative democracy again emphasizes that to address climate change, values-based selection, collection and analysis of data to form the evidence base is required. A public official applying self-interest, or reflecting slightly broader vested interests, will preferentially seek and use data favouring those interests, whereas public officials loyal to the public interest will identify the wide range of data relevant to sustainability and the potential impacts of climate change, ensure that such data is collected and subject it to thorough analysis.

Public officials who deliberately reduce or abandon the collection of data relevant to the effects of climate change do so in direct contradiction of the public interest and their fiduciary obligations to their communities. One of the starkest recent examples was the 2014 closure of the Australian Climate Commission, which, during its three-and-a-half-year life, published reliable, informative reports on climate change science, health impacts, international action and renewable energy. Its wanton destruction was a latter-day expression of the burning of books of learning conducted by tyrants seeking to consolidate power, from Hitler back at least two millennia. Less stark but similarly contrary to the public interest is the reduction in the capacities of bodies to collect and process information as a result of the partial or total withdrawal of funding to both public institutions and non-governmental organizations.

Ethical processes; ethical policies

The repudiation, emasculation or destruction of sources of information and advice relates to processes of policy rather than the policies themselves. Although it is conceptually possible to adopt ethically acceptable policy notwithstanding inadequate public-sector resources, it is a dereliction of the public sector's responsibility to rely on belief or faith in one's beliefs rather than evidence. Ethical conduct of policy processes requires that public-sector leaders inform themselves fully within available information, including that to be gleaned from democratic participatory processes.

For the public-sector employee, the information, advice and recommendations made to political leaders, whether directly or indirectly via other officials, is subject to the same responsibilities to act ethically. Nor do non-public-sector consultants and advisers to the public sector escape an obligation to act ethically. Their contracts are funded by the state, which creates an obligation to act in the public interest rather than accommodating partisan or other vested interests. Indeed, it is for such a reason that supreme audit bodies (comptroller-general, auditor-general, etc.) are increasingly given 'follow the dollar' authority to audit the expenditure of public funds by contracted private organizations.

The actual policies themselves take ethical responsibility to a higher level as their implementation has real-world effects. In the case of policy affecting carbon emissions, these effects extend beyond political boundaries to the global atmosphere, and thus to people in every other polity. To fail to take effective action is to reject the moral nature of threats posed by climate change, in particular the fiduciary duty that public-sector leaders owe to act to protect the public trust.

The ethical treatment of policy processes described above has been observed to be vulnerable to subversion and compromise by a range of factors, including a simple desire to find favour with a decision-maker, an attempt to win political support, responding to extraordinary hospitality, favouring a donor of campaign funds, succumbing to the wishes of economically powerful interests, and outright bribery.

Evaluation of policy outcomes and review of policies are integral to good governance regimes, as with the UK Department of Energy & Climate Change, monitoring and evaluation assist in deciding if a policy is working, revising policy to make it more likely to meet the public sector's objectives, facilitating further development of policy and providing evidence for future policies, whether in the same or related areas (Department of Energy and Climate Change (UK) 2012).

The risks of unethical behaviour are at least as high as in the policymaking stage. At least in the latter, the outcomes and real-world effects are hypothetical. Once policy has been implemented, the evidence of its effects is starkly apparent. Thus, in an Australian example, an emissions trading scheme (ETS) was repealed and a Direct Action Plan (DAP) introduced in its stead in mid 2014. The potential effectiveness of the latter was not supported by any reputable authority and was widely predicted to fail to curb Australian emissions. However, those predictions could only be confirmed some time after implementation of the DAP. At that point, it would be especially unethical to deny the failure of policy and persist with it nonetheless.

That situation has been reached in a completely unrelated area of social policy – 'drugs' policy. It is abundantly clear that decades of attempts to prevent the recreational use of banned drugs have succeeded in doing little except criminalize the production, distribution and consumption. Since Portugal

> decriminalized the use and possession of all illicit drugs on 1 July 2001 . . . contrary to predictions, (it) did not lead to major increases in drug use. Indeed, evidence indicates reductions in problematic use, drug-related harms and criminal justice overcrowding.
>
> (Hughes and Stevens 2010, p. 999)

Yet, notwithstanding the massive social, law enforcement and other costs of failed drugs policies elsewhere, the evidence has not thus far been acted upon. Public-sector policymakers have given priority to other issues.

Policies that remain unaffected by the evidence base are evidence that the ethical implications of priority setting have been avoided, except insofar as the time for participation by stakeholders, law reform and changes to administrative arrangements should be acknowledged.

The anthropogenic factors largely responsible for climate change add moral dimensions to the consequences of policy outcomes. These anthropogenic factors are pliable to effective regulatory policies by mankind's social institutions – led by the public sector as the sector with the monopoly on the legitimate use of regulatory powers. That being the case, there is an ethical responsibility to use that power to monitor and evaluate the outcomes of the use of, or failure to use, powers with the potential to avert catastrophic climate change, and to improve policies accordingly.

Conclusion

The great moral challenge of climate change is becoming more serious and a greater challenge to mankind's governance as each new research finding is revealed. This gives ever-greater significance to the ethical bases of decisions made by public officials from the most to the least powerful. Those ethical bases must address the imperative of re-conceptualizing 'progress' as progress towards a sustainable low-carbon economy.

To do otherwise is to stumble along with local policies and actions that jeopardize mankind's survival by further damage to the atmosphere with worldwide effects. To stumble along is to repudiate the fiduciary duty that decision-makers owe to act to protect the public trust in serving the interests of the people on whose behalf they act.

Decisions by heads of government, members of legislatures and public officials appointed to exercise discretionary powers all contribute to whether mankind's impact places our survival at increasing risk. Even the smallest, most incremental impact, adverse or beneficial, has ethics at its base. A vote allowing increased carbon emissions is making a decision that puts short-term considerations ahead of later deaths. Approving construction of one wastefully designed house is making an ethical decision that will cause incremental damage. Decision-makers must take inspiration from cultures in which it is unethical to damage their environment.

However, the responsibility goes beyond simply making policies that would be effective if fully implemented. Responsibility extends to adopting and applying principles of political action that will facilitate the development of policies supported by the community in each instance. There are ample successful examples of deliberative democracy and integrated governance that can be adapted for this purpose. Again, ethical approaches require public officials to discharge their obligations by discovering, learning and applying innovative forms of governance.

The challenge is great; that dictates that public officials have an especially strong moral responsibility to tackle it ethically.

References

Arnstein, S.A. (1969) 'A ladder of citizen participation', *Journal of the American Institute of Planners*, 35(4): 216–24.

Ban Ki-moon (2014a) Opening remarks at United Nations 2014 Climate Summit.

Ban Ki-moon (2014b) 2014 Climate Change Summary – Chair's Summary.

Bolivia (2011) *Law of Mother Earth*, Bolivia, Law 071 of the Plurinational State, passed by Bolivia's Plurinational Legislative Assembly in December 2010.

Cameron, D. (2014) UN Climate Summit 2014: David Cameron's remarks. Part of: Reducing the impact of climate change in developing countries, Supporting international action on climate change and Climate change, 23 September, available at: www.gov.uk/government/speeches/un-climate-summit-2014-david-camerons-remarks.

Castro, D. (2010) Buddhism & Sustainability: A Conference on Buddhist Ecology, Seattle University, 7–8 May.

Celsias (2011) *The Rights of Mother Earth: Ecuador and Bolivia Enshrine Her Rights*, available at: www.celsias.com/article/rights-mother-earth-bolivia-ecuador-enshrine/.

Coghill, K. and Samaratunge, R. (2013) 'Integrated governance and adaptation to climate change', in H. Ha and T.N. Dhakal (eds), *The Palgrave Macmillan Governance Approaches to Mitigation of and Adaptation to Climate Change in Asia* (pp. 163–81), Basingstoke: Palgrave Macmillan.

Court of Appeals of the State of Oregon (2014) In the Court of Appeals of the State of Oregon, Olivia Chernaik, a minor and resident of Lane County, Oregon; Lisa Chernaik, Guardian Of Olivia Chernaik; Kelsey Cascadia Rose Juliana, a minor and resident of Lane County, Oregon; and Catia Juliana, guardian of Kelsey Juliana, Petitioners-Appellants, v. John Kitzhaber, in his Official Capacity as Governor of the State of Oregon; and State of Oregon, Respondents-Respondents.

Davis, W. (2009) *The Wayfinder: Why Ancient Wisdom Matters in the Modern World*, Toronto: House of Anansi Press.

Department of Energy and Climate Change (UK) (2012) 'Energy Security Strategy' Cm 8466, London: The Stationery Office.

Feaver, D. (2012) 'Fiduciary principles and international organizations', in K. Coghill, C. Sampford and T. Smith (eds), *Fiduciary Duty and the Atmospheric Trust* (pp. 166–86), Farnham: Ashgate.

Federal Agency for Nature Conservation Federal Republic of Germany (2014) BfN Facts, available at: www.bfn.de/index+M52087573ab0.html.

Federal Republic of Germany (1994) *Basic Law for the Federal Republic of Germany, Article 20a (Grundgesetz, GG)*, Federal Law Gazette, Germany.

Finn, P. (2012) 'Public trusts and fiduciary relations', in K. Coghill, C. Sampford and T. Smith (eds), *Fiduciary Duty and the Atmospheric Trust* (pp. 31–42), Farnham: Ashgate.

Fox-Decent, E. (2012) 'From fiduciary states to joint trusteeship of the atmosphere: The right to a healthy environment through a fiduciary prism', in K. Coghill, C. Sampford and T. Smith (eds), *Fiduciary Duty and the Atmospheric Trust* (pp. 395–418), Farnham: Ashgate.

French, R. (2011) 'Public office and public trust', *Seventh Annual St Thomas More Forum Lecture*, Canberra.

Holy See (2006) Holy See Address on Development and Ecology, 'Not Only an Important Ethical and Scientific Problem', delivered on 26 October to the Second Committee of the 61st session of the UN General Assembly on sustainable development and ecology, available at: www.zenit.org/en/articles/holy-see-address-on-development-and-ecology.

Hughes, C.E. and Stevens, A. (2010) 'What can we learn from the Portuguese decriminalization of illicit drugs?', *British Journal of Criminology*, 50(6): 999–1022.

Jotzo, F. (2014) 'China heads for price on carbon; energy market overhaul is next', *The Conversation*, 19 September, available at: http://theconversation.com/china-heads-for-price-on-carbon-energy-market-overhaul-is-next-31119.

Kemf, E. (ed.) (1993) *Indigenous Peoples and Protected Areas: The Law of Mother Earth*, London: Earthscan.

Lansing, J.S. (1987) 'Balinese "water temples" and the management of irrigation', *American Anthropologist*, 89(2): 326–41.

Macknay, R. (2012) 'Trust in public office', 18th *Annual Public Sector Fraud and Corruption Conference*, Melbourne.

Marinova, D., Hossain, A. and Hossain-Rhaman, P. (2008) 'Islam on sustainability', *International Journal of Environmental, Cultural, Economic and Social Sustainability*, 4(5): 123–30.

McNeely, J.A. (1993) 'People and protected areas: Partners in prosperity', in E. Kemf (ed.), *Indigenous Peoples and Protected Areas: The Law of Mother Earth* (pp. 249–57), London: Earthscan.

Meadows, D.H. (1972) *The Limits to Growth: A Report for the Club of Rome's Project on the Predicament of Mankind*, New York: Universe Books.

Mitleton-Kelly, E. (2003) 'Ten principles of complexity & enabling infrastructures', in E. Mitleton-Kelly (ed.), *Complex Systems & Evolutionary Perspectives of Organisations: The Application of Complexity Theory to Organisations* (pp. 23–50), London: Elsevier.

Morales Ayma, E. (ed.) (2011) *The Rights of Nature: The Case for a Universal Declaration of the Rights of Mother Earth*, Ottawa: The Council of Canadians, Fundación Pachamama Global Exchange.

Nancy, J-L. (1991) *The Inoperative Community* (translation of La communauté désoeurée), Minneapolis, MN: University of Minnesota Press.

Nash, R. (1989) *The Rights of Nature: A History of Environmental Ethics*, Madison, WI: University of Wisconsin Press.

Obama, B. (2014) Remarks by the President at U.N. Climate Change Summit, available at: www.whitehouse.gov/the-press-office/2014/09/23/remarks-president-un-climate-change-summit.

Our Children's Trust (2014) 'Atmospheric Trust Litigation' – US Court of Appeals.

Parolin, P.C. (2014) Statement by His Eminence Pietro Cardinal Parolin, Secretary of State (Holy See), UN Summit on Climate Change, 23 September, New York.

Pugliese, A. and Ray, J. (2009) Awareness of Climate Change and Threat Vary by Region', available at: www.gallup.com/poll/124652/Awareness-Climate-Change-Threat-Vary-Region.aspx.

Roberts, N. (2004) 'Public deliberation in an age of direct citizen participation', *American Review of Public Administration*, 34(4): 315–53.

Rolston, H., III (1975) 'Is there an ecological ethic?', *Ethics*, 85(2): 93–109.

Ross, H. (1992) 'Culture in ecosystems: Australian ways', Symposium on Culture and Environment organised by UNESCO and the Indonesian National Commission for UNESCO, Bogor, Indonesia.

Rudd, K. (2007) 'Climate change: The great moral challenge of our generation', *YouTube*: 1:02:00.

Sampford, C. (2012) 'Trust, governance and the good life', in K. Coghill, C. Sampford and T. Smith (eds), *Fiduciary Duty and the Atmospheric Trust* (pp. 43–67), Farnham: Ashgate.

Smith, T. (2014) 'Integrity in politics? Public office as a public trust? Is there hope?', *Accountability Round Table*, Hawthorn: University of the Third Age.

The Lectric Law Library (2014).

Touchton, M. and Wampler, B. (2014) 'Improving social well-being through new democratic institutions', *Comparative Political Studies*, 47(10): 1442–69.

Transparency International (2009) *National Integrity System*, Berlin: Transparency International.

United Nations Framework Convention of Climate Change (2012) *Article 3: Principles*.

Weeramantry, C.G. (1997) 'Separate opinion', Gabcikovo-Nagymaros Project, International Court of Justice, The Hague, 25 September 1997, available at: www.icjcij.org/icjwww/idocket/ihs/ihsjudgement/ihs_ijudgment_970925_weeraman.htm.

Wood, M.C. (2012) 'Atmospheric trust litigation across the world', in K. Coghill, C. Sampford and T. Smith (eds), *Fiduciary Duty and the Atmospheric Trust* (pp. 99–164), Farnham: Ashgate.

17

THE UNDISCOVERED COUNTRY

Establishing an ethical paradigm for space activities in the twenty-first century

Christopher J. Newman

Introduction

There was a time, in the middle decades of the twentieth century, when any discussion of space activities was inherently laden with images of Apollo rockets taking pioneering astronauts to the moon. Such imagery has, in the twenty-first century, given way to more prosaic questions regarding the regulatory framework of activities undertaken for the exploration of space. Part of the reason is that the world geopolitical situation has fundamentally changed (Blount 2011–2012). Where once two giant superpowers staged evermore grandiose projects to demonstrate the dominance of their competing systems, there are now a diverse range of stakeholders involved either directly or indirectly in space activities. There are state actors and private companies, civilian and military, scientific and commercial ventures all seeking to utilize the benefits that access to space can bring.

This chapter will argue that the motivations and underpinning philosophy behind space activities are unclear and the certainties that underpinned regulatory oversight mechanisms during the Cold War have been overwhelmed by instability and self-interest. Accordingly, there is now a need to focus on the ethical underpinnings for space exploration. This discussion will attempt to highlight the difficulties faced by those within public-sector organizations when trying to review the regulation of space activity, and it is recognized that there will need to be certain limitations on any such inquiry. The inquiry will not be concerned with proposals to change the substantive institutions or make bold suggestions for reforming space governance. Instead, the focus will be upon identifying the ethical problems facing the institutions and then analysing the current regulatory framework, illustrating how lasting reform of these mechanisms is not achievable without first establishing a normative ethical standpoint.

Space activity: an ethical vacuum?

Identifying a normative ethical position to cover all space activity is no small undertaking, and as such:

> In its simplest form, a code of space ethics would be a guide to what we should and should not do in space . . . In terms of space exploration and development space ethics would cover, for example, the impact of our actions in space on individuals, on property, on the Earth and on the space environment itself.
>
> (Williamson 2006, p. 182)

This inquiry is, therefore, predicated on two core concerns. The first is that, following on from the above assertion by Williamson, there is a lack of definition of the current values that underpin national space activity. Identification of the current values underpinning space activity, however, is problematic. Individual space agencies have overarching mission statements under which they operate; indeed, NASA, as a large public-sector employer, has a code of ethics.[1] These both tend to be focused on the corporate environment, regulating the behaviour of their employees or on the benefit that the agency concerned will be able to bring to a nation or region by means of space activity. Such organizational goals can be found in NASA's latest strategic plan. This plan espouses the core values of Safety, Integrity, Teamwork and Excellence, and a stated mission to: 'Drive advances in science, technology, aeronautics, and space exploration to enhance knowledge, education, innovation, economic vitality, and stewardship of Earth' (NASA 2014). Such statements provide no real indication of an underpinning set of values, much less indicating adherence to pre-established international norms. The treaty establishing the European Space Agency (ESA) is a little more explicit:

> ESA's purpose shall be to provide for, and to promote, for exclusively peaceful purposes, cooperation among European States in space research and technology and their space applications, with a view to their being used for scientific purposes and for operational space applications systems.
>
> (Art II, Purpose, Convention of Establishment of a European Space Agency, SP-1271(E) 2003)

The European Space Agency is, however, a radically different organization to NASA, serving instead to coordinate the activities of the various member states. So despite trying to provide for and promote space activity for exclusively peaceful purposes, their role in ensuring this is limited to the projects that operate under the ESA umbrella. ROSCOSMOS, the Russian Space Agency, according to Messier

(2013), has recently undergone significant reorganization and will act as a federal executive body and contracting authority for space programmes, with no mention apparent of the values or ethics underpinning their space activity. Ethical policy within the individual space agencies therefore would appear to be focused around national or regional interest rather than normative values.

The area of space ethics is not a new or novel area of contemplation, and there is a considerable body of literature dedicated to trying to identify normative concepts that can inform and guide those responsible for space policy. Pompidou (2000) tried to explore some of the issues in a report written for the UNESCO World Commission on the Ethics of Scientific Knowledge and Technology. This report identified a number of key questions, such as who is to determine the priorities and choices of science and space technologies on the basis of which objectives? The report concluded that outer space is part of the shared heritage of mankind and space activities must be freely accessible for the benefit of all mankind, with a focus on the need for the fragile environment to be protected to ensure sustainability. The report goes on to aver that space activities require a precise legal framework, with each substantive provision subtended by an ethic designed and clearly accepted by all players in the field. Pompidou (2000, p. 25) evinces that the corollary is that an ethical code must precede the creation of any new legal instrument to entrench normative values, and that:

> ethical principles should be applied to every phase of development of the space instrument and they should underlie the strategic plans of the space agencies . . . the establishment of an ethical code should flow from international consultation to harmonize practices and possible legislation in order to avoid the proliferation of norms specific to each country.
>
> (Pompidou 2000, p. 25)

The report is clear that the establishment of ethical norms in space must be undertaken collectively by the international community and must provide the guidance for a legally binding framework based on harmonized practices. Pompidou states that without the necessary international consensus, each spacefaring nation will pursue its own agenda. Rather than being embedded within an international framework, rules for space exploration will fracture along national lines.

The search for normative values will, therefore, lead inevitably to the legal framework governing international space law. It will be shown in the course of this inquiry that in international space law, rather than the ethics shaping the regulation, it is the law that seemingly has come to ordain the values that underpin space activity. The contours of these values can be detected in the Outer Space Treaty (OST), the fundamental pillar of the regulatory framework. A historical examination of events at the time of the drafting of the OST illustrates that imposing these values may well have been the only way to ensure any form of adherence to normative standards by the two superpowers. The resulting regulatory framework also, however, left significant latitude for states to act within their own interests rather than looking to be bound by an international, normative standard, thereby limiting normative behaviour and wider consideration of generally applicable ethical standards. As Moltz (2014) explains, while cooperation and peaceful exploration of space is advantageous and can bring economic and technological benefits, the scientists and administrators ultimately receive their funding from governments, who may be somewhat reticent to cooperate with states who are their competitors.

The second hypothesis that runs throughout this chapter is that this current regulatory regime not only lacks an ethical underpinning, but also that it fundamentally fails to take account of the realities of the modern space environment. As has already been identified, space regulation was negotiated when the only states with active space programmes were opposing binary power blocs. Space activity now encompasses numerous state actors and private corporations engaged in the exploration of space, each with their own motives and goals. The major space powers, such as China, the United States and Russia, view space as another theatre of foreign policy, and pursue both military and economic strategic goals as only their economies can. Aspirational states, such as India, Japan and the European states, continue to develop their capacity to fund economic growth. A few egregious nations see space activity as a way of exerting military muscle, such as Iran and North Korea. Others, such as Malaysia and South Korea, focus on the economic benefits afforded by engaging in space activity and look to develop nascent spacefaring capacity. West (2007) states that, in 1967, the time when the OST came into force, there were seven states that had satellites in space. By 2007, this had grown to 47.

As well as being predicated on maintaining the balance of power between two superpowers, the current regulatory framework presupposes, and indeed mandates, that the exploration and utilization of space is fundamentally a state-based activity. Such an approach is, however, not reflective of the current picture of space exploration. As Foust (2014) recognizes, the financial and technical risks, not to mention the risks to human life, appeared to put exploration beyond the reach of the private sector. Commercial activity was restricted to NASA subcontracting parts of a large project out to tender where the bidders would inevitably be big aerospace companies (see Chaikin 1994 for details of the involvement of companies such as Grumann, Lockheed-Martin and Boeing in the Apollo programme).

In the post–Cold War world, however, commercial and corporate involvement has become a common feature of space activity. In the US, the Launch Services Purchase Act of 1990 compelled NASA to outsource provision of launch services to private companies with legislation in 1998 and 2004, furthering this move to commercialize US space activity. Seemingly empowered, companies themselves have started to look to provide commercial space services that operate independently of the main space agencies. The biggest of these, Space X, is already looking to develop a competitive fleet of space launchers and provide a completely private space transportation service (Perrett 2014). The existing international regulatory framework has been criticized as inhibiting commercial activity, for example by limiting the exploitation of lunar resources (see Tronchetti 2009 for a detailed discussion on this). Consequently, this reduces the incentive for private companies to develop space technologies (Hickman 2007). This shift, however, from state actors to a multi-sectored space sector poses difficult regulatory questions that will need to be addressed in any underpinning ethical code. Fundamentally, the different values that underpin state activity and commercial activity will need to be recognized and in some way reconciled.

Having identified the multi-sectored nature of space activity, it is also germane to point out the limits of this inquiry. One readily identifiable core value that runs through the history of space governance is the aspiration that space activity should be peaceful. This may seem somewhat counter-intuitive, given that early space exploration was driven by militaristic competition. Yet, one of the undoubted successes of space regulation has been the prevention of an arms race in space (Gabrynowicz 2004). The OST explicitly prohibits the stationing of nuclear weapons in space. There has also been significant cooperation among states.[2] Article IV of the OST explicitly outlaws nuclear weapons in space, and the whole thrust of the governance framework is focused towards civilian and scientific use of space. This discussion will, therefore, restrict itself to examination of what can be categorized as 'civil space' and commercial space (Moltz 2014).

There are also sound practical reasons for not including consideration of military space activities within the search for normative behaviour. Fundamentally, military activity is focused around state self-interest. Whereas civilian activities are openly administered by space agencies, often in conjunction with commercial companies, military activity is almost exclusively conducted and administered by the armed forces (although sometimes this is in conjunction with companies and space agencies, the military are almost always the lead agency and will demand high levels of secrecy). The ethical underpinning of individual national military strategy, of which space activity is a subset, is not the focus of this discussion. The inquiry will instead focus upon the civilian space administrations and commercial companies looking to develop space activities for peaceful, economic purposes.

As with other areas where ethical policy is under discussion, the aim of this discussion is the codification or identification of shared norms relating to organizational policies, procedures and practices. These norms will then ordain behaviour that is recognized as being right or wrong (Raile 2013). In respect of the activities of space exploration, these norms are inevitably interlaced with questions of technological advancement, increasing commercial activity and, perhaps crucially, national interest. The structure of this chapter will identify areas where civilian space activity operates specifically human spaceflight and planetary exploration. The chapter will then examine the waste product of this activity, orbital debris. When dealing with each of these themes, the inquiry will look to draw out the ethical issues that arise and evaluate the regulatory solutions in place to deal with them.

The inquiry will then go on to examine the current legal framework. This will encompass the historical drivers that shaped the regulation. It will then evaluate the difficulty faced by the ever-increasing number of space actors. The chapter will demonstrate that the current governance framework is in need of rebalancing to take into account the competing interests of state and commercial actors. The key challenge is for the identification of normative values that will be accepted by all stakeholders, thereby creating optimal conditions for sustainable activity to repair the damage done to the fragile space environment. Williamson (2003) states that establishing a code of ethics for space conduct is crucial, and such difficulties will need to be surmounted if serious and irreparable damage to the space environment is to be avoided. This chapter will conclude that the only way such a code can be established is identification of key ethical values by involving all stakeholders in shaping the regulatory framework.

Ethics and space exploration: establishing the frontiers

As has already been demonstrated, establishing the broad contours of the ethical position that should be adopted is no easy task. The first obvious question is moot: should humans explore space? Space exploration is occurring and space activity shows no sign of regressing among the scientific community, as well as the national and international space agencies. Schwartz (2011) goes further, articulating the view that space exploration is not only desirable, but is an activity that we, as a species, are morally obligated to undertake to ensure our long-term survival. Others who have addressed such concerns from an ethical standpoint agree that while the moral case for space exploration is unequivocal, there are questions that need addressing. Lin states that as well as fundamental ethical issues surrounding environmental and safety concerns, there are deeper concerns, such as how to deal with property rights in space, and goes on to state, 'what we do not want to happen is to rush into orbit and the settlement of space without a "big picture" strategy' (Lin 2006, p. 12). It is the contention of this inquiry that, before looking at the bigger picture, a necessary first step has to be establishing fundamental values in respect of the environment and safety.

Notwithstanding any philosophical justifications, there are, de facto, a number of nations actively engaged in the exploration of space, and this number is only going to increase (Moltz 2014). Having accepted that basic premise, it is more helpful to consider whether it is possible to identify a normative position to act as a guide to the overarching regulation of space activity. Following on from that, the question of utility remains, specifically the extent to which such a position can be embedded at the centre of all space activity or whether different ethical positions are contingent on the nature of the activity and the theatre in which those activities occur. A crucial step in trying to evaluate the ethical underpinning of space governance, this discussion will identify the key issues facing policymakers and public-sector administrators before going on to examine the legal and regulatory framework against which these issues will be administered.

Designing the ethical underpinning for the ongoing development of the space environment, however, is critical given the expansion of commercial and state-based activity in space (Horikawa 2014). It is, therefore, necessary to identify the key areas of activity that can be codified and embed them within an ethical code. These developmental areas can be broken down into three broad categories. The first area of inquiry is the normative values within the field of human spaceflight activity and how the management of human spaceflight activity needs underpinning with an ethical approach to risk management. The next matter of concern relates to the protection of celestial bodies that may be untainted by human activity yet are the subject of considerable scientific interest.[3] Finally, and perhaps the most significant of the issues to consider, is that of orbital debris. This crystallizes the issues of the previous two discussions: there is the need to efficiently exploit the obvious benefits that exist in terms of both commercial activity and physical resources. This needs to be balanced against the need to protect the orbits of the Earth from becoming cluttered with the debris of half a century of space activity (Williamson 2003).

Astronauts: risk and ethics in human spaceflight programmes

One area that would appear at first instance to be separate from international discourse is the methods and policies employed by which space agencies who manage the risk that is inherent within their individual missions (Macauley 2005). Each area of space activity carries risks of different magnitude and significance, but, as with the other areas of space governance, it will be shown that rather than building policies and practices from a sound ethical base, most risk is managed on an ad hoc and iterative basis. The management of risk in respect of human spaceflight is a key area where space administrations need to entrench ethical considerations. As in all areas of administration, it is desirable that there should be an explicit relationship between good ethical practice and thorough risk management (Francis and Armstrong 2003). In respect of human spaceflight, the reason for this is clear: the work undertaken by space agencies is unique and any failure of organizational management to adequately manage the risks almost invariably leads to consequences that are both high profile and result in death. It is argued that managing these risks with clear ethical underpinnings should be an essential element of any ethical code designed to inform space activities and will ensure an enduring basis for human spaceflight activity.

Macauley (2005) states that managing human risk in space is an important but overlooked area of public policy. Macauley was speaking almost exclusively about US space policy, given the relative success of the Soyuz programme in Russia and the lack of verifiable data from China. It is uncertain, therefore, whether this statement holds good in respect of other countries with human spaceflight capability. It should also be noted that no other space programme has had to undergo the intense public scrutiny that NASA has endured. There have been a number of accidents within the US space programme that have led to fatalities, such as those resulting in the loss of the Apollo 1,[4] Challenger[5] and Columbia spacecraft, each of which resulted in high-profile public inquiries. What such occurrences served to illustrate was that even in the midst of ambitious, high-profile programmes using the best engineers and after exhaustive testing, it is impossible to eliminate risk totally from human space exploration. Macauley (2005, p. 135), citing the findings of the Columbia Accident Investigation Board (CAIB), stated that '[the] operation of the Space Shuttle, and all human spaceflight, is a developmental activity with high inherent risks'.[6]

The criticisms of the risk management procedures in the CAIB report pointed to both fundamental organizational failures but also procedures predicated on ensuring financial efficacy and adherence to deadlines rather than rooted in an ethical concern for reducing the risk of death or serious injury of its astronauts (Berger 2003). Ironically, the report also found that the collapse of the Soviet Union indirectly contributed to the disaster as well. Removal of the political imperative for a robust space programme saw cuts to the funding of NASA. Berger (2003) points out that efficiency and savings became the key drivers, with NASA outsourcing various programme responsibilities, including safety oversight. Engaged in a high-risk, high-profile operation, an overstretched NASA diverted money that should have been spent on enhanced safety procedures to ensure it could meet the burgeoning commitments surrounding building and operating the International Space Station (ISS).

It may be, however, that the increased momentum and discussion regarding a human voyage to Mars (Zubrin and Wagner 2011) has encouraged, and will continue to drive, the public-sector regulators to address the area of risk and ethics in human spaceflight activity. One need only examine the ferocious pace of technological development under NASA's Apollo programme to appreciate how quickly ambitious plans can be brought to fruition (see Chaikin 1994). The Apollo programme, however, represented unprecedented civilian investment in a single project. Lafleur (2010) estimates that, all in, the Apollo programme costs were approximately $20.4 billion (equivalent to $109 billion in 2010 dollars).[7] It is unlikely that such direct investment will ever be seen on that scale again. Indeed, it is likely that current and future activities in space will involve the public and private sectors working together. Such collaboration will need a mixture of legislation, regulatory bodies managing the risk, and cooperation both international and transnational in nature.

Despite these concerns, and away from NASA, the transnational and international public bodies have attempted to address the legal and ethical framework of human spaceflight. In 2004, UNESCO brought together representatives of the European Center for Space Law, the legal department of ESA, as well as various academics, to discuss these issues. The resulting report of this symposium offered much by way of encouragement for those desiring an ethical foundation for human spaceflight. Faugére (2004) explicitly recognized that commercial and economic imperatives will be hard to resist as human spaceflight activities become more collective, and that establishing and calibrating normative ethical values as regard the exploration of space will be crucial.

Konrad (2004) takes the discussion one step further and emphasizes that the commercial and economic context of space exploration sits alongside the aspirational and idealistic underpinnings that are inherent with those who work in the space industry. She suggests that any formulation of space ethics in respect of the future of human spaceflight will need to look beyond individual organizations and recognize the different cultural norms of the relevant participants. If the organizational failings of NASA highlight the danger of space agencies prioritizing political imperatives over technical development and appropriate management of risk, then in the new collaborative space age, finding normative values to underpin each of the new organizational structures becomes even more important.

An ethical consensus: treatment of alien biospheres

Human spaceflight activity is high profile, with failure resulting in fatality, invariably leading to atrophy and organizational stress within the space agency responsible. It is, therefore, tempting to place undue weight on the ethical issues of such high-profile ventures, even when they exist only in theory or the early stages of development. It is not, however, only the human aspect of spaceflight governance that needs ethical consideration. Viikari (2008) states that space exploration is an inherently polluting industry. The actual exploration of space, either by humans or robotic probes, gives rise to two interrelated risks that need to be managed. The first is the avoidance of 'back contamination' by safeguarding Earth's biosphere by ensuring no exposure to alien pathogens when spacecraft return from other planets with samples. The second related aspect is prevention of 'forward contamination', by ensuring that organisms from Earth do not despoil otherwise sterile planets. Such pollution would remove much of the scientific value of exploring these extraterrestrial environments (Robinson 2006).

McArthur and Boran (2004) focus upon the impact of human contamination on an environment that has not been subject to any previous terrestrial influence. They engage in a wide-ranging discussion examining which terrestrial moral conceptions can be extrapolated sufficiently to guide humanity in the journey beyond Earth. They build inter alia on the work of Marshall (1993) and advocate an agent-centred restriction on interference with sterile environments. Clearly, a key aspect of exploration is to monitor and analyse planets and celestial bodies other than Earth. Such activity means there is a risk that such exploration will despoil the previously untainted environment of other planets, pose risks to as yet unidentified life within such biospheres and, perhaps more alarmingly, jeopardize life on Earth.

There is an apparent consensus among spacefaring nations that such contamination poses a risk that needs managing. As pointed out by Billings (2006), such consensus is restricted to measures restricting contamination of the environment rather than any underlying agreement as to the way that territory and resources should be utilized following on from these initial steps. This may be no bad thing, with Schwartz (2014) providing a compelling argument that scientific interests should underpin the exploration of space rather than a desire to colonize and consume based on national interests or characteristics.

The ethical position in respect of contamination of biospheres is one that has been well trodden in academic discussions. Williamson (2003, 2006), Butler (2006) and Robinson (2006) have all considered in detail the ethical and legal implications of interplanetary exploration. Robinson states that contamination control is only as strong as the weakest effort made by any of the nations involved in interplanetary exploration. Perhaps more than any other area of space governance, the issue of planetary protection has seen a truly international approach adopted, almost from the outset. International guidance in respect of measure to avoid contamination is provided by the Committee on Space Research (COSPAR),[8] an adjunct of the International Council for Science (ICSU). COSPAR advises the UN in respect of the standards for planetary protection, and is the focal point of international efforts to coordinate a response to the risk posed by forward and back contamination (Butler 2006).

The COSPAR guidelines operate by placing all space missions into one of five discrete categories depending upon the amount of planetary interference involved. Category I missions are the lowest risk and target the Moon or Venus, celestial bodies that are thought to be sterile. Category II covers missions to the majority of planets in the solar system, asteroids and comets. Category III covers exploration of celestial bodies that may contain life, but where the mission does not involve direct contact with the planet. Category IV currently has three sub-strata, and involves landing on planets where scientists believe there is a good chance of life existing (EN Mars, Europa and Enceladus). These first four recommendations deal with the risks posed to alien biospheres. Category V missions are those that pose a risk to the Earth by human visits to other celestial bodies and the return of samples.

For each category of mission, there are detailed recommendations regarding the steps that need to be taken in respect of sterilization and decontamination of spacecraft. A number of space-active nations have unmanned planetary exploration, and this diversity is reflected within COSPAR. Such diversity, strengthened by the high international regard in which COSPAR is held, has ensured that the planetary protection guidelines are now the accepted standard for space exploration. Butler (2006) makes a powerful case that COSPAR's recommendations need to be moved into the sphere of hard international law. He argues that this should not be difficult, given the consensus that already exists. It is also pointed out that foregoing contamination and protection procedures could reduce overall programme costs by 10 per cent on high-risk missions. For emerging nations with low budgets, and even the larger agencies such as China and Russia, looking to compete with NASA, Butler suggests that planetary protection measures could be one of the casualties in an effort to make dwindling public-sector funds go further. Additionally, as private-sector firms motivated by profit look to explore space, even the most persuasive and well-regarded voluntary code may be sacrificed. Terrestrial environmental law has illustrated that companies usually need legally binding regulation, backed with appropriate sanctions. It may be that rather than relying on altruistic compliance with COSPAR, there will need to be some underpinning strength added to their recommendations if planetary protection is to be fully realized.

Despite concern surrounding the lack of policing, these recommendations have been praised as being 'a very consistent and highly developed system of recommendations by an independent and international body of scientists' (Bohlmann 2003, p. 24). They do not, ultimately, have the force of hard international law. Instead, they are 'soft law' and part of the matrix of non-binding, voluntary codes that are crucial in the management and governance of space activities. That the COSPAR guidelines are non-binding is not unusual. There are a myriad of soft instruments that regulate space activity, such as the UN Debris Mitigation Guidelines and the ITU regulatory framework governing the regulation of communications satellites.

The arguments about the efficacy and indeed legality of soft provisions is not restricted to space activities, but so much of space activity operates on an international canvas, inevitably this begets questions surrounding the efficacy and extent to which states are bound by soft instruments (Chinkin 2000). Goh (2009) provides a thorough consideration of the role of soft law within the regulation of space activity and points out that this tapestry of soft regulation varies in degrees of differences in form, language, objectives and enforceability. More fixed, binding treaties are often the result of protracted, lengthy negotiations, and, as such, ambient developments in technology, science and engineering capability can shift the fragile ground upon which such negotiations are based.

In addition, and perhaps crucial to understanding why so many states appear to comply with non-treaty agreements, Su and Lixin (2014) point out soft instruments can serve to act as effective confidence-building measures. Such agreements establish a broad consensus without requiring the commitment of a more binding treaty. Space exploration is a collaborative venture, and very often soft codes are often the only way to try to establish normative rules when there is substantial disagreement among states. Goh (2008, p. 728) states that soft law solutions provide 'all of the functional aspects of substantive discussion without the legal import of a binding treaty framework, these non-treaty agreements are generally recorded in declarations that evince a workable compromise'.

While seemingly an ideal solution, Listner (2014), writing in relation to the Draft ICoC for Outer Space Activities, heralds a warning that such agreements could inadvertently become part of the fabric of customary international law. Customary international law emerges from established state practice as opposed to law arising from negotiated treaties. As Listner (2014, p. 57) goes on to point out, 'potential exists for what was supposed to be a non-legally binding measure to affect a legally binding international treaty that is the foundation of international space law'. Despite this (admittedly marginal) concern, states are generally eager to engage in collaborative agreements in the realm of space activity. Such non-treaty agreements, given the benefits of technology transfer and cost sharing, are ultimately viewed as being beneficial.

It is the efficacy of these non-treaty agreements that illustrates the value of constructing an overarching ethical code to underpin space activity. When considering the ethical dimensions of planetary protection of this nature, Robinson (2006) suggests that the primary concern of those charged with regulating this area is out of a self-interested anxiety for the Earth's ecosystem. Even when considering the infection of a new planet, the main disquiet appears to be the contamination of scientific studies of worlds that are untainted by terrestrial life rather than an inherent regard for such worlds stemming from altruism. As already stated, the COSPAR guidelines have no force of law, and as such states can ignore them when they feel it is in their best interests to do so. The fact that they are largely adhered to shows the strength of respect for the scientific advice they are based upon and, perhaps more significantly, the value of obtaining a broad consensus when operating on an international palate.

Clear and present danger: combatting the threat of orbital debris

This discussion has so far examined the risks of human spaceflight and the growing ethical consensus regarding the exploration of other planets. Of all the issues, however, that highlight the need for ethical underpinning of space activity, the threats posed by orbital debris are the most pressing. The concerns about space debris mirror much of the concerns regarding global warming. Indeed, as Button (2012–2013) states: 'Earth's orbit is a vital component of the ecosystem of the planet and it has become heavily polluted by debris'. Su and Lixen (2014) go on to state that the space environment has worsened to a critical point and degradation will soon be irreversible. Williamson (2003, p. 182) offers a potential reason for this decline, stating 'because space has proved so challenging to "conquer" . . . relatively little consideration has been accorded to the space environment in terms of the detrimental effects of space exploration and development'. The ethical challenge faced by the international community is clear: states and companies must move from the national and commercial interests outlined above, and give primacy to environmental considerations (Button 2013). Unfortunately, as recent attempts to address climate change on Earth have shown, issues on division of responsibility, burden sharing and different national aspirations all tend to provide significant obstacles to progress. Sadly, this is as true for orbital debris as it is for other environmental issues.[9]

The Inter-Agency Space Debris Coordination Committee (IADC) defines orbital debris as 'all man-made objects, including fragments and elements thereof, in Earth orbit or re-entering the atmosphere that are non-functional' (IADC 2013). This definition means, therefore, that *everything* launched into space has the potential to become debris. This encompasses non-functioning satellites through to flecks of paint and tools dropped by astronauts during space walks (Viikari 2008). While discussions about alien biospheres remain largely abstract and the focus of very few missions, orbital debris has the potential to affect all aspects of space activity, and more significantly, if unchecked, could cause severe disruption to the Earth.

The problem with orbital debris, unlike issues of back and forward contamination, is that Earth's atmosphere has already been subject to over 50 years of near-constant space activity. Hobe (2012) states that the amount of debris and its projected growth in the vicinity of the Earth have caused considerable alarm in the international space community. Such alarm is well placed. According to Horikawa (2014), of the 6,000 satellites launched since Sputnik in 1958, there are currently 1,000 that are still operational and over 2,000 are orbiting but non-functional. As a result of either intentional or accidental collision, there are now more than 20,000 trackable pieces of debris. As Viikari (2008) states, the danger from such debris is that impact velocities in orbit are very high, with debris travelling many times faster than bullets out of machine guns. Due to these extreme velocities, even the smallest particle of debris can prove disastrous for a functioning satellite and, perhaps even more serious, fatal for any space traveller.

It is not merely the functionality of satellites and the well-being of an elite few space travellers, however, that are of concern. The orbit of the Earth is a crucial part of the planetary environment. Like all such environments, there are natural mechanisms in place to ensure that debris in the orbit (such as meteors and comets) is dealt with through natural decay. Weeden (2011), however, points to the work done by NASA scientists Donald Kessler and Burt Cour-Palais, who predict that man-made space debris will hit a tipping point where it will grow faster than the Earth's natural capability to deal with it. There will then be a 'collisional cascading' process whereby debris will collide and break up, increasing the population of orbital debris exponentially. This would be a traumatic environmental event, and consequently the cost and risks of engaging in space activity would increase significantly.

Clearly, there are a number of ethical issues that arise out of this and would need addressing in any underpinning code of conduct. These discussions on space debris echo wider environmental debates, and indeed encompass many of the same obstacles to resolution (Viikari 2008). The first is the apparent lack of legally binding requirements to ensure that the amount of debris is mitigated (that is measures to limit the amount of space debris at the design stage of the mission, thereby making sure that the amount of debris from a space mission is minimal). The second, and technically more challenging, area is that of debris remediation (the active removal of debris from densely populated orbit regions). Given the dangers, it is perhaps not surprising that the major space agencies have acknowledged that best practice is to be found in the UN Space Debris Mitigation Guidelines, even if this falls short of full-scale adoption. These guidelines speak about mitigation of debris but do not actually speak about the remediation aspect (Hobe and Mey 2009), and are recognized as being a prudent first step towards a solution.

The UN states clearly that these are guidelines and are not legally binding under international law (Hobe and Mey 2009, p. 395). There has been much conjecture among space lawyers as to the extent to which the current legal framework prohibits the creation of orbital debris (Hobe 2011; Viikari 2008). As Hobe (2011) suggests, if the 'soft' guidelines are discounted, the OST does not explicitly render the creation of space debris unlawful. It cannot be said, however, that the public-sector space agencies have been inactive in response to the threat. IDAC is an international governmental forum designed to coordinate a worldwide response to space debris. IDAC operates as a mechanism to integrate research conducted by the individual space agencies, and membership is drawn from the space agencies of all major spacefaring nations. On an institutional level, NASA has established the Orbital Debris Program Office at the Johnson Space Centre,[10] which conducts research into all aspects of the management, mitigation and remediation of orbital debris. ESA coordinates European research into orbital debris via the ESA Space Debris Office.[11]

The area of orbital debris has previously been described as 'an unregulated vacuum devoid of law, responsibility and common sense' (Williamson 2006, p. 272). Recent international activity by public-sector bodies would appear to indicate that there is no shortage of consensus that orbital debris is a problem, and this has led to international collaboration on the mitigation or remediation measures. Coupled with the wider discussions occurring within the UN, it would seem that there is some small cause for optimism. A nascent ethical position in respect of orbital debris is clearly emerging, based around the need to reduce current debris and an aim to limit future debris. Such a position needs to be clearly articulated by all of the main space actors and must influence the underpinning governance of space activity if environmental degradation is to be halted and space activity is to remain sustainable.

The Outer Space Treaty: space governance shaped by Cold War conflict

The discussion has, thus far, identified the distinct yet interrelated areas of concern regarding risk management, planetary protection and space debris. States appear to recognize that the preservation of the space environment is a worthwhile exercise and that orbital debris poses a risk to all space users. This consensus has led to the major space nations formulating some suggested guidelines for the prevention of future debris. Despite the best intentions of administrators, however, pragmatism and commercial imperatives tend to override even the most noble of ethical considerations. For the next stage of the inquiry, having identified the areas where ethics and space activity intersect, the focus will shift on to the recognized normative instruments for managing space activity and examine the extent to which these reflect the concerns outlined above.

Any consideration concerning the legal framework governing space activity must begin with an examination of the Treaty on Principles Governing the Activities of States in the Exploration Use of Outer Space including the Moon and Other Celestial Bodies.[12] More commonly known as the Outer Space Treaty (OST), this is the principal legal instrument that provides the context and operational framework for space agencies on a national and international level. An instrument of international law, the OST has, to date, been ratified by over 100 members of the

United Nations[13] and provides the codified framework by which current activities in space are regulated (Cheng 1997). Recognized by leading space lawyers as a key development in the creation of a set of binding principles underpinning space governance (Lachs 1992) and the cornerstone of international space law conventions (Qizhi 1997), the OST draws on a number of previously non-binding UN Resolutions in respect of space exploration.[14]

It is impossible to consider the provisions of the OST without considering the historical backdrop against which the treaty was drafted and signed. The OST was negotiated against the backdrop of the Cold War and two superpowers, the US and the Soviet Union, seeking to establish dominance, both technical and political, over the other (Gabrynowicz 2004). The two major stakeholders, and at that time the only two spacefaring nations, the US and USSR both had ambitions to be the first nation to land a human being on the moon, and there needed to be formal regulation of activities in outer space before that happened. Negotiations for the treaty were largely the remit of the UN Committee for the Peaceful Uses of Outer Space (COPUOS), a committee formed in 1958 when the General Assembly of the UN created a bespoke committee tasked with fostering international consensus on matters of space law and policy while also recognizing that a specialist committee would be needed to deal with the unique issues posed by human space activity (Lyall and Larsen 2009). It has been said that given the geopolitical environment in which the OST was drafted, the treaty, and other space-related treaties signed by UN members, are essentially 'security treaties' (Blount 2011–2012, p. 520). The OST is, however, also a forward-looking treaty that tries to prevent the conquest of space resembling a colonial free-for-all (West 2007). The preamble to the OST speaks, in aspirational terms, about state parties being '*inspired by the great prospects opening up before mankind as a result of man's entry into outer space*'.

The body of the OST, however, is more pragmatic. Article I of the OST[15] mandates that there must be free access to all areas of celestial bodies, while Article II[16] explicitly places outer space beyond the claims of sovereignty. The OST represented the start of a period of consolidation of customary international law for space governance (Hobe 2010). Rather than being a substantial ethical statement of intent, however, it represents the basic requirements of a treaty designed to prevent annexation of near-Earth celestial bodies by the two superpowers (West 2007). Article IV explicitly prevents the use of space for the deployment of weapons of mass destruction and Article V establishes the role of the astronaut not as a combatant or adjunct of the military, but as an envoy of all mankind.

As stated above, the OST was the start of the process of codification of international law. Following on from it, there were an additional four treaties that spoke to more specific areas of concern: the Agreement on the Rescue of Astronauts, the Return of Astronauts and Return of Objects Launched into Outer Space (the Rescue Agreement 1968), the Convention on International Liability for Damage caused by Space Objects (the Liability Convention 1972), the Convention on Registration of Objects Launched into Outer Space (Registration Convention 1975) and the Agreement Governing the Activities of States on the

Moon and other Celestial Bodies (Moon Treaty 1979).[17] These five treaties form the body of International Space Law and were all negotiated within COPUOS.

These instruments of international law provide a troubling paradox within the context of this inquiry, seeking, as it does, an ethical lodestar for space activities. When viewed through the prism of history, these treaties represent a realistic response by COPUOS to the ambitions harboured by both superpowers at the time the treaty was drafted (Gabrynowicz 2004). The treaties had a specific job to do, in respect of preventing a colonial battle being fought in space and beyond this. Blount (2011–2012, p. 524) states that the OST 'sets out core values and aspirations that are still at the heart of international space law, many of which may have solidified into custom'. What the OST does is embody and codify the explicit and implicit values of the superpowers at the time of drafting the OST. As stated at the outset of this inquiry, space activity is a manifestation of either national ambition or, more recently, an extension of commercial opportunities. Given Pompidou's assertion that the legal framework should follow on from the ethical code governing space activities, it is concerning that the main guidance for normative behaviour in regard of space exploration is to be found in the substantive legal instrument itself. What the OST and related treaties emphatically do not do, rooted as they are in pragmatism and diplomatic compromise, is provide any kind of shared values that can provide the ethical underpinning for space exploration.

It can be seen that the OST provides the *corpus juris spatialis*, 'a solid trunk from which other branches of space law can grow' (Butler 2006, p. 1377). The treaty, however, imposes a regulatory duty upon the wider international community and the signatory states themselves. This is done in two crucial ways. Article III of the OST ensures that the existing body of international law is brought within the way in which states conduct their activities in space. In addition, and perhaps the defining characteristic of the OST, is that by virtue of Article VI, member states are assigned international responsibility for national activities in outer space. This extends to both governmental and non-governmental bodies. Similarly, under Article VII, each member state that launches an object into outer space retains responsibility for that object, and that state will be liable for the damage caused either in space or on the Earth, a principle extended by the 1972 Liability Convention.

Given that the OST imposes responsibility upon states, it is to the states and the space-active nations that we must look for the *lex specialis* in respect of their operating framework for space activities. Each nation with a space programme will have, in some way, incorporated their responsibilities under the OST within their national law. In this respect, it is instructive to consider the assertion by Lyall and Larsen (2010, p. 2) that space law is a 'label attached to a bucket that contains many different types of rules and regulations rather than as denoting a conceptually coherent single form of law'. Space law can be considered a term of function and has largely grown up on an ad hoc basis, responding to advances in technology, the shifting needs of national interest and the ever-increasing drift to international and transnational collaboration in space activities. Despite Pompidou's plea that law should flow from a revivified ethical framework, it might, therefore be too late as the tendrils of the legal framework are already firmly embedded on a national and international level. The binding legal framework was shaped by the values and concerns of the time and reflects the implicit values of the drafters, that of security, non-militarization and state accountability. In the post-Cold War world, the OST *is* the value set from which space governance flows.

The OST and the related treaties represent the primary phase of the development of normative rules for space exploration. Wessel (2012) suggests that the signing of these treaties represented only the first stage of the development of the overarching framework to manage space activities. He goes on to suggest that the later years of the twentieth century saw the development of the UN Principles on Outer Space. With the coming of the first decade of the twenty-first century, states focused on refining the meaning of the earlier space treaties and, crucially, developed guidelines on the proliferation of orbital debris and the use of nuclear power sources in interplanetary space probes. Such development, however, was against the backdrop of change. With new actors emerging in the area of space activity and technological developments making space evermore accessible, the traditional mechanisms of governance appeared ill-suited to the new world order.

Emerging space agencies: back to the future

Thus far, the discussion has outlined the legal framework for space governance and highlighted three key areas where a coherent ethical framework underpinning all regulation would provide a sustainable lodestar for regulatory development of key areas of present and future space activity. The OST and the wider *corpus juris spatialis* established principles that have been broadly accepted. As technical expertise and scientific awareness has developed, key areas of consensus regarding space travellers and the space environment have followed. Representing this as the complete picture, however, is Panglossian in the extreme. In order to fully appreciate the difficulties in trying to promulgate and maintain a consistent ethical approach to space exploration, this section will look at the difficulties faced by emerging space nations and how the consensus regarding environmental regulation poses an ethical quandary in respect of inhibiting access to space for some nations.

The OST and the underpinning regulatory framework, as has been illustrated, are children of the Cold War. Space exploration and the regulation of space activities undertaken at the time all occurred in this context. The organizational behemoths such as NASA and the Russian space agency, ROSCOSMOS, charged with organizing the space activities did not differentiate nor prioritize their space activities. Instead, they sought to demonstrate their dominance in every area of space travel, viewing the conquest of space as key indicators of national pride. Billings (2006) identifies that since the turn of this century, this situation has changed fundamentally. As well as the traditional space actors seeking a role in the expansion of space activities, there are now a number of nations who wish to engage in space activities and develop nascent space programmes. There are considerable benefits for a nation to develop some form of space capability. While the buying in of capacity such as remote-sensing capabilities or communication provisions may be cost-effective, such a policy also leaves a state vulnerable to the whims and caprices of international politics and shifting alliances.

Emerging space programmes are trying to develop in an arena where there has already been 50 years of space activity. This poses two key problems for the embryonic space actor. First, there is the matter of access to the most desirable part of space, geostationary orbit (GEO). Schwartz (2014) highlights that while Article I of the OST provides for free exploration of outer space by all states, this does stretch to regulating popular orbits. It follows that since there is only a finite amount of room in GEO, it will only be those states who have active space programmes, or access to space, that will be able to populate the desirable orbits.[18] The second problem for the emerging space nation, as identified by Fihn and Irsten (2014, p. 121) is that when the USSR and US first engaged in space activities, there were very few limitations and restrictions governing them. This meant that the resource envelope could be stretched further, focusing on developing the technology rather than on any environment issues. The result was that states could create orbital debris without having to be mindful of the consequences (Welly 2010).

Emerging space actors consequently are reluctant to enter into legally binding agreements that make utilization of space costlier and impinge on the chances of them developing much-needed capacity in this area. Elatawy (2014) states that any regulation of outer space activities needs to aim at improving the outer space environment and make it accessible for everyone. This, he argues, can be achieved by greater transparency. He suggests that technology-sharing measures promoting best practice would reduce the financial burden on the developing states. Lee and Chung (2011, p. 228), writing about the emergence of the South Korean space programme, state that late-starting space nations 'cannot handle the whole area of space development but need to focus on the most important and urgent areas'. They identify that the main goal of Korean space activity is commercial in focus and looking to enhance industrial competitiveness. Such aims are typical of the many developing space programmes that seek to explore and develop some sort of presence in space.

Even if the quandary posed by emerging space nations is set aside, the key perceived deficiency of the OST regime remains: the lack of explicit, hard-law attention to environmental issues in outer space. This is a critical area of oversight; however, the essence of the concerns is that utilitarian and pragmatic approaches to space activity have predominated. According to Viikari (2008, p. 4), this has led to a manifestation of the 'tragedy of the commons', where individual states have received benefits from individual missions while damaging the 'global commons' (Welly 2010, p. 279). This lack of explicit, legally binding regulation has created a largely unfettered environment that individual actors can freely despoil without having to pay regard to the consequences. Listner (2011) suggests that voluntary and non-binding codes of conduct predominate in this area, and as such it is an ideal area to harmonize collective behaviour and, perhaps more importantly, identify normative ethical values upon which a sustainable governance regime can be constructed.

The European Union[19] has attempted to address some of the difficulties by drafting the International Code of Conduct for Outer Space Activities (ICoC). First promulgated in 2008, there have been a number of iterations, with the latest being discussed in 2013. Section 1.3 of ICoC states that the Code seeks to form a regime of transparency and confidence-building measures with the aim of creating mutual understanding and trust, with the aim of preventing confrontation and fostering stability. The Code goes on to state specifically that it is complementary to the normative framework regarding outer space activities. Critically, s 1.4 states subscription to the Code is open to all states on a voluntary basis and explicitly provides that the Code is not legally binding. The Code itself provides, in Part II, for measures to deal with space operations and the mitigation of orbital debris. In Part III, there are details on the cooperation mechanisms, which include notification requirements of outer space activities, the provision of information regarding space activities to other states and also consultation mechanisms to resolve disputes.

International response to the Code has been mixed. According to Su and Lixin (2014), many states feel that they have not received sufficient consultation on the drafting or shaping of the policies therein. Additionally, there is the concern that while the Code is explicitly not a legal instrument, there is a possibility that widespread and continued adherence to it may see the provisions absorbed as customary international law. This concern, although not trivial, is a remote one (Listner 2014), given the nature of international law and the way in which such customary international law arises. Nonetheless, this is one of a number of impediments to wider endorsement of the ICoC. Perversely, some states[20] object to the very fact that the ICoC does reside in the category of soft law provision, preferring to see a treaty with more teeth to tackle space security and debris-related issues. Despite a cautious optimism, most commentators (see Listner 2014; Su and Lixin 2014) believe ICoC is far from the finished article and therefore not yet ready to augment the existing space governance mechanisms.

Conclusion

This discussion started by identifying a lack of explicit normative values underpinning space activities. This necessitated an examination of the key ethical dilemmas that public-sector space agencies face in the twenty-first century in respect of human spaceflight, planetary exploration and the damage to the environment caused by the detritus of space activity. The intrusion of private, commercially focused actors into the arena crucially, under the current system of space governance, does not relieve states of ultimate liability for such activity. Despite the real advances made by companies such as Space X, it is the public-sector space agencies that are still the focal point of discussions surrounding the administration of space activity, and will remain so for the foreseeable future.

This inquiry has reaffirmed that the most pressing ethical dilemma faced by space agencies is the balancing of pragmatic realities against environmental imperatives. This echoes similar ethical debates in other areas of environmental regulation, specifically surrounding the issue of climate change. Orbital debris, however, should not be viewed as separate from those discussions. The Hardinian 'tragedy of the commons' is equally applicable to the orbit of earth as it is to any other part of the planet. Debris poses a significant threat to the safety of space travellers, to the operation of satellites, the sustainability of space activity and also to the general welfare of the earth's biosphere. All space actors need to recognize the necessity of dealing with this issue as an overriding concern. Agencies must act to limit the extent to which parochial national interests should be allowed to interfere with ensuring this most fundamental of environmental concerns. Commercial operators must be incentivized to ensure their activities do not aggravate the situation.

The OST, a relic of the Cold War, is resolutely silent on the need to control and remove space debris, and even non-treaty agreements serve only to try and limit future damage rather than removal of objects that are already in orbit. There is a clear ethical imperative to deal proactively with the waste product of over half a century of environmentally unfettered space activity. Different actors will, if unchecked, dispute resource allocation and shun individual responsibility in favour of self-interest. Only when the requirement to act is broadly accepted can the regulatory framework be shaped accordingly.

There is similar regulatory ambiguity surrounding the encroachment of the private sector into space tourism and possibly providing 'for-profit' launch services. An unsuccessful test flight of the Virgin Galactic Spaceship 2 resulted in the death of one test pilot and serious injuries to another.[21] This served as a reminder that despite technical advances, space remains a high-risk environment. Space agencies will need to ensure there are robust procedures in place to ensure that commercial necessities do not endanger the lives of space travellers.

The key to resolving all of these issues lays in each national space agency adopting an open and outward-facing approach to establishing a new code of normative behaviour. In this respect, lessons can be learned from the COSPAR guidelines on planetary protection, whereby a broad and inclusive approach to drawing up a voluntary code has seen widespread acquiescence. As Welly (2010, p. 277) states: 'Scholars have pointed to the prohibition on state appropriation in the Outer Space Treaty to suggest that space belongs to no one. Yet quite the contrary is true – space belongs to everyone'.

Recognition of this need for broad stakeholder involvement would embolden established space powers to assist emerging nations seeking space capability. This in turn would prevent the need for emerging states to contribute to environmental degradation by reaping the fruits of the preceding 50 years of space activity. In all cases, such a response, if accompanied by appropriate incentives to reward positive engagement, would undoubtedly invigorate the private sector in the respective nations. It is not, however, sufficient for the established space nations to dictate what they feel normative ethical standards should be, nor is it sufficient for the technology to lead and for the regulation to catch up in a piecemeal fashion. This was the case when the OST was drafted, and the result is clearly unsatisfactory.

This new space age will see numerous actors, each with their own goals and requirements in respect of space activity. The principal method for establishing normative values leading to the effective regulation of space activity needs to be one of inclusion. A wide range of public and private stakeholders must become involved in shaping the regulatory framework. Given the current multi-sectored space environment, it can no longer be appropriate in respect of negotiating instruments of regulation, for the large, self-interested space powers to unilaterally decide how best to protect the fragile environments in space.

The operation and ongoing exploration of space under the OST regime is predicated on the existence of two, superpower, state actors. The stillborn nature of the Draft ICoC provides a clear illustration of why there is a need for an underpinning contemporary statement of normative ethical values. Without such a platform, to both inspire exploration and shape the regulation of space activities, there is likely to be little success in negotiating effective and meaningful non-binding guidelines, much less hard international law. The result will be an atrophied regulatory framework whereby space debris continues to accrue and the safety of space travellers is balanced against deadlines and profit. Only from broad agreement from all users of space can effective governance of space activities be built. From such foundations, the institutions and mechanisms can be constructed. From this sustainable and environmentally sensitive exploration may well be the fruits of twenty-first-century space activity. Basing this on such a sound ethical base could prove to be as enduring a legacy as the rockets of Apollo, if not quite as evocative.

Notes

1 Full details of NASA's ethics policy can be found here: www.nasa.gov/offices/ogc/general_law/ethics_resources_page.html#.VKrz_8Zz1lI (accessed 25 January 2015).
2 An example of this would be the Apollo-Soyuz Test Project (see Scott *et al.* 2004 for full details of this collaborative venture between the US and USSR).
3 Such a category would include the Moon, although there are numerous unmanned probes that have impacted on the Moon and may have contained microbes and bacteria from Earth (Butler 2006).
4 In respect of Apollo 1, the three members of the crew died while training for the first flight in the Apollo programme. A fire broke out on the launch pad and the crew was trapped in the space capsule on the launch pad. The investigations detailed in Chaikin (1994) found that a combination of poor design, the use of a pure oxygen atmosphere in launch pad tests and a failure in quality control procedures caused the death of the three astronauts.
5 The Space Shuttle Challenger was destroyed on 28 January 1986 following an explosion 73 seconds after launch, killing all seven astronauts on board. The mission was extremely high profile, with one of the astronauts being the first 'teacher in space', Christa McAuliffe. The Presidential Commission on the Space Shuttle Challenger Accident, chaired by William P. Rogers, included Neil Armstrong, Sally Ride, Richard P. Feynman and Charles 'Chuck' Yeager. It found that the accident was caused by a failure in the seal of

a joint on one of the shuttle's solid rocket boosters. The failure of the joint was down to a flawed design that was susceptible to variations in temperature. This design flaw was exacerbated by NASA's decision to proceed with the launch notwithstanding very low temperatures and warnings from engineers at Morton Thiokol, the company contracted to design and build the SRB. The Challenger disaster and subsequent inquiry has been the subject of numerous books and documentaries. The full report is available here: http://history.nasa.gov/rogersrep/genindex.htm (accessed 25 January 2015).

6 The Space Shuttle Colombia disintegrated on re-entry to the Earth's atmosphere on 1 February 2003, killing the seven astronauts on board. The report of the Columbia Accident Investigation Board is available here: www.nasa.gov/columbia/home/CAIB_Vol1.html (accessed 25 January 2015). The CAIB found that the spacecraft broke up after a failure of the heat shield designed to protect the craft from the extreme temperatures experienced when re-entering the Earth's atmosphere. The breach of the heat shield was caused when it was impacted by a breakaway piece of foam insulating the main fuel tank, which occurred 81.7 seconds after lift-off. As well as the physical cause of the disaster, the CAIB made a number of scathing observations about the management culture within NASA, with the report saying: 'the NASA organizational culture had as much to do with this accident as the foam'.

7 By way of comparison, Lafleur states that the Shuttle programme cost a total of $198 billion, but this was spread over 41 years (1972 to the end of 2012). Given that there were 134 Shuttle flights, the cost of each of them works out at $1.4 billion. Compare this with the six successful moon landings, each costing around $18 billion each.

8 See the COSPAR website (https://cosparhq.cnes.fr; accessed 25 January 2015) for further details.

9 See the discussions on the Lima Climate Change Conference in December 2014 at: www.bbc.co.uk/news/science-environment-30468048 (accessed 25 January 2015).

10 See http://orbitaldebris.jsc.nasa.gov (accessed 25 January 2015).

11 See www.esa.int/Our_Activities/Operations/Ground_Systems_Engineering/ESA_Space_Debris_Office (accessed 25 January 2015).

12 The 1967 OST was adopted by the General Assembly of the UN on 19 December 1966 by virtue of Resolution 2222 (XXI). It opened for signature on 27 January 1967 and entered into force on 10 October 1967.

13 As of 1 January 2014, 103 states have ratified the OST, with a further 25 non-ratified signatories, according to the UN Office for Outer Space Affairs (OOSA): www.oosa.unvienna.org/oosa/en/SpaceLaw/treatystatus/index.html (accessed 25 January 2015).

14 Resolution 1962 (XVIII) of 13 December 1963 A/RES/1962 *Declaration of Legal Principles Governing the Activities of the States in the Exploration and Use of Outer Space.*

15 Article I of the OST states inter alia that outer space, including the Moon and other celestial bodies, shall be free for exploration and use by all states without discrimination of any kind, on a basis of equality and in accordance with international law, and there shall be free access to all areas of celestial bodies.

16 Article II of the OST 1967 states: 'Outer space, including the Moon and other celestial bodies, is not subject to national appropriation by claim of sovereignty, by means of use or occupation, or by any other means.'

17 These treaties are available at: www.oosa.unvienna.org/pdf/publications/ST_SPACE_061Rev01E.pdf (accessed 25 January 2015).

18 The regulation of GEO has fallen to the International Telecommunications Union (ITU). It is not the purpose of this discussion to critique the role of the ITU; for further discussion on the fairness of space activity from a Rawlsian perspective, see Schwartz (2014).

19 As opposed to the European Space Agency, which, although working closely with the EU, is a distinct body. See Mazurelle *et al.* (2009) for details of the complex interplay between these two European bodies.

20 Specifically India (see Listner 2011).

21 See Amos (2014).

References

Amos, J. (2014) *Will Crash Set Back Space Tourism?*, available at: www.bbc.co.uk/news/science-environment-29858964 (accessed 4 January 2015).

Berger, B. (2003) *Columbia Report Faults NASA Culture, Government Oversight*, available at: www.space.com/19476-space-shuttle-columbia-disaster-oversight.html (accessed 23 August 2014).

Billings, L. (2006) 'How shall we live in space? Culture, law and ethics in spacefaring society', *Space Policy*, 22(4): 249–55.

Blount, P. (2011–2012) 'Renovating space: The future of international space law', *Denv. J Int'l L & Poly*, 40(1–3): 515.

Bohlmann, U. (2003) 'Planetary Protection in Public International Law', American Institute of Aeronautics and Astronautics (AIAA), Proceedings of the 46th Colloquium on the Law of Outer Space, October, Bremen, Germany.

Butler, J. (2006) 'Unearthly microbes and the laws designed to resist them', *Ga. L. Rev.*, 41: 1355–95.

Button, M. (2012–13) 'Cleaning up space: The Madrid Protocal to the Antarctic Treaty as a model for regulating orbital debris', *Wm. & Mary Envtl. L. & Pol'y Rev*, 37: 539–68.

Chaikin, A. (1994) *A Man on the Moon* (1st edn), New York: Viking.

Cheng, B. (1997) *Studies in International Space Law* (1st edn), Oxford: Clarendon Press.

Chinkin, C. (2000) 'Normative development in the international legal system', in D. Shelton (ed.), *Commitment and Compliance: The Role of Non-Binding Norms in the International Legal System* (1st edn) (pp. 21–42), Oxford: Oxford University Press.

Elatawy, M. (2014) 'ICoC: Recommendations for further elaboration', in R. Rajagopalan and D. Porras (eds), *Awaiting Launch: Perspectives on the Draft ICoC for Outer Space Activities* (1st edn) (pp. 45–50), Observer Research Foundation, available at: http://orfonline.org/cms/export/orfonline/modules/report/attachments/AwaitingLaunch_1397728623369.pdf (accessed on 25 January 2015).

EU ICoC (2013) *International Code of Conduct for Outer Space Activities*, available at: http://eeas.europa.eu/non-proliferation-and-disarmament/pdf/space_code_conduct_draft_vers_16_sept_2013_en.pdf (accessed 25 January 2015).

Faugere, J-P. (2004) 'Report of the Symposium', in ECSL, ESA, UNESCO Joint Symposium (2004) *Legal and Ethical Framework for Astronauts in Space Sojourns*, Paris, available at: http://unesdoc.unesco.org/images/0013/001397/139752m.pdf (accessed 25 January 2015).

Fihn, B. and Irsten, G. (2014) 'Addressing challenges in space through new multilateral processes', in R. Rajagopalan and D. Porras (eds), *Awaiting Launch: Perspectives on the Draft ICoC for Outer Space Activities* (1st edn) (pp. 119–23), Observer Research Foundation, available at: http://orfonline.org/cms/export/orfonline/modules/report/attachments/AwaitingLaunch_1397728623369.pdf (accessed on 25 January 2015).

Foust, J. (2014) *The Future of NASA's Commercial Partnerships*, available at: www.thespacereview.com/article/2515/1 (accessed 30 August 2014).

Francis, R. and Armstrong, A. (2003) 'Ethics as a risk management strategy: The Australian experience', *Journal of Business Ethics*, 45(4): 375–85.

Gabrynowicz, J. (2004) 'Space law: Its Cold War origins and challenges in the era of globalization', *Suffolk UL Rev.*, 37: 1041–66.

Goh, G. (2008) 'Softly, softly catchee monkey: Informalism and the quiet development of international space law', *Neb. L. Rev*, 87: 725–46.

Gonzalez, R. (2014) *NASA Sets a 2018 Launch Date for the Rocket That Will Take Us to Mars*, available at: http://io9.com/nasa-sets-a-2018-launch-date-for-the-rocket-that-will-t-1628809899?utm_campaign=socialflow_io9_twitter&utm_source=io9_twitter&utm_medium=socialflow (accessed 30 August 2014).

Hickman, J. (2007) *Still Crazy after Four Decades: The Case for Withdrawing from the 1967 Outer Space Treaty*, available at: www.thespacereview.com/article/960/1 (accessed 25 January 2015).

Hobe, S. (2010) 'Impact of new developments on international space law (new actors, commercialisation, privatisation, increase in the number of space-faring nations)', *Unif. L. Rev.*, 15: 869–82.

Hobe, S. (2012) 'Environmental protection in outer space: Where we stand and what is needed to make progress with regard to the problem of space debris', *Indiana Journal of Law and Technology*, 8: 1–10.

Hobe, S. and Mey, J. (2009) 'UN space debris mitigation guidelines/Die UN Richtlinien zur Verhutung von Weltraumtrummern/Lignes Directrices Relatives a la Reduction des Debris Spatiaux', *ZLW*, 58: 388–403.

Horikawa, Y. (2014) 'ICoC and long term sustainability of outer space activities', in R. Rajogopalan and D. Porras (eds), *Awaiting Launch: Perspectives on the Draft ICoC for Outer Space Activities* (1st edn) (pp. 19–26), Observer Research Foundation, available at: http://orfonline.org/cms/export/orfonline/modules/report/attachments/AwaitingLaunch_1397728623369.pdf (accessed on 25 January 2015)..

IADC (2013) *Inter-Agency Space Debris Coordination Committee (IADC): Key Definitions*, available at: www.iadc-online.org/index.cgi?item=docs_pub (accessed 5 September 2014).

Konrad, M. (2004) 'On knowledge intermediaries and knowledge spaces in contemporary space science', quoted in ECSL, ESA, UNESCO Joint Symposium (2004) *Legal and Ethical Framework for Astronauts in Space Sojourns*, Paris, available at: http://unesdoc.unesco.org/images/0013/001397/139752m.pdf (accessed 25 January 2015).

Lachs, M. (1992) 'The treaty on principles of the law of outer space, 1961–1992', *Netherlands International Law Review*, 39(3): 291–302.

Lafleur, C. (2010) *Costs of US Piloted Programs*, available at: www.thespacereview.com/article/1579/1 (accessed 22 August 2014).

Lee, J. and Chung, S. (2011) 'Space policy for late comer countries: A case study of South Korea', *Space Policy*, 27(4): 227–33.

Lin, P. (2006) 'Viewpoint: Look before taking another leap for mankind – ethical and social considerations in rebuilding society in space', *Astropolitics*, 4(3): 281–94.

Listner, M. (2011) *The Space Review: EU Code of Conduct – Commentary on Indian Concerns and Their Effects*, available at: www.thespacereview.com/article/1977/1 (accessed 7 September 2014).

Listner, M. (2014) 'Customary international law: A troublesome question for ICoC?', in R. Rajagopalan and D. Porras (eds), *Awaiting Launch: Perspectives on the Draft ICoC for Outer Space Activities* (1st edn) (pp. 53–60), Observer Research Foundation, available at: http://orfonline.org/cms/export/orfonline/modules/report/attachments/AwaitingLaunch_1397728623369.pdf (accessed on 25 January 2015).

Lyall, F. and Larsen, P. (2009) *Space Law* (1st edn), Farnham: Ashgate.

Macauley, M. (2005) 'Flying in the face of uncertainty: Human risk in space activities', *Chi. J. Int'l L.*, 6: 131–48.

Marshall, A. (1993) 'Ethics and the extraterrestrial environment', *Journal of Applied Philosophy*, 10(2): 227–36.

Mazurelle, F., Wouters, J. and Thiebaut, W. (2009) 'Evolution of European space governance: Policy, legal and institutional implications', *Int'l Org. L. Rev.*, 6: 155–90.

McArthur, D. and Boran, I. (2004) 'Agent-centered restrictions and the ethics of space exploration', *Journal of Social Philosophy*, 35(1): 148–63.

Messier, D. (2013) *Rogozin: Russia to Consolidate Space Sector into Open Joint Stock Company at Parabolic Arc*, available at: www.parabolicarc.com/2013/08/30/rogozin-interview-kommersant/ (accessed 3 January 2015).

Moltz, J. (2014) *Crowded Orbits* (1st edn), New York: Columbia University Press.

National Aeronautics and Space Administration (2014) *NASA Strategic Plan*, Washington, DC: NASA.

Perrett, B. (2014) *SpaceX Proves Challenging To China's Long March Launcher | Space Content from Aviation Week*, available at: http://aviationweek.com/space/spacex-proves-challenging-chinas-long-march-launcher (accessed 4 January 2015).

Pompidou, A. (2000) *The Ethics of Space Policy*, UNESCO World Commission on the Ethics of Scientific Knowledge and Technology (COMEST).

Qizhi, H. (1997) 'Outer Space Treaty in perspective', *J. Space L.*, 25: 93–100.

Raile, E. (2013) 'Building ethical capital: Perceptions of ethical climate in the public sector', *Public Administration Review*, 73(2): 253–62.

Rajagopalan, R. and Porras, D. (2014) *Awaiting Launch: Perspectives on the Draft ICOC for Outer Space Activities* (1st edn), Observer Research Foundation, available at: http://orfonline.org/cms/export/orfonline/modules/report/attachments/AwaitingLaunch_1397728623369.pdf (accessed on 25 January 2015).

Robinson, G. (2006) 'Forward contamination of interstitial space and celestial bodies: Risk reduction, cultural objectives, and the law/Zur Kontamination des Weltraums: Risikobeschrankung, Kulturelle und Rechtliche Fragen/La Contamination de l'Espace Extra-Atmospherique: Reduction des Risques, Questions Culturelles et Juridiques', *ZLW*, 55: 380.

Schwartz, J. (2011) 'Our moral obligation to support space exploration', *Environmental Ethics*, 33: 67–88.

Schwartz, J. (2014) 'Fairness as a moral grounding for space policy', in Cockell, C. S. (ed.), *The Meaning of Liberty Beyond Earth* (1st edn) (pp. 69–90), Switzerland: Springer.

Scott, D., Leonov, A. and Toomey, C. (2004) *Two Sides of the Moon*, New York: Thomas Dunne Books.

Su, J. and Lixin, Z. (2014) 'The European Union draft Code of Conduct for outer space activities: An appraisal', *Space Policy*, 30: 34–9.

Tronchetti, F. (2009) *The Exploitation of Natural Resources of the Moon and Other Celestial Bodies*, Leiden: Martinus Nijhoff.

UN Office of Outer Space Affairs (2010) *UN-Space Debris Mitigation Guidelines*, Vienna: UNOOSA, available at: www.oosa.unvienna.org/pdf/publications/st_space_49E.pdf (accessed 25 January 2015).

Viikari, L. (2008) *The Environmental Element in Space Law* (1st edn), Leiden: Martinus Nijhoff.

Weeden, B. (2011) 'Overview of the legal and policy challenges of orbital debris removal', *Space Policy*, 27(1): 38–43.

Welly, N. (2010) 'Enlightened state-interest: A legal framework for protecting the common interest of all mankind from Hardinian tragedy', *J. Space L.*, 36: 273.

Wessel, B. (2012) 'Rule of law in outer space: The effects of treaties and nonbinding agreements on international space law', *Hastings Int'l & Comp. L. Rev.*, 35: 289–322.

West, J. (2007) *Back to the Future: The Outer Space Treaty Turns 40* [online] thespacereview. com, available at: www.thespacereview.com/article/982/1 (accessed 25 January 2015).

Williamson, M. (2003) 'Space ethics and protection of the space environment', *Space Policy*, 19(1): 47–52.

Williamson, M. (2006) *Space* (1st edn), Reston, VA: American Institute of Aeronautics and Astronautics.

Zubrin, R. and Wagner, R. (1996) *The case for Mars* (1st edn), New York: Free Press.

PART VII

Conclusion

18

TOWARDS A GLOBAL ETHICS

Wishful thinking or a strategic necessity?

*Alan Lawton, Leo Huberts and
Zeger van der Wal*

Introduction

This concluding chapter builds on the individual chapters and adds a number of overarching topics to reflect upon. A central question is whether a 'global' ethics is possible. This relates to classic discussions between proponents of 'universalistic ethics' versus 'ethical relativism'. In addition, a number of developments in governance and society seem appropriate to take into account, including the involvement of different actors in the provision of public services. These developments may seem to complicate possible convergence towards a global ethics both in theory and in practice. A second question concerns the communities of researchers and practitioners involved in ethics, integrity and anti-corruption. At all levels, many are involved in the topic, in discussions about the content, but also on the institutions and policies that might help to curb corruption, protect integrity and promote ethics. A fierce debate on what helps is on many agendas. Is research in the field characterized by convergence or divergence? Is there a paradigm for research in this field?

The last question will be addressed briefly, focusing on our field of study, on the community of researchers. Optimism and progress can be signalled: more involvement in research in a multitude of disciplines, with bodies of knowledge with a stronger empirical basis. We also acknowledge the discovery of new territories that are explored, even moving 'into space'. We nevertheless also signal a number of fundamental issues and dilemmas, bringing along a challenging agenda for future research and theory development.

Ethical relativism and/or a global ethics?

Ethical relativism is the view that ethical principles or judgements are relative to the individual or culture, and that it does not make sense, therefore, to pursue the goal of a universal ethics. Ethical principles are relative insofar as they are practised in specific situations. Thus, the injunction 'don't lie' can be overturned if lying averts greater moral harm in a particular context. At the same time, it can be argued that we should welcome diversity in moral thinking and exposure to different views than our own. This is all part of human flourishing.

It follows from the point of view of ethical relativism that we are less willing to pass judgements on others in case we are accused of moral imperialism or arrogance. What right do we have to assert that our values are the 'true' values? At the same time, does this mean that we cannot criticize anyone? With regard to terrorists, for example, can we still condemn the act even though we might have little to say about the motives that drove them? Are we left in a moral vacuum where we might wish to respect the autonomy of others, but then make no claims on the rightness or wrongness of the outcomes of individual actions?

For ethical relativists, there is no independent test or expert opinion to use in judging the behaviours of others. It is just our individual preferences that determine our ethical behaviour and judgements: we cannot say that X is better than Y, but rather we prefer X to Y.

We may try to persuade other people that understanding the world in a particular way is correct, and this is the point that Macaulay makes in Chapter 4, in his discussion of myth, but it is misleading to suggest that we can do so on the basis of some independent assessment that it is the best account currently available (Johnston 1999, p. 107).

Despite the strength of these views, scholars have tried to reconcile culturally specific ethics with a universal ethic, and at least offer some minimal conception of a universal ethic:

> When all allowance has been made, then, for the possible diversity of moral systems and the possible diversity of demands within a system, it remains true that the recognition of certain general virtues and obligations will be a logically or humanly necessary feature of almost any conceivable moral system: these will include the abstract virtue of justice, some form of obligation to mutual aid and to mutual abstention from injury and, in some form and in some degree, the virtue of honesty.
>
> (Strawson 1961, p. 12)

In the same vein, Walzer (1983) argued for a minimal universal ethics based upon an intercultural sharing of a minimum of common values such as justice, which you may recall is at the heart of good government in the Lorenzetti fresco that we discuss in the Preface. Apel (2000) argues both for the need and the possibility of a global ethic, through the route of intercultural justice and co-responsibility, and which needs to move beyond a concern with, for example, universal human rights:

> But a conception of universal ethics as a response to the globalization process should be more than just an agreement on a certain enumeration of words for values (or even norms) that can be made the subject of a declaration, although such a declaration could be very useful and even politically influential, as has been shown by the UN declaration of human rights of 1948.
>
> (Apel 2000, p. 153)

Apel recognizes the importance of empirical inductive studies to identify commonalities, complemented by discourse ethics that recognizes that we engage with others in a public discourse, and while there will be differences and dissent, a public discourse will, at least, seek consensus about the reasons for dissent (see also Bauman 1993).

At the same time, Stensöta, in Chapter 2, argues for a public ethics of care, nurturing relationships, that can be applied across a whole range of policy areas. As Richard Rorty puts it: 'So it is best to think of moral progress as a matter of increasing sensitivity, increasing responsiveness to the needs of a larger and larger variety of people and things' (1999, p. 81).

State and society in transition

At the formation of the modern state, it was Edmund Burke, parliamentarian and conservative philosopher, who wrote, in consideration of the role of the state and the contract or partnership with its citizens:

> As the ends of such a partnership cannot be obtained in many generations, it becomes a partnership not only between those who are living, but between those who are living, those who are dead, and those who are to be born.
>
> (Burke 1790/1968, pp. 194–5)

Clearly, Burke is raising the issue of who the state is responsible for, and we come back to this point later. However, we also need to consider how the state may have changed since the eighteenth century and, in particular, the shift from government to governance.

Governance, a broad concept applied to many different public and private contexts, can be applied to a whole range of related concepts, including power, authority, politics, policy, administration, government, steering, management and organization (Kjaer 2004). The attractiveness of the governance concept is that it locates decision-making, power, authority and the delivery of public services outside of government alone, and it accounts for decentralization, deconcentration, dispersal in the direction of many types of public, semi-public and private bodies, as well as private corporations. This is a more accurate description of public services as we saw in Parker's case study in Chapter 14 and Lawton and Rayner's discussion of networks in Chapter 15. To offer a simple illustration, taking care of citizen safety, once seen as essentially a state task, has now become the responsibility of a network of public and private organizations, including profit-seeking companies. In other words, more people, groups and organizations have become responsible for acting in the interests of safety, and have become involved in the 'governance of safety and security'. The concept of governance, being relatively new, broad, dynamic, fluid and elusive, is thus perfect as an umbrella concept for this type of development (Huberts 2014, pp. 67–9).

The strength of the governance concept is that it points to the dynamics of (the division of) power and authority in both government and corporations. No longer is it just about government. Clearly, government has a crucial role to play (Frederickson 2010; Lynn *et al.* 2001), but Pierre and Peters (2000, p. 12) define governance as the articulation and pursuit of collective interests in the 'post-strong state' era, while stressing that the state still plays an important role in governance processes by setting priorities and defining objectives. Heywood (2002, p. 424), in contrast, proposed that governance lies at a greater distance from the state, defining it as 'the various ways in which social life is coordinated, of which government is merely one' and describing government 'as the mechanism through which ordered rule is maintained; the machinery for making and enforcing collective decisions in society and elsewhere'. Thus, Coghill, in Chapter 16, argues that public officials need to 'discover, learn and apply innovative forms of governance'.

The concept of governance is not only popular in academic circles; it also features in discussions involving the institutions responsible for governing social problems. For example, newer institutions especially, such as the European Union (EU) and privatized bodies in the fields of health, welfare and housing, embrace the concept because, as clearly and convincingly put forward in an EU White Paper on European Governance (2001), it justifies their involvement in key policy areas much more than traditional concepts such as 'government' and 'politics'. As Huberts (2014, p. 201) puts it, governance is 'authoritative policy-making on collective problems and interests and implementation of these policies'. Besides explicitly mentioning both policymaking and policy implementation, this definition contains the important element 'collective', a term that implies the involvement of some type of collectivity, which can be a local or national community, but also a corporation or organization. Governance, therefore, is about addressing collective problems and interests, possibly by one actor, or by a network of public and private actors. We might also wonder about the extent of the collectivity itself. Newman, for example, in Chapter 17, argues for multi-sectoral governance over and above the state. A second important element is 'authoritative', a term referring to the governing actor(s), together with the collectivity involved, that distinguishes governance from the random exercise of power. 'Governance', therefore, although it has meaning for the publics involved, differs from 'government', which refers to the *territorial* authoritative governance system equipped with the unique *powers* to use force and to tax.

Globalization

Globalization can be defined as the opening up of international trade, foreign aid or reducing the sense of isolation. And yet, for some, it has not brought the expected benefits, nor reduced poverty, nor increased stability, but rather, critics argue, is in fact Westernization by proxy, destroying the environment in the meantime. Not only that, but international institutions such as the IMF and the World Bank have promoted a particular view of globalization (e.g. privatization) as a cure to perceived public-sector ills (Stiglitz 2002). Kerkhoff and Wagenaar, in Chapter 5, warn us of the dangers of such universalism.

Indeed, scholars do question the Western or cultural bias in many discussions of ethics and integrity, and in perceptions of corruption (De Graaf et al. 2010; Mungiu-Pippidi 2006). Sissener (2001), for example, in proposing an 'anthropological perspective on corruption', claimed that Western approaches to corruption are often exactly that: they are peculiarly Western, influenced as they are by Weber's famous ideal type of bureaucracy and not easily applied to non-Western societies. In countries such as Bangladesh, China or Nepal, for instance, the public official who issues favours for a remuneration of some kind within an established network is not corrupt; his or her actions are simply a social obligation to help, and such transactions within such a network are considered normal (Sissener 2001). The definition issue thus raises questions of cultural bias. Accordingly, Chadda (2004, p. 122) was particularly outspoken on the use of Transparency International's definition in developing countries: 'To judge transactions originating in the traditional sphere as corrupt because they clash with the requirements of the legal rational order can be seen as simply an ideological argument for the rapid destruction of the traditional sphere'.

We do well to heed the words of historian Eric Hobsbawm, who suggests that 'globalisation does not simply sweep away regional, national and other cultures, but combines with them in a peculiar way' (2013, p. 24). However, others argue for the 'great convergence' and identify a 'consensual cluster of norms' (Mahbubani 2013). Mahbubani identifies four key pillars of convergence – environmental, economic, technological and aspirational. There are new norms driven by modern science, rationality, free-market economics, multilateralism and the transformation of the social contract between the rulers and the ruled. He also suggests: 'Yet there is also no doubt that over time our sense of the moral community that we belong to has grown steadily in size (Mahbubani 2013, p. 255). Yet, to what extent is there evidence of global convergence?

Convergence or divergence in ethics?

Convergence can be described as the tendency for countries to grow more alike, to develop similarities in structure, processes and performance (Bennet 1991). It means moving from different positions to a common point (such a common point may be one that is normative and considered desirable by international agencies such as the World Bank). It is temporal rather than spatial. Convergence is a process; it is dynamic. We are interested, then, in common patterns and relationships and regularities. One area where this has received much attention is in public-sector reform. We can look at the example of New Public Management to illustrate the claims that have been made regarding convergence:

> The claims to universality are said to depend upon a number of conditions. First, the adoption of the same set of doctrines (e.g., Hood's seven doctrines introduced above) as the means to solve the problems of traditional public administration. Second, that reforms are apolitical and are supported by politicians of all hues. Third, that problems in one country are similar, and linked to, problems in other countries. Fourth, that there is a new global paradigm replacing commonly held assumptions and bringing in a new agenda, values and policies. All of these are contested.
>
> (Lawton and Six 2012, p. 418)

Thus, the claims concern a common set of doctrines, common political support, common problems, common solutions. Yet, it is not obvious that key aspects of NPM in terms of content, beliefs and values are commonly found. There appears to be general agreement that reforms have been more readily accepted in some countries (e.g. Australia, Canada, UK), but that in others, they were merely a continuation of historical managerial interventions aimed at trimming down the size of government, such as the US (Lynn 2006; Pollitt and Bouckaert 2011) and have informed government practices.

Pollitt (2001) examines the notion of convergence with respect to public-sector reforms in more detail and identifies four stages of convergence. These are, first, *discursive convergence*, such that language is converging and more and more people are using the same concepts (cf. also Kettl's 2005 phrase 'global public management revolution'). Second, *decisional convergence*, where different governments adopt similar organizational forms or management practices. Third, *practice convergence*, insofar as organizations begin to work in similar ways. Fourth, *results convergence*, where the outputs and outcomes of public service organizations begin to look similar. Pollitt argues that while there may be convergence in discursive and decisional convergence, there is less evidence of convergence in terms of practice or results.

If we turn to ethics, do we find the same? According to Ghere (2005, p. 352), the prospect of adopting a global ethic – a framework for defining right and wrong that knows no social, economic or political borders – remains far in the future. Notwithstanding that, scholars have found commonalities.

In an attempt to identify the core values explicitly advocated, or implicitly assumed, among global actors and examine the reasoning underlying such values, Yoder and Cooper (2005) examined a large number of international treaties, pacts, agreements, conventions and programmes going back to the 1970s.

They summarized their findings into an 'emerging global standard for public ethics' that consists of five core values:

- *the right to self-determination* (with transparency as a requisite for people to secure this right individually and collectively);
- *freedom* (including freedom of information, autonomy of economic choice and autonomy of political choice);
- *honesty by government* (making accountability possible);
- *trust* as the essential glue that holds democratic governance and market economies together (in essence, a product of freedom and honesty); and
- *stability (and predictability)* as a by-product of freedom, honesty and trust.

As support for these five core values, they cited recognition of an increasingly interdependent world and a growing global commitment to market economies and democratic governance. This begs the question of whether market economies and democratic governance require such values or whether market economies and democratic governance are the inevitable consequences of holding such values.

Similarly, Bossaert and Demmke (2005) examine EU member policies on ethics and integrity, which primarily addressed the challenges experienced by EU states attempting to develop a uniform European Code of Ethics. One surprising similarity they reported is that, despite differences in general ethical perceptions, the civil servants' obligations regarding ethical behaviour are remarkably similar in all 25 national public services of the enlarged EU. This similarity is evident in the ethical requirements determined by both laws and disciplinary actions. Moreover, the traditional values of national civil services (such as neutrality, respecting the rule of law, confidentiality, impartiality and avoiding conflicts of interest) have remained unchanged for decades. These values are echoed in Palidauskaite's (2006) research on Eastern European countries, which concluded that the purported values for public servants are legality, serving the public, loyalty to the constitutional government, impartiality, competence, professionalism, honesty, integrity, disinterestedness, political neutrality, transparency, and openness. More recently, however, Demmke and Moilanen (2011, p. 30) found evidence of more change and variety in values, concluding that, over time: 'New values such as transparency, diversity, sustainability, and flexibility have also been added to the classical values. [Seemingly, therefore], the future will be dominated by more value conflicts and newly emerging values'.

In a recent comparison of codes of conduct in different parts of the world, Beck Jørgensen and Sørensen (2013) found that these 'codes of good governance', as they called them, focus on the proper role of the state, its public sector, and public servants in general, which makes them useful for answering questions about the similarities and differences in 'national governance values'. More specifically, in 14 national codes of good governance, the authors identified a very interesting set of apparently global public values (which also happen to reflect ideals from constitutionalism and rational bureaucracy): public interest, regime dignity, political loyalty, transparency, neutrality, impartiality, effectiveness, accountability, and legality. These values, they pointed out, match the international code from the UN and the model code from the European Council, as well as conceptions of good governance promoted by the OECD, IMF, World Bank, UN and EU. Consequently, the authors suggested, they constitute a set of *global public values*.

An area of research, into ethical leadership, has provided a rich field in the search for common ethical values through empirical research. Research into ethical leadership has explored the notion that certain attributes of leadership can be found in different parts of the world, and the findings are revealing.

A good example of this notion is provided by the major research programme the GLOBE project (Global Leadership and Organizational Behavior Effectiveness) that explored the effects of culture on a range of organizational outcomes, including leadership, in 61 different societies (House *et al.* 2002). The framework for cultural values was derived from Hofstede's (1980, 2001) well-known cultural dimensions: uncertainty avoidance, power distance, institutional collectivism, in-group collectivism, gender egalitarianism, assertiveness, future orientation, performance orientation, and humane orientation. House and his colleagues found that charismatic/value-based leadership and integrity attributes of leaders were positively endorsed in all the societies included in their study (House *et al.* 1999).

Likewise, Resick *et al.* (2006), who also used data from the GLOBE Research Program, grouped these dimensions in 10 clusters: Anglo, Confucian Asia, Eastern European, Germanic European, Latin American, Latin European, Middle Eastern, Nordic European, Southeast Asian and Sub-Saharan African. Certain dimensions were cross-culturally endorsed, notably character/integrity and altruism, and viewed by the different cultural clusters as behaviours and characteristics that contribute to a person being an effective leader across cultures. A later study, using a qualitative research methodology, looked for examples of convergence and divergence in six countries (Resick *et al.* 2011) and found, similarly, cross-cultural convergence regarding character, consideration and respect for others.

Similarly, Den Hartog *et al.* (1999) found trustworthiness, fairness and honesty to be common. They also found differences; charismatic/transformational leadership attributes such as being enthusiastic, taking risks, ambition, self-effacement, self-sacrifice, sincerity, sensitivity and compassion seemed to be perceived as culturally contingent.

Thus, in the case of ethical leadership, there does appear to be evidence that demonstrates that certain traits are found universally. Given this, what are the dynamics, the processes and the institutions that might facilitate convergence?

Convergence of strategies for ethical promotion and regulation

Convergence may be facilitated by the imposition of reforms by international agencies on, sometimes reluctant, recipients. Critics have long lamented the impact of international organizations such as the World Bank, OECD (PUMA) and IMF. Such organizations have promoted an international vocabulary of public-sector reform with terms such as 'agentification', 'contractualization', 'performance measurement' and 'privatization' (Pollitt and Bouckaert 2011). Can the same phenomena be observed in the field of ethics? Clearly, there are a number of organizations and protocols that address ethical issues. Among the former are Transparency International and the World Bank; among the latter are the UN General Assembly Resolution on Corruption and the OECD Convention on Combating Bribery of Foreign Public Officials. We might also wonder to what extent there is an 'ethics industry' (Huberts 2014) and its various best practices, leading countries to adopt a strategy of creating an independent/autonomous anti-corruption agency with substantive judicial powers.

However, apart from the promotion of a common vocabulary, are there measures of, in Pollitt's terminology, decisional convergence? Lawton *et al.* (2009) explore a taxonomy of policy issues in a comparative study of the UK and Lithuania ethical policymaking. They identify a number of factors in the policy process:

1 *Policy push*, which refers to the reasons for putting in place an ethical framework. Thus, it could result from demands made by international agencies, such as the EU, for whom an anti-corruption framework is required as a condition of membership.
2 *Policy issues* are those that are addressed by the introduction of the ethical framework, and may include identifying conflicts of interest, fighting corruption and fraud, improving standards of behaviour, and combatting cronyism and nepotism.
3 *Policy goals* are what the policy is trying to achieve, from the punishment of individual transgressions to the elimination of systemic corruption.
4 *Policy objects* are those individuals or institutions to whom, or what, the policy is to be applied to, and will, in different countries, include the police, members of the judiciary, central civil service, and central or local politicians.
5 *Policy instruments* are the tools that are used to achieve the policy goals, and will include laws and regulations, codes of conduct, anti-corruption agencies, and training. Various chapters in this book have examined these instruments.
6 *Policy implementation* will depend upon leadership and the role of key individuals such as ethics officers, resources, capacity and capability. It will also reflect the extent to which reforms are planned, emergent or incremental.
7 *Policy styles* will reflect the extent of central direction and local discretion; unitary or federal systems of government will also reflect the regime changes that will result in different policy styles being adopted.

At the same time, we need to recognize that individual countries have different experiences of ethical behaviour on the part of their public officials and have different policy instruments in place.

Here, we draw upon the work of Six and Lawton (2013), who in turn utilize Misangyi *et al.* (2008) and the notion of institutional logic. In exploring local integrity systems, Six and Lawton (2013) identify four different categories of countries that have different institutional logics:

1   A *dominant ethical institutional logic*, found in such countries as Finland, which has consistently high ethical performance and does not need formal rules and agencies to combat unethical conduct.
2   A *dominant corrupt institutional logic*, found in such countries as Bulgaria, which has put in place anti-corruption measures but has yet to overcome traditions of corrupt behaviour.
3   *From corrupt to ethical institutional logic*, found in, for example, Hong Kong and Singapore, where corruption reform has worked.
4   A *dominant ethical institutional logic with occasional lapses*, for example the UK, where every so often there is a major scandal such as the MPs' expenses in 2009. New measures are introduced and are likely to work because of the prevailing logic.

Six and Lawton (2013) argue that different combinations of measures to combat unethical conduct will work in different countries, and that countries can be clustered together depending upon their ethical institutional logic. This suggests that different countries, or clusters of countries, might be on different ethical trajectories, and these differences need to be recognized when developing measures to combat corruption and unethical behaviour. Thus, transplanting a Hong Kong ICAC to another country might not necessarily work. At the same time, there will be a common set of measures to choose from, including anti-corruption agencies, ethics training, independent auditors and so on, configured differently and reflecting the prevailing institutional logic.

Even where there are similarities, such as in Singapore, Hong Kong and, to a lesser extent, South Korea, is this due to practice convergence or results from extraneous other factors such as a general rise in wealth or developments in citizen education?

Organizational responses to unethical behaviour have been discussed by Monaghan and Graycar in Chapter 6, by Hoekstra in Chapter 9 and by Maesschalck and De Schrijver in Chapter 12. The authors present frameworks for developing the ethical organization and, along with Heywood and Rose in Chapter 11, advise a nuanced approach to the use of different tools and formal and informal instruments within the organization. At the same time, we need remind ourselves that organizations exist within a wider set of values, and we should consider, as Heres does in Chapter 10, extending stakeholder involvement. Indeed, the boundaries of the organization are porous, and unethical behaviour of public officials may need to be evaluated by both internal and external stakeholders.

The contributions in the book signal the fierce debate that characterizes our field on this topic. In the Introduction, we referred to 'that old chestnut of rules versus values' and the recognition, increasingly, that most integrity regimes will include a combination of both. This more or less illustrates the state of the art on our ideas and knowledge on the configuration and combination of the different tools, institutions and processes that seem to work best in any given situation. Is it ethical leadership that makes the difference? How important are separate institutions that focus on ethics and integrity? Is the code of conduct and ethics training an effective tool in our repertoire? Involved practitioners and institutions tend to be self-satisfied about their role, adopting a 'the more the better' attitude. Hence, more reflection and research on what works is essential, in terms of not only agencies, but also instruments and systems. Nothing seems to work as a panacea, combinations offer perspective, but what really works should be high on the agenda for our community of researchers to make progress, in empirical work as well as theoretical development. In addition, further reflection on what 'an effective tool' is seems important. Do we focus on the 'process' of governance and the criteria on the (ethical) quality of decision-making and policy implementation, or do we concentrate on the societal results (on sustainability, including climate change, social equality, justice, etc.)? Both are building blocks towards an integrated (ethical) governance network.

Ethics research and theory

As scholars, we need to attend to, as Macaulay reminds us in Chapter 4, both normative and empirical questions (Cooper 2004). There have been a number of empirical studies that have drawn comparisons between different countries across a wide range of indicators. Goel and Nelson (2010) examine the role of historical factors, geographic influences and the government on corruption. Using data from approximately 100 countries, they found that greater government intervention in a country's economy leads to more corruption; larger government size leads to less corruption; and greater regulatory activity increases the opportunities to engage in corrupt behaviour. Both old countries and new countries have similar tendencies to induce corruption, with urban-centred countries likely to have less corruption. Goel and Nelson argue that as nations become more prosperous, then the degree of corrupt behaviour goes down. This is an interesting argument since it does not take into consideration the impact of inequalities within the same country. Thus, Wilkinson and Pickett (2010) argue that inequality within countries leads to a whole host of social, economic, health and educational problems and can be correlated with low levels of trust within society. They argue that the inequalities that affect the way people treat each other within their own societies also affect the norms and expectations they bring to bear on international issues. Thus, if we get it right nationally, will that then spill over into the international sphere?

There are also a number of sets of indicators that try to assess globally various aspects of governance (e.g. the Good Society Index) (Holmberg and Rothstein 2014). The index ranks 146 countries against a number of indices clustered together under a number of themes, including the social, health, economic and political indicators such as quality of government, trust, the political system, the economy, the environment, education, and so on. Also well known, and disputed by some, are the World Bank Worldwide Governance Indicators (Kaufmann *et al.* 2010).

Nevertheless, Fukuyama (2013) argues that the existing quantitative measures used in evaluating quality of governance in large complex societies are inadequate, no matter how advanced some of the composite indicators have become. He argues that there are at least four broad approaches to evaluating the quality of governance – procedural measures, input measures, output measures and measures of bureaucratic autonomy. He suggests that the quality of governance is a function of the capacity of government, in terms of resources and the professionalization of staff, and autonomy.

Notwithstanding such disagreements, a key question is to what extent both scholars and practitioners learn from each other. If we take organizations and practitioners first, organizational learning in what works is critical for both policy and theory development. In the 10 years or so since Prange (1999) argued that organizational learning was desperately seeking theory, a wealth of literature on organizational learning and the learning organization has been produced. Yet, comparatively few studies have investigated the relationship between organizational learning and ethics. A systematic literature review of public service organizational learning identified 131 relevant papers, none of which pertained to ethics or ethical learning (Rashman *et al.* 2009).

Where ethics and organizational learning have been brought together, the results form a diverse range of studies. Verbos *et al.* (2007, p. 25) argue that organizational learning is a key element of successfully building a positive ethical organization: 'the dynamic nature of organizations and their members commands an open system in which learning derives from interactions with the environment and informs moral reasoning throughout'. Verbos *et al.*'s (2007) insistence on the positive nature of ethical organizational learning serves as an interesting contrast with earlier studies, such as Zajac and Comfort (1997), which argues that such learning takes place in the wake of ethical failures within organizations. Recently, there has been an increased call to address the gaps in the literature:

> While organizational learning regarding efficiency and effectiveness is well developed, there is a need for more theory describing organizational moral learning. A review of existing research on organizational moral learning reveals a lack of empirical evidence on learning processes within and between organizations.
>
> (Spitzeck 2009: 157)

One key distinction is that *organizational learning* is different to the *learning organization* (Sun 2003). The unit of analysis in the latter is the organization itself, how it is designed to create and sustain continuous improvement and learning. Organizational learning, as Easterby-Smith *et al.* (2000) suggest, is more than the sum of its individual parts, and point to the emergence of a debate about the learning network. Recognizing that the boundaries between organizations become blurred and that organizations work with each other through networks and partnerships, this debate realigns the unit of analysis as the network rather than the individual or the organization. Indeed, this is very much supported by Hoekstra in Chapter 9, who highlights the possibilities of learning through networks.

A further vehicle for learning could be communities of practice. Wenger (1998) focuses upon the idea of a community of practice, and he sees such community as self-organizing and informally bound; it might involve some kind of joint enterprise, and mutual engagement. It is not just a set of relationships, as in a network, but has a purpose. Knowledge is created, shared, organized, revised and passed on. It can also provide a space for identity. One advantage of a community of practice is to provide a home for like-minded people from other organizations. Such a description might fit the academic community as we seek to learn from each other, and through our papers, books and conferences disseminate our research.

This book illustrates the commitment of many scholars and scientific disciplines on the ethics and integrity of public policy and management. It also clarifies that this, our, topic is important to understand contemporary governance. In terms of 'learning', this brings along a challenging agenda for the scholars involved, as well as for the broader mainstream field of research and theory development. The diversity of the community of researchers in this field, the presence of the variety of theories and (empirical) research communities, encourage optimism on the progress, including 'multidisciplinary learning' to be made. At the same time, we should not overestimate the actual interest for our topics within the mainstream focus in our fields of study. This supports an agenda towards more exchange and interrelationships in our own community, as well as a strategy to clarify that 'ethics' matters to be able to understand public management and policy process and outcomes.

Conclusion

The study of global ethics is not, of course, limited to US and EU researchers, and it would be informative to have a true global perspective on these and other issues. Some significant contributions have been made, for example, by Australian scholarship (to name but one other country), including Graycar and Smith (2011), Miller et al. (2005), Preston and Sampford (2002), Sampford and Preston (1998), and Sampford et al. (2006). Even more importantly, however, a real globalization seems to be needed in the involvement of public administration scholars and practitioners. At present, optimism about a global standard for public ethics and integrity is at odds with those who criticize the World Bank, International Monetary Fund (IMF) and the UN as simply the implementation arm of Western ethical culture, or the more moderate who doubt that good governance concepts and policies can be distinguished that apply to all contexts and countries (Andrews 2010; Doig and Theobald 1999; Huberts et al. 2008).

While recognizing the different positions, what is required is a more nuanced approach, and that requires, as Becker and Talsma, in Chapter 3, put it, that we put some colour into our black-and-white thinking.

We began our discussion of the modern state with Burke, and wondered at the responsibilities of the state. Coghill's chapter on the environment change raised further issues. One view sees the state as moral agents with responsibility for issues that affect us all. Weijers *et al.* (2010) argue that states have responsibility for dealing with climate change based upon which states have the ability to pay, and the amount of existing pollution 'culpably caused' by them. But we argue that it is also about reciprocity as well as responsibility. We might do worse than to return to Hannah Arendt's conception of the public realm:

> What unites people in a political community is . . . not some set of common values, but the world they set up in common, the spaces they inhabit together, the institutions and practices which they share as citizens.
>
> (d'Entrèves 2000, p. 75)

The importance of the 'commons' is identified by Peiffer and Marquette in Chapter 7.

In the meantime, public administrators can re-professionalize their ethics in a manner that incorporates global humanitarian concern. To do so, practitioners need researchers to map globalization's ethical terrain and to recommend approaches for globally pertinent actions that are just, prudent and feasible. At the same time, as several of our contributors remind us, we need to listen to how practitioners frame their understandings. We also need to remind ourselves, as Menzel does in Chapter 8, that there are good people who work in our public services, and that good government has not succumbed to the Tyrant of Lorenzetti's depiction.

To explore unethical behaviour, fraud and corruption, but also virtues, good behaviour and how organizations can promote good government, seems crucial to progress in theory and practice on government and governance. Lorenzetti reminds us of the appalling consequences that follow from bad government and the importance of justice to ensure good government. It is a lesson that is no less relevant today.

References

Andrews, M. (2010) 'Good government means different things in different countries', *Governance*, 23(1): 7–35.

Apel, K-O. (2000) 'Globalization and the need for universal ethics', *European Journal of Social Theory*, 3(2): 137–55.

Bauman, Z. (1993) *Postmodern Ethics*, Oxford: Blackwell.

Beck Jørgensen, T. and Sørensen, D-L. (2013) 'Codes of good governance: National or global public values?', *Public Integrity*, 15(1): 71–95.

Bennett, C.J. (1991) 'What is policy convergence and what causes it?', *British Journal of Political Science*, 21(2): 215–33.

Bossaert, D. and Demmke, C. (2005) *Main Challenges in the Field of Ethics and Integrity in the EU Member States*, Maastricht: European Institute of Public Administration.

Burke, E. (1790/1968) *Reflections on the Revolution in France*, Penguin edition edited by C.C. O'Brien, Harmondsworth: Penguin.

Chadda, M. (2004) 'India: Between majesty and modernity', in R.A. Johnson (ed.), *The Struggle Against Corruption* (pp. 109–43), New York: Palgrave Macmillan.

Commission of the European Communities (2001) 'European Governance: A White Paper', COM(2001) 428 Final, Brussels.

Cooper, T.L. (2004) 'Big questions in administrative ethics: A need for focused, collaborative effort', *Public Administration Review*, 64(4): 395–407.

De Graaf, G, Wagenaar, F.P. and Hoenderboom, M.P. (2010) 'Constructing corruption', in G. de Graaf, P. Von Maravić and P. Wagenaar (eds), *The Good Cause: Theoretical Perspectives on Corruption* (pp. 98–114), Opladen: Barbara Budrich.

Demmke, C. and Moilanen, T. (2011) *Effectiveness of Good Governance and Ethics in Central Administration: Evaluating Reform Outcomes in the Context of the Financial Crisis States*, Maastricht: European Institute of Public Administration.

Den Hartog, D.N., House, R.J., Hanges, P.J., Ruiz-Quintanilla, S.A., Dorfman, P.W. et al. (1999) 'Culturally specific and cross-culturally generalizable implicit leadership theories: Are attributes of charismatic/transformational leadership universally endorsed?', *The Leadership Quarterly*, 10(2): 219–56.

d'Entrèves, M.P. (2000) 'Public and private in Hannah Arendt's conception of citizenship', in M.P. d'Entrèves and U. Vogel (eds), *Public & Private: Legal, Political and Philosophical Perspectives* (pp. 68–90), London: Routledge.

Doig, A. and Theobald, R. (1999) *Corruption and Democratisation*, London: Routledge.

Easterby-Smith, M., Crossan, M. and Nicolini, D. (2000) 'Organizational learning: Debates past, present and future', *Journal of Management Studies*, 37(6): 783–96.

Frederickson, H.G. (2010) 'Searching for virtue in the public life: Revisiting the vulgar ethics thesis', *Public Integrity*, 12(3): 239–46.

Fukuyama, F. (2013) 'What is governance?', *Governance: An International Journal of Policy, Administration, and Institutions*, 26(3): 347–68.

Ghere, R.K. (2005) 'Globalization and public-service ethics: Some directions for inquiry', in H.G. Frederickson and R.K. Ghere (eds), *Ethics in Public Management* (pp. 328–55), Armonk, NY: M.E. Sharpe.

Goel, R.K. and Nelson, M.A. (2010) 'Causes of corruption: History, geography and government', *Journal of Policy Modelling*, 32: 433–47.

Graycar, A. and Smith, R.G. (eds) (2011) *Handbook of Global Research and Practice in Corruption*, Cheltenham: Edward Elgar.

Hobsbawm, E. (2013) *Fractured Times: Culture and Society in the Twentieth Century*, London: Little Brown.

Hofstede, G. (1980) *Culture's Consequences*, Beverly Hills, CA: Sage.

Hofstede, G. (2001) *Culture's Consequences: Comparing Values, Behaviors, Institutions, and Organizations across Nations* (2nd edn), Thousand Oaks, CA: Sage.

Holmberg, S. and Rothstein, B. (2014) *Correlates of the Good Society*, Working Paper Series 2014:13, Quality of Governance Institute (QOG), University of Gothenberg, Gothenberg, Sweden.

House, R.J., Javida, M., Hanges, P. and Dorfman, P. (2002) 'Understanding cultures and implicit leadership theories across the globe: An introduction to project GLOBE', *Journal of World Business*, 37(1): 3–10.

House, R., Hanges, P., Ruiz-Quintanilla, S., Dorfman, P., Javidan, M., Dickson, M. and 170 co-authors (1999) 'Cultural influences on leadership and organizations: Project

GLOBE', in W. Mobley, M. Gessner and V. Arnold (eds), *Advances in Global Leadership, Vol. 1* (pp. 171–233), Stamford, CT: JAI Press.

Huberts, L. (2014) *The Integrity of Governance: What it Is, What We Know, What is Done and Where to Go*, Basingstoke: Palgrave Macmillan.

Huberts, L.W.J.C., Maesschalck, J. and Jurkiewicz, C.L. (2008) 'Global perspectives on good governance policies and research', in L.W.J.C. Huberts, J. Maesschalck and C.L. Jurkiewicz (eds), *Ethics and Integrity of Governance: Perspectives across Frontiers* (pp. 239–64), Cheltenham: Edward Elgar.

Johnston, P. (1999) *The Contradictions of Modern Moral Philosophy: Ethics after Wittgenstein*, London & New York: Routledge.

Kaufmann, D., Kraay, A. and Mastruzzi, M. (2010) *The Worldwide Governance Indicators: Methodology and Analytical Issues*, Policy Research Working Paper 5430, World Bank.

Kettl, D.F. (2005) *The Global Public Management Revolution*, Washington, DC: Brookings Institution.

Kjaer, M. (2004) *Governance: Key Concepts*, Cambridge: Polity Press.

Lawton, A. and Six, F. (2012) 'New Public Management: Lessons from abroad', in D.C Menzel and H.L. White (eds), *The State of Public Administration: Issue, Challenges and Opportunities*, Armonk, NY: M.E. Sharpe.

Lawton, A., Macaulay, M. and Palidauskaite, J. (2009) 'Towards a comparative methodology for public service ethics', EGPA Conference, Malta 2–5 September, PSG VII: 'Ethics and Integrity of Governance'.

Lynn, L.E., Jr. (2006) *Public Management: Old and New*, New York: Routledge.

Lynn, L., Jr., Heinrich, C. and Hill, C. (2001) *Improving Governance: A New Logic for Empirical Research*, Washington, DC: Georgetown University Press.

Mahbubani, K. (2013) *The Great Convergence: Asia, the West and the Logic of One World*, New York: Public Affairs.

Miller, S., Roberts, P. and Spence, E. (2005) *Corruption and Anti-Corruption: An Applied Philosophical Approach*, Upper Saddle river, NJ: Pearson Prentice Hall.

Misangyi, V.F., Weaver, G.R. and Elms, H. (2008) 'Ending corruption: The interplay among institutional logics, resources and institutional entrepreneurs', *Academy of Management Review*, 33(3): 750–70.

Mungiu-Pippidi, A. (2006) 'Corruption: Diagnosis and treatment', *Journal of Democracy*, 17(3): 86–99.

Palidauskaite, J. (2006) 'Codes of ethics in transitional democracies: A comparative perspective', *Public Integrity*, 8(1): 35–48.

Pierre, J. and Peters, B.G. (2000) *Governance, Politics and the State*, Houndmills: Macmillan.

Pollitt, C. (2001) 'Clarifying convergence: Striking similarities and durable differences in public management reform', *Public Management Review*, 3(4): 471–92.

Pollitt, C. and Bouckaert, G. (2011) *Public Management Reform: A Comparative Analysis – New Public Management, Governance, and the Neo-Weberian State* (3rd edn), Oxford: Oxford University Press.

Prange, C. (1999) 'Organisational learning: Desperately seeking theory?', in M. Easterby-Smith, J. Burgoyne and L. Araujo (eds), *Organizational Learning and the Learning Organization* (pp. 23–43), London: Sage.

Preston, N. and Sampford, C., with Connors, C. (2002) *Encouraging Ethics and Challenging Corruption: Reforming Governance in Public Institutions*, Sydney: The Federation Press.

Rashman, L., Withers, E. and Hartley, J. (2009) 'Organizational learning and knowledge in public service organizations: A systematic review of the literature', *International Journal of Management Reviews*, 11(4): 463–94.

Resick, C.J., Hanges, P.J., Dickson, M.W. and Mitchelson, J.K. (2006) 'A cross-cultural examination of the endorsement of ethical leadership', *Journal of Business Ethics*, 63(4): 345–59.

Resick, C.J., Martin, G.S., Keating, M.A., Dickson, M.W., Kwan, H.K. and Peng, C. (2011) 'What ethical leadership means to me: Asian, American and European perspectives', *Journal of Business Ethics*, 101: 435–57.

Rorty, R. (1999) *Philosophy and Social Hope*, London: Penguin.

Sampford, C. and Preston, N. (eds) (1998) *Public Sector Ethics: Finding and Implementing Values*, London: Routledge.

Sampford, C., Shacklock, A., Connors, C. and Galtung, F. (eds) (2006) *Measuring Corruption*, Hampshire: Ashgate.

Sissener, T.K. (2001) 'Anthropological perspectives on corruption', Chr. Michelsen Institute Working Paper 2001: 5, Bergen, Norway.

Six, F. and Lawton, A. (2013) 'Towards a theory of integrity systems: A configurational approach', *International Review of Administrative Sciences*, 79(4): 639–58.

Spitzeck, H. (2009) 'Organizational moral learning: What, if anything, do corporations learn from NGO critique?', *Journal of Business Ethics*, 88: 157–73.

Stiglitz, J. (2002) *Globalization and Its Discontents*, London: Penguin.

Strawson, P.F. (1961) 'Social morality and individual ideal', *Philosophy*, 36(January): 1–17.

Sun, H.C. (2003) 'Conceptual clarifications for "organizational learning", "learning organization" and "a learning organization"', *Human Resource Development International*, 6(2): 153–66.

Verbos, A.K., Gerard, J.A., Forshey, P.R., Harding, C.S. and Miller, J.S. (2007) 'The positive ethical organization: Enacting a living code of ethics and ethical organizational identity', *Journal of Business Ethics*, 76: 17–33.

Walzer, M. (1983) *Spheres of Justice: A Defense of Pluralism and Equality*, New York: Basic Books.

Weijers, D., Eng, D. and Das, R. (2010) 'Sharing the responsibility of dealing with climate change: Interpreting the principle of common but differentiated responsibilities', in J. Boston, A. Bradstock and D. Eng (eds), *Public Policy: Why Ethics Matters*, Canberra: ANU E Press, Australian National University.

Wenger, E. (1998) *Communities of Practice: Learning, Meaning, and Identity*, New York: Cambridge University Press.

Wilkinson, R. and Pickett, K. (2010) *The Spirit Level: Why Equality Is Better for Everyone*, London: Penguin.

Yoder, D.E. and Cooper, T.L. (2005) 'Public-service ethics in a transnational world', in H.G. Frederickson and R.K. Ghere (eds), *Ethics in Public Management* (pp. 297–327), Armonk, NY: M.E. Sharpe.

Zajac, G. and Comfort, L.K. (1997) '"The spirit of watchfulness": Public ethics as organizational learning', *Journal of Public Administration Research and Theory*, 7(4): 541–70.

INDEX